There Would Always Be a Fairy Tale

There Would Always Be a Fairy Tale

More Essays on Tolkien

Verlyn Flieger

The Kent State University Press
Kent, Ohio

© 2017 by The Kent State University Press, Kent, Ohio 44242
ALL RIGHTS RESERVED
Library of Congress Catalog Card Number 2017000823
ISBN 978-1-60635-308-0
Manufactured in the United States of America

LIBRARY OF CONGRESS CATALOGING-IN-PUBLICATION DATA
Library of Congress Cataloging-in-Publication Data
Names: Flieger, Verlyn, 1933- author.
Title: There would always be a fairy tale : more essays on Tolkien / Verlyn Flieger.
Description: Kent, Ohio : The Kent State University Press, 2017. | Includes bibliographical references and index.
Identifiers: LCCN 2017000823 (print) | LCCN 2017001133 (ebook) |
    ISBN 9781606353080 (pbk. : alk. paper) | ISBN 9781631012884 (ePub) |
    ISBN 9781631012891 (ePDF)
Subjects: LCSH: Tolkien, J. R. R. (John Ronald Reuel), 1892-1973--Criticism and interpretation. | Fantasy fiction, English--History and criticism. | Fairy tales--History and criticism. | Middle Earth (Imaginary place)
Classification: LCC PR6039.O32 Z6466 2017 (print) | LCC PR6039.O32 (ebook) |
    DDC 823/.912--dc23
LC record available at https://lccn.loc.gov/2017000823

*In loving memory of Vaughn Howland,
who pushed me to do this book.*

Contents

Acknowledgments	ix
Introduction	xi
Style, Usage, and Abbreviations	xiii
Note to the Reader	xvii

PART ONE: "A PERILOUS LAND": DEFINING *FAËRIE*	1
"There Would Always Be a 'Fairy-tale'": J. R. R. Tolkien and the Folklore Controversy	5
But What Did He Really Mean?	17
Re-creating Reality	32
War, Death, and Fairy Stories in the Work of J. R. R. Tolkien	49
Eucatastrophe and the Dark	59

PART TWO: "FAËRIE BEGINS": THE NUTS AND BOLTS OF SUB-CREATION	67
Words and World-making: The Particle Physics of Middle-earth	71
Myth, History, and Time-travel: *The Lost Road* and *The Notion Club Papers*	76
Politically Incorrect Tolkien	90
The Jewels, the Stone, the Ring, and the Making of Meaning	100
Making Choices: Moral Ambiguity in Tolkien's Major Fiction	113

PART THREE: "ARRESTING STRANGENESS": MAKING IT DIFFERENT	125
The Forests and the Trees: Sal and Ian in Faërie	129
How Trees Behave—Or Do They?	145
Myth and Truth in Tolkien's Legendarium	157
Fays, Corrigans, Elves, and More: Tolkien's Dark Ladies	165

PART FOUR: BOILING BONES; SERVING SOUP   179
   Tolkien, *Kalevala,* and Middle-earth   183
   Tolkien's Celtic Connection   196
   Tolkien's French Connection   203
   Drowned Lands   213
   Voyaging About: Tolkien and Celtic *Navigatio*   221

Permissions and Acknowledgments   229
Notes   231
Works Cited   240
Index   248

Acknowledgments

Thanks go to the members of the Tolkien Symposium, who for nigh on thirty years now have listened patiently and criticized constructively as I tried out my ideas on them. Further thanks go to the wider audience of participants in conferences on Tolkien and fantasy, who have done the same. Thanks above all to J. R. R. Tolkien, whose unparalleled imagination got me started seventy years ago.

Finally, my thanks to the late Vaughn Howland, always, for everything.

Introduction

The title for this book and the titles for each individual section are drawn from that gold mine for Tolkien scholars, his wide-ranging yet highly focused, erudite and idiosyncratic essay "On Fairy-stories." As much, in its own way as his fiction, Tolkien's essay is a testament to his enduring love for fairy tales and to his bedrock belief in their value. "On Fairy-stories" is both detailed and discursive, but at its core is Tolkien's challenge to the myth theory of nineteenth-century anthropologists, philologists, and folklorists that fairy tales were naïve or "primitive," or represented the "childhood" of humanity and its personification of natural forces as gods. With his customary confidence in his own ideas, Tolkien argued that this was "the truth almost upside down." It was not the phenomena that gave rise to the gods, asserted Tolkien; rather, it was the gods, in their humanity and personality, who were needed to give life to the phenomena. His dictum, with the hammer-wielding Norse thunder god Thórr as his example, gave me my title. "*[T]here would always be a 'fairy-tale'* as long as there was any Thórr. When the fairy-tale ceased, there would be just thunder, which no human ear had yet heard" (*MC* 124; my emphasis).

In making this sweeping, over-the-top assertion, Tolkien was consciously going against the critical grain, privileging the character over the phenomenon and championing the story over the theory. We need the story, he said, in order to know the phenomenon; without the story we have no key to what is going on. If we don't have a name for what we hear, we don't know what we are hearing. Thus, we may hear it as a god whose name means "thunder" or call it the sonic boom of expanding air. Either will do. What is essential is that we give it a name, for it is the name that generates its own story.

Tolkien regarded humans beings as involuntary story-tellers, not just able to tell stories, but unable to not do so. "To ask what is the origin of stories," he said, " . . . is to ask what is the origin of language and the mind" (*MC* 119). For him, these three components—mind, language, and story—were one inclusive concept. Together they formed a web of interlocking and reciprocally vibrating strands that wove the tapestry of story. As long as there existed a perceiving human mind and the language to weave that mind's expression, there would always be a story, a fairy tale. Tolkien's intellectual life was dedicated to that principle, and his imaginative life was dedicated to its practice. This book is devoted to Tolkien the teller of tales and cocreator of the myths they brush against. It is concerned with his lifelong interest in and engagement with fairy stories, with the special world (which he called Faërie) they both create and inhabit, and with the elements that go to make that world the special place it is.

As with its predecessor, *Green Suns and Faërie*, the essays in this book were mostly written to fit the parameters of specific conferences or anthologies, sometimes both together. I have not revised them, although (again like *Green Suns*) I have tried to group them loosely by theme. They are in essence an unpatterned mosaic whose tiles touch a variety of subjects from myth to truth, from social manners to moral behavior, from textual history to the microparticles of Middle-earth. When I assembled the individual pieces, however, what I saw taking shape was a more coherent picture than I had anticipated, a picture of a man as complicated as the books that bear his name; a man in love with the past, acutely aware of the present, and wary of the future; an independent and unorthodox thinker who was both a believer and a doubter, able to maintain conflicting ideas in tension; a teller of tales both romantic and bitter, hopeful and pessimistic, in equal parts tragic and comedic. a man whose work does not seek for right or wrong answers so much as a way to accommodate both; a man of antitheses, as his biographer Humphrey Carpenter described him. I hope you will like him. I do.

Style, Usage, and Abbreviations

Any scholarly discussion of Tolkien's work, both nonfiction and fiction, poses problems of style, problems that are complicated by several additional factors. First, Tolkien was not himself consistent in his treatment of certain terms and coinages, even within a single work. Second, such inconsistencies have been complicated by variations in the many editions of his work. Third, differences in style and spelling conventions between British and American English have added yet another dimension of complexity. And finally, the treatment of terms also must reflect their function in specific contexts. When Tolkien discusses Faërie, for example, he capitalizes it to indicate the specific meaning he has given the word, and also italicizes it when he is discussing it as a term, rather than as a concept. While it is probably impossible to achieve complete consistency, I have adopted the following conventions. Direct quotations from Tolkien and others are, of course, reproduced exactly as written. In treating the terms he used or created for the creatures peopling his own world—for example, elves, men, dwarves, hobbits, orcs, ents, and huorns—I have followed his lead in capitalizing them when they are being used to refer to the people or race, but lowercasing them when they are referring to specific subgroups or individuals belonging to those peoples or races. Words given specific meanings by Tolkien (such as *Faërie*), together with his own coinages (such as *eucatastrophe* and *dyscatastrophe*), retain his choice regarding capitalization. However, terms used by others as well as Tolkien, such as *fairy tale, fantasy, primary world,* and *perilous realm,* are spelled and capitalized, except in direct quotation, according to American scholarly style convention. Moreover, italics (except in direct quotation, where all italics are the author's own unless otherwise indicated) are reserved for discussions of words as terms or to express emphasis. I have applied similar conventions in the discussion of the work of other authors, such as Philip Pullman.

The wide selection of editions of Tolkien's fiction likewise has implications for usage. This is particularly true of *The Lord of the Rings* in all its various editions—one-volume, three-volume, trade paperback, mass-market paperback, faux leather, deluxe edition, illustrated edition, all with differing paginations. This broad selection makes for a scholar's dilemma—which edition to cite and how—and a bibliographer's nightmare. The usual way is to cite the hardcover second edition, and—since even one-volume editions of *The Lord of the Rings* still carry the titles of the original three volumes, and are divided into six books—to list volume title, book number, chapter number, and page number. Thus a reference to or quotation from the opening lines of chapter 1 of *The Fellowship of the Ring* is cited parenthetically as (*FR* I, i, 29), the idea being that whatever edition readers may use, this road map will bring them pretty close.

But then there are *The Silmarillion* and the Silmarillion, two works separated (apparently) only by typography—italic vs. roman. Actually, they are substantially different from one another. The former denotes the one-volume book selected, arranged, and edited by Christopher Tolkien and published in 1977. The latter is Tolkien's own inclusive term for the drafts of his entire mythology in all its stages (including *The Lord of the Rings*), which Christopher Tolkien edited and published serially from 1983 to 1996 in twelve separately titled volumes with the series title The History of Middle-Earth. Again, the simplest way to cite is by title, with an italic *S* standing for the published *Silmarillion*, the roman HOME standing for the whole series, and separate abbreviations for separate titles within the HOME series—*BLT* for *Book of Lost Tales*, for example, or *LB* for *The Lays of Beleriand*. Tolkien's essays published in larger volumes are cited by the title of the volume in which they appear, such as *MC* for *The Monsters and the Critics and Other Essays* or *TOFS* for *Tolkien On Fairy-stories*. All other books are cited by author unless an author has more than one, in which case citation will be by title key word; Richard Dorson's *Peasant Customs and Savage Myths*, for example, is cited as *Peasant Customs*, and Tom Shippey's *The Road to Middle-earth* is cited as *Road*, while his Author of the Century is cited as *Author*. All works referred to in the text are listed under author and complete title in the Works Cited.

Works by Tolkien

The Adventures of Tom Bombadil—*ATB*
The Annotated Hobbit—*AH*
"Beowulf: The Monsters and the Critics," in *The Monsters and the Critics and Other Essays*—*MC*
The Book of Lost Tales, Part I—*BLT I*
The Book of Lost Tales, Part II—*BLT II*

"English and Welsh," in *Angles and Britons—A&B*
The Fall of Arthur—FoA
The Fellowship of the Ring—FR
The History of Middle-Earth [series]—HOME
The Hobbit—H
"Ides Ælfscyne" in *Songs for the Philologists—SP*
The Lay of Aotrou and Itroun—A&I
The Lays of Beleriand—LB
The Letters of J. R. R. Tolkien—Letters
"Looney," *The Oxford Magazine—OM*
The Lord of the Rings in one volume—*LotR*
The Lost Road and Other Writings—LR
A Middle English Vocabulary—Vocabulary
The Monsters and the Critics and Other Essays—MC
Morgoth's Ring—MR
"Mythopoeia" in *Tree and Leaf, Including the Poem* "Mythopoeia"—*T&L*
The Notion Club Papers in *Sauron Defeated—SD*
"On Fairy-stories" in *Essays Presented to Charles Williams—EPCW*
"On Fairy-stories" in *The Monsters and the Critics and Other Essays—MC*
"On the Kalevala" in *The Story of Kullervo—SK*
The Peoples of Middle-earth—Peoples
The Return of the King—RK
The Return of the Shadow—RS
"The Rivers and Beacon-hills of Gondor," in *Vinyar Tengwar—VT*
Sauron Defeated—SD
The Simarillion—S
Smith of Wootton Major, ed. Flieger—*SMW*
Songs for the Philologists—SP
The Story of Kullervo, ed. Flieger—*SK*
Tolkien On Fairy-Stories, ed. Flieger and Anderson—*TOFS*
The Treason of Isengard—TI
Tree and Leaf, Including the Poem "Mythopoeia"—*T&L*
The Two Towers—TT
Unfinished Tales of Númenor and Middle-earth—UT
The War of the Jewels—WJ
The War of the Ring—WR
Words, Phrases and Passages in Various Tongues in The Lord of the Rings—*WPP*

Note to the Reader

This book is not one continuous argument on a single subject. Rather, it is a collection of discrete essays, each written for a particular occasion and meant to be read here one by one and in no particular order. It could be said, however, that in the broadest sense I am always making a continuous, albeit multivalent, argument about the essential aspects of Tolkien's legendarium—about its nature as a secondary world, its emphasis on Faërie, its re-creation of medieval and (despite his disclaimers) Celtic and French material. Thus, some of the same ideas and concepts I judge essential to understanding Tolkien's work are discussed in more than one essay, and not infrequently in very nearly the same words. An example of such overlap is the etymology of the word *Faërie*, which comes up in several essays, in each case because I deemed it necessary to the discussion at that point. Another overlap concerns his term *Faërian Drama*, which he uses to denote an important and little-analyzed concept that I discuss at length in "But What Did He Really Mean?" (37–44) and more briefly but still necessarily in "The Forest and the Trees" (192–93). Discussion of Tolkien's use of medieval Celtic and French (often related) motifs in part 4 presents another such overlap.

Although I have tried to trim unnecessary repetition, for the most part I've left these discussions as they were when first written, judging each to be necessary to the argument of the particular essay in which it is embedded. If, as seems not unlikely, you are already familiar with the ideas, feel free to skip the discussions.

PART ONE

"A Perilous Land"

Defining *Faërie*

> Faërie is a perilous land, and in it are pitfalls for the unwary and dungeons for the overbold.
>
> —J. R. R. Tolkien, "On Fairy-stories"

Tolkien's famous essay "On Fairy-stories" begins with a warning: there are pitfalls and dungeons for the unwary and overbold. The words sound both ominous and cautionary, and taken together suggest more than peril; they predict reprisal. This is not an expected consequence of the reading of fairy tales. But Tolkien knew what he was talking about. Wary or unwary, bold or overbold, he'd been there. As a reader, he knew the power over the imagination of what he called Faërie, the state of enchantment, and the fate of those who lose themselves within it. As a scholar, he knew it was perilous to try to define fairy stories, to discover where they came from, to interrogate their relationship to "real life," to analyze the unanalyzable craft of sub-creation, or to defend the value of fantasy; nevertheless, he proceeded to do all of those things, as the essays in this section show.

His statement, later in "On Fairy-stories," that "there would always be a 'fairy-tale,'" forms the main title and is the focus of my essay on his essay, putting the latter in the context of the myth and folklore controversies of the nineteenth and early twentieth centuries. My next essay, "But What Did He Really Mean?" examines the contrasting and sometimes contradictory statements that Tolkien made over the years about Faërie, about the amount of conscious Christianity in his work, and about the integrity of his sub-creation. "Re-creating Reality" is a further examination of his theory and practice of fantasy. "War, Death, and Fairy Stories in the Work of J. R. R. Tolkien" takes as its premise Tolkien's statement in *The Silmarillion* that death is the "gift" of the godhead and examines his various and sometimes perplexing treatments of death in *The Lord of the Rings*. "Eucatastrophe and the Dark," written for an MLA handbook on teaching Tolkien, discusses my strong belief as a teacher at both graduate and undergraduate levels in the importance of introducing students to Tolkien's fiction through the competing lenses of his two landmark essays, "On Fairy-stories," which emphasizes the happy ending, and "*Beowulf:* The Monsters and the Critics," which focuses on the inevitability of death and final darkness. Together, these two sides of his vision set up the polarity and tension between light and dark that I see as a hallmark of his fiction.

"There Would Always Be a 'Fairy-tale'"
J. R. R. Tolkien and the Folklore Controversy

In March of 1939, with the Second World War about to begin, a middle-aged professor of Anglo-Saxon at Oxford University with a private hobby of inventing myth and languages took time out from both occupations to deliver the annual Andrew Lang Lecture at St. Andrews University in Scotland. Surprisingly, Tolkien's talk was the first in the series to deal with Lang's work in myth and folklore. He called his lecture, which he later expanded and published as an essay, "Fairy-stories." In it, he recalled that his own taste for fairy stories was "wakened . . . on the threshold of manhood, and quickened to full life by war" (*MC* 135).

The war to which Tolkien referred was not the one about to start but its predecessor, soon to be known as the "First" World War. Nevertheless, it is not difficult to track the connections that might have linked fairy stories, the past war, and the one ready to start as he spoke at St. Andrews. World War I began in August 1914. In September of that year, John Ronald Tolkien, then a twenty-two-year-old student at Oxford awaiting military call-up, wrote a fairy-tale poem titled "The Voyage of Eärendel," about a celestial mariner who sails the night sky to seek peace for Middle-earth. It was the beginning of his invented mythology (Carpenter, *Tolkien* 71; *BLT* II 267, 277n).

Tolkien's so-called mythology for England has been much discussed among scholars of his work, and his own words about his motive in undertaking such a project have usually been taken at face value:

> I was from early days grieved by the poverty of my own beloved country: it had no stories of its own (bound up with its tongue and soil), not of the quality that I sought and found (as an ingredient) in legends of other lands.

5

> There was Greek, and Celtic, and Romance, Germanic, Scandinavian, and Finnish (which greatly affected me); but nothing English, save impoverished chap-book stuff. . . . I had a mind to make a body of more or less connected legend . . . which I could dedicate simply to: to England; to my country. . . . I would draw some of the great tales in fullness, and leave many only placed in the scheme, and sketched. The cycles should be linked to a majestic whole, and yet leave scope for other minds and hands, wielding paint and music and drama. (*Letters* 144–45)

The concept is clear, and the entirety of Tolkien's Silmarillion cosmology as published in The History of Middle-earth fits the description like Cinderella's slipper. However, the historical and intellectual background from which that concept emerged has been too little considered.

The two coincident events mentioned earlier, the start of Tolkien's mythology and the start of World War I, were themselves coincident with a third—not a beginning this time, but an end. This was the close of what Richard Dorson calls the "golden century" of British folklore studies, 1813 to 1914 (*Peasant Customs* ix). More than mere chronology connects all three. While the start of war was not the inspiration for Tolkien's mythology, which had been taking shape in his mind for some time, the immediacy of the conflict and its threat to European national identities if Germany should prevail may well have acted as a spur. The outbreak of hostilities had the opposite effect on folklore studies. The exigencies of war slammed the door on the first burst of international cooperation in this area of research.

Tolkien's often-republished essay "On Fairy-stories" is usually read in the context of his own work as his creative manifesto, explicating the principles he was even then putting into practice in his own mythological fiction. In the last month of 1937, over a year before his St. Andrews lecture, he had begun the sequel to *The Hobbit* requested by his publisher, George Allen and Unwin, a work that, after long labor, became *The Lord of the Rings*. Begun as "the new Hobbit" (*Letters* 112), this project began almost immediately to veer away from the juvenile tone and content of the earlier book, gravitating toward the older and much darker material of the Silmarillion mythology originally intended "for England." It seems reasonable to suppose that Tolkien's theoretical discussion of fairy stories would be colored by his practice and that the standards he set out in the lecture would be those he was even then engaged in developing through his own experience.

There is, however, a wider and more complex intellectual and historical background into which both the lecture and the fiction fit, for the principles set forth in his essay were not just the working template for his own story but also a direct reply to and argument against the current major folklore theories. At the time Tolkien spoke at St. Andrews, the golden century—the first fine, careless rapture of folklore studies—was long over. Nonetheless, the questions that had concerned the folklorists—according to Dorson, "[t]he origin and dispersion of the Aryans, the mythopoeic view of early man, the animistic philosophy of savages, the survivals of primitive belief among peasants" (*Peasant Customs* x), together with the Sherlockian search for answers and the close-up inspection of trees that left researchers unable to see the forest— were all still operable factors. By 1939, it was time to review and reevaluate the state of the question, and Tolkien, no folklorist but a myth-maker, felt (though he modestly denied it) equal to the task. Much of his argument in "On Fairy-stories" was both a capsule history of and a rebuttal to the theories of the folklore movement.

The issues over which the folklorists disagreed are precisely the topics Tolkien addresses in his lecture, and that he counters with his own more imaginative analysis of the nature and appropriate uses of fantasy. To enter the debate, Tolkien selected three names representing the major and contending schools of theory that had generated and sustained the controversy. From comparative philology, he took Max Müller and his follower, George Webbe Dasent, and from evolutionary anthropology, he took Müller's chief opponent, Andrew Lang.

Tolkien faulted all of them and the theories they represented for "using the stories not as they were meant to be used, but as a quarry from which to dig evidence, or information, about matters in which they are interested" (*MC* 119). In his view, these folklorists were not reading stories at all; they were examining data, a process which to him was a gross misuse of the enchantment, what he called the quality of Faërie, that he found in fairy tales. His response began with a discussion of what fairy stories were not, followed by his judgment of what they were and how they worked. The result was an on-the-spot forging of his own working theory, hammered out on the anvil of the folklore controversy.

From each contending school of thought, Tolkien plucked a phrase or idea to address, which he then used in topic sentences in his lecture. From Müller, he took the concepts of nature myth and solar mythology, and the idea of mythology as a disease of language (Müller 2: passim), all of which were staples of Müller's groundbreaking first essay, "Comparative Mythology," published in 1856. From Lang, he took the idea of human maturation as the model for cultural evolution, an idea that had led Lang to conclude that the matter of fairy stories was primitive, and that consequently the stories themselves were fit only for children, concepts he spelled out in one of his most widely read books, *Custom and Myth*. From Dasent's introduction to his translation of Moe and Asbjørnsen's collection of *Norske Folke-eventyr* (rendered in English as *Popular Tales from the Norse*), Tolkien took an extended metaphor, the "soup" of story and the "bones of the ox" from which it is boiled (Dasent 7).

Some background is necessary here. The origins of folklore research go back to the gentleman antiquaries of the sixteenth and seventeenth centuries, John Leland, William Camden, and John Aubrey. To begin with, their investigations into the antiquities of England were chiefly topographical and included Stonehenge, Avebury, and a variety of other monuments, mounds, long barrows, and standing stones. The first great literary flowering came in the eighteenth century with the ballad collections of Thomas Percy and Francis Child. Late in the eighteenth century, the German Johannes Gottfried von Herder argued persuasively for oral traditions rooted in the language of the unlettered "folk" as the repository of any country's cultural identity. It was an idea whose time had come, and by the early nineteenth century the hunt was on, no longer for physical ruins but for narrative folk traditions as reservoirs of national spirit.

This was Dorson's "golden century," the era of the great collectors. The brothers Grimm in Germany, Moe and Asbjørnsen in Norway, Elias Lönnrot in Finland, and in the British Isles, John Francis Campbell of Islay in Scotland, Sir John Rhys in Wales, Thomas Croker and Jeremiah Curtin in Ireland, and Thomas Keightley in general all turned to the "folk" to discover a mythic past. Their research was coincident with a resurgence of interest in cultural and national identity. Germany had not long been a united nation when the Grimms began looking for philological material to validate that unity. Likewise, Ireland, Scotland, and Wales, the Celtic outposts in the British Isles, were reaching for and finding evidence of a cultural history independent of English hegemony. An especially notable success was that of Elias Lönnrot, whose collection of Finnish folk songs, arranged and published as *Kalevala*, gave his native Finland, for centuries the shuttlecock of Russia and Sweden, a national identity.

Despite all this nationalistic fervor, however, once the stories were collected and set down it became uncomfortably clear that they were made of pretty raw material: incest, rape, bestiality, child murder, cannibalism, and the like. Two of the Grimms' stories Tolkien mentions in his lecture—"The Frog-King" and "The Juniper Tree"—amply illustrate this. "The Frog-King" is about a princess who promises to marry a frog if he will retrieve her ball from a well. When he does indeed fetch her the ball, she is faced with the disagreeable prospect of fulfilling her promise and admitting the frog to her bed. The fact that the frog magically and at the last minute turns into a handsome prince is irrelevant to the real frisson of the story, the monstrous notion of a young woman going to bed with a frog. This is made explicit in the narrative when the frog jumps on to her pillow as she prepares for the night and demands to share her bed.

"The Juniper Tree" hinges on cannibalism. The story tells of a wicked stepmother who murders, cuts up, stews, and serves her young stepson to the boy's father for dinner. The boy's stepsister (a more loving relative than her mother) saves the bones from the stew and buries them under a tree in the yard, from whence the boy is resurrected as a bird. This "gay and vengeful bird-spirit," as Tolkien describes it (*MC* 128), brings about the death of the stepmother by dropping a millstone on her. As in "The Frog King," the taboo is not violated, for the father, though ignorant of the content of the soup, inexplicably loses his appetite. Nevertheless, the concept is introduced.

The proper Victorians were properly horrified at such goings-on, prompting a search for anything that could explain or justify such barbarities as child murder, anthropophagy, and bestiality and such logical inconsistencies as just how a union between a girl and a frog could be consummated. In Britain, the battle lines were drawn between the mythologists and the anthropologists, specifically represented by Max Müller and Andrew Lang. Müller used comparative philology, relying heavily on Greek and Vedic sources, and found the origins he sought in evidence from Sanskrit, Homeric Greek, and in comparisons of Indo-European (or as he termed them "Indo-Aryan") languages. The search for Aryan roots was full of pitfalls, and it did not take long for some collectors to fall into them, and to look for what they wanted to find instead of finding whatever was there. Nazi Germany was the extreme and ugly culmination of the early Indo-Aryan theory.

Müller introduced his argument in an epochal essay, "Comparative Mythology" (1856), later reprinted as volume 2 of his four-volume *Chips from a German Workshop* (1867–75). Here he proposed that myths as we have them arose through verbal misapprehension (Dorson, *Peasant Customs* 67), the late misunderstanding of early, primarily Sanskrit Vedic names for celestial phenomena. According to Müller, the concepts of the Aryan gods arose in the "mythopoeic" age (qtd. in Dorson, *British Folklorists* 162). As the migrations of the Indo-Aryan people splintered them into separate groups, so their language and its related mythology splintered into various offshoots. During this process, the original true, "nature/solar" meanings were forgotten, surviving only in mythical words and phrases that were retained although their original referents were forgotten.

The stories and names that then developed to explain these phrases constituted Müller's notion of mythology as "a disease of language": that invalid understanding from which new stories—the myths as we know them—were created (Dorson, *British Folklorists* 162). The natural phenomena originally referred to—sun, sky, dawn, night, earth, wind—were replaced by heroic personifications—Apollo, Zeus, Eos, Nyx, Gaia, and others. Müller's conclusion was that by tracing the words back to ancient forms it was possible to arrive at their original referents. However, he was constrained by his own catchphrases, for his interpretation of mythology as a disease implied a previous state of health, a state presumably expressed in the "original" language of solar mythology. Moreover, the assumption that there had been an "original," therefore "true" solar meaning that had been lost, had the predictable but deplorable consequence of elevating the "Aryan" peoples and languages to primacy, and, by implication, denigrating the non-Aryan "others."

When you look for things, you are apt to find them, and pretty soon Müller was finding solar mythology everywhere and seeing solar heroes in every myth he examined. Any time a hero went into a cave, or traveled from east to west, or died in battle, that was the sun setting. A hero vanquishing a dragon was the rising sun conquering the night. And so on. Those who followed in Müller's wake elaborated his theory but stuck to his methods. Adalbert Kuhn, a German scholar described by Dorson as "one of the foremost of the philological mythologists" and the chief proponent of the "lightning school" (*British Folklorists* 171), proposed a variation that substituted lightning for the sun and found electrical phenomena in Zeus and Indra, and lightning-related fire in the story of Prometheus. Kuhn expanded Müller's theory to include a variety of weather phenomena—clouds, lightning-bolts, thunder—but did not substantially change its direction.

Müller's philological principle ruled uncontested for nearly a decade before it was, as Tolkien put it, "dethroned from the high place it once held in this court of inquiry" (*MC* 121). The dethroner was Andrew Lang, who opposed Müller vigorously and vociferously for more than twenty years and finally toppled him. Lang's *Custom and Myth* attacked comparative mythology for its self-limitation to Aryan-speaking peoples and replaced philology with anthropology. To his credit, Lang avoided the Aryan/racial pitfall, but only to fall into the trap of social Darwinism, a pit of almost equal size and naïveté. His approach was grounded in the notion that humanity had evolved culturally from a "primitive" to a "civilized" state. He "demolished the hypothesis of disease-of-language . . . and filled the vacuum with a continuous chain of savage survivals" (Dorson, *British Folklorists* 197).

In Lang's view, the rawer aspects of the tales were the relicts not of some lost language of celestial mythology but of "primitive," therefore "savage," cultural practices. His evidence was assembled from studies of contemporary, so-called primitive peoples such as Native Americans, Australian Aborigines, Zulus, Hottentots, Melanesians, Polynesians, Samoyeds, and West Highlanders. Not the history of Indo-Aryan languages, said Lang, but the ritual and totemic customs of contemporary primitive societies can explain the seemingly irrational, at times horrific subject matter of myths and fairy stories. "The origin of the irrational element in myth and tale is to be found in the qualities of the uncivilized imagination" (qtd. in Dorson, *Peasant Customs* 297). Lang's view of "the uncivilized imagination" as the earliest or childhood stage of human cultural development led directly to the concomitant assumption that in a post-childhood, that is to say, modern, world, fairy tales would only—indeed, could only—be enjoyed by children.

Although by the time he gave his lecture the golden century was long over, Tolkien was by no means the only member of his generation to respond (whether negatively or positively) to the intellectual climate of opinion arising out of the controversy. Others had read the folklorists and taken their words to heart. The first novel in C. S. Lewis's so-called space trilogy, *Out of the Silent Planet*, has his protagonist, a philologist, taking notes on the language of Malacandra (the planet Mars). In the next volume, *Perelandra* (i.e., Venus), this language turns out to be Old Solar, an original speech common to the entire solar system but now entirely lost on Earth.

It is not difficult to hear an echo of Indo-Aryan theory in the antiquity and originality of Lewis's lost tongue, or of Müller's solar mythology in the name Lewis bestows on his fictive language. Lewis's good friend and (along with Tolkien) his fellow-Inkling, Owen Barfield, devoted much of his B. Litt. thesis, later expanded and published as *Poetic Diction*, to addressing Müller's theory. Tolkien, the one bona fide mythmaker in the group, was unique only in basing his answer on practice as well as theory.

Let us turn now to Tolkien's lecture, which left neither the philologists nor the anthropologists much room to maneuver. Addressing Müller, and through him his followers, Tolkien dealt summarily with disease as either a cause or a result. He first rejected Müller's famous phrase and then reversed it: "Mythology," he maintained, "is not a disease at all.... It would be more near the truth to say that languages, especially modern European languages, are a disease of mythology" (*MC* 121–22). But the idea that either was a "disease" of the other was countered by his proposal that language, myth, and human consciousness arose together, simultaneously and indivisibly.

This was to him so central and important an idea that he returned to it several times. "To ask what is the origin of stories, however qualified," he said, "is to ask what is the origin of language and the mind" (*MC* 119). In his view, myth-making is neither a late nor a degenerate function of language separated from its roots. A myth is not a cutting grafted onto a new stem but an organic and self-consistent whole, with its own inner consistency of reality. Having established the point, Tolkien nevertheless made it again. "The incarnate mind, the tongue, and the tale are in our world coeval" (*MC* 122). Language, story, and human imagination are inborn faculties in the human organism. No one of them has a pathological relationship to any of the others.

That said, Tolkien next addressed the concept of "solar" or "nature" myth. In his view, Müller's notion—that gods were originally natural forces that over time diminished to legends and finally dwindled to fairy stories—would be "the truth almost upside down. . . . The gods may derive their colour and beauty from the high splendours of nature, but it was Man who obtained these for them, abstracted them from sun and moon and cloud; their personality they get direct from him. . . ." (*MC* 123). His counter example, a gage thrown down to Müller and his Greek and Sanskrit etymologies, is from a mythology that he vastly preferred, the Norse.

Using Müller's own weapon of philology and expanding the argument to include the "lightning school," he offered Thórr as a typical case of "Olympian nature myth," glossing Thórr's name as the Norse word for thunder and suggesting Thórr's hammer, Miöllnir, as lightning. He then went on to point out what to him was the important and obvious fact: that beyond these characteristics, Thórr had a personality that was absent from thunder or lightning. The question of which came first, the phenomenon or the character, Tolkien suggested, is a meaningless one. Take Thórr as far back as you can and you will still find a story about a recognizably human personality, for, he declared, "there would always be a 'fairy-tale' as long as there was any Thórr. When the fairy-tale ceased, there would be just thunder, which no human ear had yet heard" (*MC* 124).

Turning to George Dasent, Tolkien took Dasent's metaphor of "the soup," elaborated it, and then reapplied it, saying that "we must be satisfied with the soup that is set before us, and not desire to see the bones of the ox out of which it has been boiled." He went on to imply that Dasent had said the right thing for the wrong reason. He dismissed Dasent's "soup" as "a mishmash of bogus pre-history founded on the early surmises of Comparative Philology" and found little to value in his "bones," which he described as "the workings and the proofs that led to these theories" (*MC* 120).

I suggest that it was not mere coincidence that led Tolkien to make such a statement in 1939. Dasent's stance was blatantly and stridently racist, described by Richard Dorson as "praising the Aryans and denigrating non-Aryans in the crassest racist terms" (*Peasant Customs* 572). Dasent had seized on the "Aryan" component of the Indo-Aryan theory to make chillingly explicit in his own discussion what may have been implicit in the work of his folklore peers. Where Müller had focused on language, Dasent focused on race. Such phrases as "the popular literature of the race," by which he meant the Norse or Germanic, and "tales which England once had in common with all the Aryan race" (qtd. in Dorson, *Peasant Customs* 598, 599) make his position clear.

There was nothing to stop Dasent from publishing his opinions, and while they seem clearly indefensible now, at the time, they reflected the cultural chauvinism of many scholars of his generation. But by the time of Tolkien's lecture, such opinions were no longer simply the theories of folklorists but the explicit principles behind Nazi Germany and its war machine, just then gearing up for action. I don't think it is stretching too much to read in Tolkien's words an implicit condemnation of the exemplar and worst illustration of Dasent's Aryan emphasis. Tolkien countered by focusing on the story rather than on its ancestry (whether "Aryan" or not). He declared that by the "soup" he meant "the story as served up by its author or teller," which he found effective, and by "desire to see the bones" he meant its sources or component material, which he did not (*MC* 120).

Tolkien then elaborated Dasent's extended metaphor of soup, ox, and bones, adding the pot or cauldron of story and also the cook (the largely unknown story teller), but only to illustrate the futility of inquiry into origins. Despite his own taste for philology, he felt that desire for the bones was not the most desirable purpose of reading, and that it worked to the detriment of the story itself. While conceding that fairy stories are "very ancient indeed" and that they are found "wherever there is language" (*MC* 121), he very quickly dealt with the major questions of independent evolution (which he called invention), diffusion (which he called borrowing in space—that is, through migration), and inheritance (which he called borrowing in time). Not surprisingly, Tolkien, himself an inventor, privileged invention: "To an inventor, that is, to a story-maker, the other two must in the end lead back . . . At the centre of the supposed diffusion there is a place where once an inventor lived. . . . While if we believe that sometimes there occurred the independent striking out of similar ideas . . . we simply multiply the ancestral inventor, but do not in that way the more clearly understand his gift" (*MC* 121).

Having dealt with Müller and Dasent, Tolkien turned to Lang, who was, after all, the occasion for his lecture. "Children's taste," Lang had declared, "remains like the taste of their naked ancestors thousands of years ago" (qtd. in *MC* 134). If anything, this outraged Tolkien even more than the solar theory, and he took strenuous exception to Lang's words. "[D]o we really know much about these 'naked ancestors,'" he inquired, "except that they were certainly not naked? Our fairy-stories, however old certain elements in them may be, are certainly not the same as theirs" (*MC* 134). As an adult who read and wrote fairy stories, he regarded it as both trivializing and patronizing to propose, as Lang did, that 1) the prehistoric period at which fairy stories may be said to have arisen was analogous to "savage" cultures, and that 2) it was therefore the "childhood" of human development.

Tolkien rejected out of hand the notion that "children are the natural or specially appropriate audience for fairy-stories." The fact that fairy tales are "a natural human taste" does not necessarily mean, he declared, that this taste is natural to all humans, nor that it is more natural to children than to adults (*MC* 136). Since his own taste for fairy stories had been awakened in young manhood and quickened to full life by war, it followed that what fairy stories had to offer was adult fare. The bowdlerized fairy tales being offered to children in his own time were sanitized versions, with all the gore and mayhem excised. If they had to be edited down for children, it followed that they could hardly have been originally intended for them. He vigorously criticized Lang's own literary fairy stories for their double vision—a patronizing attitude toward the child audience and a conspiratorial glance over the children's heads at any listening adults.

He praised "The Juniper Tree" precisely for its "beauty and horror," for "its exquisite and tragic beginning, the abominable cannibal stew, the gruesome bones, the gay and vengeful bird-spirit coming out of a mist that rose from the tree " (*MC* 128). Yet he found the story's chief attraction to be its immense antiquity, resident chiefly in the very elements that so disturbed the Victorians—the child-murder and cannibalism. "I do not think," he declared, "[that] I was harmed by the horror *in the fairy-tale setting*, out of whatever dark beliefs and practices of the past it may have come. Such stories have now a mythical or total (unanalysable) effect, an effect quite independent of the findings of Comparative Folklore, and one which it cannot spoil or explain" (*MC* 128–29).

The outbreak of World War I sharpened the sense of cultural nationalism even as it threatened to obliterate it. At the same time, it closed the golden century that had awakened that national sensibility. Its effect in both directions coincided with and may have spurred Tolkien's first efforts at a fictive myth for England modeled on the primary myths he was even then discovering. He had written of *Kalevala*, "I would that we had more of it left—something of the same sort that belonged to the English" (Carpenter, *Tolkien* 89). Distressed at the poor showing of England in the folklore stakes, he desired to remedy this deficiency by doing for England something similar to what Lönnrot had done for Finland. Out of this came the notion of a mythology for England, something that would give his own country a mythic (albeit in his case entirely fictive) identity of its own.

With World War II about to break out as he gave his lecture, Tolkien revisited the subject, recapitulating and at the same time replying to the controversy by reaffirming myth's intrinsic value as story, not as source for extrinsic information. That Tolkien loved fairy stories is plain to anyone who has read his work, and in a purely personal context perhaps we need look no further to explain his lecture. "[W]hen we have done all that research . . . can do," he said, "when we have explained many of the elements commonly found embedded in fairy-stories . . . there remains still a point too often forgotten: that is the effect produced *now* by these old things in the stories as they are" (*MC* 128).

But in a larger context, it is not unreasonable to speculate that just as the First World War had quickened Tolkien's taste for fairy tales and aroused his ambition to create a mythology for England, so the shadow of the Second World War falling across his lecture moved him to rehearse the specific values he looked for and found both in fairy stories and his own mythology. Add to these the more intellectual background of the folklore controversy and the combination will point us back to Tolkien's own writing, deepening and widening the context in which this work can be understood.

And in this historical and intellectual context we should not overlook the folklore controversy as the whetstone that honed Tolkien's own mythology at the same time that it sharpened his defense of the worth of fairy stories "as they are"—that is to say, as stories, not as rocks containing fossils more valuable than the matrix from which they may have been pried. He defended fairy stories for their gift of enduring values to readers of any age. These values included recovery, escape, consolation, and eucatastrophe—the last a word coined by Tolkien himself to describe the "sudden joyous 'turn'" in a fairy story when victory is plucked from defeat, life is rescued from death, and joy triumphs over sorrow (*MC* 153). And in an added context, those values cannot but have had a special and timely value not just to Tolkien but to his audience in relation to the two world wars—the one so recently over and the next about to start.

In both these contexts, it is easy to agree with Tolkien that it matters less where fairy stories came from, or what they might originally have referred to, than what they have to give the reader in that *now* which he so strongly emphasized. For just as there will always be war, so, in Tolkien's view, there will always be fairy stories, even if he has to write them himself. If we have the one, we surely need the other. We need fairy stories to give us those very things that he listed so carefully—recovery of a more hopeful reality, escape from the imminent shadow of death, and consolation for sorrow through the eucatastrophe that turns catastrophe to joy.

Without the fairy story, there will be just thunder, which no human ear will have heard.

But What Did He Really Mean?

> A coherent personality aspires, like a work of art, to contain its conflicts without resolving them dogmatically.
> —Judith Thurman, *Secrets of the Flesh*

Almost from the date of its publication, *The Lord of the Rings* has been subject to conflicting interpretations, appealing equally to neopagans who see in its elves and hobbits an alternative to the dreary realism of mainstream culture and to Christians who find an evangelical message in its imagery of stars and light and bread and sacrifice. Tolkien was more patient with enthusiasts from both groups than many authors would have been, but their fervor did lead him to make ambiguous and even contradictory statements—as, for example, in comments in his letters as to whether there was intentional Christianity in *The Lord of the Rings*, or in his essay "On Fairy-stories" (written before *The Lord of the Rings* but strongly influencing it) as to whether elves (aka fairies) are real. Thus he could write to Robert Murray that *The Lord of the Rings* was "fundamentally" religious and Catholic (*Letters* 172) and to W. H. Auden that he felt no obligation to make it fit Christianity (*Letters* 355). He could, in "On Fairy-stories" and its rough drafts, argue for elves as real, yet on the same page—sometimes in the same paragraph—call them products of human imagination. He could in one breath talk about Faërie as an actual place and in the next say it was the realm of fantasy. There are many such turnabouts in Tolkien's writings, reversals of direction that not only make him appear contradictory but invite contradictory interpretations of his work, permitting advocates with opposite views to cherry-pick the statements that best support their positions.

One result of Tolkien's ambiguity is that the same cherries can be picked by both sides to support contending positions. For example, the same passage in a letter to Robert Murray is cited by Joseph Pearce to defend Tolkien's Christian orthodoxy, and by Patrick Curry to support his intentional paganism (109, 117–18). Maybe this is what Tolkien intended; maybe not. Michael Drout's 2005 article "Towards a Better Tolkien Criticism" points out that the "over-reliance of critics upon the *Letters* guides Tolkien scholarship down the narrow channel" of finding a single theological meaning in Tolkien's works (21). Therefore, the question in my title for this chapter, "But What Did He Really Mean?" is not intended to resolve the ambiguity but to use it as a guide to what may have been issues as unresolved for Tolkien as they were for his admirers. My discussion has three sections: the first on the question of intentional Christianity in Tolkien's fiction, the second on the reality (or unreality) of elves and Faërie, and the third on the related meaning of his term *Faërian Drama*.

Christianity

As with any correspondents Tolkien tailored his letters to their particular addressees, although, as we will see, he went farther in this than do many letter writers. His most definite—and most negative—statement came in a 1951 letter to Milton Waldman of the publishing firm William Collins, Sons, and Co. The letter was written to persuade Waldman that Collins should publish Tolkien's fictive mythology, the Silmarillion, together with the then-unpublished *Lord of the Rings*, and is therefore more descriptive and rhetorical than conventionally chatty. It is important to note that although Waldman was a fellow Catholic, Tolkien did not use shared Catholicism or even shared Christianity as a selling point for his work. In fact, he went in the opposite direction, telling Waldman that what disqualified the "Arthurian world" as England's mythology was that it was "involved in, and explicitly contains the Christian religion." While conceding that "[m]yth and fairy-story must, as all art, reflect and contain in solution elements of moral and religious truth," he argued that such elements should not be "explicit, not in the known form of the primary world," which explicitness seemed to him "fatal" (144). The word *fatal* is the key, and means exactly what it says—"lethal," "death-dealing." Connecting a fictional mythology to one from the real world would literally kill the fiction, reducing it to a gloss on another story. Robbed of independence, it would become allegory in which every element would point to the other story.

Yet in a letter to another fellow Catholic, Robert Murray (who had read galley proofs of *The Lord of the Rings*), Tolkien took the alternative position (often cited as evidence of Christian content in his fiction) that his book was "a fundamentally religious and Catholic work; unconsciously so at first, but consciously in the revision" (*Letters* 172). We should consider the possibility that since by this time the book had not only had been accepted for publication (by Allen and Unwin) but was well on its way to publication, Tolkien now felt more confidant in affirming a Christian stance. Yet he followed this affirmation with a rather odd explanation: "*That is why* I have not put in, or have cut out, practically all references to anything like 'religion', to cults or practices, in the imaginary world. For the religious element is absorbed into the story and the symbolism" (172; my emphasis). This takes some unpacking. At first glance it seems to be saying that the work is so suffused with Christianity that explicit reference is superfluous. However, a closer look reveals words so carefully arranged to say both everything and nothing that they practically invite competing arguments. Joseph Pearce uses them to show that Tolkien meant *The Lord of the Rings* to be "theologically orthodox" (109), while Patrick Curry cites them to support the book's blend of "Christian, pagan, and humanist ingredients" (117). Pearce calls the statements paradoxical (109). Curry describes them as "syncretism" (117).

Pearce is not far off the mark. It is paradoxical to say the religiousness of a work is your motive for cutting out religion, rather like telling a loved one that the existence of your love means you don't have to declare it. Moreover, for an author who emphatically disavowed allegory to invoke the "symbolism" of a work seems disingenuous, to say the least. But Curry is not wrong either. To omit all reference to religion opens the door to a wider, more syncretistic and inclusive audience, allowing Curry, for example, to point out that the Valar "are related to the ancient elements (fire, earth, air, and water) in a characteristically pagan way" (110–11). Such widely differing readings may tell us as much about the scholars as it does about Tolkien, but it cannot be overlooked that Tolkien opened the door to both.

The key to this apparent inconsistency may lie not just in the differing philosophical adherence of the interpreters, but also in the relationship of the writer to the addressee. While the 1951 letter is addressed to Milton Waldman, Tolkien was speaking through him to William Collins, chairman of the publishing firm. Tolkien's wording makes it plain that he was seeking to have what he knew was a highly idiosyncratic work accepted on its own terms, and was thus forestalling comparison. He likened his Valar to "the 'gods' of higher mythology, which can be accepted—well, shall we say baldly, by a mind that believes in the Blessed Trinity" (*Letters* 146), pointing out the difference, not the similarity. He may also have had in mind the explicit Christian content of *The Lion, the Witch, and the Wardrobe*, C. S. Lewis's children's fantasy (published just one year earlier), which he disliked.

The addressee of the other letter, with its more orthodox statements, was Father Robert Murray, a grandson of Sir James Murray, first editor of *The Oxford English Dictionary*, on which Tolkien worked in 1919–20. At the time at which Tolkien wrote and for many years after, Fr. Murray was a priest, a member of the Society of Jesus. His close friendship with the Tolkien family was instrumental in his conversion to Catholicism in 1945–46. Clearly, then, for Tolkien and Murray, Catholicism was more than a shared religion; it was a basis for their friendship. Tolkien prefaced his statements about *The Lord of the Rings* by telling Murray that he had "even revealed to me more clearly some things about my work" (*Letters* 172). To reply to Murray's comments by saying what he said to Waldman would have been not just uncalled for, it would have been insensitive and inappropriate.

Yet to tell Murray that his revision was "consciously" Catholic (*Letters* 172), and to tell W. H. Auden a year and a half later that he had "very little . . . conscious . . . intention in mind at any point" (211) is so striking a change of position that it calls into question either Tolkien's memory or his sincerity, for if one of these statements is true, the other must be false.[1] Either Tolkien didn't know his own mind, or he was cutting his cloth to fit the wearer, telling each correspondent what he wanted to hear. We can test this by switching the statements and judging their fit, which is uncomfortable. It is highly unlikely that Tolkien would have responded to Murray by saying he had no conscious intent in writing his book, or that he would have told Waldman that the book was consciously Catholic. Nevertheless, since Tolkien was neither a hypocrite nor a liar, something more than artful dodging must be going on here. It seems possible that in each case he meant what he wrote at the time that he wrote it, and, of course, he had no reason to go back and check his letter to Murray, a fellow Catholic, when he wrote to Auden, a fellow writer and poet. The identity of the addressee determined the content of the letter, as it does for most letter writers.

For example, when Murray wrote that he found *The Lord of the Rings* compatible with "the order of Grace" and compared Galadriel to the Virgin Mary (*Letters* 171–72), he was clearly invoking "the known form of the primary world" that Tolkien had repudiated in his earlier letter to Waldman. Yet to Murray, Tolkien responded, "I think I know exactly what you mean by the order of Grace; and of course by your references to Our Lady, upon which all my own small perception of beauty both in majesty and simplicity is founded" (172). With Murray, he avoided the uncompromising "fatal" he had used to Waldman in favor of gentler phrases, like "perception of beauty" and "I know what you mean," which can convey understanding but not necessarily endorsement. It was a way to say yes but not yes. The same agreement without endorsement can be found in his 1958 letter to Deborah Webster where he cited one critic's association of lembas with the Eucharist, and another's assertion that the character of Galadriel was "clearly related to Catholic devotion to Mary" (*Letters* 288), which sounds suspiciously like "the known form of the primary world." Note, however, that here, unlike his remarks in the letter to Murray, Tolkien was citing other people's opinions, not his own. He did not commit himself, merely commenting that "far greater things may colour the mind in dealing with the lesser things of a fairy story" (*Letters* 288). But he did not say whose mind was being thus colored.

The Galadriel-Mary equation was a popular one with readers. A 1971 letter from Ruth Austin prompted Tolkien to respond that he "was particularly interested" in her remarks "about Galadriel." As with all the letters, we don't know what Austin remarked, only what Tolkien replied, which was: "I think it is true that I owe much of this character [Galadriel] to Christian and Catholic teaching and imagination about Mary," from which we may infer that Austin had made the Galadriel comparison. While this response sounds like the same sort of agreement without endorsement he had used with Webster, this time Tolkien went further, cautioning, "but actually Galadriel was a penitent: in her youth a leader in the rebellion against the Valar.... At the end of the First Age she proudly refused forgiveness or permission to return" (*Letters* 407). Parsing the grammar, we see the declarative "it is true," followed by the conjunction "but" introducing the corrective "actually," followed by "Galadriel was a penitent." Since Catholic dogma holds that Mary was conceived without sin, Tolkien's "but actually" really means "on the contrary." It separates Galadriel's penitence for wrongdoing from Mary's sinlessness. The distinction is doctrinal, and his use of doctrine rather than diplomacy to discourage an attribution of this element of Christianity in his work is notable.

In his 1967 interview with Henry Resnick, he came close to repudiating intentional Christian reference, commenting, "You don't have to be Christian to believe that somebody has to die to save something. As a matter of fact, December 25th occurred strictly by accident, and I let it in to show that this was not a christian [sic] myth anyhow. It was a purely unimportant date, and I thought, Well there it is, just an accident" (43). Note that Tolkien doesn't say it isn't Christian, just that it doesn't have to be. He echoed this in a letter to Houghton Mifflin, writing that, "the 'Third Age' was not a Christian world" but "a monotheistic world of 'natural theology'" (*Letters* 220), and in one to W. H. Auden, writing, "I don't feel under any obligation to make my story fit with formalized Christian theology, though I actually intended it to be consonant with Christian thought and belief" (*Letters* 355). It scarcely needs pointing out that "fundamentally religious," "consonant with," and "strictly by accident" show a wide spectrum of positions.

While such yes-but-not-yes tactics can be perplexing, we may give Tolkien credit for negotiating his way across the minefield of public opinion, addressing a variety of readers—many of them complete strangers—without alienating any of them. But where among them does Tolkien situate himself? The answer is, he doesn't. To arrive at his undeclared position, we must read between the lines and watch the language carefully as it jumps from "fatal" to "fundamentally religious," from "I know what you mean" to "but actually." It seems clear that at one level he simply wanted his book to be taken on its own terms as an original creation, not predicated on or tethered to a real-world mythos. He had a model in the *Beowulf* poet, who, he said, was a Christian "creating ... the illusion of surveying a past, pagan but noble and fraught with a deep significance" (*MC* 27). While this is probably what he meant when he said that the Third Age was not a Christian world, at a deeper level he was in sympathy with both codes, being devoutly Christian but with a deep-seated yearning for the old pagan heroic culture Christianity had replaced.

Yet there is one instance where Tolkien actually defended a heterodox aspect of his secondary world rather than curtseying to his orthodox opponent's position. This occurred when Peter Hastings, manager of the Newman Bookshop in Oxford, took exception to the reincarnation of Tolkien's Elves. Since Church doctrine teaches resurrection in the body, the notion of one soul inhabiting more than one body was unorthodox to say the least. Hastings suggested that Tolkien might have "overstepped the mark in metaphysical matters," and gone "beyond the position of a sub-creator" (*Letters* 187). Tolkien's reply was (for once) unequivocal and unevasive: "I do not see how ... any theologian or philosopher, unless very much better informed about the relation of spirit and body than I believe anyone to be, could deny the *possibility* of re-incarnation as a mode of existence prescribed for certain kinds of rational incarnate creatures" (*Letters* 189). Such heresy might well have sparked disagreement, if not doctrinal outrage, which may be why Tolkien didn't send the letter. His note says, "It seemed to be taking myself too importantly" (*Letters* 196), but he may also have wanted to avoid a theological argument with Hastings.

I suggest he didn't want a theological argument with anyone, and so expressed his more adventurous views with caution, ultimately keeping them to himself and to his fiction. He certainly espoused orthodox Catholicism, but his letters and his fiction show an imagination capable of transcending Christianity without disagreeing with it. Elven reincarnation remained a staple of his mythos, even in such late writings as the appendices to the "Athrabeth Finrod ah Andreth," where he insisted that the reincarnation of the Elves "seems an essential element in the tales" (*MR* 363).

Elves and Faërie

This brings us to elves and their place in his thought and work. Here the same yes-but-not-yes dynamic is in play, with the difference that Tolkien's correspondents are not actual people but hypothetical naysayers whose arguments he imagines. It seems obvious that he was torn between his desire for the reality of elves as supernatural companions to humanity and his fear of ridicule if he expressed it. The paragraphs in the Waldman letter describing his mythology are introduced by, "Do not laugh!" and concluded with, "Absurd." The early pages of the letter vacillate between eagerness to share a cherished enthusiasm and apology for its naïveté: "my crest has long since fallen," "such an overweening purpose" (*Letters* 144–45). He once told an interviewer apropos *The Hobbit*, "If I hadn't done that [said it was written for children] . . . people would have thought I was loony" ("J. R. R. Tolkien Dead at 81").

His adjective recalls the title of his poem "Looney," published in the *Oxford Magazine* in 1934, in which an unnamed speaker, asked where he has been and what he has seen, tells of his trip to fairyland and return to an uncomprehending world. "To myself I must talk, for seldom they speak, men that I meet" (340). When the publication date of *The Lord of the Rings* approached, Tolkien told Robert Murray, "[I]t will be impossible not to mind what is said. I have exposed my heart to be shot at" (Carpenter, *Tolkien* 218). He dreaded the kind of response that in fact he got from such leading lights as Edmund Wilson, whose "Oo Those Awful Orcs!" gave a voice to the uncomprehending world that "Looney" encountered on his return. It was after the publication of Wilson's review that Tolkien rewrote "Looney," removing the opening questions and the words "must" and "seldom" from the final couplet to make the speaker's isolation total.

"On Fairy-stories" confronts the same issue more prosaically, with Tolkien standing in for Looney and the reading audience replacing the "men that I meet." Anticipating a skeptical reception, Tolkien tries in the essay, as in his letters, to have it both ways, on one hand treating elves as real beings independent of humanity, and on the other saying that they are products of human imagination. The overwhelming impression is very much like that of the "Looney" poem—that he is talking to himself. In the essay he declares, "if elves are true and really exist independently of our tales about them, then this also is certainly true, elves are not primarily concerned with us, nor we with them" (*MC* 113, *TOFS* 32), but he then backtracks in a footnote: "This is true, even if they [elves] are only creations of Man's mind, 'true' only as reflecting in a particular way one of Man's visions of Truth" (*MC* 113, note 2; *TOFS* 32). A few pages further on, he uses the same side step, saying, "it is from [elves] that we may learn what is the central desire and aspiration of human Fantasy—even if the elves are, all the more so in so far as they are, only a product of Fantasy itself" (*MC* 143; *TOFS* 64).

Earlier drafts show him struggling to articulate the same ideas. In Manuscript B he wrote, "I will tell you what I think . . . If fairies really exist—independently of Man—then very few of our 'Fairy-stories' have any relation to them. . . . They are a quite separate creation living in another mode" (*TOFS* 254), which is exactly the situation in "Looney," where the voyager senses the presence of the fairy inhabitants but cannot connect with them. Yet some pages later in the same draft, he raises the question of "whether *faierie* [sic] exists independent of man, or whether it is creation" (*TOFS* 268). This is not unlike the either/or "consciously Catholic" vs. "little conscious intention" of his statements to Murray and Auden. Either elves are a separate creation (meaning they have a real existence) or elves are made from human desire for subcreative art (meaning they don't). Can they be both? We learn from them *even if* they are only creation—that is to say, even if we make them up.

If Tolkien is saying we learn from our own creativity he could say it more simply. He doesn't. Instead he says, "I will tell you what I think." And he does. The following "if . . . then" argument, echoing "if elves are true" in the published essay, is what he thinks. The "you" he is talking to comprises the uncomprehending men that Looney meets at the end of that poem. For this motif of "if elves are true" recurs so persistently that it is hard not to conclude that at some level Tolkien wanted to believe in elves and allowed himself to argue for their real existence. Otherwise, why is the trueness of elves or Faërie even an issue? Nothing in the essay or the draft requires such belief to undergird the argument. In both it would surely be easier, and would certainly be safer, to simply write about elves as imaginary beings or literary conventions. He would then be free to say anything he liked without risking refutation.

Tolkien's ambivalence about elves/fairies is matched by his ambivalence about fairyland. While the essay begins by declaring that "Faërie is a perilous land," it is safe to assume that most readers take this as a figure of speech. Tolkien is not talking about a "real" place, but about, as he says a few lines later, "the realm of fairy-story"—that is to say, imagination. And though much of the ensuing discussion centers on the nature of Faërie, the "realm or state in which fairies have their being," nothing in these opening pages says fairies are real or Faërie is actual. Superficially, he bowed to conventional skepticism, but on Folio 18 of Manuscript B he wrote,

> What is this *faierie*? It reposes (for us now) in a view that the normal world, tangible visible audible, is only an appearance. Behind it is a reservoir of

power which is manifested in these forms. If we can drive a well down to this reservoir, we shall tap a power that can not only change the visible forms of things already existent, but spout up with a boundless wealth forms of things never before known—potential but unrealized. (*TOFS* 270)

This suggests that at a deeper level Tolkien believed in the reality of what he described. The concept of the "normal world" as "only an appearance" posits a paranormal otherworld with "a reservoir of power" to change existing forms and create new ones. But the published essay declares more cautiously that the "Reality . . . of elves and men is the same, if differently valued and perceived" (*TOFS* 63), which seems to say that it's all in how you look at it.

Faërian Drama

The most provocative passage in the essay introduces the term *Faërian Drama*, a phrase I have found in only three instances in all of Tolkien's writings: once in the published essay, once in Manuscript B of the essay, and once, obliquely, as "Elvish drama" in Part One of *The Notion Club Papers*. The paragraph in the published essay is both the most revealing and the most puzzling of all Tolkien's statements on the subject. Here he writes that,

> "Faërian Drama"—those plays which according to abundant records the elves have often presented to men—can produce Fantasy with a realism and immediacy beyond the compass of any human mechanism. As a result their usual effect (upon a man) is to go beyond Secondary Belief. It you are present at a Faërian drama you yourself are, or think that you are, bodily inside its Secondary World. The experience may be very similar to Dreaming. . . . But in Faërian drama you are in a dream that some other mind is weaving, and the knowledge of that alarming fact may slip from your grasp. To experience *directly* a Secondary World: the potion is too strong, and you give to it Primary Belief, however marvellous the events. You are deluded—whether that is the intention of the elves . . . is another question. They . . . are not themselves deluded. This is for them a form of Art, and distinct from Wizardry or Magic, properly so called. They do not live in it, though they can, perhaps, afford to spend more time at it than human artists can. The Primary World, Reality, of elves and men is the same, if differently valued and perceived. (*TOFS* 63)

Like Bottom awaking from his enchantment in *A Midsummer Night's Dream*, Tolkien is trying to describe the indescribable. Unlike Bottom, he expects the reader to understand, or at least to recognize, the experience he is talking about. It is a safe bet that not all readers do. Few will even ask the question, "What exactly is a Faërian Drama?" and fewer still will wonder what "abundant records" recount their presentation to men.[2]

I will tell you what I think. A Faërian Drama is a fantastic, illusory performance put on by fairies/elves for a specific audience—human beings. It is a kind of waking dream. Tolkien's statement that "You are in a dream some other mind is weaving" is very like the statement in David Lindsay's *A Voyage to Arcturus* made by the medium Backhouse, "[a] fast-rising star in the psychic world" (15): "I dream with open eyes . . . and others see my dreams" (16). Tolkien had read *A Voyage to Arcturus* (*Letters* 34). To dream with open eyes is to be in a trance state. Although Tolkien says, "you are deluded," I am loth to call it "hallucination," since that word is strongly negative and implies a pathology, which is undercut by his mention of "abundant records." But what are these abundant records to which he refers? He does not mention any, so again, I will tell you what I think. The "records" are those stories, ballads, and lays of mortals in the fairyland, accounts like the Middle English story of Sir Orfeo, who goes into fairyland to win back his wife, like the ballad of Thomas Rymer, beguiled by the queen of fairyland to spend seven years in her kingdom, or like the aforementioned dream of Bottom the Weaver enchanted by Puck in Shakespeare's play. Indeed, the central portion and locale (the wood) of the play, the multiple enchantments of the pairs of lovers, of Bottom, and of Titania herself, are a Faërian Drama. A more modern example would be Keats's knight at arms enthralled by "La Belle Dame Sans Merci." Faërian Dramas are half-real, half-visionary experiences enshrined in literature. As Theseus describes it in Shakespeare's *A Midsummer Night's Dream*,

> The poet's eye, in fine frenzy rolling,
> Doth glance from heaven to Earth, from Earth to heaven;
> And as imagination bodies forth
> The forms of things unknown, the poet's pen
> Turns them to shapes and gives to airy nothing
> A local habitation and a name. (*MND* 5.1.14–19)

Though the term is never used within his fiction, Tolkien creates more than one Faërian Drama. The feasting Wood Elves in Mirkwood—a Faërie realm if ever there was one—who appear and disappear so tantalizingly in *The Hobbit*, are clearly staging a Faërian Drama for Bilbo and the Dwarves, one into which Thorin Oakenshield "fell like a stone enchanted" as he stepped into their midst (*H* 138–51). The tone of the narrative is light-hearted, and the description of the episode is playful, but the enchantment is clear. Frodo apparently experiences a Faërian Drama when he hears elven singing in the Hall of Fire at Rivendell: "visions of far lands and bright things that he had never yet imagined opened out before him; and the firelit hall became like a golden mist above seas of foam that sighed upon the margins of the world. Then the enchantment became more and more dreamlike, until he felt that an endless river of swelling gold and silver was flowing over him. . . . Swiftly he sank under its shining weight into a deep realm of sleep" (*FR* II, i, 245–46). Something like this happens to Ramer in *The Notion Club Papers*, where he describes "dream-storywriting. For it is not, of course, writing, but a sort of realized drama," to which another character, Jeremy, replies, "Elvish Drama," but is shouted down before he can proceed (*SD* 193). Christopher Tolkien's note on this is of interest here:

> # 43 *Elvish Drama*. In [MS] A it is Ramer himself who speaks of "elf-drama" ("it is not writing but elf-drama"), and again in [MS] B, which has:
> "... For it is not of course writing, but a sort of realized drama. The Elvish Drama that Lewis speaks of somewhere."
> "Not Lewis," said Jeremy. "It comes in one of those essays of the circle, but it was by one of the minor members." (*SD* 216).

Elvish Drama and *Faërian Drama* are interchangeable terms. Jeremy's attribution of the phrase to "one of the minor members" and the noisy reaction of the Notion Club seem intended to evoke those Inklings meetings where, according to Christopher Tolkien, a reading of *The Lord of the Rings* "would begin with Hugo lying on the couch and lolling and shouting and saying 'Oh, God, no more elves!'" (qtd. in *A Film Portrait of J. R. R. Tolkien*). An inside joke. Yet the passage is also a way to say something without saying it. The fictive voices of Ramer and Jeremy, as well as that of Guildford, the Club's recorder, stand between Tolkien and Elvish Drama in *The Notion Club Papers*, whereas in the essay nothing stands between him and the "strong potion" that invites primary belief.

Frodo's "visions of things . . . never yet imagined" recalls Manuscript B's "things never before known that spout up." Another passage in Manuscript B uses the term, and comes close to Frodo's experience: "The real desire is not to enter these lands . . . as a natural denizen (as a knight, say, armed with a sword and courage adequate to this world) but to see them in action and being as we see our objective world—with the mind free from the limited body: a Faërian Drama" (*TOFS* 294).

Seeing a Faërian Drama "in action and being" means as an *observer* "with the mind free from the limited body"—not as a participant but as an audience, as at a play. Certainly this is what happens to Frodo in the Hall of Fire. It is likewise what happens to Looney in the Faërie land, as the poem's opening questions, "Where have you been? What have you seen?" make clear.

The vividness of Frodo's and Looney's and Ramer's experiences in the fiction is matched in the essay by Tolkien's grammar. The verbs are in the present indicative, not the conditional mood: "You *are* deluded," not "you *would be* deluded." "You *are* [not *would be*] in a dream," "you *give* [not *would give*] to it Primary Belief." He then he muddies the water by adding that "whether that [delusion, dream] is the intention of the elves (always or at any time) is another question." And muddies it further when he adds that "[t]hey at any rate are not themselves deluded. This is for them a form of Art, and distinct from Wizardry or Magic, properly so called."

So what does this really mean? In the case of Frodo, the Elven song may be enchanting (or deluding) him, though this seems more a by-product of Art than its intention. In the case of Looney, the voyage and the enchantment are hallucinatory and uncommunicable. In the case of Ramer, the delusion (or dream) seems to be entirely within himself. The passage from "On Fairy-stories" is so vivid and intense it is hard not to imagine that it had its origin in Tolkien's personal experience of an altered state, whether trance or daydream or hallucination, a transportation to an other world the experience of which was actual, whether its reality was or not. And then he adds the puzzling concluding sentence. "The Primary World, Reality, of elves and men is the same, if differently valued and perceived" (*TOFS* 63). But what does this really mean?

Without knowing the question, Tolkien's collaborator and former student, Simone D'Ardenne, offered an answer in her essay "The Man and the Scholar": "I said to him once: 'You broke the veil, didn't you, and passed through?' which in fact he did and which he readily admitted. No wonder, therefore that he could recapture the language of the fairies. . . . Tolkien belonged to that very rare class of linguists, now becoming extinct, who like the Grimm brothers could understand and recapture the glamour of 'the word'" (34–35). To break the veil and pass through is "to see . . . in action and being as we see our objective world—with the mind free from the limited body: a Faërian Drama." This is what happens to Frodo, who sees "visions of bright things." This is what happens to Looney, who hears song but sees no singers, and even more to the speaker in "The Sea-bell," who cries, "Why do you hide? . . . Answer my call! . . . Show me a face!" and finally concludes, "I have lost myself" (*ATB* 59). This is what happens to Ramer, who sees "realised drama."

D'Ardenne's phrase *glamour of the word* may be the key. The OED defines *glamour* as "magic, enchantment, spell." It is a Scottish variant of *grammar*, altered from Fr. *grammaire*, ME *gramer(e)*, "letters," from I-E *gerebh-*, "to scratch" [Cp. *graffiti, graphite, telegraph*]. The "glamour of 'the word,'" then, would be its power to alter perception, to "break through" the veil separating realities and reveal the connections between them.[3] I suggest that this what Tolkien meant when he said that the "Reality . . . of elves and men [was] the same, if differently valued and perceived" (*TOFS* 63). Does that mean he actually believed in fairies?

One passage in Manuscript B suggests strongly that he did. Here, as with his unsent letter to Hastings, in the private company of only his pen and paper Tolkien seems to have allowed himself the luxury of writing what he really thought. I quote the passage, edited for brevity but with sense intact. It begins with the familiar "if" motif, but the ensuing discussion shows Tolkien transcending the hypothetical to speak out of his deepest meditation.

> If fairies exist. . . . They are a quite separate creation living in another mode. . . . For lack of a better word they may be called spirits, *daemons*, inherent powers of the created world . . . subject to Moral Law, capable of good and evil. . . . They are in fact non-incarnate minds (or souls) of a stature and even nature more near to that of Man . . . than any other rational creatures, known or guessed by us. They can take form at will, or they could do so: they have or had a choice.
>
> Thus a tree-fairy (or dryad) is, or was a minor spirit in the process of creation who aided as "agent" in the making effective of the divine Tree-idea or some part of it, or of even of some one particular example: some tree. He is therefore now bound by use and love to Trees (or a tree), immortal while the world (and trees) last—never to escape, until the End. It is a dreadful Doom (to human minds if they are wise) in exchange for splendid power. What fate awaits him beyond the Confines of the World, we cannot know. It is likely that the Fairy does not know himself. It is possible that nothing awaits him—outside the World and the Cycle of Story and of Time. (*TOFS* 254–55)

This passage is remarkable in its openness to ideas conventionally dismissed, even ridiculed, by skeptics. It shows Tolkien thinking outside the limit of ordinary human perception and open to the ultramundane extension of Creation beyond the visible world. Plato would have understood this passage, as would Augustine. Patrick Curry would love it. It is foreign to the everyday, rational mid-twentieth-century culture in which Tolkien lived and wrote, but not beyond the scope of Christian mysticism, though a dryad rather than Holy Spirit suggests a non-Christian perspective. It is no wonder that Tolkien did not publish this passage. The wonder is that he wrote it.

Conclusion

But you may ask: what difference does it make that Tolkien trimmed his sails to meet winds from different directions? He wouldn't be the first to do so, and with or without them, there is still *The Lord of the Rings* in all its richness and multivalent texture, a book from which readers have been taking what they need and want for almost sixty years and show no signs of stopping. I propose that it does make a difference, for the trimming reveals a deep ambivalence in the man that produced a creative tension in his fiction. He was neither the Christian mythmaker that some would like, or the literary spokesman for a neopagan world that others would make him. He was a more complex individual than critics on either side have been willing to acknowledge, a man deeply conflicted, balancing faith against experience, and orthodoxy against an inner perception that broke the veil and reached the other side of the visible world.

All these statements, in the letters and in the essay, are voices in a conversation that continued over many years in Tolkien's own mind as well as on paper. It tried to harmonize his work's originality and his own imagination with Christian orthodoxy, and to situate his often unorthodox views within the narrower confines of his religion without abandoning either. It seems clear that he also anticipated the ridicule and scorn of the literary lions and antiromantics who dominated the literary landscape during the time in which he wrote and for long after: not just friends like Hugo Dyson, who tired of elves, but hostile critics like Edmund Wilson, who willfully misunderstood what he was trying to do, and Germaine Greer, who dismissed his readers as "a tribe" of women sporting puffed sleeves and carrying teddy bears, and thus shot at his heart long after he was dead.

Conflict about elements so central to his life and work recalls Humphrey Carpenter's statement that he was "a man of antitheses" (*Tolkien* 95). Since Carpenter is the only one besides Christopher Tolkien to have read Tolkien's diaries, we should pay attention to his words. The diaries, says Carpenter, reflected Tolkien's "second side," his "deep uncertainty," his "black moods" and feelings of hopelessness and despair, both for himself and the world (*Tolkien* 129). Yet the antitheses that Carpenter saw provided that "five minutes later in the company of a friend he would forget his black gloom and be in the best of humour" (*Tolkien* 129). This is not surprising. To be able to savor fully the joys in human life, one must know what it is to be without them; contrast deepens perception and sharpens appreciation. Tolkien put it another way when he wrote to his son Michael, "You have to understand the good in things, to detect the real evil" (*Letters* 55).

To be a man of antitheses is not necessarily a bad thing, and to contain paradox without resolving it is the mark of an inclusive mind. Uncertainty leaves room for flexibility, while its opposite, single-mindedness, can mean consistency but also intransigence. As the epigraph to this essay states, "A coherent personality aspires, like a work of art, to contain its conflicts without resolving them dogmatically" (Thurman xvi). Tolkien's personality allowed him to contain his conflicts without resolving them. This was an advantage, not a defect. Conceding yet contesting, he found a way to maintain a public balance between alternatives without compromising his private opinions.

His Catholic faith was central to his life, but at a level beyond doctrine he also believed in fairies, and might, like Frodo and Looney and Ramer, have had direct experience of the "strong potion" of Faërian Drama. The conflict between faith and imagination fueled his art, creating what he called the "complex, rather bitter, and very terrifying romance" that is *The Lord of the Rings* (*Letters* 136). Resolving that conflict might have removed the bitterness and the terror, but it also would have removed the power and tensile strength of a story whose virtue is its indeterminacy, a story in which Frodo can be both guilty and innocent, in which Boromir is both admirable and culpable, and in which Sam is both beneficent and destructive. We see Éowyn at her best when she follows her desire to be a warrior-maiden but also when she decides to be a healer. Is it Gandalf or Saruman who silently appears at the edge of Fangorn Forest to the Three Hunters, Aragorn, Legolas, and Gimli, and then just as silently disappears? Gandalf says they certainly did not see him, so it must have been Saruman. But the horses neigh joyfully, the mystery is never solved, and it seems clear that ambiguity is what Tolkien intended.

But why? What did he really mean? What purpose would be served by deliberately conflating or confusing Gandalf and Saruman? I suggest it is the idea, so much a part of Tolkien's worldview and his story, that good and evil are two sides of the same coin, and that it is all too easy to mistake one for the other—in either direction. His is not a story about good and evil but a story in which good can become evil, a story whose strength lies in the tension created by deliberately unresolved situations and conflicts. Leaving such conflicts unresolved allowed their author to tap into that "reservoir of power" below the visible world. It enabled him to "not only change the visible forms of things already existent, but spout up with a boundless wealth forms of things never before known" (*TOFS* 270).

Re-creating Reality

Let us begin by acknowledging the obvious: fiction by its very nature is escapist. The imaginary characters and events of a novel or a play or a poem or a short story, as well as the world within which they occur, have no existence outside the work that creates them. A reader immersed in such a world, however realistic it may seem, is escaping his or her experienced world for the one created on the page. That being the case, then what is popularly called "escapist" literature—fantasy, fairy tale, horror, science fiction—is different only in scale from its less fanciful literary cousins. Such escapist works are distinguished from other fiction chiefly by the greater extent to which they diverge from observable reality into what J. R. R. Tolkien called a secondary world, a world where things happen that could not happen in real life. The difference is more of degree than of kind.

Yet the term *escapist* has had negative connotations that are hard to shake off, having been deployed by skeptics to dismiss a whole mode of literature for being at best fanciful and lightweight, at worst improbable and delusive. As fanciful and lightweight, such material is passed as acceptable for children but not for adults, who, reading for enjoyment the same book or story, risk severe censure for their unhealthy preference for illusion over reality. While this is a current and still-popular critical judgment, it would seem (to borrow a phrase from Tolkien's 1939 essay, "On Fairy-stories") to be "almost the truth upside-down" (*MC* 123). Surely it is adults, with an experience of the "real" world greater than that of children, who most benefit from the leavening effect of fantasy on the reality for which it is not so much an escape as a re-configuration. This notwithstanding, the exact nature and, more important, the appropriateness of fantasy as adult reading remain the subjects of an ongoing conversation.

As early as 1956, Edmund Wilson labeled *The Lord of the Rings* "juvenile trash" and professed himself "puzzled to know why the author should have supposed he was writing for adults. . . . [E]xcept when he is being pedantic and also boring the adult reader, there is little in *The Lord of the Rings* over the head of a seven-year-old child. It is essentially a children's book—a children's book which has somehow got out of hand" (312). Some three decades later but in much the same spirit, Germaine Greer deplored in outraged prose the results of a 1997 Waterstone's Bookstore poll in which *The Lord of the Rings* topped the list of the hundred greatest books of the twentieth century. "Ever since I arrived at Cambridge as a student in 1964 and encountered a tribe of full-grown women wearing puffed sleeves, clutching teddies and babbling excitedly about the doings of hobbits, it has been my nightmare that Tolkien would turn out to be the most influential writer of the twentieth century. The bad dream has materialised. . . . The books that come in Tolkien's train are more or less what you would expect; flight from reality is their dominating characteristic" (2–9). Greer's consternation, her fastidious disdain for puffed sleeves and teddies, serve only to elaborate on Wilson's dismissal. No longer merely juvenile, like Wilson's hypothetical seven-year-old, Greer's babbling "tribe of full-grown women" has been regressed to a quasi-infantile state that seems more pathological than childish. While serious Tolkien scholars (neither wearing puffed sleeves nor clutching teddies) might challenge her view, it seems safe to suggest that they could not change it.

That so significant a branch of modern fiction as fantasy should be so misconstrued says more about the naysayers than about the works themselves, whose visions of alternative reality—exemplified in the works of J. R. R. Tolkien but also in those of such writers as Ursula Le Guin, Philip Pullman and George R. R. Martin—have been and still are read by adults and children alike. Although "On Fairy-stories" anticipated Wilson and Greer by several decades, Tolkien's argument shows that he was well aware of the elitist intellectual high ground claimed by both. "On Fairy-stories" directly confronts such disdain with two arguments: first pointing out that the distinction between those who appreciate imaginative literature and those who do not is more a difference of taste than of age (*MC* 130), and second refuting the equally unexamined assumption that escape implies denial rather than distance and instead asserting that the latter can offer perspective and foster new perception. Far from avoiding reality, Tolkien declares, fantasy works to let us see it more clearly. "We should meet the centaur and the dragon, and then perhaps suddenly behold, like the ancient shepherds, sheep, and dogs, and horses—and wolves" (*MC* 146).

His essay is long and discursive and covers a host of related topics, ranging from fairy stories to theories of language to a mini-history of myth and folklore studies. While acknowledging its scope, I will consider most specifically the subsection titled "Fantasy," in which Tolkien directly addresses the uses of imagination. It is important to recognize that his discussion, like that of Aristotle on drama, is not prescriptive but descriptive, not a "how-to" set of rules but a thoughtful consideration of what works, and how. With this in mind, we can assess the extent to which Tolkien's own fiction fits his description of fantasy. And finally, we can appraise the effect of both his fiction and his essay on representative works by those who came after (and therefore in the very largest sense, because of) him.

The Essay

The essay is roughly divided into three unequally proportioned sections on the nature, origin, and function of fairy stories, with the most time and space devoted to this last, their usefulness to the reader. Tolkien proposes that the function of the fairy tale (and, by implication, fantastic literature in general) and one of its greatest values is precisely its ability to provide escape, to create a secondary world into which the reader can enter. He launches his campaign with the accurate observation that fairy stories are not stories about fairies but stories about Faërie, "the realm or state in which fairies have their being," and about the "*aventures*" of men with this secondary world (*MC* 113). The italicized word *aventures*—mistakenly and misleadingly misspelled *adventures* in *The Tolkien Reader*)—is in its correct spelling important here. *Aventure*, close in sound and spelling to Old French *avant*, "forward," goes beyond *adventure* to connote moving into danger, the perilous unknown, the extraordinary, and ultimately the supernatural; that is to say, the secondary world or otherworld called by medieval poets *la forêt des aventures* and by Tolkien the perilous realm of Faërie.

It is clear that the word *Faërie* is of primary importance to Tolkien's vision. It conveys the most important concept in the essay and may well be the most significant term in Tolkien's lexicon. Faërie is the key to both his theory and his practice, for it is exactly this secondary world, an alternate reality whose magic is that of imagination, that is dismissed as childish by the critics. An older, less conventional spelling of the word—*fayery*—may help to clarify his usage. The addition of the verbalizing suffix, *ery*, to the base noun *fay/fée* (Old

French "fairy"), extends and subtly transforms the import, adding a kinetic quality to the noun, as, for example, in *slavery* (both the practice and the condition) or *bakery* (both the practice and the product). Thus *fay-ery/faërie* means at once the creation of enchantment, the storial world of imagination thus created (fairyland/Faërie, the otherworld), and the mental/psychological condition of those enchanted—the readers of the story.

Admitting that "in criticism [Escape] would seem to be the worse the better it succeeds" (*MC* 148), Tolkien nevertheless champions the term (and with it his own fiction), calling escape "one of the main functions of fairy-stories" (*MC* 147–48). Moreover, he states, "creative Fantasy is founded upon the hard recognition that things are so in the world as it appears under the sun; on a recognition of fact but not a slavery to it" (*MC* 144). Even more simply and unequivocally, he declares that "Fantasy is made out of the Primary World" (*MC* 147). These are powerful and practical statements, and those who find fantasy to be juvenile or childish would do well to heed them.

The secondary world of fantasy, as Tolkien understood it, was built on and created in support of the primary, the "real" world, and the "hard recognition" of its condition "under the sun," that is, in the circumstances of everyday life. In order to succeed, he maintains, escapist literature must acknowledge, must indeed build on, the world it seeks to transcend. In this regard, his "escapist" world of Middle-earth is as realistic as Conan Doyle's London. Both are founded on and grounded in observable reality, in the facts of everyday life "under the sun," yet both are distinct from this "real" world and free from its demands in that they never have and do not now exist in actuality but only in imagination. Thus 221b Baker Street is no more and no less "real" than Bag End, and Sherlock Holmes's world, though we may find its street and place names familiar, is as much a secondary world as is Tolkien's Hobbiton or his Lothlórien. Though one has a real-world corollary and the other does not, the difference is not one of category but of degree.

Tolkien calls fantasy a "sub-creative art," practiced in imitation and acknowledgment of a prime creator. The essay's discussion of the adjective as incantatory, "a part of speech in a mythical grammar," asserts that it is capable of changing reality or creating a new reality (*MC* 122). That the vehicle for such sub-creation is language, that the building blocks of a secondary world are the words of the primary world, is one of the essay's most important points. The practice of "combining nouns and redistributing adjectives" (*MC* 143) can invent "new form" (*MC* 122) by creating in the reader's imagination the world they describe. When Tolkien talks later about ""inheriting the fantastic device of human language" (*MC* 140), he is using the word *fantastic* in its literal sense, not as an intensifier but as an exact description of the power of words to transform by making us see that which they name or describe. His example of "taking green from grass" and putting it on a man's face to "produce a horror" is a practical illustration of the simultaneously creative and alienating power of words to produce fantasy by rearranging reality. If an imagined world has a green sun, for example, that world must conform to its own "inner consistency," by which Tolkien means that the world of the story must obey its own rules. A world with a green sun will have color values different from our own. It is in such fantasy, says Tolkien, that "new form is made; Faërie begins; Man becomes a sub-creator" (*MC* 122). The secondary world has invited us to escape from the confines of the primary world, but the new form makes us appreciate the familiar one.

It is this context that Tolkien lays out his requirements for a successful fairy tale: that it provide its readers with recovery, escape, and consolation. Recovery, by which he means not so much recuperation (as from illness) as the regaining of a clear view, is the getting back of something lost. It describes the reading experience of seeing as if for the first time familiar things in a new setting that makes them appear strange and new. The poet Marianne Moore's concept of real toads in imaginary gardens comes to mind. In complete agreement with Moore, Tolkien proposes that "We should look at green again . . . and be startled anew by blue and yellow and red" (*MC* 146). Tolkien meant his readers to look at his imaginary Elves and Hobbits and be startled anew by seeing ourselves in them. The "fantastic" personnel of *The Lord of the Rings*, whether short or tall, beautiful or ugly, eager or world-weary, are most familiar when they are most strange. Even the Orcs reveal all too identifiable aspects of humanity, most familiar when least desirable. They treat each other with as much disrespect as humans do each other, resent their bosses, and speak a gutter slang recognizable from a host of modern and postmodern films, plays, and novels. They are, if not real toads, at least realistic ones in a garden that seems less and less imaginary the more you look at it.

This process of reappreciating the familiar as unfamiliar explains itself, allowing Tolkien to move on to the larger question of escape. Here he must argue against the intellectual attitude, prevalent in his day and no less prevalent in ours, that discounts the value of escapist literature—one typified by Wilson and Greer. The time and care Tolkien expends in his discussion are the measure of his engagement with the question. His argument is a reaction against not just literary realism, with its focus on the ordinary, often seamy aspects of modern life, but also the real grime and mechanistic dehumanization that were the byproducts of the industrial state. The extreme reaction against industrialism pervading this part of the essay is in part a result of the astonishing speed with which the slow-moving rural world of his Warwickshire childhood was overtaken and superseded by the rapid developmental pace of technology. While he had no desire to catch up, he nevertheless felt caught up and swept along on the tide of industrial progress. With this as his position, Tolkien contrasts to its advantage the "Escape of the Prisoner with the Flight of the Deserter" (*MC* 149). The desire to avoid unpleasant circumstances, by whatever means and for however short a time, is a natural human impulse.

"But," continues Tolkien, "there are also other and more profound 'escapisms.'" He insists that it is neither inappropriate nor unworthy to want to go beyond what he calls the "ancient limitations" of the human condition to fulfill "old ambitions and desires" (*MC* 151): to sound the depths and heights of sea and sky like fish and bird, to communicate with other species and thus to transcend the separation of humans from the other creatures of their world, from the whole world of nature. The fairy-story motif of the talking animal provides this escape and achieves this transcendence. And finally there is what Tolkien calls "the Great Escape: the Escape from Death" (*MC* 152), exemplified by Beauty's dying Beast, who resurges from his death as her handsome prince, or by Snow White's or the Sleeping Beauty's awakening from a deathlike sleep by a prince's kiss.

To this escape, Tolkien adds the further element of consolation, the final necessity of the fairy tale embodied in its requisite and traditional happy ending. Whatever dire events take place in the course of the narrative, the tale will end happily. In a very real sense, this is the one essential component. It is what the unexamined term *fairy story* means to most people. No matter how close the protagonist comes to disaster, everything will be all right. To explain the full meaning of consolation, Tolkien invented a word, *eucatastrophe*, to signify the "sudden joyous 'turn'" or lift (*MC* 153) when the story unexpectedly reverses its direction. While the word is Tolkien's invention, it is legitimately built on an existing term borrowed from Greek tragedy, *catastrophe*, whose components are Greek *kata*, "down," and *strephein*, "turn." In a tragedy, the catastrophe is the downward turn, the change in fortune when, for example, Oedipus learns the circumstances of his birth and thus his true and doom-laden identity. Adding to *catastrophe* the prefix *eu*, "good," Tolkien keeps the concept but changes the direction. In order for the turn to occur, there must be the imminent possibility of *dyscatastrophe*, another word of Tolkien's invention, this one reinforcing the downward direction by adding the prefix *dys* (from Greek *dus*, "bad or evil"). Without this portent of "sorrow and failure," (*MC* 153) the turn has no impact. The possibility of these is what creates the joy of deliverance and leads to the happy ending.

The Fiction

The relevance of all of this to Tolkien's own fiction would seem obvious, but is in fact more complex and complicated than at first appears. There is no question that both *The Hobbit* and *The Lord of the Rings* are Fantasies in that they transcend observable reality to create a secondary world. But this classification has led to some surprising errors in critical judgment based on the assumption that fantasy as such is a genre for children rather than adults. *The Hobbit*, a children's book, has been praised as a fairy story, albeit a complex and to some extent parodic one, while *The Lord of the Rings*—which its author declared to his publisher was "quite unfit for children" (*Letters* 136)—has been dismissed as both children's book and fairy story (a double whammy intended to roundly discredit it) by critics who neither like nor understand what Tolkien was trying to do.

The Hobbit

Looking first at *The Hobbit*, we have no difficulty in acknowledging that it is a story for children. Even without knowing that Tolkien began it as a story told to his own children—a fact now generally known—we can recognize by its tone, comparable to that of other children's books of the period (see, for example, the fantasies of E. Nesbit), that it addresses a juvenile audience. We also have no trouble acknowledging that by anyone's standard it is a fairy story, setting its unlikely hero on a quest for lost treasure and pitting him against such traditional fairy-tale figures as trolls, goblins, and elves. That it is a fairy story by Tolkien's more exacting standards is likewise clear, for it bears what he called "the trade-mark *Of Faërie*" (*MC* 135) indelibly stamped upon it.

Two aspects of Faërie concern us here. The first is the encompassing secondary world of the book as a whole, a world into which the reader enters by way of the famous first sentence: "In a hole in the ground there lived a hobbit" (*H* 11). At once we know that we are out of this world and into another marked (indeed, almost created) by the unfamiliar word *hobbit*, and the succeeding paragraphs lead us deeper into that world. It is an otherworld, a secondary world, but one so firmly grounded in the primary one that we can recognize the links. It is a world where imaginary creatures called Hobbits live dull boring lives, get letters in the mail, enjoy pipe-smoking but neglect the washing-up, and forget their pocket-handkerchiefs. Reversing Marianne Moore, we might describe Bilbo Baggins as an imaginary toad in a real garden. Yet this same world is also an imaginary garden in which this individual, quite ordinary except for his species, can hobnob with Dwarves and Wizards, converse with an eagle and a dragon, possess a magical key to unlock a mountain, and wear a ring of invisibility.

The juxtaposition of such disparate elements, a juxtaposition employed partly for humor but also to create what Tolkien calls the "arresting strangeness" (*MC* 139) that is the hallmark of fantasy, is a vivid illustration of his theory of recovery. To find domestic chores and mundane occupations occupying the same narrative space as the paraphernalia of magic and fairy story is to reimagine both categories, and see each in terms of the other. The act of casually saying "Good morning" to a passing wizard makes that ordinary phrase extraordinary even as it domesticates the wizard. The result in both cases is estrangement followed by recovery, a new appreciation of what we have taken for granted.

The second aspect of Faërie is that experienced by the hobbit hero himself, as this seemingly ordinary fellow leaves his familiar/unfamiliar and surprisingly conventional hobbit hole to venture out into a world inhabited by the paraphernalia of fairy tales—trolls with talking purses, shape-changing were-bears, dark forests inhabited by white deer (a standard medieval sign of the otherworld), peopled by partying elves who appear and disappear at will, and threaded by rivers causing enchanted sleep. Escape, in both aspects of Faërie, follows naturally from recovery. We as readers escape from our ordinary world into the secondary world of the book and are at once enchanted by hobbits and wizards. In parallel with the reader, Bilbo escapes his ordinary, somewhat humdrum life and transcends his Baggins nature to enter a Tookish faërian world,[1] one that introduces him not just to the "arresting strangeness" of Mirkwood and Smaug but to the long-suppressed, arrestingly strange and Tookish side of himself. His dream on the rock shelf after rescue by the eagles, a dream of wandering through the different rooms of his own house looking for something he cannot find or remember, is a scarcely veiled—and, for a fairy story, surprisingly psychological—depiction of his burgeoning awakening to a new self.

It hardly needs pointing out that *The Hobbit*, whose very human hero talks with an eagle and exchanges riddles with a dragon, qualifies in this respect as a fairy story. But can we find in Tolkien's story a true eucatastrophe and happy ending? The answer is both yes and no, for *The Hobbit* is an idiosyncratic fairy story whose tone and ethos shift markedly halfway through. C. S. Lewis's comment on this shift, that it is as if Badger had suddenly started talking like Njal,[2] is apt and insightful. What began as a mock fairy-tale quest to There and Back Again changes when the dwarves reach the Lonely Mountain and rouse the wrath of Smaug into a mini-epic more like *Beowulf* than "Snow White," albeit one in which the hero plays a less-than-heroic part. Tolkien even deprives Bilbo of the deed that should be his by right, the slaying of the dragon, assigning this instead to the later-entering Bard the Bowman, whose kingly credentials are hurried into the story almost as an afterthought.

The last third of the book shifts away from conventional fairy tale to a surprisingly contemporary (albeit fanciful) study of greed, politics, war, and moral ambiguity. The book's climax and denouement, the Battle of Five Armies, is played out among competing groups—Elves, Dwarves, and Men—that have been on the brink of war with one another until threatened by the Wolves and Goblins, when they perforce unite against their common foes. Written in the early thirties of the last century and published late in 1937, the story has the memory of World War I and the looming shadow of World War II scarcely hidden below the surface of the fantasy. In this regard we must acknowledge that *The Hobbit* takes an unexpected left turn that brings its secondary world perilously close to the primary one.

The last-minute eagles-to-the-rescue device may qualify as eucatastrophe, but only in a limited sense. It ends the war, but it does not end the story. This goes on to chronicle, in a more *Beowulf*ian than fairy-tale mood, the fatalistic farewell and death of Thorin Oakenshield, who goes to the halls of waiting after telling Bilbo that "if more of us valued food and cheer and song above hoarded gold, it would be a merrier world" (*H* 243). Note that Thorin is not saying merry ever after, just merrier than the world he has known. Bilbo's subsequent homecoming to Bag End, laden with treasure, rounds off the journey and the story, but while this is a happy ending, it is somewhat lacking as a eucatastrophe, since he has never been in any real peril. It is not a turn but a re-turn, a restoration of fairy-tale order. We may say that *The Hobbit* is an atypical hybrid composed in roughly equal parts of fairy tale and epic but not wholly of either genre. It has many of the requisite elements—secondary world, fantasy, recovery, escape—but these are imperfectly blended and lacking in the essential resolution of eucatastrophe and therefore the happy ending that should tie them together. In the final analysis, *The Hobbit*'s greatest importance lies in its foreshadowing of things to come.

THE LORD OF THE RINGS

The sequel to *The Hobbit* that over time became *The Lord of the Rings* had precisely that advantage—time in which to become—that its precursor had lacked. It also allowed Tolkien to apply the lessons learned in writing the previous book. Ideas, motifs, and characters only half-developed in *The Hobbit* or hurried to completion in too few pages were now better prepared for and more fully fleshed out. Starting work in the months immediately following publication of *The Hobbit*, Tolkien launched an abortive first effort (initially referred to as the "new Hobbit") perhaps as early as December 1937.[3] However, the gestation of *The Lord of the Rings* took twelve laborious years (1937–49), a stop-and-start process[4] during which time (as he later noted in the foreword to the second edition) he changed his house, his chair, and his college (*FR* 6). Yet this protracted process allowed Tolkien to more carefully develop and put into practice what he had learned in the process of writing its predecessor and had codified into principles in the essay that followed so soon after it.

Let us establish at the start that *The Lord of the Rings* is not a book aimed at or intended primarily for children. Its position as the sequel and continuance of *The Hobbit* has led readers to assume the same audience for both, but although that was initially the case, the "new Hobbit" very quickly outgrew its predecessor "in the matter of atmosphere, tone, or audience addressed" (*Letters* 138)[5] to become what Tolkien also described to his publisher as "an immensely long, complex, rather bitter, and very terrifying romance, quite unfit for children" (136). He was wrong only in the last four words, unless by "children" he meant people under the age of eight or nine. *The Lord of the Rings* can be and has been read by many children of that age and older, just as fairy stories can be enjoyed by readers of any age. But as with any good story, the more mature the readers, the more they are likely to get out of the story.

So multilayered and complexly interlaced a narrative as *The Lord of the Rings*, extending with appendices to more than a thousand pages, cannot be fully analyzed within the brief compass of an article. The best that can be done is to select for examination representative elements that conform to the requirements of fairy story and fantasy as outlined in Tolkien's essay. Let us start with Faërie/fantasy. As in *The Hobbit*, the entire world of *The Lord of the Rings* is a secondary world. The little world of Hobbiton and the Shire—Tolkien's nostalgic re-creation (with the addition of Hobbits) of the world of his own early childhood—functions as a sentimental journey for him and as fantasy for his modern readers. If they have read *The Hobbit*, this new work will remind them of its enchantment, and if they have not, its arresting strangeness will lead them into Faërie.

As with *The Hobbit*, but with far more skill and subtlety, the narrative of *The Lord of the Rings* leads its protagonists into its own secondary world, into Faërie. The presence of the supernatural Ring scarcely qualifies the unsupernatural Shire as Faërie, though for the reader the presence of Hobbits makes it a secondary world. Far more faërian is the Old Forest, the first and in many respects the most perilous of Tolkien's perilous realms. Leaving Bag End, Frodo, Sam, and Pippin spend their first night out of doors and fear no danger, for they are still "in the heart of the Shire" (*FR* I, iii, 81)—no secondary otherworld to them, but the primary world with which they are trustingly familiar. Leaving Crickhollow two days later, the four hobbits make the first and most explicitly depicted crossing into the otherworld of the book. They follow the tunnel as it dives under and crosses beneath the Hedge, emerging aboveground on the other side to hear the ominous *click* as the gate shuts behind them. Merry announces with finality that they have "left the Shire" and are now "outside, and on the edge of the Old Forest" (*FR* I, vi, 120). They have left *their* primary world to enter into and participate in a secondary one. It is plain that a threshold has been crossed and that what the hobbits (and we as readers) are about to enter is *la forêt des aventures*.

Nevertheless, the Old Forest relies on realism for its fantasy, and (with the exception of Old Man Willow) simply behaves like a forest. Roots trip the travelers, branches drop or snag, paths disappear, brambles block the way and force the travelers to change direction. Cynthia Cohen's excellent discussion of the Old Forest in her article "The Unique Representation of Trees in *The Lord of the Rings*" (Cohen 105–11) makes the point that the hobbits' growing sense of unease, the aura of menace they perceive, relies more on their own subjective impressions than on any explicit account of the trees' intention. Yet this rather adds to than detracts from the Old Forest as Faërie, since Tolkien's point in the essay is that the enchantment of Faërie resides to a large degree in the altered state of the reader. Faërie, he explains, "contains many things besides elves and fays . . . it holds the seas, the sun, the moon, the sky; and the earth and all things that are in it: *tree* and bird . . . and ourselves, mortal men, *when we are enchanted*" (*MC* 113; my emphases). Old Man Willow merely takes the process a step further, and Cohen suggests that he may not in fact be a tree, but rather "an entity living with or associated with a tree—some sort of spirit, or perhaps a Fairy" (Cohen 111).[6]

What was implicit in the collective trees of the Old Forest and in the hinted-at sentience of Old Man Willow becomes explicit in Tolkien's portrayal of Treebeard/Fangorn, whose name is both individual and collective. While technically the Ents are not trees per se but tree shepherds, the distinction is an arbitrary one, and most readers respond to them as walking, talking trees. The subliminal awareness of Old Man Willow is with Treebeard given voice and personality; he is presented as not so much a tree fairy as a tree of Faërie. In his persona is embodied all the otherness it previously took Tolkien an entire woodland to convey. Paradoxically, his strangeness is conveyed through familiarity. Where Old Man Willow sang enchantment at the edge of perception, Treebeard converses with Merry and Pippin in the

Common Speech and on their own terms. Like strangers meeting, he and the hobbits exchange introductions.

In contrast to both the Old Forest and Fangorn, the other woodland we encounter, Lothlórien, seems to embody the conventional notion of "fairyland," its otherworldly beauty designed with every artifice at the storyteller's command to cast a spell. Bounded by water which the fellowship must cross, filled with mallorn trees with silver trunks and golden leaves, inhabited by the tree-dwelling Elves, suffused with the palpable presence of what Sam calls magic, Lothlórien seems to fulfill Tolkien's definition of *Faërie* as "the realm or state in which fairies have their being" and to be intended to enchant both the reader and the members of the fellowship. Unlike the Old Forest, where Tolkien used the natural behavior of woodlands to establish the otherness to humanity of *la forêt des aventures*, or Fangorn, where he embodied that otherness in a single character, in Lothlórien he goes out of his way to create a secondary world within his secondary world.

Although it contains nothing that is not in the "real" world (if you accept Elves as aspects of humanity), although it lacks the aura of otherness and the sense of estrangement that give the Old Forest so much of its power, Lothlórien carries more clearly than any other region of Middle-earth the trademark "*Of Faërie*." Much of this comes from its treatment of time, for Lórien, like the fairylands of mythology and folktale, is not bound by the laws of time and space—two of the "ancient limitations" Tolkien's essay lists—that rule the primary world. Since I have discussed elsewhere Tolkien's efforts to temporally differentiate Lórien from the world around it,[7] I will observe here only that Tolkien conveys, through the perception of Frodo, the notion that Lórien exists in a different time frame from that of the outside world. Entering it, Frodo feels as if he has "stepped over a bridge of time into a corner of the Elder Days" and is in "a timeless land" (*FR* II, vi, 364, 365).

It is this that enables Tolkien to move seamlessly from escape to recovery, for in the timeless land of Lórien Frodo's sharpened senses experience the familiar world as fresh and new. Blindfolded on the path through the wood, he can smell the trees and the grass trodden under his feet. He can distinguish different notes in the rustle of the leaves, the murmur of the river, the "thin clear" voices of the birds (*FR* II, vi, 363). At Cerin Amroth and without the blindfold, Frodo finds this experience not just repeated but heightened. "All that he saw was shapely . . . at once clear cut . . . and ancient. He saw no colour but those he knew . . . but they were fresh and poignant, as if he had at that moment first perceived them" (*FR* II, vi, 365). If this is not recovery, I don't know what is.

Where *The Lord of the Rings* most profoundly challenges the fairy-story ethos of Tolkien's essay is in the last and most essential requirement, that of consolation. Certainly there is a turn and a eucatastrophe. The moment at the Cracks of Doom when Frodo claims the Ring is catastrophe pure and simple, a sudden disastrous downturn that leads the story and the protagonist to the brink of tragedy. Gollum's attack and biting off of Frodo's finger, followed so immediately by his fall into the fire, provide a turn so stunning and so unexpected that it leaves the first-time reader breathless. It is a perfect eucatastrophe, and it leads to Aragorn's coronation, his planting of the sapling of the White Tree, his marriage with Arwen, the only slightly subordinate marriages of Faramir to Éowyn and Sam to Rosie Cotton, and the fruitful harvest year of 1420. It is an extended, undeniable happy ending, very much the "happily ever after" ending for his book envisioned by Bilbo at Rivendell. Sam's joyous question when he wakes in Ithilien and sees Gandalf alive, "Is everything sad going to come untrue?" (*RK* VI, iv, 230), seems to demand a "yes" for its answer. Far more than in *The Hobbit,* Tolkien has given his story a resolution that seems to conform in all particulars to his own criteria for the fairy-story happy ending.

Except for Frodo.

The *Beowulf*ian note sounded by the death of Thorin Oakenshield as *The Hobbit* approached its end becomes in *The Lord of the Rings* the far greater and more tragic fall of Frodo, who succumbs, as he cannot help doing, to the power of the Ring. While Thorin's death is bleak, it brings grief but not tragedy to the protagonist of *The Hobbit,* Bilbo, whose story then continues to its happy end. In contrast, the great and tragic irony of *The Lord of the Rings* is that the events at the Cracks of Doom bring about a happy ending for everyone but the protagonist and center of the story. While everyone else rejoices, marries, and settles down to a postwar life of fulfillment and security, Frodo alone derives no personal benefit from his sacrifice; indeed, he suffers permanent damage. In addition to losing his finger, he has lost his innocence, his home, and his sense of himself. Most damaging of all, both physically and psychologically, he has lost the Ring. He has given everything he had and has recovered nothing, bringing back from Mount Doom only a maimed hand and his knowledge of his own failure.

The book's long-drawn-out coda, encompassing the homecoming of the original four hobbits, the scouring of the Shire, its regreening by Sam, and its postwar rebuilding, is intended to chronicle the effects of war on the home front, but even more it is intended to show the post-traumatic stress suffered by Frodo. Now, post-traumatic stress is not a regular feature of the conventional fairy story, and Tolkien's insistence on including it is the measure of his honesty, and of how far his story transcends conventional fairy tale, epic, even tragedy. The theorist of the fairy tale has gone beyond eucatastrophe, beyond the happy ending, to show us that, as his essay acknowledges, "there is no true end to any fairy tale" (*MC* 153), and that the consequences of any story reach beyond the pattern of the plot.

Does such treatment challenge or support the popular notion of escapism? We may say that *The Lord of the Rings* does both. It certainly challenges the notion with regard to Frodo, whose escape into the wider world beyond Hobbiton and the Shire has resulted not in recovery but in his "hard recognition" (*MC* 144) of his own weakness and fallibility, and whose tragedy is a signal to the reader that not all tales have happy endings. His remark to Merry near the end of their return, that it feels like "falling asleep again" (*RK* VI, vii, 276), is the measure of how far he has come, but also of what he has lost. In other respects, the book has much to support the notion of escape. Readers have escaped from the primary world into a secondary world of such enchantment that many want to live there, assume Middle-earth identities and do their best to superimpose the secondary world onto the primary one. At the same time, it is exactly that enchantment that has enabled readers to recover the beauty, the wonder, and the possibilities of their own primary world out of which the secondary one has grown.

There has been as well a literary corollary to this process of recovery. It is inevitable that the desire to do again what Tolkien has done will create an audience hungry for new enchantment, and will inspire writers to sub-create their own secondary worlds to satisfy that hunger. In the wake of both will come new theorists whose analysis will extend or modify or codify the ground rules.

The Inheritors

Tolkien's secondary world is so complete, the events in it so compelling of what he called secondary belief, that his book stands alone in the realm of modern fantasy, towering above the many imitators who have come after it. Yet the power and beauty of *The Lord of the Rings* have inspired several generations of post-Tolkien fantasists to try to do likewise, with varying degrees of success. Early examples following hard on the heels of Tolkien's success include Terry Brooks's *Sword of Shannara* and Stephen Donaldson's Thomas Covenant novels, with each author extending the three-volume format of Tolkien's so-called trilogy (actually a continuous narrative) to multivolume series. In the 1970s, Tolkien's success also sparked renewed interest in the work of Evangeline Walton. Walton had written a four-volume reworking of

The Mabinogion in the 1930s and 1940s, but only the first volume was published then. Only after Tolkien's success were the subsequent three volumes published in the early 1970s to take advantage of growing interest in myth-inspired fiction. This same surge of interest in the 1970s and early 1980s helped Susan Cooper, Lloyd Alexander, and Alan Garner to draw on Celtic myth for their neo-Tolkien fantasies

Building on the increasing demand for such escapist literature, second and third generations of post-Tolkien fantasists have refined without fundamentally changing Tolkien's criteria for fantasy, while the term itself has become more canonically acceptable than it used to be. Scholars around the world are exploring the value, the techniques, and the philosophy of fantasy. The ongoing conversation has carried Tolkien's rather broad concepts of Faërie, enchantment, and secondary worlds into ever more precisely defined categories, as for example in the classification system provided by Farah Mendlesohn's *The Rhetorics of Fantasy*. Mendlesohn's taxonomy divides modern fantasy literature into four categories, which are (roughly) four varieties of escape, each defining a different relationship of the protagonist (and the reader) to the fantasy world. They are "the portal-quest, the immersive, the intrusive, and the liminal. These categories are determined by the means by which the fantastic enters the narrated world. In the portal-quest we are invited through into the fantastic, in the intrusion fantasy the fantastic enters the fictional world, in the liminal fantasy the magic hovers in the corner of our eye, while the immersive fantasy allows us no escape" (xiv).

C. S. Lewis's *The Lion, the Witch, and the Wardrobe* is Mendlesohn's primary example of portal-quest fantasy, the wardrobe being the portal, the point of entry into the other world. Yet she also cites *The Lord of the Rings* as a portal-quest, seeing in it a transition "from a mundane life" in which the fantastic is either far-removed or unknown, to the protagonist's "direct contact" (xix–xx), when he or she (and the reader) is "invited through into the fantastic" (xiv). This, of course, is precisely what happens to the four hobbits when they leave Crickhollow for the wider world of strangeness and peril outside the Shire. This wider world, however, is simply a continuation of the Middle-earth they already live in, with phenomena differing in degree from the Old Forest to the Barrow Downs to Shelob's lair.

While her taxonomy provides concrete tools for analyzing techniques of fantasy, the very exactness of Mendlesohn's categories may hamper their application, since it is quite possible for a work of fantasy to transcend a category or to fit into more than one, in which case just how useful are the categories? *The Lord of the Rings* cannot be limited to portal-quest, for example, since a case can be made for any of the four categories. It can fit the category of intrusion, since the most fantastic object in the story, the Ring (in Mendlesohn's terms, "the beast at the bottom of the garden" [xxi]), has already entered the Shire when the story begins. Liminality comes into play in Lórien, where what for Sam feels like magic (for he cannot see it directly) is explained as mere technology by the elves who practice it. As for the immersive fantasy, Mendlesohn explains it as "present[ing] the fantastic without comment as the norm both for the protagonist and for the reader" (xx), and further comments that "we sit on the protagonist's shoulder and . . . have access to his eyes and ears" (xx); this is exactly what readers experience on entering the world of *The Lord of the Rings*. In Mendlesohn's taxonomy, the immersive fantasy allows us "no escape" (xiv). But in Tolkien's terms, it is this very circumstance—our being drawn entirely into the sub-created world—that provides the escape.

In contrast, Philip Pullman's His Dark Materials trilogy, *The Golden Compass* (originally published in the UK as *Northern Lights*), *The Subtle Knife*, and *The Amber Spyglass*, has created alternate yet recognizable worlds with many of the actual world's familiar features—Oxford's Jericho, the colleges, houseboats on the river, the Pitt-Rivers Museum; the vaguely familiar Mediterranean coastal town of Cittàgazze, with its palm trees, sidewalk cafes and hills in the distance—and inserted into them a sprinkling of unfamiliar features, such as daemons, the alethiometer, the subtle knife, holes in the world, the Dust. Yet these are strange precisely because we see them in the context of familiar surroundings. The Oxfords and Cittàgazze of Lyra and Will are secondary worlds wholly dependent for their existence on the reader's knowledge not just of the real world, but of specific places within it. Thus Pullman's secondary worlds, in particular the Oxford of *The Golden Compass* and the tangential Oxford and Cittàgazze of *The Subtle Knife*, are so like to the world we know that there is in either book little scope for escape or recovery in Tolkien's terms.

Pullman seems to want to meld the fantastical with the starkly realistic: to make, as it were, the primary world into a secondary world. We might better call this alienation than escape, for it is a deliberate attempt to disorient the reader by defamiliarizing the ordinary and destabilizing the expected. Mendlesohn describes this technique as liminal fantasy, maintaining that "[i]n the liminal fantasy we are given to understand, through cues to the familiar, that this is our world" (xxiii). We do not escape the primary world; rather, we discover it as (in Tolkien's term) Faërie, an unsettling Faërie, to be sure, but, since Faërie is meant to unsettle (read "enchant"), essentially true to its kind.

Pullman has stoutly maintained that the books composing His Dark Materials are "not fantasy but stark realism." The fantasy does not exist for its own sake, but is "there to support and embody," as he insisted in a December 1998 interview, "matters that might normally be encountered in works of realism"—"what it means to be human, to grow up, to suffer and learn" (unattributed interview). In answering a question about the series posted on his website on March 6, 2009, Pullman added that it was about a "universal human experience, namely growing up" of "real people" rather than "beings that don't exist" ("Questions and Answers").

But the fact is that Will and Lyra are no more "real people" with "universal human experience" than are Tolkien's hobbits. All are fictive constructs, Lyra and Will more easily recognizable perhaps, but with no more reality than Pullman's overtly fantastic elements—daemons (vols. 1, 2, 3), Specters (vol. 2), and donkeys on wheels (vol. 3)—who easily qualify as "beings that don't exist" in the real world. Like C. S. Lewis's *The Lion, the Witch, and the Wardrobe*—Mendlesohn's primary example of portal-quest fantasy—Pullman's *The Subtle Knife* offers a gateway into another world, but with the difference that, unlike Lewis's wardrobe, the parallel world of Cittàgazze, into which Will scrambles through a hole in the Oxford night and to which Lyra crosses over her father's bridge, is clearly meant, like the world they leave, to be an alternative version of their own world. To compound the alienation, the Oxford to which they both return from the parallel world of Cittàgazze is the "real" world for Will, but a parallel and fantastic Oxford for Lyra.

In Mendlesohn's taxonomy, this Oxford is liminal for the reader, a portal-quest entry for Lyra, and an intrusion for Will. Pullman is one example among many of writers whose imagined reality offers itself to readers for escape and to critics for analysis. Mendlesohn's book covers a large number of authors, including Lloyd Alexander, Stephen Donaldson, John Crowley, C. S. Lewis, China Mieville, and Peter Beagle, as well as J. R. R. Tolkien and many others. Whether her categories are helpful in understanding the uses of fantasy is up to the reader.

It seems clear that as time passes the appetite for fantasy shows no sign of slacking, and the audience grows ever larger. As more and more fantasies are written, filmed, translated into games and virtual realities, traded from computer to computer and website to website, the theoretical conversation will do its best to keep up. The psychology and techniques of the fantastic are sure to be more and more deeply studied. But for Virginia Woolf's Common Reader, neither scholar nor critic but one who reads for pleasure, the works will outlast the criticism as the sub-creators will outlast the theorists.

Except for Tolkien, who was both sub-creator and theorist, and who used his fiction and his theory to inform one another. The effect of each on the other is plain to see.

War, Death, and Fairy Stories in the Work of J. R. R. Tolkien

On 6 May 1944, during World War II, J. R. R. Tolkien replied to a letter from his son Christopher, then undergoing pilot training in South Africa and apparently deeply disturbed by the stupidity and complexity of bureaucratic activities in camp. Tolkien responded, "I think if you could begin to *write* . . . you would find it a great relief. I sense amongst all your pains . . . the desire to express your *feeling* about good, evil, fair, foul in some way: to rationalize it and prevent it just festering. In my case it generated Morgoth and the History of the Gnomes" (*Letters* 78). Tolkien may have overstated the case for frustration as inspiration. The History of the Gnomes was the germ of the Silmarillion, Tolkien's invented mythology, which certainly had deeper sources than life in a military camp. Nevertheless, the Silmarillion and its offshoot, *The Lord of the Rings,* do indeed express his feeling about some very big issues of "good and evil, fair and foul," and his writing probably did much to prevent them festering. Among other things, Tolkien's war experience helped to sharpen his developing interest in what might seem the opposite of the gritty world of war, the world of imagination. "A real taste for fairy-stories," he wrote, "was wakened by philology on the threshold of manhood, and quickened to full life by war" (*MC* 135).

I'll leave philology for another day, but I do want to explore Tolkien's war-quickened taste for fairy stories (and by extension myths) in the context of his suggested solution to Christopher's perceived pains. His word *rationalize* in the letter is important, for it connotes a conscious process. We think of the word as meaning justification, or excuse, but it also has the quite literal meaning (as given in def. 2, *OED*), "to render conformable to reason; to explain on a rational basis." By this definition, to rationalize is to defend against the irrational, the meaningless. In seeming contrast, Tolkien's choice of fairy stories—a genre not conventionally associated with rationality—as the vehicle for dealing with good and evil says much about the importance to him of imagination as a road to understanding. It has been said that myths are the meaning of history, that it is the stories we tell about events that invest them with significance and make great happenings applicable to ordinary people. If that is the case, then Tolkien's invented myth should tell us something about how his writing of it "rationalized" the real history he experienced in order to prevent it "festering." And it does, but in ways that sometimes appear more complicated than clarifying, and more mystical than rational.

To learn more, we must go back to another letter, this one about death, which is the third item in my title list after fairy stories and war. I have discussed this letter elsewhere (*Green Suns and Faërie*), but it bears revisiting in the present context. Written some three decades earlier than the letter to Christopher, this one was composed in and about another war, World War I, and about the death in that war of one of Tolkien's closest friends, Rob Gilson. The letter is addressed to another close school friend, Geoffrey Smith. Together with a third friend, Christopher Wiseman, the four had been a fellowship since schooldays, continuing through university and into the war. They called themselves the TCBS, initials for Tea Club Barrows Store, after the site of their meetings in downtown Birmingham. All four had artistic ambitions—Tolkien and Smith were burgeoning poets, Wiseman, a musician, and Gilson, a visual artist with an interest in architecture. Like many romantic, idealistic young men of their generation, they had seen themselves as a special group, a latter day Pre-Raphaelite brotherhood. Now all four were in the armed forces: Wiseman in the navy and Tolkien, Smith, and Gilson in the army. For the foreseeable future, their high-flown ambitions were not forgotten but temporarily suspended. It is in this context—war versus ambition—that Tolkien composed his letter to Smith. Here is what he wrote on 12 August 1916 in response to the death of Rob Gilson.

> My dear old Geoffrey,
> . . . I cannot get away from the conclusion that it is wrong to confound the greatness which Rob has won with the greatness which he himself doubted. . . . I now believe that if the greatness which we three certainly meant . . . is really the lot of the TCBS, then the death of any of its members is but a bitter winnowing of those who were not meant to be great. . . . The greatness I meant was that of a great instrument in God's hands—a mover, a doer, even an achiever of great things. . . . The greatness which Rob has found is in no way smaller—for the greatness I meant and tremblingly hoped for as ours

is valueless unless steeped with the same holiness of courage suffering and sacrifice—but is of a different kind. . . . What I meant . . . was that the TCBS had been granted some spark of fire . . . that was destined to kindle a new light . . . destined to testify for God and Truth in a more direct way even than by laying down its several lives. . . . (*Letters* 9–10)

There's a lot packed into this—grief, survivor's guilt, ambition, greatness, sacrifice, truth, God, destiny, above all, the nature of meaning and the meaning of death. A lot of festering feeling. Tolkien was no stranger to death; his father had died when he was three, his mother when he was twelve. But the death of parents, while an immeasurable loss, can at least be understood as the passing of an older generation, and in that respect fitted into the continuum of human life. The unlooked-for death by violence of a contemporary (Gilson was actually a year younger than Tolkien) is a quite different thing, underscoring one's own mortality and raising the question of the place of death in everyday experience.

Gilson was killed while leading his men into battle on the first day of the Somme, one of the greatest battles of World War I and the most destructive of human life. On that day, 1 July 1916, wave after wave of English soldiers were ordered out of their trenches to cross no-man's-land and attack the German trenches. They had no idea what they were getting into. They had been told the barbed wire protecting the German trenches had been cut. It hadn't. They had been told the German machine-gun emplacements had been taken out. They hadn't. The advancing English were simply mowed down by merciless machine-gun fire, and, each burdened with sixty-five pounds of equipment, were unable to fire back. They had little protective covering fire. On that day, twenty thousand English troops were killed and another forty thousand wounded. In all, as the battle continued over the next four months, one million men were killed or wounded—on both sides—and no lasting advantage was gained by either side.

And yet less than two years previously there had occurred the spontaneous "Christmas truce" of 1914, when the firing stopped and soldiers from both sides ventured into no-man's-land, where they mingled, exchanging food and souvenirs and singing carols. Troops from both sides were also friendly enough to play games of football with one another. It was a rare moment of peace on earth, good will toward men. But it was no way to fight a war, and when the top brass heard about it, they took steps to see that it did not happen again. Orders went forth from the vested interests of both sides, the bureaucrats and commanders, forbidding such contact on the very reasonable grounds that men who had met and begun to know each other might no longer want to kill one another on orders. After the carnage of the Somme, there were no more Christmas truces.

Tolkien's letter, full of implied and unanswered questions, must be read in both contexts, read in light of the Christmas truce as well as measured against the fact that the battle in which Gilson died was inconclusive. How "conformable to reason," then, was Gilson's death? ("rationalize," def. 2 *OED*). There was ample cause, certainly: the war, the battle, the German guns. But we see Tolkien struggling to find a reason, to rationalize something so patently irrational. How reasonable was Gilson's "sacrifice" if men who fought and killed each other could also sing and play and celebrate together? If no victory was gained?

Most important, if Gilson's death had no effect on the Great War, what effect did it have on the TCBS? What did his death mean to and for the other three? What did it say about his "greatness"? About his destiny? The words *great* or *greatness* occur nine times in this short passage from Tolkien's letter; the word *meant* occurs five times, each time changing slightly according to context: "[t]he *greatness* which we three . . . *meant*," "those . . . not *meant* to be *great*," "the *greatness* I [Tolkien] *meant*," "the *greatness* which Rob has found," "[*greatness*] of a different kind," "the *greatness* I *meant* and tremblingly hoped for," "[w]hat I *meant* . . . was." The stronger word *destined* occurs twice: "*destined* to kindle a new light" and "*destined* to testify for God." Beneath these words one can sense Tolkien struggling to reconcile his boyhood sense of destiny with his devout Catholic belief in order to find meaning in the death of Rob Gilson—patently meaningless in light of the fact that the battle that killed him achieved nothing except the deaths of twenty thousand men.

Although he never comes out and says it, behind Tolkien's tortured reasoning is the question of God's role in human life, and behind that is another question: what is the personal meaning of Gilson's death in the context of that "destiny" that Tolkien had envisioned as being "a great instrument in God's hands"? Did Gilson die because he was not meant to be a great instrument in the same way as the others? Was Gilson meant to die and therefore not meant to be a great instrument? If Tolkien survived, was that because he was meant to be a great instrument and therefore not meant to die? These are huge questions, and we can see Tolkien, in the throes of survivor's guilt, struggling to find answers.

His problem was intensified by a later letter, this time *from* Smith, who wrote to Tolkien, "If I am scuppered [killed] tonight, . . . may you say the things I have tried to say long after I am not there to say them" (Carpenter, *Tolkien* 86). On 3 December 1916, four months after Gilson's death, Geoffrey

Smith also was dead, of wounds from a random shell that hit him while he was walking down a road behind the lines. This accidental death offered even less meaning than Gilson's, who at least was killed in a battle where death was the intent, and it raised the same questions. But it gives added weight to Tolkien's ruminations. Smith's exhortation that Tolkien "say the things I have tried to say" is not just the passing of a torch; it is tantamount to a directive, almost a command. Was it also a destiny? Was Smith, like Gilson, meant to die? Had Tolkien survived because he was meant to speak for Smith?

Tolkien's response to all these questions was the same one he recommended to Christopher thirty years later. He began to write. Sent back to England with trench fever at the end of 1916, he began, within a month of Smith's death, to write what was to become the Silmarillion, to "generate Morgoth and the History of the Gnomes," to create Middle-earth and its cosmology. It took a while. It was not until some three years later that he wrote the first draft of his creation story, the "Music of the Ainur" or "Ainulindalë." This gave Tolkien the opportunity to create one of the boldest and most provocative aspects of his invented mythology—that is, its treatment of death. This is, to put it mildly, an unorthodox approach, in which Tolkien has his godhead Ilúvatar give Men the "gift" of death (*S* 42). The notion of death as the gift of God is clean contrary to Tolkien's own Catholic faith, which rests on the belief that death is "the wages of sin" and an "enemy" to be overcome by the Resurrection (Rom. 6:23; 1 Cor. 15:26). But within his invented world, Tolkien was free to push speculation beyond the conventions of belief. One of the advantages of the imaginative fiction that was Tolkien's preferred mode is that it need obey no rules but its own. Another advantage is that it allows leeway for unorthodox replies to orthodox questions.

This idea of death as a gift is not a caprice but a conscious foray into uncharted territory, and is, as far as I know, unique among both real and imaginary mythologies. Tolkien was not proposing a revision of orthodox belief, but offering a fictive answer to the fantasist's perennial question, "What if?" as well as to his own questioning, in his letter to Smith, of God's plan. Here is how his cosmology works. His imaginary world is peopled by Elves and Men, two races clearly patterned on humanity but separated from one another by opposing destinies. Elves are immortal, tied to the circles of the world for as long as it lasts and bound to the pattern of the Music that has created the world. Men are given the "gift" of death with no promise of an afterlife. Writing many years later to a reviewer of *The Lord of the Rings* (and thus indirectly to its readers), Tolkien variously explained, "I am only concerned with Death as part of the nature, physical and spiritual, of Man, and with Hope without guarantees" (*Letters* 237).

Much has been written about this aspect of Tolkien's world, and I do not propose to go into the theology of it. But it seems at least worth considering that this most extraordinary feature of his invented mythology gave him a way to inquire into the meaning of death in general, and thereby to explore the apparently senseless deaths of Rob Gilson and G. B. Smith in what was patently a useless war, since it flared up again twenty years later. He couldn't rationalize their deaths in real life—but in Middle-earth he could. One of his rationalizations involved an inquiry into the drawbacks of "deathlessness." To that end, his Elves are presented as suspended in perpetual deathlessness, able to be killed but bound to return to life in the same identity over and over.

Writing of the "Escape from Death" that characterizes fairy stories, he speculated that, "the human stories of the elves are doubtless full of the Escape from Deathlessness" (*MC* 153). He said it less playfully in a draft of a letter to a reader, where he wrote, "The real theme for me is about something . . . permanent and difficult: Death and Immortality: the mystery of the love of the world in the hearts of a race 'doomed' to leave and seemingly lose it; the anguish in the hearts of a race 'doomed' not to leave it, until its whole evil-aroused story is complete" (*Letters* 246). In both iterations, this sounds rather simple. Deathlessness will turn out to be a burden. Death remains a mystery. Unsurprisingly, Tolkien found the mystery more fruitful to write about, but—also unsurprisingly—not so simple, as we will see when we look closely.

Tolkien's searching treatment of death and its opposite, deathlessness, suffuses his entire mythology—not just the Silmarillion but *The Lord of the Rings*—and is a huge topic, far beyond the scope of this paper. For brevity's sake (though I will touch on some long-reaching questions), I will keep chiefly to some characters in *The Lord of the Rings* to whom Tolkien, standing in for Ilúvatar, give the mysterious gift of death. Who are they? And how do they die? Death rides several different horses in Tolkien's mythos. Death comes to a surprising range of people, both good and not so good, and Tolkien devises several kinds (grades?) of death, some of which raise troubling moral questions. Some people seek death and find it—like Theoden and Denethor and Aragorn. Some find death who do not seek it, like the man of Harad to whose anonymous death Sam is witness during the skirmish in Ithilien.

I'll start with the deaths of Theoden and Denethor, two deaths given prominence in the moral world of Middle-earth. Theoden goes into battle expecting be killed—and he is. His death is a heroic one, fitting to him and to his warrior culture, and while it is mourned, it is also praised. Tolkien's word for him is *fey*, meaning "death-ripe" or "death-directed." In this respect, his death is not unlike that of Denethor, who is also death-ripe, death-directed. Yet Denethor's death is given a different moral context and undergoes a moral judgment not applied to Theoden's. We may say that the "meaning" of Theoden's death is heroism, and the "meaning" of Denethor's is—not cowardice, for he is a brave man—perhaps misguidedness. He should not have died, and his death is condemned by both Gandalf (directly) and Tolkien (as authorial arbiter). "Authority is not given to you, Steward of Gondor, to order the hour of your death," says Gandalf (*RK* V, vii, 129), and it is safe to say most readers would agree. Death is a gift that comes with conditions. No authority, no death.

But wait a minute. A closer look reveals a puzzling discrepancy in Gandalf's/Tolkien's stance if we look at it in the light of yet another death, that of Aragorn. Ordering the hour of his death is exactly what Aragorn does, as we are told in "The Tale of Aragorn and Arwen" in Appendix A of *The Lord of the Rings*. Arwen, who has renounced her elven immortality in order to marry Aragorn, begs him to stay, to which he replies, "To me has been given the grace to go at my will." He explains that his willed death is to avoid his becoming "unmanned and witless" (*RK* App. A, 343). In other words, his death will allow him to avoid the less attractive aspects of old age. Considered side by side, the two deaths of Denethor and Aragorn raise some troubling questions. Both Denethor and Aragorn die of their own volition, taking their deaths into their own hands. Both are, at the time, in good health, so that natural death is not imminent, and both deaths will be used to forestall future consequences. In practical terms this is euthanasia, a notion contrary to Catholic doctrine, especially in Tolkien's pre-Vatican II world. So it would seem that Tolkien was using the freedom of his invented world to push the boundaries pretty far.[1] What exactly, we may ask, is the difference between the *grace* given to Aragorn and the *authority* withheld from Denethor? Is the purposeful termination of life permissible when a good guy does it but not when a morally ambiguous guy does it? Or does the reason behind each death affect its moral position? Each of these deaths is given a "rationale." Each death has a motive, and the motive is to avoid an undesired outcome. Each death is an achieved goal. I suggest, however, that each raises some difficult questions about the other. I suspect that when it came to it, Tolkien found his own invention more complex than he imagined. It is not just death versus deathlessness; it is also one person's death versus another person's death, and one kind of death versus another kind. The "gift" seems to come with strings attached.

The deaths of Denethor and Aragorn, so similar in intent yet treated so differently, complicate the notion of any transcendent mythic meaning. As an alternative, I propose to examine another death, this one unsought, in the treatment of which Tolkien abandons his transcendent approach for a more personal and intimate one, and which is all the more effective for his doing so. This is the death of the man of Harad killed in the skirmish with Faramir's troops in Ithilien. It is neither heroic and fitting like Theoden's nor defiant and wrong-headed like Denethor's; nor is it carefully considered like Aragorn's. In terms of the story, it is not a "big" death but a very small one. But in terms of Tolkien's overall theme, it looms large, and terms of his treatment of death, it is by far the most moving and therefore the most successful. I want to look closely at Tolkien's treatment of this death, because it seems to me to come the closest in spirit of any in *The Lord of the Rings* to the death in battle of Rob Gilson. It doesn't answer Tolkien's questions. But it frames them. Here is how Tolkien describes it.

> ... suddenly straight over the rim of their sheltering bank, a man fell, crashing through the slender trees, nearly on top of [Frodo and Sam]. He came to rest in the fern a few feet away, face downward, green arrow-feathers sticking from his neck below a golden collar. His scarlet robes were tattered, his corslet of overlapping brazen plates was rent and hewn, his black plaits of hair braided with gold were drenched with blood. His brown hand still clutched the hilt of a broken sword.
>
> It was Sam's first view of a battle of Men against Men, and he did not like it much. He was glad that he could not see the dead face. He wondered what the man's name was and where he came from; and if he was really evil of heart, or what lies or threats had led him on the long march from his home; and if he would not really rather have stayed there in peace ... (*TT* IV, iv, 269)

This vignette is one of Tolkien's most vivid passages of description, and it doesn't take much to imagine that Rob Gilson's death might have happened in much the same way—struck down in battle, crashing, falling on his face, rent and tattered and drenched in blood. Nor is it too far-fetched to speculate that Tolkien might have had that real death in mind when he created this fictive one. Battlefields are marked chiefly by dead bodies, whether in France in 1916 or in Middle-earth in the Third Age. The details of this scene, presented through Sam's eyes—the green and scarlet and black and gold; the feathers, the robe, the corslet, the collar; and most of all the blood drenching the man's braids of hair—have the immediate impact of a film close-up. Sam has heard the war. Now he can see it, and it puts a new face on a conflict he has up to now taken for granted as being between the good guys and the bad guys. That war may be directed by double-dyed bad guys like Sauron, but it is being fought by ordinary people, neither wholly bad nor wholly good but wholly human, men who have made the "long march" from their homes to suffer death in a strange country.

Sam's reaction comes straight from Tolkien's heart and recalls the 1914 Christmas truce alluded to earlier, when soldiers from both sides—neither heroes nor cowards but ordinary men in extraordinary circumstances—stopped killing each other and came together to celebrate a shared holiday, to sing carols, play football, exchange photos, and discover one another's humanity and recognize that they were not "evil of heart." Especially telling is Sam's speculation, upon seeing the death of the man of Harad, that he might have been lied to or threatened by those above him with a vested interest in promoting a war, and that he might rather have "stayed in peace" than gone into battle. It is worth remembering that this passage was written by a man who joined the army because he had to, not because he wanted to, and who would much rather have stayed in peace if that had been an option; a man who had a grudge against "that ruddy little ignoramus Adolf Hitler" for "[r]uining, perverting, misapplying, and making forever accursed, that noble northern spirit" which he loved (*Letters* 55–56).

In the end, I suggest that Tolkien found no easy answers to the tortured questions implied in his letter to Smith. I propose, moreover, that his attempts at juxtaposing Death and Deathlessness resulted in a succession of incidents with separate meanings that raised yet more questions. He wrestled with those questions, and with the idea of death, throughout the years of his creative life without coming to a definitive answer. "Many that live deserve death," Gandalf tells Frodo. "And some die that deserve life. Can you give it to them? Then do not be too eager to deal out death in judgement" (*FR* I, ii, 69). In the end, Tolkien found no secure meaning in the deaths dealt out to Gilson and Smith—and surely both young men deserved life. My conclusion is that Tolkien's mythos does not really rationalize death, in the conventional sense of "justify." Nor does it, in the literal sense, render death "conformable to reason" ("rationalize," defs. 1 and 2, *OED*), for it isn't always. Instead, and most tellingly, the vignette in Ithilien simply memorializes death. Unable, finally, to give it a one-size-fits-all transcendent meaning, Tolkien was most successful when he simply presented it.

Ernest Hemingway called death "that thing we all must do." And so it is. But each of us will do it differently, within the context of our own story. The death of the man of Harad and Sam's reaction to it gave death a vivid and moving context within Tolkien's fairy-story world of Morgoth and the Gnomes, that world whose creation was Tolkien's response to the overwhelming events whose meaning he struggled to understand. By including in his search for meaning not just the deaths of the great, like Theoden and Denethor and Aragorn, but also the death of this Unknown Soldier of Middle-earth, Tolkien found a way to deal with his festering feeling about "good and evil, fair and foul." He gave it to Sam, whose questions about the man of Harad are not the big transcendent inquiries into meaning that occupied Tolkien in 1916 but the little, personal questions that everyone asks. What was his name? Where was he from? What brought him here? Did he want to come? Did he want to fight?

And in that gift to Sam, Tolkien found a way to pay homage to those denied greatness by his other gift, the mysterious and unfathomable gift of Ilúvatar.

Eucatastrophe and the Dark

Faced with a classroom full of expectant students, most of whom have read *The Lord of the Rings*—some many times—before signing up for the course, the teacher of Tolkien's work should have clearly in mind what aspects of that multivalanced work he or she wants to emphasize. Will it be the completeness and integrity of his sub-created world? The medieval roots of his narrative? Its surprising modernity? Its relation to the world of modern fantasy? While all of these are valid, and I take care to include them in the course, my own special goal is to help students discover what gives the book its extraordinary ability to move its readers, why they keep coming back again and again to a story that he himself called "complex, rather bitter, and very terrifying" (*Letters* 136). For me, the gateway into *The Lord of the Rings* and the key to its power are to be found in the tension between his two great essays, "On Fairy-stories" and "*Beowulf:* The Monsters and the Critics."

The essays are contradictory. They mark the opposite poles of Tolkien's creative imagination, one celebrating the magic of fairy tales and their archetypal happy ending, the other exalting the heroic *Beowulf*ian battle with the dark that ends in defeat. Yet while they seem both emotionally and philosophically at odds, they also exist in a curious kind of creative tension with one another. The same man wrote both essays, understood and believed both points of view, and made both part of his fiction. The tension between these extremes is what gives his book much of its energy and its power to move the reader. In any course I teach on Tolkien, my path into his work is through these essays, and though it is a winding way, I have found that following it results in a richer appreciation of the books than my students and I might otherwise arrive at.

Starting off with the two essays, however, is a challenging beginning, for it throws students in at the deep end and requires them to swim. That many are already more or less familiar with Tolkien's fiction makes little difference to their experience of the essays, which are predicated on a level of knowledge about literatures—myth, folklore, fairy tale, and early English epic—rarely offered these days in English syllabi. Thus the teacher must not only translate the occasional phrase from Greek or Anglo-Saxon but must also explain and contextualize two contrasting genres and fill in the history of scholarship in both fields. Then we can begin.

"On Fairy-stories"

Written at the time of transition from *The Hobbit* to *The Lord of the Rings* (1938), the fairy-story essay should be read in two contexts. The first, the necessary background history of the myth and folklore movement, shows where Tolkien was coming from and how he was entering the debate. The second context is that of the essay's importance as a working explication of Tolkien's creative process. As the latter, "On Fairy-stories" sets up a number of concepts easy to recognize in Tolkien's work—Faërie, enchantment, sub-creation, the secondary world, fantasy, the inner consistency of reality. I am not alone in having discussed these at greater length in other works, so I will just say here that once we have got past the problem of definition (what is or is not a fairy story and how do you know) and the questions of origins and importance (Where do they come from? Why are they good reading? Are they for adults as well as children?), the key concept is the notion of Faërie, which leads to all the others mentioned above.

My class spends some time on the derivation of the word *faërie* (from Old French *fae* or *fée*, meaning "fairy," with the suffix *ery/erie* extending the root noun to a process or state, as *fay-ery*, meaning "the practice of enchantment or the state of being enchanted"). This is what Tolkien calls the secondary world, the otherworld of fairyland that readers experience when they read the book. Further etymology will add a darker aspect by tracing the word back to Latin *fàta* (the Fates), plural of *fàtum* (Fate), which explains why Tolkien called Faërie a perilous realm, and illuminates his treatment of the otherworlds of his fiction, from Mirkwood to the Old Forest to Lothlórien to Fangorn Forest. The Hobbits' encounters with Old Man Willow, with Tom Bombadil and Goldberry, and with the Elves of Lórien, are journeys into Faërie in both its light and dark aspects.

These characters and scenes are fantastic in that they are no part of the observable "real" world, yet they preserve in the secondary world the inner consistency of reality that makes them believable. In the Old Forest, Old Man Willow is a tree, and his character extends only a little beyond what trees really do. He puts out obtrusive roots, his leaves flutter and murmur, the great cracks in his trunk have the mysterious terror of a child's nightmare. His nemesis, Tom Bombadil, defies definition, but Tom's benevolent nature, as well as Tolkien's specific comments about him in his letters, allies him with the vanishing English countryside whose loss Tolkien mourned. Moreover, Tom's immunity to the Ring defines the nature of its power, which is to dominate other wills—not a usual characteristic of the natural world. Of all the otherworlds, Lórien in its timeless Elvish beauty is the most purely Faërie-like, the most enchanting of the otherworlds, both to the Hobbits and to Tolkien's readers.

I have found that students really enjoy putting two and two together—applying the theory of Tolkien's essay to the practice of his fiction, seeing both in action, so to speak—and coming to an understanding of Tolkien's use of his working model. The fairy-story essay defines *The Lord of the Rings* as a secondary world—in effect a fairy story, one writ extra-large, no question, but a fairy story nonetheless. Yet all this is window-dressing, is, in a sense, prologue to what is for Tolkien (and must be for students) the heart of the matter: the use of fairy stories, the rewards that fairy stories give their readers. These Tolkien lists as recovery, escape, and consolation, with special emphasis on the happy ending, the final reward of the fairy story. In this respect, *The Lord of the Rings* both conforms to the essay and transcends it. Students find escape (entry into a secondary world) and recovery (seeing the familiar as if it were new) easy enough to apply, and come to the consolation of the happy ending expecting this combination to be equally easy.

Then we tackle *eucatastrophe,* defined by Tolkien as "the good catastrophe, the sudden joyous 'turn'" (*MC* 153), that takes the story from dark to light, from potential disaster to the happy ending. And it is here that the influence of "On Fairy-stories" on *The Lord of the Rings* becomes complicated, for the turn, which Tolkien calls a "sudden and miraculous grace: never to be counted on to recur" (*MC* 153), depends for its effect on the imminent *dyscatastrophe* that generates the very real possibility that no happy ending will come. Not just the escape but the hairbreadth narrowness of the escape achieves the effect, and the "sudden and miraculous grace" cannot be a god from the machine, but must conform to the inner consistency, and thus the credibility, of the world and the events. It is easy to recognize both in Tolkien's stunning and extraordinary denouement, the one-two punch of Frodo and Gollum at the Cracks of Doom that saves Middle-earth. Tolkien's insistence that fantasy must have the "inner consistency of reality" comes into play here. Given the circumstances, Frodo can do no otherwise than what he does. Given the circumstances, Gollum can do no otherwise than what he does. The actions of both together move the narrative with startling suddenness from the dyscatastrophe that is Frodo's claiming of the Ring to the eucatastrophic "turn" of Gollum's attack and the Ring's consequent destruction. Both lead to the happy ending. At this point, however, there is a departure from the "On Fairy-stories" model, for this outcome is a qualified and bittersweet happy ending. It is just here that the story suddenly swings from fairy story to the opposite pole of Tolkien's imagination, the *Beowulf* essay, and shifts from eucatastrophe to the opposite concept: actual, not narrowly escaped tragedy, and the fate of being human.

"*BEOWULF:* THE MONSTERS AND THE CRITICS"

Differing in scope and subject matter ("On Fairy-stories" is a wide-ranging discussion of a genre, the *Beowulf* essay a narrowly focused examination of a single work), the two essays yet employ the same strategies of argument—previous scholars' misreading of the texts as background for why Tolkien's reading is the correct one. Since today's students are rarely conversant with early *Beowulf* scholarship, we have first to explore why Tolkien's reading of *Beowulf* is important: how his defense of the monsters as central to the theme not only revealed the poem to be a coherent work of art but in the process dramatically redirected *Beowulf* scholarship. More important to students of Tolkien's work, the essay's emotional and critical position leads straight to *The Lord of the Rings* and Frodo's struggle with the monsters represented both by Gollum and by the Ring itself. The heart of Tolkien's *Beowulf* essay and the key to his art lie in his focus on "that battle with the hostile world and the offspring of the dark which ends for all, even the kings and champions, in defeat" (*MC* 18). Tolkien's statement that "*lif is læne: eal scæceð liht and lif somod*"—"life is loan: all perishes, light and life together"—captures the essence of what the poem meant to him (*MC* 19).

In class we read the essay as a guide to "Tolkien's *Beowulf*," a two-part meditation on the theme of courage and defeat. The young warrior's victory over Grendel is balanced against the final defeat of the death-ripe old king in the fight with the dragon. But *The Lord of the Rings* is a long and multileveled book, and only when students have read it in light of the *Beowulf* essay can they connect Tolkien's understanding of the Old English poem with the sense of doomed heroism and inevitable loss that permeates his own book. Then we read *The Lord of the Rings* not as a fairy story but as a tragedy, the tragedy of Frodo, whose struggle against his inner monster (externalized as both the Ring and Gollum) ends in defeat. Gollum's unforeseen but inevitable attack at the Cracks of Doom turns the dyscatastrophe of Frodo's capitulation to the Ring into a happy ending. In part. It is a happy ending for everyone but the hero, since the *eucatastrophe* benefits Middle-earth in general and Aragorn and Faramir and Éowyn and Merry and Pippin and Sam in particular. But it does not benefit the one (or the two, Frodo and Gollum) whose actions brought it about. The catch in the necessity of *dyscatastrophe* for the *eucatastrophe* to work is that except insofar as it frees him from the power of the Ring, the *eucatastrophe* does not benefit Frodo, who, stuck in the *dyscatastrophe*, pays a high price for everyone else's joy. Tolkien's uncompromising honesty (based almost certainly on his own experience of war and its aftermath) will not permit Frodo to emerge from his struggle with the dark unscathed. Instead, Tolkien goes back again to *Beowulf. Lif is læne: eal scæceð liht and lif somod.* Frodo is wounded, traumatized, bereft of his health, his home, and what has become the most important thing in his life—the Ring.

Tolkien called the structure of *Beowulf* "essentially a balance, an opposition of ends and beginnings." So too the structure of *The Lord of the Rings* rests on a balance—not so much chronological as thematic—of light and dark, of Faërie and enchantment as over against inevitable loss. This is most movingly manifest in what happens to Frodo over the course of the book as he moves from fairy tale to epic tragedy. Reading *The Lord of the Rings* though Tolkien's *Beowulf* essay allows students to see in his own fiction the same perspective he found in the poem, "a new perspective [on] an ancient theme: that man, each man and all men, and all their works shall die" (*MC* 23). Such a perspective helps prepare students for what really happens to Frodo—no fairy-tale happy ending but unhealed wounds and loss of all he holds dear. Tolkien does not have Frodo die, but what he does arrange for his hobbit hero is in many ways a crueler fate. We have only to note Frodo's recurrent illness or hear his words to Gandalf—"I am wounded with knife, sting, and tooth, and a long burden. Where shall I find rest?" (*RK* VI, vii, 268); to Sam—"I am wounded . . . wounded; it will never really heal" (*RK* VI, ix, 305); or, most poignant of all, to Farmer Cotton—"It is gone forever . . . and now all is dark and empty" (*RK* VI, ix, 304).

This is a bitter pill for some readers to swallow, and it is not unusual to encounter students who refuse to accept it, who argue in the teeth of the evidence that the story really *is* a fairy tale, that there *is* a happy ending, that Frodo succeeds in his quest and lives happily in some post-*Lord of the Rings* ever after. This makes for some pretty intense class discussion, with students passionately defending one position or the other and talking to one another instead of to me (an action I applaud and encourage). Citation of Tolkien's letters stating that the quest "was bound to fail" (*Letters* 234), that "Frodo 'failed'" (*Letters* 252, 326), that "the power of Evil in the world is *not* finally resistible by incarnate creatures, however 'good'" (*Letters* 252), that Valinor is "a kind of purgatory" (*Letters* 328) rather than a version of Heaven, often meets with intransigence. I usually let the debate run for five minutes or so before announcing that I will simply put the question on the final exam or make it part of the final paper assignment and invite students to argue pro or con, insisting only that they support their position with evidence from the book and both essays. If they make a good case, which often turns on interpretation of the word *fail*, I give them full credit.

It is important for students to realize that studying Tolkien does not result in "right" or "wrong" answers. It results in understanding how in writing *The Lord of the Rings* Tolkien expressed his view of the human condition and its paradoxical union of joy and beauty with loss and pain. This paradox, not just in his general treatment but in his specific treatment of a particular character, Frodo, is what gives the story not just its power but its poignance. I do not say Tolkien reconciled the paradox, for I believe that the contradiction is in the man as well as in his works and remains unresolved. But it is just this unresolved conflict that gives *The Lord of the Rings* its curious power to engage and hold the reader. It combines final defeat and eucatastrophe, *Beowulf* and fairy story, in interconnection and interdependence, and gives students the framework within which to understand the extraordinary depth of Tolkien's vision. Frodo does not, cannot, live happily ever after, and his alienation from home and friends is the final defeat in which the tragic ethos of the *Beowulf* essay opposes, though it does not negate, the joy of "On Fairy-stories." The tension between the two is what keeps alive a story that is, in fact, exactly as Tolkien described it, "complex, rather bitter, and terrifying." I want my students to know that.

Pedagogical Strategies

Since both essays demand a knowledge of history and scholarship above the classroom experience of most undergraduates, and are dense with references and allusions, a good way to begin is by inviting students to air their difficulties with the texts. This also gives the teacher cues as to where and how to engage them with the material. Ignorance and confusion are useful springboards, enabling students to discover with relief that they are not alone, and giving them courage to express their opinions. My exams draw evenly from the texts and from what comes up in discussion. Exams are open book and open notes. The object is not to test students' memory but to foster the learning process by inviting them to read carefully, think deeply, and write informedly. A midterm might ask the students to identify and write an essay on quotations from the essays, for example:

> as in a little circle of light about their halls, men with courage as their stay went forward to that battle with the hostile world and the offspring of the dark which ends for all, even the kings and champions, in defeat.

and/or

> I will call it *Eucatastrophe*. The *eucatastrophic* tale is the true form of fairy-tale, and its highest function.

Another question might ask:

> What are Tolkien's chief criteria for fairy stories, and how well do they fit his own work? Where and how do you see evidence of Faërie in *The Lord of the Rings*?

A final exam or final paper assignment might ask students to reflect on something like the following:

> In his biography of Tolkien, Humphrey Carpenter described him as "a cheerful, almost irrepressible person with a great zest for life." But Carpenter also said he was "capable of bouts of profound despair [and] a deep sense of impending loss. Nothing was safe. Nothing would last." Write an essay exploring the relevance of Carpenter's statements to *The Lord of the Rings*.

or

> In "On Fairy-stories" Tolkien writes that "the sudden, joyous 'turn' . . . does not deny the existence of . . . sorrow and failure." In fact, he says, "the possibility of these is necessary to the joy of deliverance." Discuss "deliverance" and "sorrow and failure" as opposing themes in *The Lord of the Rings*. Is the balance between these extremes even?

PART TWO

"Faërie Begins"

The Nuts and Bolts of Sub-creation

> [I]n such 'fantasy', as it is called, new form is made; Faërie begins; Man becomes a sub-creator.
> —J. R. R. Tolkien, "On Fairy-stories"

Sub-creation was Tolkien's term for the art of making or Gk. *poiesis*. The essays in this section explore what was for him the heart of the matter, the practical, nuts-and-bolts process by which he constructed what he called his secondary world. This includes the use of words as "parts of speech in a mythical grammar" (*MC* 122), exploration of the process of transmission of texts over time, examination of the importance of talismanic artifacts, of distinct and often clashing cultures, and standards of conduct.

"Words and World-making: The Particle Physics of Middle-earth" looks at Tolkien's deployment of words, specifically different names in his invented languages for the same things, to enrich and deepen the fabric of his invented world. "Myth, History, and Time-travel: *The Lost Road* and *The Notion Club Papers*" is a look at Tolkien's two ventures into science fiction as possible framing devices for the transmission of his invented mythology. "Politically Incorrect Tolkien" examines the mores and manners of the various societies depicted in Tolkien's *The Lord of the Rings*, their ignorances, prejudices, and unexamined assumptions about themselves and other societies.

"The Jewels, the Stone, the Ring, and the Making of Meaning" traces the development in Tolkien's work of the idea of the magical talisman or artifact, from the Arkenstone of *The Hobbit* to the Silmarils of *The Silmarillion* to the One Ring of *The Lord of the Rings*, showing how Tolkien refined and polished the concept. "Moral Ambiguity in Tolkien's Major Fiction" examines the moral dilemmas Tolkien deliberately constructs in *The Lord of the Rings* for Frodo, Sam, Boromir, Gandalf, and Aragorn in order to illustrate the complexity and interdependence of apparent good and evil.

Words and World-making

The Particle Physics of Middle-earth

Two major components of any world are its geography and its people. A necessary third is language, by which to define and bond the other two. Without language, geography has no context and people no expression. Without language, there is no way to take the measure of a world, to know its dimensions or its qualities. But measurement—of any kind, at any level—brings complications, for as it defines and describes it, so it also creates the thing measured, so that it is not quite what it was before the measurement. At the level of particle physics, this is Heisenberg's principle of indeterminacy, formulated to account for the interaction and reciprocal effect upon one another of the observer and the particle in the act of measurement, blurring the boundary between the observer and the thing observed.

Princeton physicist John Wheeler called this "changing the universe," and concluded that the old Cartesian idea of the universe as something distinct from the people in it is no longer valid. We can no longer think of the universe as something out there, observable at a distance from behind a plate-glass window. We are part of what we see, and we change it by looking at it. Even to observe so small as a thing as an electron, says Wheeler, we have to shatter that glass. "We have to reach out and insert a measuring device. . . . to measure position, or insert a device to measure momentum, but the insertion of one prevents the insertion of the other." Whichever it is, he continues, "it has an unpredictable effect on the future of that electron, and to that degree the future of the universe is changed. We changed it." His response is to change the language. "We have to cross out that old word 'observer' and replace it with the new word 'participator'" (Wheeler 689). If we measure position, we will disrupt momentum; if we measure momentum, we must forgo position.

The measurement of either forecloses the measurement of the other. But whichever we measure, we change the future of the electron, and to that degree the universe is a work in progress, one in which we are participators, not external observers. Wheeler's thesis, paralleled in the metaphysical writings of theoretical physicists such as David Bohm and Fritjof Capra,[1] is that the world is process, in continuous and creative interaction with the conscious observer or participator, and that this interaction is always at work, shaping and reshaping both consciousness and the world.

I propose to retain both Heisenberg's principle and Wheeler's thesis, but shift them from the microcosm to the macrocosm and apply them to Tolkien's fictive world of Middle-earth. In my analogy, the particles are the phenomena of his world, the measuring device, the words used to name those phenomena, and the participators, the users of those words, the inhabitants who generate and speak the languages of Middle-earth. While such an analogy would work for any fantasy—indeed, for any fiction—it is particularly appropriate for Tolkien since his invented languages are a formative and important element in his fiction, contributing materially to both the fantasy and the reality of his secondary world.

Tolkien's well-known statement that he created his world in order to justify the languages appears more valid with each new iteration of his mythology. Early readers of *The Lord of the Rings* read Strider's recitation of the tale of Tinúviel (if they read it at all; some didn't) as poetry, not history, and certainly not as what Strider said it was, a "rough echo" in the Common Speech of a poetic form called *ann-thennath* among the Elves (*FR* I, xi, 205)—in other words, as a translation from another language. In a discussion of this very poem in their article "Three Elvish Verse Modes," Patrick Wynne and Carl Hostetter note that "[t]here is no evidence that Tolkien ever wrote any of the original Elvish poems said to underlie these 'translated' versions, but such references provide an additional layer of depth to the sub-created world, implying that Middle-earth was home to a vast body of authentic Elvish verse of which we are shown only tantalizing glimpses" (114).

With the complete History of Middle-earth now at our disposal, and with the ongoing work on Tolkien's invented languages, we can see more clearly that for Tolkien there was no world without a language, no language without a people who spoke it, no "people" without a common language to both bind them and describe them. Tolkien's preoccupation, his "Secret Vice," was the invention of languages (*Letters* 374); that hobby became a vocation when the invention of languages necessitated the invention of a world. Certainly, then, the world was made for the languages. But it would be equally true to say that the world was made out of the languages.

Tolkien was by profession a philologist, but beyond that he was a philosopher of language, having much in common with language philosophers such as Ernst Cassirer, Owen Barfield, and Benjamin Whorf, all of whom explored language as a way into the minds and worldviews of its speakers.[2]

Including as parts of a coherent gathering all of the published narratives of Middle-earth—*The Hobbit, The Lord of the Rings, Unfinished Tales, The Silmarillion,* and The History of Middle-earth—we can cite as languages spoken at one point or another within the texts and appendices Proto-Eldarin (also called Qenya and later Quenya), Sindarin, Adûnaic, Dwarvish, Entish, Orcish, and Hobbitish, in addition to ones merely mentioned, such as Goldogrin and Rohirric. Each of these languages reflects through its syntax, vocabulary, and phonology the worldview and perception of its native speakers. In reading these words, we are experiencing the worldviews of their speakers, and thus seeing Tolkien's multivalent world in each moment through new and different eyes, appreciating the facets of the jewel and thus its variety as well as its integrity.

An example is Gimli's catalogue of names for the Misty Mountains when the Fellowship first sees them on the distant horizon.

> They stand tall in our dreams: Baraz, Zirak, Shathûr. Only once before have I seen them from afar in waking life, but I know them and their names, for under them lies Khazad-Dûm, the Dwarrowdelf, that is now called the Black Pit, Moria in the Elvish tongue. Yonder stands Barazinbar, the Redhorn, cruel Caradhras, and beyond him are Silvertine and Cloudyhead: Celebdil the White and Fanuidhol the Grey, that we call Zirak-Zigil and Bundushathûr.... There the Misty Mountains divide, and between their arms lies the deep-shadowed valley which we cannot forget: Azanulbizar, the Dimrill Dale, which the Elves call Nanduhirion. (*FR* II, iii, 297)

For a dwarf of few words, this is a flood of them, and its torrent of names—the first set actually given only in the shortened form, as Gimli then elaborates and tacks on endings—prompts Sam's comment that dwarf-language must be a "fair jaw-cracker" (298). But both catalog and comment have a function beyond exoticism and comic relief. They inject new perception into the narrative. Tolkien was giving a glimpse into the many layers of language and perception in his world, layers contained in Gimli's list of names in Dwarvish, Elvish (Sindarin), and Common Speech (English), as well as in Sam's perception of their strangeness.

Tolkien has Gimli remark that he knows the mountains and their names, suggesting that to know different names for things is to know the things differently.

The passage includes three sets of names for the same three mountains in three different languages; a bumper crop of four names—Khazad-Dûm, Dwarrowdelf, Black Pit, Moria—for the cavern under them; and three for the valley—Azanulbizar, Dimrill Dale, Nanduhirion.[3] A close look, or, better still, an attempt to pronounce the names—try it yourself—will show that what seems, as Wheeler says, "to sit safely out there" (689) is neither safe nor sitting out there, but is interacting linguistically with each observer, changing perception with each different name. Thus Dwarvish *Barazinbar* > Sindarin *Caradhras* > Common Speech *Redhorn*; Dwarvish *Zirak-Zigil* > Sindarin *Celebdil* > Common Speech *Silvertine*; Dwarvish *Bundushathûr* > Sindarin *Fanuidhol* > Common Speech *Cloudyhead*. But the English names have not the arresting strangeness of those in the invented languages, nor do they mean quite the same thing.

In the notes and glosses at the end of *The Road Goes Ever On*, Tolkien explains *fanui* as "cloudy" and *dhol* as "head. "Cloudyhead" is thus a literal translation of the Sindarin word *Fanuidhol*. But literal translations, as any translator knows, do not always best convey the nuances of the original word. *Fana*, the root of *fanui*, has a primary meaning of "veil." Thus, a close approximation of the meaning of *Fanuidhol* might be "head veiled in clouds," not simply "cloudy," which sounds more like a weather forecast. Tolkien explains further that *fana* also has a special sense of "bright" or "radiant," as "suffused with a light from within," a sense derived from its use in *fanar*, the veils or raiment worn by the Valar when they appear to Elves and Men.

Embedded in this cluster of meanings, *Fanuidhol* clearly means something more than and something different from mere "Cloudyhead." To Elves looking at the mountain, the name conveys the veiled brightness associated with the Valar. The mountain Fanuidhol, then, has for Elves a special, almost supernatural aspect that the mountain Cloudyhead does not have for Men, nor Bundushathûr "head in clouds" for Dwarves. The words change the phenomena; the Elves do not see the mountain differently from Men and Dwarves. They see a different mountain.

Here's another example from Gimli's list of jaw-crackers, a list of names for one of the most important sites in Middle-earth, the lost Dwarf kingdom of Moria. *Khazad-Dûm* is the Dwarvish name, *Dwarrowdelf* is an Old English construction, *Black Pit* is Common Speech, and *Moria* is Sindarin. They are all names for the same underground complex. Or is it the same? The sound of each name falls as differently on the ear as the appearance strikes the beholding eye, and the meaning enters the mind. *Khazad-Dûm* is exotic, the *kh* slightly guttural as in Arabic or Hebrew. *Dwarrowdelf* is archaic but vaguely familiar, composed of almost-recognizable elements. *Moria* is liquid, lilting, darkly musical. *Black Pit* is wholly negative. Sound supports meaning, for each name carries the differing perception of its users.

In Dwarvish, *Khazad-Dûm* means "Mansions of the Khazad"—that is, the Dwarves. It is their name for their own place as seen through their own eyes; it reflects their sense of their own grandeur. *Dwarrowdelf,* archaic English, means "Dwarf-delving," and reveals a striking difference in perception. What to Dwarves is magnificent and palatial, is seen by non-Dwarves as simply digging, excavation. And it is something worse in Common Speech. A delving could be any kind of digging, but a black pit is for falling into, either through accident or despair. And *Moria,* for all its music, is a compound of *mor,* S. "dark," and *ia,* S. "void, abyss," suggesting dark, bottomless emptiness or even a black hole.

Different names, different perceptions, different perceivers, and as a consequence subtly different things. Such differences work on the reader to convey a world richly complex with meanings, all the more arresting because these meanings rub against one another, even sometimes overlap or compete. No one, not even Gimli, argues for one name as the correct one against all the others. Instead we are given an impression of one physical actuality embodying many places, seen from many points of view. We are shifted among realities, from that of the Dwarves whose home this is (or was) to the view of their work by outsiders to the physical result of that work to a vision of the dark vacancy that is hollowed out. The particle has been measured in different ways, and each way has changed Tolkien's world.

Thus, the concrete reality of Middle-earth depends, paradoxically, on its fluidity, its capacity to alter, to be perceived as one thing, then another, and another, as language creates and changes meaning. This is especially true for the intended final recipient of all this linguistic information, for the process extends beyond the closed fictive world to draw the reader into participation in this participatory universe. For just as Tolkien created Middle-earth, so do we, his readers create it with him. In the act of reading we collide with the particles, changing them and being changed by them. By the act of measurement we are measured. In reading *The Lord of the Rings,* we participate in a continuous, reciprocal act of creation by Tolkien, by his characters, and by ourselves as we read.

Myth, History, and Time-travel
The Lost Road *and* The Notion Club Papers

Although they are usually regarded as secondary works, lesser addenda to his legendarium and therefore comparatively little studied, J. R. R. Tolkien's two unfinished time-travel stories, *The Notion Club Papers* and its precursor, *The Lost Road*, occupy a unique and important place in his canon. This is not just because they are science fiction rather than the fantasy for which he is known, but also because they cross boundaries of time and space, their action taking place half in the present and half in the past, half in the "real" and half in the fantasy world. While *The Notion Club Papers* is so drastic a revision of *The Lost Road* as to be in effect a completely new story, the two works are nevertheless interdependent in some ways, expressing the same ideas, and following, in intention if not in execution, the same concepts of serial identity and inherited memory. Both stories, together with their accompanying notes and outlines, have been edited and published by Christopher Tolkien in his History of Middle-earth, *The Lost Road* appearing in volume 5 in 1987 and *The Notion Club Papers* in volume 9 in 1992.

The stories are important for several interrelated reasons. First, they mark the introduction into Tolkien's legendarium of the downfall of the island nation of Númenor, his Atlantis.[1] The drowning of Númenor altered the geology, politics, and history of Tolkien's imaginary world, changing its shape from flat to round, and giving its history a line of kings culminating in Aragorn son of Arathorn, Isildur's son, heir of Elendil. A second point of importance about the stories is that they connect Tolkien's mythology for England to aspects of his personal life. Third but far from least, between the two of them the stories supply an elaborate, highly structured framing mechanism to account for the transmission of his storied history from the deep past of his legendarium to his own time and place. The web of relationships among these elements is complex, and over the years that Tolkien worked on his so-called mythology for England, the strands crossed and recrossed in often confusing ways as his ideas developed and proliferated.

Númenor: The Missing Link

The whole enterprise began with a friendly yet challenging bargain between two old friends and colleagues. As recounted by Tolkien (*Letters* 209, 342, 347, 378), the genesis of the time-travel idea was a coin toss between himself and C. S. Lewis, conjecturally dated by Christopher Tolkien to circa 1936–37 (*LR* 7–8). Agreeing that there was not enough of their favorite kind of reading (fantasy and science fiction), Tolkien and Lewis decided to write more themselves and did a heads-or-tails coin toss to see who should take space travel and who, time travel. Lewis got space travel, promptly packed his hero into a spaceship and sent him off to Mars, and a scant two years after the bargain, published his story as *Out of the Silent Planet*, the first book of his so-called Space Trilogy. Tolkien got time travel and found a more psychological and credible way to take his protagonists from one time to another. He wrote four chapters in which a present-day English father and son, Alboin and Audoin Errol, dreamed their way back through time from modern-day Cornwall to his newly invented prehistoric Númenor, where they reappeared as Elendil and Herendil. Tolkien intended Númenor to be "the 'missing link'" between the Elder Days of his mythology and the Age of Men (*Letters* 232). He described it as his "personal alteration of the Atlantis myth and/or tradition, and accommodation of it to my general mythology" (*Letters* 361). The idea was to bridge the gap between the England of Tolkien's own time and the Middle-earth of his imaginary past by a regression through receding time of ever-earlier dreams. Simple enough in synopsis, the idea was complex in its concept and would have been (had Tolkien ever finished it) equally complex in execution. As he described *The Lost Road* in 1964:

> The thread was to be the occurrence time and again in human families . . . of a father and son called by names that could be interpreted as Bliss-friend and Elf-friend. . . . It started with a father-son affinity between Edwin and Elwin of the present, and was supposed to go back into legendary time by way of an Eädwine and Ǽfwine of circa A.D. 918, and Audoin and Alboin of

Lombardic legend, and so to the traditions of the North Sea concerning the coming of corn and culture heroes. . . . In my tale we were to come at last to Amandil and Elendil leaders of the loyal party in Númenor. (*Letters* 347)

While the notion of a sequence of dreams seems to have been Tolkien's own, his use of dream as a vehicle for time travel was in a literary tradition popular in the nineteenth- and early twentieth centuries. Salient examples are Charles Dickens's *A Christmas Carol* (1843), Edward Bellamy's *Looking Backward* (1887), William Morris's *A Dream of John Ball* (1888) and *News From Nowhere* (1890), and Mark Twain's *A Connecticut Yankee at King Arthur's Court* (1889). In 1891, the year before Tolkien was born, George Du Maurier's *Peter Ibbetson* told a story of lovers separated in real life who travel together through time in their dreams. In 1935, the year just preceding the coin toss, Tolkien had read with interest J. W. Dunne's *An Experiment with Time*, a nonfiction work that proposed time as a field-like space where an "observer" in a dream state can move in any direction. Dunne's ideas influenced a generation of English writers, from J. B. Priestley to Rumer Godden to J. R. R. Tolkien.

The elaborate nature of Tolkien's "thread" concept may be one reason *The Lost Road* was abandoned, but another reason must surely have been the looming publication of *The Hobbit*, followed almost immediately by Tolkien's start on the "new Hobbit" that turned into the time-consuming *Lord of the Rings*. Whatever his reasons for breaking off work on his time-travel project, it lay fallow for another eight years. Tolkien picked it up again in late 1944, writing to his publisher that he had "in a fortnight of comparative leisure round about last Christmas written three parts of another book, taking up in an entirely different frame and setting what little had any value in the inchoate *Lost Road*" (*Letters* 118). Thus the time-travel idea got a new lease on life as *The Notion Club Papers*, with the same purpose of bridging the gap between Tolkien's imaginary past and his own time. But after a promising start, it too was abandoned, probably because, as Tolkien wrote to his publisher, he was "putting *The Lord of the Rings* . . . before all else" (*SD* 145).

The plots of both stories (insofar as they are written) seem simple enough. In each, a pair of modern-day Englishmen deeply interested in both myth and travel through time experience increasingly intense flashes of extrapersonal memory connected to their long-ago Middle-earth avatars and ancestors. These flashes of memory contain scattered bits of information, scraps of unknown languages, incomplete accounts of some great disaster. Narrative style differs from story to story. *The Lost Road* is related through straightforward third-person narrative. *The Notion Club Papers* are couched as the minutes of Notion Club meetings reported in the first person by the club's recorder and thereby acquiring an immediacy that *The Lost Road* lacks. The fact that both stories break off just as the main action—that is, the time journey—gets under way makes it difficult to imagine just how Tolkien might have planned to bring either story to a satisfactory close.

While the dream mechanism is less overt in *The Notion Club Papers* than in *The Lost Road*, in both stories modern Englishmen were to enter Tolkien's imaginary world. As Tolkien handles it, the time-travel device moves characters and readers, often violently, between his twentieth-century England and the fictional prehistoric world of his mythology, with no advance notice and no perceptible transition. His use of serial memory to achieve this seems more psychological or even psychic than science-fictional.

The opening two chapters of *The Lost Road* take place in an unspecified present that is clearly Tolkien's own time, and in a specific place, Cornwall, that is unabashedly Tolkien's own Britain, where live Oswin and Alboin Errol, a father and son with a strong interest in history, languages, and the history of languages. Opportunity for confusion arises here, as, having introduced one father-and-son pair, Tolkien then passes the torch to the following generation. Oswin dies and the new father-and-son pair, Alboin Errol and *his* son Audoin, take over, as in Tolkien's description, cited above. As both Alboin and Audoin fall asleep, the story jumps from the Errols in modern Cornwall to Elendil and Herendil (not Amandil as in Tolkien's description) in Tolkien's Númenor. There are hints that the times overlap. We are told that Alboin has had since childhood the desire "*to go back*. To walk in Time, perhaps, as men walk on long roads" (*LR* 45). But the connection between past and present seems narratively remote. Alboin has dream conversations with a shadowy figure who reminds him of his father, but who announces himself as Elendil, and who tells him he may have his desire "to go back" (*LR* 48). The closest the story gets to what is clearly intended as the denouement, the downfall of Númenor, is when Alboin falls asleep, saying 'There is storm over Númenor" (*LR* 51), and the closest it gets to actual time travel is when he says later, "We start when the summons comes" (*LR* 53).

Although *The Lost Road* must be credited with getting Tolkien started on time travel, he later apologized to his publisher for sending him a draft, noting, "I hope it is forgotten" (*SD* 145). He was probably right to apologize, in that the playing out of the thread would have resulted in an overlong series of flashbacks, a cumbersome, step-by-step transition such as is handled more efficiently in films by dissolve. In *The Notion Club Papers*, Tolkien went further, making his real-world events take place in his own Oxford, but at two specific periods in the future of his own time, 1980–90 and 2012. Nevertheless, *The Lost Road* is important for contributing to *The Notion Cub Papers* both concept (Englishmen traveling into a fictive past) and mechanism (dream as a vehicle). Tolkien's interim writing experience—he was "on the last chapters" of *The Lord of the Rings*" (*SD* 12–13)—materially improved his craft, so that *The Notion Club Papers* is a more skilful piece of work than its predecessor.

While the father-son thread of *The Lost Road* is not wholly abandoned in *The Notion Club Papers*, it is relegated to the backstory, and the reclusive, philologically inclined Errols in Cornwall are replaced by a larger, more variegated cast of characters. The members of the Notion Club are friends and colleagues who drink, joke, argue, carouse (occasionally breaking furniture), and give no quarter in debate. They are voluble, opinionated, analytical, passionate, fond of wordplay and given to outrageous puns. In their own scholarly way, they are a rowdy bunch. Their dialogue, caught on the hoof as it were, has the immediacy, the energetic give-and-take, the bite of actual speech. While they are presented as contemporary Englishmen, the major characters are also, like those of *The Lost Road*, avatars of their Númenorean forebears. But more so than in *The Lost Road*, the balance between the periods is uneven. The energy of the story and the force of the narrative lie far more in the modern characters and their interactions than in their Númenorean avatars. This is partly because the Númenorean episodes are barely sketched, being hardly more than intrusions into the present-day narrative, but also because the modern Englishmen are livelier and more interesting than their Middle-earth counterparts.

As in *The Lost Road*, the island nation of Númenor is the terminus of the time travel, and its drowning in a geological catastrophe is the event that was to change the direction of Tolkien's mythology, reshape his world from flat to round, alter its relationship to its god-figures, the Valar, and provide the quasi-theological concept of the Straight Road to Valinor, best known as the path taken by Frodo's ship as it sails down the Firth of Lune. Coincident with each time-travel story is a separately written account of the drowning of Númenor. For *The Lost Road*, it is *The Fall of Númenor*; for *The Notion Club Papers*, it is *The Drowning of Anadûnê*. Both stand in a similar relationship to the better-known *Akallabeth* published in *The Silmarillion*. *The Drowning of Anadûnê* also introduced a new language, Adunaic,[2] which apparently entered the legendarium with part 2 of *The Notion Club Papers*, comparatively late in the development of the mythology.

Strongly Biographical Elements

Christopher Tolkien has noted the presence of "strongly biographical" elements in *The Lost Road* that were "closely modelled" on his father's own life (*LR* 53). These include the academic career and linguistic interests of one of the characters, Alboin. *The Notion Club Papers* likewise contains biographical elements, but the references are on two different planes, one social and one psychological. The Notion Club is modeled on Tolkien's own informal Oxford club of the Inklings (Inkling=Notion). Early drafts of *The Notion Club Papers* show Tolkien assigning (and reassigning) specific Inklings identities to specific Notion Club characters. C. S. Lewis was first "Ramer" and then "Frankley." Tolkien also was "Ramer" at one point, but he too was changed, in this case to "Latimer," before finally emerging as "Guildford," who, not by accident, is the Club's recorder and thus the author of the minutes of the meetings which make up the *Papers*. Hugo Dyson seems consistently to have been the model for "Lowdham," and Humphrey Havard was "Dolbear." But this preliminary casting was almost certainly modified, and it ultimately receded as the fictional characters developed lives of their own. In any case, in the earliest draft—what Christopher Tolkien calls manuscript A—Tolkien addressed a "Preface to the Inklings" in which he both acknowledged and disclaimed intended resemblances to real persons, for "the mirror is cracked," and the countenances "distorted," with "noses and other features" distributed without attribution (*SD* 148–49). And it may be that what Tolkien was drawing on was as much a dynamic of speech and social interaction as of specific character per se.

It is through the concept of the destruction of Númenor that more autobiographical reference enters the story. Unsurprisingly for Tolkien, this is conveyed through names and the meanings of names. It begins with *The Lost Road*, whose father-and-son pairings—Alboin (Ælwine, "Elf-friend") and Audoin (Eädwine, "Bliss-friend")—include grandfather Oswin (Anglo-Saxon "God-friend"). The "friend" component is the chief autobiographical clue, for it is echoed in the names in Tolkien's own family. Tolkien's father Arthur, Tolkien himself, and all four of his children have as a middle name Reuel, a Hebrew name that means "friend" or "God-friend." The parallel between Tolkien's fictive grandfather-father-son "thread" with names containing the "friend" element—God-friend, Elf-friend, Bliss-friend—and a similar "friend" name passed from grandfather to father to son in his own family is too striking to be accidental.

The destruction of Númenor also carries an autobiographical reference, this one more deeply personal and psychological, perhaps even psychic. In several of his letters, Tolkien described a recurrent dream, which he called his "Atlantis complex," or "Atlantis-haunting," and which he characterized as a "dim memory of some ancient history" (*Letters* 347). This was of being inundated by a great wave, which swept over him and threatened to drown him and from which he awoke "gasping, out of deep water" (*Letters* 347). It was the inspiration for his island nation of Númenor, which exists (apparently) only so it can be destroyed in an oceanic cataclysm that changes the shape of the world. The dream was "[p]ossibly inherited," he wrote to W. H. Auden, "though my parents died too young to transfer such things by words. Inherited from me (I suppose) by only one of my children [his second son, Michael (*Letters* 445n)], though I did not know that about my son until recently, and he did not know it about me" (*Letters* 213). In a draft of a letter to a "Mr. Thompson," he repeated the story. "That vision and dream has been ever with me—and has been inherited (as I only discovered recently) by one of my children" (*Letters* 232).

Possibly inherited by Tolkien from his parents. Inherited from him by one of his children. One certain instance and a conjectural second of inherited memory in one family, a memory across (perhaps) three generations of an event that none of the dreamers, apparently, had experienced in real life. It is no great stretch to imagine that Tolkien might have wanted to believe not only that he had inherited as well as passed on the dream but also that it was in fact "the dim memory of some ancient history," an actual event. If this were indeed the case, it would underpin his structural concept of the familial father-son thread by which he proposed to bring his prehistoric mythology into his modern-day England. In any event, he seems to have got it out of his mind by writing it into his fiction, releasing, as he wrote in a letter, "some hidden 'complex'" (*Letters* 232), which was "now exorcised by writing about it" (*Letters* 347). "I don't think I have had it [the dream]," he wrote to W. H. Auden in 1944, " since I wrote the 'Downfall of Númenor' as the last of the legends of the First and Second Age" (*Letters* 213).

While this is persuasive evidence for the link between life and art, it is circumstantial evidence, and raises questions about just how to connect the dots. The letters in which Tolkien talks about the dream are obviously later than the time of the discovery itself, but how much later is unknown, and "recently" is too vague a term on which to posit a coherent sequence. Tolkien's discovery that his son had had the same dream may have come before or after he introduced Atlantis and the dreaming fathers and sons into the story. There is no way to know. His speculation that he himself may have inherited it from a parent is just that—speculation, which may be why the first-generation figures in both stories, Oswin in *The Lost Road* and Edwin in *The Notion Club Papers*, have little or no role in the actual time travel.

Autobiographical reference does not stop here. The *Lost Road* grandfather, Oswin, is replaced in *The Notion Club Papers* by father Edwin (Eädwine, Audoin), who is Alwyn (Ælfwine, Elendil) Lowdham's father. (The pattern of proliferating and overlapping names is part of what makes Tolkien's underlying concept so difficult to sort out.) Edwin Lowdham, a voyager who disappears at sea and who has no role in the action, is the apparent source for a mysterious page in "Númenorean script" dropped by Lowdham at the end of one meeting. It turns out to be a translation of the Adunaic account of the Fall of Númenor. To compound the autobiographical references, the translation is identified by "old Professor Rashbold at Pembroke" as "Old English of a strongly Mercian (West Midland) colour" (*SD* 257). Now *Rashbold*, as Tolkien trivia experts know, was Tolkien's translation of the German form of his own surname, *toll*, "rash, foolhardy," *kühn*, "keen, eager, bold," while Pembroke College was his first faculty position at Oxford, where he was Rawlinson and Bosworth Professor of Anglo-Saxon. He has allowed himself a cameo appearance in his own fiction, no doubt thoroughly enjoying the inside joke.

The Frame Is Part of the Picture

Part 1 of *The Notion Club Papers* (subtitled "The Ramblings of Ramer") is a largely theoretical discussion of framing devices for space travel, a topic of lively debate. How you get to the unknown planet must be of a piece with the rest of the story, must indeed be an integral part of the story. H. G. Wells's time machine and gravitation insulator, David Lindsay's "back-rays" and C. S. Lewis's crystal torpedo are all roundly criticized as being poorly integrated, unbelievable contraptions, ill-fitting frames for the stories they contain. At one point in the argument, Guildford actually says that in "normal probability" the only means for landing on a new planet is "by being born" (*SD* 170). In view of the transmission (already discussed) of the great wave memory from generation to generation to generation, it does not take a great leap of imagination to suppose that Tolkien might have thought "being born" would work just as well for landing in a new time.

In addition to drawing on actual characters to provide verisimilitude, Tolkien gave the story an elaborate multiframe design, to impart a sense of reality to what is in fact fantasy. The central and most fantastic episode, the actual travel backward in time, is nested within the minutes, kept by Nicholas

Guildford, of the fictive but realistic Notion Club. These minutes in turn are framed as a bundle of papers discovered in the basement of the Oxford Examination Schools by a Mr. Howard Green and edited by him. The whole is then presented as published in a "Second Edition," with history, notes, and editorial commentary by J. R. Titmass, an historian; W. W. Wormald, a "Bibliopolist"; and D. N. Borrow, a linguist. The *Papers* thus belong to the found manuscript genre of fantasy and science fiction, a tradition that stretches from H. Rider Haggard's *She* to Margaret Atwood's *The Handmaid's Tale*. The fact that the Papers are the "minutes" of fictitious meetings and thus spread over a sequence of numbered nights gives Tolkien some leeway. His task is less to develop a plot than to chart the progress of an argument.

As edited by Christopher Tolkien, the narrative falls into two parts. Part 1 is dominated by Michael Ramer, part 2, by Arundel Lowdham and Wilfred Jeremy. All three are well-realized personalities, psychologically and psychically complex, with hidden and largely unsuspected depths. There are supporting characters Philip Frankley and Rufus Dolbear, plus a cast of minor club members, bit players who complicate discussion but do not affect the action. The story opens with discussion of Ramer's just-read (but not included) story. This provokes a discussion of "frame," the device by which a story is carried from one place or time to another—specifically, in this context, how science fiction (their word is *scientifiction*, a term introduced Hugo Gernsback, publisher of *Amazing Stories*, "The Magazine of Scientifiction," in 1926) manages travel from one planet to another. Forced by the club to defend himself, Ramer acknowledges the clumsiness of his framing device; it is this that brings on the discussion of vehicles for both time and space travel and results in the club's criticism of Wells's time machine). Commanded by Dolbear to "Comes clean!" Ramer reveals that the story is an account of his actual self-induced and controlled dream wanderings to other, apparently extraterrestrial worlds.

This sets the stage for part 2 of *The Notion Club Papers*, subtitled "The Strange Case of Arundel Lowdham." Here Tolkien gets down to business, and the conversation turns from space travel to time travel. Time travel leads to history, and history leads to myth and the point where they intersect. Lowdham has increasingly intense flashbacks to what appears to be Númenor, in which he curses Zigūr, the Adunaic name for Sauron. Lowdham also has dreams of Númenor, and more particularly of strange languages, which he calls A and B, or Avallonian (Quenya) and Adunaic. In the course of one night's discussion, Jeremy raises the question: "If you went back [in time] would you find myth dissolving into history or history into myth? . . . Perhaps," he suggests, "the Atlantis catastrophe was the dividing line?" (*SD* 249). *The Notion Club Papers* suggests that Tolkien's answer is "yes." With the "Atlantis catastrophe," his dream of the great wave as an inherited "dim memory" enters the story (*Letters* 347), and his fictive mythology joins his personal, therefore contemporary, history. Lowdham and Jeremy are gradually revealed (first to the reader and then to themselves) as avatars, direct descendents and psychic and psychological reincarnations of Númenorean figures in Tolkien's own mythology. In one night's discussion, they are overtaken and engulfed by a sudden, unexpected storm of terrifying proportions, and we are to understand that it is happening simultaneously in Oxford and Númenor, and that it is in fact the Drowning of Anadûnë. They are possessed by their Númenorean identities of Nimruzir (the Adunaic form of Anglo-Saxon *Ælfwine*) and Abrazan (the Adunaic form of Anglo-Saxon *Tréowine*).

It is this night's discussion, storm, and crisis of identity that precipitate the actual time travel. Interestingly, however, Tolkien inverts the process, and instead of the characters moving into past time, a past event (the destruction of Númenor) erupts into their present lives, and their past identities take charge of their present selves. In a sort of waking dream, the two men go on an extended search for more information, relying for guidance on their dreams. When they return, Lowdham narrates one such dream experience to the Notion Club, a first-person account, in the persona of Ælfwine, of the mythic story of King Sheave (*SD* 273–76). So powerful is the spell Tolkien casts that when Lowdham ends the story by returning to his Oxford self with the words, "And with that, I think I must end for tonight," the reader is startled by the abrupt transition, pulled suddenly out of the world of myth into the everyday. Unfortunately, it is here that all too soon and all too frustratingly the narrative breaks off, forcing the reader to make another abrupt transition from the world of the Notion Club to the realization that this too is a story. We are left hanging: wondering, guessing, unable to be sure where the story is going or what is meant to happen. Fortunately, as with *The Lost Road,* Tolkien left rough drafts and notes—tantalizing hints of what the story might have looked like if he had finished it.

Two projected continuations of the "King Sheave" episode (carried over and fleshed out from the verse treatment in *The Lost Road* [87–91]) close the last recorded meeting of the club. Lowdham/Ælfwine and Jeremy/Tréowine set out to sea and sail West. Both continuations bring the voyagers to the Straight Road, but in both their ship is driven back by storm. The sketches break off there, with an outline following:

> Tréowine [Jeremy] sees the straight Road and the world plunging down. Ælfwine's [Lowdham's] vessel seems to be taking the straight Road and falls [sic] in a swoon of fear and exhaustion.

Ælfwine gets view of the Book of Stories; and writes down what he can remember.

Later fleeting visions.

Beleriand tale.

Sojourn in Númenor before and during the fall ends with Elendil [Lowdham] and Voronwë [Jeremy] fleeing on a hill of water into the dark with Eagles and lightning pursuing them. Elendil has a book which he has written.

His descendants get glimpses of it.

Ælfwine has one. (*SD* 279)

Also among Tolkien's notes is a single enigmatic note, a scrap of paper that reads simply, "Do the Atlantis story and abandon Eriol–Saga, with Loudham, Jeremy, Guildford, and Ramer taking part." Cryptic though it is, the note may be the best clue to what Tolkien intended for *The Notion Club Papers*, which is clearly "the Atlantis story" in which "Loudham, Jeremy, Guildford and Ramer" are principal characters. The "Eriol–Saga" was the Silmarillion mythology "for England," a work in progress from 1917 until interrupted first by *The Hobbit* in the mid-1930s and then by *The Lord of the Rings* in the late thirties and the forties. Tolkien's mythology was framed as tales told by the Elves (at first called "Fairies") to a voyager (compare Edwin Lowdham) named Eriol or Ælfwine, who carries them from Valinor back to what will become England. Christopher Tolkien has proposed that "the Eriol-Saga had been, up to this time, what my father had in mind for the further course of the meetings of the Notion Club, but was now rejecting in favour of 'Atlantis'" (*SD* 281–82). Another possibility is that Tolkien was not rejecting the Eriol-Saga outright, but was considering attaching one frame story to another, joining the Eriol-Saga to the Atlantis story (the drowning of Númenor) by way of *The Notion Club Papers* much as Jeremy suggested that myth might blend into history with "Atlantis as the dividing line."

There is no way to know just how Tolkien might have planned for Lowdham, Jeremy, Guildford, and Ramer to "take part," though we may speculate that Tolkien intended some sort of time travel for all of them. Nevertheless, in the context of this note, the outline quoted above and its mention of the "Book of Stories" and Elendil's book (and the fact that "Ælfwine has" a copy of it) must be seen not just as Tolkien's description of an imaginative concept but as his envisioning of the prototype credibility device for the whole mythological conceit, making *The Notion Club Papers* the bridge by which his imagined prehistoric mythology, connected by time travel to the Notion Club, would be brought forward in time by the discovery and publication of its minutes by Mr. Howard Green.

A Mythology for England

Dreaming fathers and sons, inherited memory, Atlantis turned into Númenor, a story passed down through time: these elements together do much to explain Tolkien's otherwise seemingly arbitrary choice of Atlantis-Númenor. He was basing this part of his mythology directly on his own experience, and although the execution may be overcomplex, the basic idea is clear enough. Thus these time-travel stories—first *The Lost Road* and second and more significantly *The Notion Club Papers*—have a formative role in Tolkien's mythology and are crucial to our understanding of it. In his commentary on *The Lost Road*, Christopher Tolkien has written,

> With the entry at this time [the 1936 *Lost Road*] of the cardinal ideas of the Downfall of Númenor, the World Made Round, and the Straight Road, into the conception of "Middle-earth", and the thought of a "time-travel" story in which the very significant figure of the Anglo-Saxon Ælfwine would be both "extended" into the future, into the twentieth century, and "extended" also into a many-layered past, my father was envisaging a massive and explicit linking of his own legends with those of many other places and times: all concerned with the stories and dreams of peoples who dwelt by the coasts of the Great Western Sea. All this was set aside during the period of the writing of *The Lord of the Rings*, but not abandoned: for in 1945, before indeed *The Lord of the Rings* was completed, he returned to these themes in the unfinished *Notion Club Papers*. (*LR* 98)

Tolkien's proposal to "do the Atlantis story" would not just bring his mythology into the present, it would in effect start it off there.

The contemporary time-travel stories, written in a style closer to that of the modern novel than of mythic history, were to be the frame for Tolkien's whole mythology for England, which would then be English because its modern English protagonists were connected by inherited memory to their Númenorean ancestors. It would cross the "dividing line" between myth and history by means of the "book" of which Elendil's "descendants get glimpses" and of which Ælfwine has a copy, and which, if the conceit of transmission via time travel had been carried through to its conclusion, would have become part of *The Notion Club Papers*, which the modern reader would then have had in hand. The page of West Mercian Anglo-Saxon transcribed (from Elendil's book?) in Númenorean script and narrating the drowning of Númenor would be evidence of the transition from myth to history.

It is clear, therefore, that although they stand a little to one side, as it were, of Tolkien's major mythological works (*The Silmarillion* and *The Lord of the Rings*), nonetheless *The Lost Road* and *The Notion Club Papers* deserve serious attention as significant elements in Tolkien's Middle-earth canon. They changed the shape of his world, and without them there would be no Elendil, no Isildur, and no Aragorn as we know him. *The Lost Road* notes and outlines give us the clearest view of Tolkien's overall vision, while *The Notion Club Papers* contains some of his most vigorous writing, as well as some of his most deeply felt insights into the workings of the human psyche. That both stories, but especially *The Notion Club Papers*, stopped short of final resolution may turn out to be one of the greater losses, not just to the reader pulled so unexpectedly out of the King Sheave tale but also to Tolkien's whole vision. Had *The Notion Club Papers* been completed, it would have provided a rounding out and summing up that might have successfully brought up to date the mythology for England that Tolkien began in 1917.

This was not to be. After *The Lord of the Rings*, the overarching concept of stories told, heard, written down, and carried forward was transferred to the "Red Book" and its attendant volumes of Elvish lore. These were then conceived as a compendium of the Silmarillion tales, *The Hobbit*, and *The Lord of the Rings*, as collected by Bilbo, completed by Sam and Frodo, passed from Brandybuck father to son, carried to Gondor, transcribed by "Findegil King's Writer," stored in Minas Tirith (*FR* Prologue, 23–24), and finally—as the Cirth and Tengwar running header and footer to the title-page of *The Lord of the Rings* tell us—translated into English by J. R. R. Tolkien. His identification of himself with Guildford as recorder in the early draft of *The Notion Club Papers* is replaced by his identification of himself in his own persona, not in the text but hidden in plain sight in the runes and script of his invented writing systems. Gone are all the Elf-friends and Bliss-friends, the Ælfwines and Treowines and Alboins and Audoins. Gone too are Guildford, Lowdham, old Rashbold of Pembroke, and Mr. Howard Green, all replaced by J. R. R. Tolkien in his own identity.

It may well have been the elaborate framing superstructure of *The Notion Club Papers* that caused the whole edifice to collapse under its own weight. Christopher Tolkien has commented that "the whole conception [had] now developed a disturbing complexity" (*SD* 280), one "so intricate that one need perhaps look no further for an answer to the question, why were *The Notion Club Papers* abandoned?" (*SD* 282). He may be right. It is difficult to imagine how such an intertangled pattern could have been sorted out, and its complexities made plain. This notwithstanding, the existence of *The Notion Club Papers* and the insight the story gives into the workings of Tolkien's mind are valuable in their own right. The *Papers* may be a failed—or at least an abortive—attempt, but they are valuable as much for what they suggest as for what they do or do not accomplish. It is Tolkien's reach, not his grasp, that serious students of his work should pay attention to here.

Politically Incorrect Tolkien

In looking at Tolkien as politically incorrect, I won't be telling you anything you don't already know, not if you have read *The Lord of the Rings*. Yet it may be that I can affect the way you know it, that I can invite you to see the familiar in an unfamiliar light. In his essay, "On Fairy-stories," Tolkien calls this process "recovery" and describes it as a "regaining of a clear view" of things once fresh but now dimmed and dulled by time and custom (*MC* 146). This recovery, he felt, was one of the chief functions of the fairy story. While my discussion will be no fairy story, it still may help to recover or give a clearer view of some of the extraordinariness in the world Tolkien called *Faërie*, a world peopled with what we think of as fairy-story elements, such as Hobbits, Elves, and Orcs. If I succeed, I will have invited you to see those elements, the very machinery and personnel of fairy tale, as less fairy-like and more human, extraordinarily like the ordinary world in which we live. I am not the first to have seen this. Both Christina Scull and Jane Chance have made the same or similar observations,[1] but their approaches are sufficiently different from mine that I trust there will not be too much overlap.

Digging into what I will call the sociology of Middle-earth, I discovered, somewhat to my surprise, that the subject revealed Tolkien's view of human nature—even the apparently lighter examples of it, such as hobbits—to be much darker than I had realized or given him credit for. So the first person to experience recovery and get a clearer view was myself.

I suppose I ought first of all to define *political incorrectness*. I mean by this term the overt exclusion, marginalization, or insulting of people who are socially disadvantaged or discriminated against; the use of language, ideas, policies, or behavior that gives offense in terms of occupation, gender, race, culture, or sexual orientation. The phrase may evoke those criticisms so often aimed by the intellectual elite at long-suffering Tolkien, who from time to time is accused of being racist or misogynist or imperialist or jingoist for displaying insensitivity to women or minorities or the economically disadvantaged. As a matter of fact, he is a poor candidate for any of these labels. He is no misogynist, having created two of the most heroic women in modern fiction, Lúthien and Éowyn; he is sensitive to minorities, championing the actions and the importance in world affairs of the overlooked and undervalued common man, the "little guy" (i.e., the Hobbit); he is no imperialist, having confessed in a letter that his political leaning was toward anarchy (*Letters* 63); and he is no jingoist, since he was fully aware that in an armed conflict there will inevitably be orcs "on both sides" (*Letters* 82).

How then, is he politically incorrect? My answer is that he is not, but that a lot of his characters are. Ted Sandyman makes fun of Sam Gamgee for being gullible enough to believe in wonders like Elves and walking trees. The hobbits in Hobbiton are suspicious of the hobbits in Buckland; the hobbits in Buckland return the favor; the hobbits in both places don't think much of Bree; and the Sackville-Bagginses don't like anybody but themselves. We will see this climate of thought writ larger when the four main hobbits—Frodo, Sam, Merry, and Pippin—move out of the Shire into the larger world, where we'll find not just hobbits looking sideways at other hobbits but elves on guard against dwarves, dwarves nursing a long-standing grudge against elves, Númenoreans feeling superior to Southrons, and even the Uruk-Hai looking down on the orcs of Mordor.

This should come as no surprise. Tolkien was not writing *Utopia*. He was writing the history of Middle-earth, and Middle-earth was meant to reflect the real world as he saw it from the perspective of one of the most turbulent, divisive, repressive centuries in history. How, then, could his secondary world be anything but politically incorrect, especially from a twenty-first-century point of view. Instead of "Politically Incorrect Tolkien," I probably should have called my talk "Politically Incorrect Elves, Dwarves, Men, and Hobbits," or "Politically Incorrect Middle-earth," since the whole place is a seething hotbed of racial and cultural prejudice, narrow-mindedness, suspicion, and animosity. Socially and politically, it is a mess. There is no governance, there are no leaders free of the taint; there is no sense of a world in civilized contact with its component parts. The few areas that have preserved themselves—Doriath, Nargothrond, Gondolin, the Shire—have done so at the cost of a dangerous political and social isolation.

Examples from both *The Lord of the Rings* and *The Silmarillion* abound, and will, I hope, give a representative picture of the state of social and political relations, or lack of them, in Middle-earth. As examples, I've chosen the Shire for its Hobbits, Thingol as the bad good guy, and the Orcs as everybody's favorite enemy. Each will, I hope, illustrate a facet of political incorrectness. I'll start with Hobbits, the most reader-favored race in Middle-earth, and the idyllic Shire, the community readers love and yearn for. At first glance, the Shire seems like everybody's nostalgic dream of the good old days. It's a nice place to visit, but a careful look should persuade you that you wouldn't want to live there. As we meet it in the opening chapters of *The Fellowship of the Ring*, the Shire has all the virtues and faults of a preindustrial rural community. The Shire (notably Hobbiton and, we may suppose, Bywater, Michel Delving, and Buckland as well) is slow-paced, peaceful, free of smog and traffic jams and engine noise. The water is clean and the air is clear. The Shire and its main communities are also ignorant, close-minded, intolerant, judgmental, and smug.

Anyone who has ever lived in a small town or village will recognize the combination, and the contradiction. The whole place is inward-looking, preoccupied with its own affairs and intentionally guarded from outside influence. The Bounders are there to keep foreign elements out of the Shire, and the maps, showing blank beyond the Shire's borders, are a visual representation of this policy. As for the hobbits who live there, as a society they are provincial, parochial, insular, politically conservative if not reactionary, self-satisfied and self-righteous. Moreover, with a few notable exceptions (Bilbo, Frodo, and Frodo's companions) they are uneducated by preference, a trait exemplified by their preference for genealogy over history and certainly over tales and legends. They are for the most part uninvolved in and unaware of matters outside their own domestic concerns. They don't even believe in fairies. The hobbits we know and like—Bilbo, Frodo, Sam, and, to a lesser extent, Merry and Pippin—do not seem representative of the type as a whole. They are atypical and, to varying degrees, outsiders in their own community.

The typical hobbit is Ted Sandyman, who in addition to not believing in fairies (i.e., Elves) also doesn't believe in dragons or tree-men and doesn't want to be told different. Equally typical is Sam's Gaffer, hoping no harm will come to Sam because of his having been taught his letters by Bilbo. A little learning is a dangerous thing, and a lot of learning is more so. The Gaffer is locked into a view of life no wider than Bagshot Row and suspicious of everything beyond it, like Tooks and Brandybucks. In that first conversation at the Ivy Bush in the opening chapter of *The Fellowship*, the Gaffer contrasts the "queer" Brandybucks with his own Hobbiton neighbors, who are "decent folk" (*FR* I, i, 30–31). In this context, *decent* means "conventional, predictable, unimaginative, conformist"—in a word, "dull." It also means given to malicious gossip and fond of a pint. As for *queer*, it means unsettlingly "different," messing about in boats and associating with wandering conjurors.

Granted this is novelistic exposition intended to set the scene, but it is Tolkien who chooses what to explain and what kind of scene to set. It is worth noting that in the conversation at The Ivy Bush, the word *queer* occurs eight times in three pages. Old Noakes of Bywater is suspicious of "Buckland, where folks are so queer" (*FR* I, i, 30); Daddy Twofoot agrees that "No wonder they're queer ... if they live on the wrong side of the ... river" (30); the Gaffer, as noted, calls them "'a queer breed" (30), and also "queer Bucklanders" (31); Ted Sandyman avers that "Bag End's a queer place, and its folk are queerer" (32); whereupon the Gaffer—politically correct for once—retorts, "If that's being queer, then we could do with a bit more queerness in these parts" (32). Hammond and Scull point out that Farmer Maggot uses the term *queer* to express his deep suspicion of some of the "folk wandering in these parts at times" (*Reader's Companion* 58), and tells Frodo "you should never have gone mixing yourself up with Hobbiton folk. . . . Folk are queer up there" (*FR* I, iv, 104). Plainly, queerness and acceptibility are in the eye of the beholder. It's all in how you look at it.

The typical hobbit is certainly not Frodo Baggins, who finds his neighboring Boffinses and Bagginses and Bolgers and Proudfoots "too stupid and dull for words" (*FR* I, ii, 71), converses with elves in Elvish, and yearns to follow Bilbo's road that goes ever on and on. Nevertheless, even Frodo is typical in some ways. His deep abhorrence of the notion of Gollum as a hobbit is an expression of his unconscious sense of racial superiority. He may be from the wrong side of the river, but he has the prejudices of his hobbit-kind, telling Gandalf that he thought the Big People were "just big, and rather stupid: kind and stupid, like Butterbur; or stupid and wicked like Bill Ferny. But then," he admits, "we don't know much about Men in the Shire" (*FR* II, i, 233). How could they, when they deliberately turn their backs on the outside world? Hobbits must be the least-traveled individuals in Middle-earth, and that includes the Ents and the Huorns. Although, like Bilbo, Frodo has a hankering to get outside the Shire and has been known to talk to elves, he still bears traces of Shire narrow-mindedness. For example, he advocates a preemptive strike and supports the death penalty for Gollum—not for what he has done but for what he may do: "What a pity that Bilbo did not stab that vile creature, when he had a chance," he exclaims (*FR* I, ii, 68). He also feels morally (and racially) superior, declaring that, "hobbits don't cheat" (64), an assertion that is patently false, as he finds out at the Forbidden Pool, when he himself has to cheat to save Gollum's life.

Hailing originally from the wrong side of the river, Frodo is an outsider in his own community, viewed with suspicion by his neighbors both before his journey to Mount Doom and after his return, having wasted his time, according to Sam's Gaffer, "trespassing in foreign parts, chasing Black Men up mountains" (*RK* VI, viii, 293). In the view of Old Noakes of Bywater, Frodo is "more than half a Brandybuck" (*FR* I, i, 30), which puts him, if not beyond the Pale, at least on its outer edge. And Lobelia Sackville-Baggins pushes him over the edge, asking Frodo, after Bilbo's disappearance, "Why didn't you go too?" and going Old Noakes one better by declaring, "You don't belong here; you're no Baggins—you—you're a Brandybuck!" To Frodo's wry comment, "That was an insult, if you like," Merry counters with, "It was a compliment . . . and so, of course, not true" (*FR* I, i, 48).

On the surface this, like the rest of the early quasi-comic treatment of Hobbits and Hobbiton, is designed to get a laugh, but as we look deeper, the levels of meaning multiply. For Lobelia to call Frodo a Brandybuck is, from her point of view and certainly by her intent, an insult, and Frodo understands it as such. As a Brandybuck himself, Merry naturally sees it as a compliment, but since he knows Lobelia is not likely to say anything nice about Frodo, the apparent compliment cannot be taken as sincere, and therefore is not true. The underlying assumptions on both sides thus pit Baggins against Brandybuck and Hobbiton against Buckland. The Hobbiton and Buckland hobbits are united only in their deep suspicion of the Breelanders, whom they call Outsiders, a word that speaks volumes about their own insularity.

The Breelanders are no better. The whole community is ripe for a takeover by any force smart enough to prey on its prejudices, which is just what happens while the four hobbits are away saving Middle-earth. Sharkey and his gang move in and take over. Even as the story begins, population upheaval and displacement are straining the bounds of hospitality. To start with, Bree is a gated community deeply suspicious of strangers, a condition that worsens in degree but does not change in kind as time passes. Even when we first meet them, the Breelanders do not welcome immigrants, and the immigrants are belligerent and aggressive. "If room isn't found for them, they'll find it for themselves. They've a right to live, same as other folk," says one traveler whom we will meet again (*FR* I, ix, 168). Harry the gatekeeper is plainly suspicious of people arriving after nightfall. Merry disarms his suspicions by identifying himself and his place of origin and remarking, "The Bree-folk used to be fair-spoken to travelers" (163). "Used to be" is the key phrase here. The world outside the Shire is under the threat of war, and war brings out hidden prejudices in former friends.

Echoing Sam's Gaffer in spirit as well as in diction, Harry the gatekeeper warns Merry, "There's queer folk about," but his attitude seems to include the four hobbits in the description. Barliman Butterbur doesn't like the looks of Strider any more than the Shire hobbits like the looks of Bill Ferny or his "squint-eyed ill-favoured" companion (*FR* I, ix, 168), the man who defended the right of immigrants to settle. I must note here that the phrase "squint-eyed" has been the cause of some confusion between English and American usage, finally resolved by an exchange of letters between Nancy Martsch and Christopher Tolkien. In response to Nancy's enquiry about the phrase, Christopher wrote that *squint* doesn't necessarily mean "slit-eyed or slant-eyed," a conventionally American reading of the phrase. He wrote that "*squint* in 'English English' always carries the idea of *obliqueness:* a *squint* is a ... disorder that causes the eye to look obliquely ... it can thus very readily come to connote character [as] 'ambiguous, dubious, suspicious, shady, fishy'" (Martsch 9). In any case, looks, whether squint or slant, are significant, and are valid criteria for judging character. The fact that Bill has a "squint-eyed" friend counts against both of them and marks them out as bad guys.

So much for the idyllic Shire and its jolly hobbits. My next example, in himself a far more presentable individual than Lobelia or Bill Ferny or his louche companion, is King Thingol of Doriath, one of the major characters in *The Silmarillion*. Thingol is among the highest of the High Eves. He is a Calaquendi, the leader whose brightness changes the Sindar from Dark Elves to Grey-elves. He has seen the Light of the Two Trees; he is the consort of Melian the Maia; he is arguably the elitest among the elite of Middle-earth. He is also and demonstrably the most overtly and publicly bigoted character in Tolkien's sub-created world. Thingol is a striking example of the psychology of bigotry. He is someone who thinks of himself as a good guy on the side of the good guys, but he is disastrously—and ultimately fatally—oblivious to the nature of his own prejudices. That is, he is aware of them, but not aware that they are prejudices, thinking instead that they are ethically and ethnically justified positions in the context of the world he lives in, which is, admittedly, a world at perpetual war with itself.

Thingol has intentionally chosen to circumscribe his world, narrowing it to the confines of Doriath for what seems to him good and defensible reasons. He doesn't want to associate with people he quite legitimately finds morally repugnant—the kinslaying Noldor. It is hard to fault him for forbidding killers entrance to his realm. But also he refuses to speak their language or allow it to be spoken. This has resonance on several levels for Tolkien, for whom language was of supreme importance and who once made the sweeping statement that "[m]ythology is language and language is mythology" (*TOFS* 181). Tolkien knew that to obliterate a people's language is to destroy their memory, their history, their mythology, their identity. It is what the English tried to do to the Celts of the British Isles—the Welsh and the Cornish, the Manx and the

Scots Gaelic and the Irish—what the Swedes tried to do to the Finns, what in America the European Americans tried to do the Native Americans. That the Welsh have held on to their language—and their legends and their poetry—and that the Irish were able to resuscitate theirs are triumphs of tenacity over persistence, of a people over a policy.

Significantly, Thingol oversees an ethnically restricted kingdom that excludes other races, specifically Men—though, as with all exclusions, there are exceptions. He graciously and generously opens his home to the exiled Túrin, son of Húrin, welcoming him as a kind of foster son. His treatment of Túrin is one of the best aspects of his story and shows Thingol in the best possible light. Over against this, he regards the entry into Doriath of Túrin's distant cousin Beren (they are both descended from Beor the Old) as "insolence." Túrin's plight brings out the best in Thingol, and his kindness and forbearance in dealing with this homeless, belligerent, and perversely intransigent refugee are exemplary. Beren, in contrast, brings out the worst in Thingol: all that is narrow, possessive, scheming, and intolerant, and that will ultimately cause his death.

The reason for the difference is simple: Beren wants to marry Thingol's daughter, Lúthien. It is this that taps into Thingol's hidden prejudice. As is the case with others who think of themselves as liberal, Thingol's liberality stops at his own family. Like many a doting father, when push comes to shove he doesn't want his daughter to marry a man of another race. He calls Beren a "baseborn mortal," invoking class superiority, and an "unhappy mortal," meaning not that Beren is sad, but that he brings bad luck, and says that his land is "forbidden to such as you" (translation: "we don't want any of your kind around here"). Looking at Lúthien, he asks, "[S]hall such as these lay hands on you, and yet live?" (*S* 165–66). The phrase "lay hands" is worth attention. It is perhaps the most explicit expression of sexual jealousy in Tolkien's work.

I said earlier that the qualities Thingol displays in this situation, and the events they set in motion, ultimately cause his death. Here is how. Thingol's possession of the Silmaril, the quest for which was intended to be the occasion of Beren's death, begins to possess him. When he gets the Nauglamír from Húrin, he hires the Dwarves to remake the necklace and set it with the Silmaril. Greed strives with greed when the Dwarves, having finished their work, claim the necklace, including the Silmaril, as their own. Thingol, "in wrath and pride" and "scorn" (*S* 233) speaks to them haughtily in Tolkien's elevated "high" style. Listen to his words: "How do ye of uncouth race dare to demand aught of me, Elu Thingol, Lord of Beleriand, whose life began by the waters of Cuiviénen years uncounted ere the fathers of the stunted people awoke?" Let's translate this into modern idiom. "How dare you low, ignorant, short people of an inferior race presume to make demands of me, an Elf? I was here before you, I'm older than you, I'm taller than you, and therefore I'm better than you." Not content with abusing the Dwarves, he tries to get out of paying them for their work. It's no wonder they feel insulted and enraged and kill him. Thingol's fall is one of the most classical Aristotelian episodes in Tolkien's mythology, a descent from high status and nobility into ruin, brought about by his own tragic error, his greed and pride. From the light of the Two Trees of Valinor, he falls both actually and metaphorically into the dark and dies in a cave underground.

My last example, the Orcs, will provide an interesting study. For most of *The Lord of the Rings,* Orcs are the enemy en masse, and it is thus okay—indeed, required—to hate them. They are most often depicted as a mass of swarming bodies yelling and screaming, as at the Falls of Rauros or at Helm's Deep. Or in uncharacteristic silence, as among the Huorns. Generically, as a people, Orcs are there only to be killed—by Boromir or Legolas or Gimli, or Aragorn, finally by the Huorns in some mysterious manner never described. Even when we do meet them as individuals, they are rude, vulgar, insulting, abusive, and contemptuous even of their fellow orcs while smugly aware of their own superiority. Grishnákh resents Uglúk, Uglúk despises Grishnákh, and both of them feel only scorn for the northern orcs of Moria. The orcs in the Tower of Cirith Ungol don't like the orc soldiers in the encampments on the plains of Mordor. Shagrat doesn't like Snaga, and neither likes Gorbag. In this, they all seem remarkably representative of a large portion of the human race, who define themselves as much by what they are not as by what they are. It is important that Orcs are recognizably human, and that very little they do is outside the realm of recognizable human behavior. Like soldiers everywhere, they march, they grouse, they bicker, they behave insubordinately, they squabble among themselves. They also snarl and murder and betray, and while this is not (one hopes) typical of the military, it is certainly recognizable as human behavior.

Orcs think of one another and of their enemies in much the same way we think of them, in terms of deprecatory generalities, not as individuals. Orcs call the men of Rohan "Whiteskins," and this is not a compliment. Uglúk calls the northern orcs "maggots" because they dwell in the deeps of Moria, and he calls the Mordor orcs "apes of Lugbúrz" because they have a different allegiance from his own. In the Tower of Cirith Ungol, Snaga refers to the Mordor orcs as "stinking Morgul-rats," while the Mordor orc who follows Gollum in book 6 calls the tracker orcs "little snufflers." The tracker orc calls the Nazgûl "filthy Shriekers." Sam's remark to Frodo that "if this nice friendliness would spread about in Mordor, half our troubles would be over" (*RK* VI, ii, 203) seems like something we could all agree with.

The Orcs are unsurpassed in Middle-earth in their use of insulting and demeaning epithets. Here, for example, is Uglúk, one of Saruman's Uruk-Hai speaking to Grishnákh, an orc of Mordor: "I don't trust you little swine. You've no guts outside your own sties" (*TT* III, iii, 49). And later, Grishnákh hisses to Pippin and Merry: "Curse you, you filthy little vermin.... I'll untie every string in your bodies" (*TT* III, iii, 59). Here's Shagrat, an orc in the Tower of Cirith Ungol, to Snaga, an orc of Lugbúrz (i.e., Barad Dûr): "[Y]ou little maggot.... Come here and I'll squeeze your eyes out.... I'll put red maggot-holes in your belly" (*RK* VI, i, 181–82). Here's one of the orc trackers to the other in Mordor: "Not much use are you...? I reckon eyes are better than your snotty noses" (*RK* VI, ii, 202). The message is clear: anybody not "us" (and that means orcs from a different community) is an animal, a pig, a vermin, a crawling worm.

"But," you will tell me, "these are Orcs. Of course they're nasty, brutish, and short. Nobody expects anything else from Orcs—certainly not polite behavior. That's not their role in the story." And that is exactly my point. Their role is to be the Others, the "Not Us" who negatively define us by exemplifying what we are not. Led, it is true, by Tolkien, we as readers patronizingly accept the assumption that Orcs are not people, or at least not people like "us." They are an order of existence so different from (and so much worse than) ourselves that we take for granted that political incorrectness is inherent in their nature. They can't be changed. Who now is being prejudiced, intolerant, and politically incorrect? Them? Or us?

I said at the beginning that Tolkien's political incorrectness makes his world more like the ordinary world we live in than the enchanted fairy-tale world many think of as the setting of his work. I also said that I found even some of the lighter aspects of his world to be darker than I had expected. I hope I have shown that both statements can be borne out by evidence. Despite the carping of his critics, Tolkien's world is anything but a simplistic fairy tale. It is, as he said of *Beowulf*, "a balance, an opposition"; it is "a contrasted description" (*MC* 28), and for contrast you need two sides. Balanced against Lórien is the Old Forest, against Treebeard, Old Willow-Man, against Gandalf, Saruman. Balanced against Frodo is Gollum.

I do not mean to suggest that there is no nobility in Tolkien's world, no kindness or compassion or generosity or sacrifice. Of course these things are present, or there would be nothing to balance. This is what Tolkien's millions of readers see and know and love in his books. It is much of what makes them the durable classics that they are. But to be best appreciated, these elements must be seen in the context of their opposites, the dark side of human nature that its heroes are fighting against both externally and within themselves. If Tolkien had not had the courage to portray his world as containing narrow-mindedness, bigotry, and ignorance as well as courage, compassion, and charity (in the biblical sense of that word), Middle-earth would not have had the "inner consistency of reality" he felt was necessary for true sub-creation, nor would it have become the enduring monument that we all know it to be.

The Jewels, the Stone, the Ring, and the Making of Meaning

In 1982, Tom Shippey asked, "what is a Silmaril?" and went on to inquire, "More acutely, what is the relationship in the story [of Eärendil] between success and failure? Eärendil's star appears to be a victory-emblem, 'the Flammifer of Westerness', and yet is associated with loss and homelessness, with the weeping of women on the 'Hither Shore'" (*Road,* rev. ed. 220). While his question is specific, highlighting how Tolkien's poetry introduces names without explaining them ("a pattern forever being glimpsed but never quite grasped" [*Road,* rev. ed. 219]), I'd like to expand it to address a larger issue, namely, "What did Tolkien mean the Silmarils to mean?" It is as good a question now as it was all those years ago, and to my knowledge no one has yet produced a satisfactory answer. Unless Tolkien is being so profoundly pessimistic that most of his readers are reluctant to see it, the jewels' essence as "unsullied light" and their function as the catalyst for great harm seem at cross-purposes. Yet what seems like pessimism may better be explained as Tolkien having taken on more than he could adequately handle, for behind the apparent contradiction there can be discerned a pattern in the making, a design that grew in coherence as the designer's skill improved through practice.

It is obvious to anyone reading *The Silmarillion, The Hobbit,* and *The Lord of the Rings* that in each work a particular treasure is the carrier of a familiar Tolkien theme: the danger of uncontrolled desire, covetousness grown to obsession. Shippey suggests "love of things" as "the besetting sin of modern civilisation," calling it "not quite Avarice and not quite Pride, but somehow attached to both" (*Road,* rev. ed. 274). As early as 1981, Randel Helms remarked on the relationship between the Silmarils and the Arkenstone and between both of these and the Ring, and marked the development from earliest to latest. In *Tolkien and the Silmarils*, he described *The Lord of the Rings* as "*The Hobbit* writ large" (77), and *The Hobbit* as "*The Silmarillion* writ small" (80). Helms's comparison touched on, but did not explore in any depth, the relative value and function of the three artifacts in their respective stories. In *The Annotated Hobbit*, the annotator of Tolkien's work, Douglas Anderson, dealt at length with that book's chief artifact, the Arkenstone, and cited the etymology and usage of the word *arkenstone/eorcenstane* in other works as possible indicators of its position and purpose in Tolkien's story (Tolkien, *AH* 293–94). John Rateliff devoted extensive coverage to the relationship between the Silmarils and the Arkenstone in his *The History of* The Hobbit, originally published in two volumes in 2007 together with the text of the original manuscript. Tom Shippey notes apparent anomalies in Tolkien's treatment over time of the Silmarils (*Road*, rev. ed. 273, 274, 275) and the Ring (*Road*, rev. ed. 87–89). No one, as far as I am aware, has devoted attention to the relative success in its particular work of each artifact in comparison to the others.

While the Silmarils, the Arkenstone, and the Ring provide a range of lessons on the danger of possessiveness, Tolkien's earliest attempt, the Silmarils, is the least satisfactory, for unless he is more pessimistic than most readers want to allow, there is a disconcerting incongruity between the light they house and the effect they have. Their light is positive; their effect is insidious and morally destructive. Tolkien's last effort, however, the Ring of Power, more successfully coordinates medium and message. The Ring is evil, and its effect—on everyone but Faramir—is insidious and morally destructive. The problematic gap is closed and the message is clear. The odd man out in this sequence is the Arkenstone. Neither good nor evil, it is poised between the Silmarils and the Ring, reminiscent of both but less than either. Unlike the other treasures, the Arkenstone has no indwelling nature, no symbolic significance, yet it displays characteristics that tie it to its predecessor and successor.

Discussing Bilbo's "Song of Eärendil" at Rivendell, Shippey points out (as noted earlier) that Eärendil's star [a Silmaril] appears to be a victory emblem, . . . *and yet* is associated with loss and homelessness, with the weeping of women" (*Road*, rev. ed. 220; my emphasis). Shippey's "and yet" highlights the disconnect—not just in the poem but also in the Silmarillion as a whole—between the positive connotations of light and the negative impact of the Silmarils. In *Arda Reconstructed* (2009) Douglas Kane went a bit farther to remark that the "holy jewels . . . alone preserved the 'pure' Light, yet also generated so much of the strife described in these tales" (23). Although Kane did not pursue the implications, his "yet also," like Shippey's "and yet," acknowledged the contradiction between preserving pure light and generating strife that distinguishes the Silmarils from the other artifacts. Tolkien's statement (*Letters* 148) that the events of his legendarium were "threaded upon the fate and significance of the *Silmarilli* ('radiance of pure light')" is not much help, for if their fate is clear, their significance is anything but.

The problem is that light, which is generally assumed to be beneficial, comes with significance already attached, as Tolkien well knew. He wrote to Milton Waldman that light "is such a primeval symbol in the nature of the Universe, that it can hardy be analysed" (*Letters* 148n). He also was surely aware that light as a concept carries specific religious, mystical, moral, and intellectual associations, stretching from the Book of Genesis to the Gospel of John to the Buddha to Locke and Hume and Voltaire. Yet his portrayal of light in his story is in direct opposition both to its significance as a "primeval symbol" and to these later associations. One has only to consider the multiple applications of the word "enlightenment" in all its contexts to spot the disjuncture between the Silmarils' inner light and their outer effect. While Tolkien does not refer to his light—whether of that the Lamps, the Trees, or the Silmarils—as "good," preferring words such as "holy," "unsullied," and "hallowed," he describes the Light of Valinor as "derived from light before any fall," and as "the light of art undivorced from reason, that sees things ... and 'says that they are good'—as beautiful" (*Letters* 148n). If the light of the Silmarils is so holy, why do they have such a negative impact? Medium and message are inconsistent with one another.

The obvious contrast is the Ring, where medium and message are consistent with each other, not least because the quality of the treasure is markedly different. The Ring contains power, not light. Power attracts, and the power of the Ring attracts Saruman, Boromir, Denethor, Galadriel, Grishnâkh, Gollum, even Sam Gamgee. We know why Sauron made the One Ring: "to rule them all," which is also why other people want it. On the other hand, we don't know why Fëanor made the Silmarils, and, as far as we know, neither does he. Is it heretical to suggest that maybe Tolkien didn't know either? The narrative says only that Fëanor was "filled with a new thought," but what that thought was is never explained. Unlike the Ring, the Silmarils confer no special benefit on their possessor—in fact, quite the opposite. Contrary to their nature, they do not enlighten; they endarken. They awaken possessiveness in Fëanor, covetousness in Morgoth, the impulse to murder in Thingol, and are the direct cause of the death of Maedhros and the perpetual self-exile of Maglor. A side effect, but worth noticing, is the departure of Melian from Doriath and Middle-earth. That's a lot of harm to be caused by light.

To address, if not to solve, this conundrum, I will examine the role of each treasure in its own story by posing three questions—what? how? and why?

The Silmarils

Let us go beyond Shippey's question, "What is a Silmaril?" to explore a larger one: What are they supposed to mean? As unique artifacts with significance beyond themselves, the Silmarils invite comparison with similar objects in myth and literature, most notably the Sampo of the Finnish *Kalevala* and the Grail of Arthurian romance. In *Kalevala*, the Sampo is an irreplaceable and mysterious object of enormous value, though it is never defined or described. It is forged by a craftsman but apparently can be made only once, and while many ideas as to its nature have been offered—it is a mill, it is a pillar, it is a treasure-chest, it is the world tree—no single one has prevailed. Whatever it is, the Sampo brings wealth and prosperity to its possessor. Louhi, Mistress of the North, first commissions the Sampo and then locks it in a mountain and refuses to share it with the heroes Väinämoinen, Ilmarinen and Lemminkainen, who retaliate by stealing it. In the ensuing tug of war, the Sampo is lost—broken up and drowned in the sea.

Similarities to the Silmarils are obvious, and I am not the first to point them out.[1] As with the Sampo, the fate of the Silmarils is clear but their significance is ill-defined. The medium (light) is not congruent with the message (greed and possessiveness). Like Louhi with the Sampo, Fëanor keeps the Silmarils "locked in the deep chambers of his hoard" (*S* 69). Like the Sampo, they are stolen, first by Morgoth and then by Beren. Originally a cluster of three, they are, like the Sampo though more metaphorically, broken up and scattered before reaching their "long homes" in earth, sea, and sky.

Similarities to the Grail are also obvious. The Grail is the symbolic center of the Arthurian story, as are the Silmarils in Tolkien's. Both have an obvious mystical dimension; both are called "holy"; and both are the objects of a life-changing quest. The Grail Quest is the search for transcendent spirituality, as the quest for the Silmarils is the effort to regain lost light. The ultimate symbol of sacrifice and redemption, the Grail is the cup of Christ's blood at the Last Supper and its receptacle when he bleeds on the Cross. The Silmarils likewise are containers, but of light, not blood; they house the last of the "unsullied" light from Aman, the "blessed land." Yet where the blood-filled Holy Grail brings healing and transcendence, and the mysterious Sampo brings prosperity, the light-filled "holy jewels" bring misfortune, injury, pain, and death. The closer you look, the harder it becomes to reconcile the Silmarils' nature with their role in the story.

This may be because the tale grew in the telling, for both the story and the Silmarils changed over the twenty or so years of their development. In their earliest appearance in the 1918 *Book of Lost Tales*, they are not what they later become, unique receptacles of the last of the light. They are simply part of a large bout of Noldorian gem-making that includes crystal, amber, chrysoprase, topaz, garnets, and rubies, emeralds, sapphires, amethysts, moonstones, beryls, and onyx, and agate, opals, and diamonds. Challenged to make something fairer (the only motive we are ever given), Fëanor creates a new gem made of "the sheen of pearls and the faint half-colours of opals" bathed in the "radiant dew" of Silpion and a "single tiny drop" of the light of Laurelin (*BLT* I 128). Pleased with his handiwork, he makes two more. All three are stolen by Melko, together with a "treasury of gems" and an apparently unrelated herd of horses (*BLT* I 145).

Days later, in an unrelated incident, the Two Trees are killed, suggesting that at this stage the jewels and the Trees were not thematically linked. Christopher Tolkien comments, "The primary motive in the later story of Melkor's desire for the Silmarils . . . is here represented only by a lust for the gems of the Noldoli in general: it is indeed a remarkable feature of the original mythology that though the Silmarils were present they were of such relatively small importance" (*BLT* I 156). This "remarkable feature" may have prompted Shippey's comment that "Tolkien's own efforts to say what *The Silmarillion* was 'about' were never completely illuminating" (*Road*, rev. ed. 276). We may suspect a pun in Shippey's well-chosen adjective.

Subsequent versions of their story increase the significance of the Silmarils. They next appear in a late revision of the 1917 "The Tale of Tinúviel,"[2] where the Crown of Melko and the setting of the Silmarils therein first appear (*BLT* II 53). Tinúviel's father Tinwelint (not yet Thingol) asks Beren (here no man but an elf) to bring him a Silmaril from Melko's crown (*BLT* II 13). The jewel now has a "holy magic" attributable to its making in Valinor "before the evil came there" (*BLT* II 34), and has acquired supernatural, moral, and spiritual value. The Silmarils are also mentioned in a fragment tentatively dated by Christopher Tolkien to early 1925 (*LB* 131) where they are

> . . . the Three . . .   thrice-enchanted
> globes of crystal   by gleam undying
> illumined, lit (*LB* 134)

Christopher writes, "It is clear that the Silmarils had already gained greatly in significance since the earliest period of the mythology" (*LB* 138).

In all these versions, the constants are their beauty, their desirability, and their theft by Melko/Melkor. The variables are the amount of light they contain, the source or sources of that light, and the exact nature of their holiness, whether (as in early versions) simply through association with Valinor, or because (as in *The Silmarillion*) the gems are "hallowed by Varda" (*S* 67).

How do they work? Another good question. Mostly, they warp people's lives, which is not what you would expect of hallowed light. Fëanor is the prime example. That light should drive its preserver into his own darkness seems a paradox too far, matched by the irony that without him the light would have been irretrievably lost.[3] Moreover, the Silmarils' effect varies from psychological (corrupting Fëanor and Thingol) to physical (burning Morgoth, Carcharoth, Maedhros, and Maglor), with their effect on Beren, Lúthien, and Eärendil being the exception to both. We might assume that one Silmaril burns Morgoth and Carcharoth and the remaining two burn Maedhros and Maglor because in each case the possession is wrongful, as if light misappropriated turns to heat. Fair enough. But by that token, the Silmaril for which he barters his daughter should also burn Thingol, whose possession is no more rightful than the others'. Yet it doesn't, even though Thingol's motive and murderous scheme for getting the jewel hardly qualify him as a worthy recipient. That same Silmaril, stolen by Beren, bequeathed to Eärendil, and borne aloft into the night sky as he voyages through the heavens, becomes the evening/morning star. It is thus visible but unattainable, and, as Shippey observes (see above), it is associated not with illumination but with loss and homelessness, and the weeping of women. If there is a message here, it is mixed.

There is one place where the message is not mixed, where Tolkien is in full command of his material and his light behaves like light, not dark. This is in *The Lord of the Rings*. Here, Eärendil's Silmaril is neither an object nor a trophy, but a beacon, a light when all other lights go out, in the phial Galadriel gives to Frodo. When Frodo advances down the tunnel in Cirith Ungol holding aloft the phial, its light does precisely what light actually does do—defeats darkness. The Silmaril's light does it again when Sam uses the phial against Shelob. It is noteworthy that both instances occur in Ungol, "unlight"—that is to say, dark. A third time the light is used (again by Sam), it is to break the will of the Watchers at Cirith Ungol, when it blazes to "grace with splendour his faithful brown hobbit-hand" (*RK* VI, i, 191), an echo of Beren's hand holding the Silmaril. What has made this treatment different from its predecessors? My answer is, time and experience. On the basis of the paper used, Christopher Tolkien dates Tolkien's drafts of the Company's farewell to Lórien and Galadriel's gift of the phial only to sometime after 1940. However, he dates the Cirith Ungol chapter more precisely to May 1944. It is hard not to suppose that, perhaps through parallel experience in handling the Ring, Tolkien had learned how to make medium and message work together to support his theme.

Which leads to my next question: Why are the Silmarils there?

The answer is mixed. They contribute materially to plot, but less clearly, perhaps less effectively, to theme. There has to be a fulcrum for the plot and the Silmarils are it. In this respect, they function as traditional fairy-tale treasures and occupy a traditional role in the story. It is clear from the early drafts that as the mythology developed their importance grew and light became a central concept. The shift of vehicle from Trees to Jewels allows for more action, for while the Trees' light shines impartially on and for all in Valinor, the Jewels' light can be and is coveted, possessed, hoarded, hidden, stolen, and transported. The problem is that their nature and their role as possessed items are at odds, and seem, confusingly, to combat rather than support one another, as light becomes both the reason for and the price of war in Middle-earth. Again I will ask: What is the message here? Is Tolkien's world is not ready for the light?

That the message is not clear (see Shippey's comments above) may be a function of the discrepancy between the height of Tolkien's ambition, the intractability of his material, and the limitations of his skill at the time. Like many poets, his reach exceeded his grasp. He aimed lower with the Arkenstone.

The Arkenstone

The Arkenstone both does and does not share salient characteristics with the treasures that bracket it, the Silmarils before and the Ring after its invention. Like them, it is beautiful, desirable, and the catalyst for a lot of trouble. Unlike them, it has no inherent characteristic such as holiness or power and confers nothing on its possessor. Moreover, it inhabits a fundamentally different work and world from those of the other two treasures. While *The Hobbit* has tangential ties to the Silmarillion and more obvious ones to *The Lord of the Rings*, it is still a lesser work than either, a children's story set in a fairy-tale world, not a mythology or an epic romance in an invented cosmos. There is no agenda behind the Arkenstone's role in the story, so the answers to my three questions are easier. As to what the Arkenstone is and means, it is a stone dug out of the mountain, shaped and polished by the Dwarves. It is an heirloom passed down from Dwarf father to Dwarf son. It becomes a coveted treasure, but with no indwelling capacities associated with light, dark, good, evil, or any other concept. No meaning beyond its beauty is suggested. Thus it can more easily fulfill the modest expectations Tolkien builds into *The Hobbit*—itself a far less ambitious effort in both intention and execution than the Silmarillion or *The Lord of the Rings*.

Like the Silmarils, the Arkenstone went through changes before settling into its identity as Thorin's much-desired heirloom. Initially unnamed, it acquired credentials as the Gem of Girion given by the king of Dale to the dwarves of the Lonely Mountain. This was later changed to the Arkenstone of Thrain, found by the dwarves in the heart of the mountain. Even then, however, its function was contrary to its eventual position as the most desirable object, for at this early stage it was meant to really be Bilbo's fourteenth share of the profits of the expedition, small and portable enough to carry in his pocket. Unlike the Silmarils, the Arkenstone is a secondary ingredient in the story Tolkien was creating, an add-on to a plot expanding beyond its original parameters. Its most direct precursor was not any artifact from the depths of myth but the Moonstone from the novel of the same name written by nineteenth-century novelist Wilkie Collins, a jewel whose theft, pursuit, and recovery by its rightful hereditary possessors form the burden of what is usually conceded to be the first English detective novel. Collins's description of the Moonstone, as shining "out of the depths of its own brightness," with a light "that streamed from it... like the light of the harvest moon" (Collins 61), is not unlike Tolkien's descriptions of both the Arkenstone and the Silmarils, and one is tempted to look no further for Tolkien's most immediate inspiration.

This immediate influence aside, it is as if Tolkien recycled material left over from the Silmarillion into *The Hobbit*, but without the extra significance. John Rateliff has argued that there was some connection in Tolkien's mind between the two, never fully defined but most clearly shown in their descriptions and the way details about one bled over into descriptions of the other.[4] Nevertheless, fully defined or not, the ghost of the Silmarils still haunts the Arkenstone. It is a "great white gem" (*H* 197), a "great jewel" with its own "inner light" (201), yet it also changes external light into "sparks of white radiance" (201). The overlap is no surprise when we recall that Tolkien worked simultaneously on both stories, putting aside the Silmarillion only when *The Hobbit* went into production. Tolkien also used a form of the word *Arkenstone* in the Old English version of the Annals of Valinor to refer to *þá Silmarillas, þæt wæron Eorclanstánas* ("the Silmarils, that were precious/holy stones") where the word element *eorclan* can mean both "precious" and "holy" (*AH* 294; Rateliff 604, 605). The presence of the word *precious* in this context is hard to ignore.

How does it work? Or more precisely, what does it do? This is easy to answer, because, unlike the other artifacts, the Arkenstone doesn't do anything. It is a patient, not an agent. The Silmarils can burn and the Ring ensnare and corrupt its possessor, but the Arkenstone has no active ingredient.

So why is it in the story? Its chief function seems to be to reveal character. Though its late introduction seems almost an afterthought, once it is there, like both Silmarils and Ring, it appeals to the inherent flaws in human nature. It makes Thorin crafty, devious, and not above a crooked deal, and it turns Bilbo into a real thief. "Now I am a burglar indeed!" he says as he shuts his eyes and pockets the Arkenstone (*H* 201). And when the hurly-burly's done, and the battle's lost and won, he tells himself, "You are a fool, Bilbo Baggins, and you made a great mess of that business with the stone" (*H* 244). At least he knows it. Fëanor never attains this self-knowledge, and for a fuller exploration of the idea we will have to wait for the fall and redemption of Boromir.

But Bilbo's fall and subsequent self-knowledge are sidebars to the story proper.[5] They do not affect the plot. Nor does the Arkenstone. We are led to expect that as a bargaining piece between Bard and Thorin it will avert a battle, and thus Bilbo's theft, though still a moral lapse, will be justified after the fact. But the bargain, though struck, is never concluded. Thorin delays payment, and the dwarves' attack to recapture the stone is aborted by the arrival of Bolg and the goblins. This forces the former foes to unite against a common enemy and precipitates the Battle of Five Armies, in which the Arkenstone plays no part.

In sum, the Arkenstone is both less meaningful and less integral to the plot than the Silmarils or the Ring in their respective works. Its role in the story, while consistent with its own nature as a beautiful object to be admired and coveted, is devoid of any greater significance. For these very reasons, it works better than the Silmarils. Moreover, it marks a kind of hesitation between Tolkien's early treatment of the Silmarils and his later and more fully realized treatment of the Ring of Power.

The Ring

In considering the Ring of Power, the answer to the "what" question is harder to pin down than with the other two artifacts, partly because the Ring, like the Silmarils and the Arkenstone, went through a series of changes before settling into its role as an instrument of power. Shippey points out a "näive note" in *The Return of the Shadow* (259), which states that the Ring is "[n]ot very dangerous, when used for good purpose" (*RS* 42). In light of its subsequent nature and function, "naive" seems too mild a word. So what is the Ring? The practical answer is that the Ring is a container.[6] It houses Sauron's power in an object outside his body (see *Letters* 153, 279), just as the soul of the demon Kastchei is hidden in an egg in the Russian fairy tale "The Firebird." But, like the equally obvious answer for the Grail or the Silmarils, this doesn't capture the Ring's real significance, which is as a power, not a receptacle. Tolkien himself, in a letter to Rhona Beare, cautioned, "You cannot press the One Ring too hard, for it is of course a mythical feature." He went on, "If I were to 'philosophize' this myth, or at least the Ring of Sauron, I should say it was a mythical way of representing the truth that *potency* (or perhaps rather *potentiality*) if it is to be exercised, and produce results, has to be externalized" (*Letters* 279). The word *mythical* here seems to betoken a nonrealistic treatment weighted with symbolic meaning. Tolkien's philosophizing is on the mark, for attempts to "press the One Ring too hard" simply show how difficult it is to define. For all Gandalf's description of its purpose, the greatest effect of the Ring, the power that it gives its possessor to "rule them all" (*FR* I, ii, 59), is barely illustrated.

How does it work? Aside from invisibility (the least of its attributes), the function of the Ring is shown far more through characters' responses to the *idea* of it than through its own powers or action. Only three times in the story do we see the Ring do what it is known for doing. Each time, it is Frodo (not desirous of power) who does not "rule them all," but only Gollum. The first time is in the Emyn Muil, where the Ring is the guarantee for Gollum's promise not to run away. "Swear by it, if you will" (*TT* IV, I, 225), Frodo tells him, and Gollum swears. The second time is at the Forbidden Pool, when Frodo uses the Ring to bring Gollum to Faramir "'Come!' he said, 'Or the Precious will be angry'" (*TT* IV, vi, 297). And Gollum comes, carrying a half-eaten fish. The last time is on the path below the Cracks of Doom when Frodo, clutching the Ring as a "wheel of fire," banishes Gollum, commanding, "Begone, and trouble me no more!" (*RK* VI, iii, 221),[7] and Gollum goes, though not for long.

So why is it present in *The Lord of the Rings*? It is in the story because it *is* the story: the power of the Ring and the corrupting effect of that power are what the story is about. But the Ring's effect appears only gradually. Bilbo's belligerence toward Gandalf and his reluctance to relinquish the Ring after the birthday party are the first illustrations of its effect. Frodo's subsequent temptation to use it at the first appearance of a Black Rider is ambiguous; is he succumbing to a natural impulse to hide or is the Ring itself compelling his behavior? The question is not answered, as Tolkien moves the Rider on before Frodo can take any action.

Early drafts had Frodo actually put on the Ring at Farmer Maggot's house, in a comic scene of disappearing beer, greatly expanded in a later version (*RS* 96–97, 292–94). This episode was scrapped in favor of the later, more pointed scene in the house of Tom Bombadil, when Frodo puts it on but stays visible to Tom while becoming invisible to Sam and Pippin. Tom himself has just put on the Ring and has not disappeared. This defines the nature of the Ring in a way that the scene with Farmer Maggot could not. The Ring works on humanity's desire to dominate. Unlike Maggot, Tom is a personified force of nature, not a conventional human being, and thus has no such desire. Power has no effect on him—and not much on Frodo at this point.

The next episode is at the barrow, where Frodo's courage and loyalty, not his susceptibility to the Ring, are tested. The Ring is less a compulsion than a practical means of escape. Frodo's temptation is not that of yielding to the Ring but of abandoning his comrades. Both the situation and Frodo's victory over himself are clear. In contrast, his action at the Prancing Pony in Bree is loaded with ambiguity. During his encore of "The Man in the Moon," Frodo has his hand in his pocket. In his final disastrous caper, he falls, his finger and the Ring connect, and he disappears. Whether this is brought about by the Ring itself or is mere accident is left deliberately ambiguous, but whatever the cause, the result is minimal. His disappearance has no effect on him beyond his being revealed to the squint-eyed Southerner.

Not until the incident at Weathertop do we see fully how and on what the Ring works,—the human psyche. Wearing the Ring on Weathertop, Frodo is invisible to Sam but visible to the Riders and he to them, for unlike in Tom's house and at Bree, here the Ring alters his perception. Wearing it makes the real world shadowy, the shadow world sharp and clear. It takes Frodo into the dark psychological world of which it is at once the embodiment, the instrument, and the gateway. It is no accident that Sam hears his master's voice coming from "under the earth" (*FR* I, xii, 209), for Frodo has entered the dark underworld of human nature.

Both this experience and the additional effect of the wound from the Morgul-knife permanently alter Frodo. Descriptions of his condition during the journey to the Ford show that though he has taken off the Ring, he is still in the shadow-world. His perception is so altered that the actual world around him loses substance. "The trees and rocks about him seemed shadowy and dim" (*FR* I, xii, 215); "every now and again a mist seemed to obscure his sight" (217); "the mist before his eyes . . . darkened, and he felt that a shadow was coming between him and the faces of his friends" (222); "during the day things about him faded to shadows of ghostly grey. He almost welcomed the coming of night, for then the world seemed less pale and empty" (224). In the final confrontation at the Ford he can, as he could on Weathertop, see the Black Riders clearly and they can see him. No longer wearing the Ring, he is still half in the Ring world.

At Rivendell, Bilbo's request to see the Ring triggers in Frodo a similar response, making him see Bilbo as a grasping creature with bony hands reaching for his treasure. It is a projection of his own inner darkness, his own desire. The image tells us about Frodo, not Bilbo, whose reaction when he sees Frodo's face is to say, "I understand now . . . Put it away! I am sorry" (*FR* II, I, 244). What Bilbo understands will be clear only after the entrance of Gollum into the story, when we will begin to see the terrible transformation that this episode foreshadows. In Moria, when Frodo first becomes aware of Gollum, he can see further into the dark than his companions.

The next significant incident is between Frodo and Boromir on Amon Hen. This episode relates less to Frodo's previous experience with the Ring than to Bilbo's with the Arkenstone. In each case, a character rationalizes his desire as his "right": Bilbo as his fourteenth share, Boromir as a Númenorean. Both characters "fall," Bilbo metaphorically, Boromir both literally, as his foot catches on a stone, and metaphorically, as he hits rock bottom in his surrender to temptation. Bilbo's self-recognition in *The Hobbit* that he is capable of theft—that he is "a burglar indeed" (*H* 201)—foreshadows Boromir's more fully integrated fall and self-realization: "What have I said? . . . What have I done? . . . A madness took me, but it has passed" (*FR* II, x, 416). Boromir's self-knowledge, his confession and apology to Aragorn, echo Thorin Oakenshield's farewell to Bilbo, when he reflects that valuing "food and cheer and song above hoarded gold" would make "a merrier world" (*H* 243).

Subsequent chapters in book IV and the beginning of book VI focus on Frodo's continuing struggle against the Ring. Tolkien does not tell us about it; instead he has Frodo tell us, through his many references to being in the dark or the dark entering his heart and through his rage at Sam in the Tower of Cirith Ungol and his remorse afterward. His cry of "What have I said? . . . What have I done?" echoes Boromir on Amon Hen, but what Boromir calls "madness," Frodo recognizes as "the horrible power of the Ring" (*RK* VI, i, 188). Nearing Mount Doom, he tells Sam, "I am almost in its power now . . . and if you tried to take it I should go mad" (*RK* VI, iii, 214). His self-knowledge has a higher price than Boromir's, whose madness passes, leaving him whole, while Frodo's possesses him, leaving him broken. It is the measure of Tolkien's skill that the moment at the Cracks of Doom when Frodo claims the Ring stuns first-time readers, yet is fully consistent with everything we have been told about the Ring's power.

To conclude, there are not just differences among the artifacts, there is marked improvement and refinement over time in Tolkien's handling of vehicle and theme. He is least successful with the Silmarils, whose role in the story is counter to their essential nature. They may be light, but they generate more heat than illumination. He is less ambitious, and therefore more successful, in his treatment of the Arkenstone. The story is a fairy tale, not an epic; the stakes are lower; and the Arkenstone itself is just a stone with no symbolism attached. Ultimately, it is less a prize than a memorial, buried with Thorin. Finally, Tolkien is most successful in both intent and execution with the Ring of Power, which acts in accord with its own nature and is consistent with its story in a way the Silmarils do not and are not.

In short, Shippey's question was not just a good one, it was the right one, and he was right to ask it. The Silmarils are not a perfect representation of what I believe Tolkien was trying to accomplish. Like the tale itself, its author's ability to corral his material and harness it to his design grew in the telling. Over the course of thirty years, Tolkien taught himself how to coordinate vehicle and theme and make them work for each other, for him, and for his audience.

Making Choices

Moral Ambiguity in Tolkien's Major Fiction

Since the first publication of *The Lord of the Rings* in 1954–55, Tolkien's treatment of good and evil, right and wrong, has too often been misconstrued as simplistic. Edwin Muir's 1954 review of *The Fellowship of the Ring* set the tone, stating that "[Tolkien's] good people are consistently good, his evil figures immutably evil" (7). Edmund Wilson was just as bad, stating in "Oo! Those Awful Orcs!" that "The hero has no serious temptations; is . . . perplexed by few problems. What we get is a simple confrontation . . . of the Forces of Evil with the Forces of Good" (313). Nothing could be further from the truth. Both critics seem to have assumed a posture of academic snobbism that regarded fantasy as insubstantial and determinedly anti-intellectual. Over the many decades since publication, Tolkien has proved them wrong. Yet despite many comments to the contrary by such literary lions as C. S. Lewis and W. H. Auden, as well as praise by several generations of later scholars, literary critics such as Muir and Wilson and others of their persuasion have had a lasting effect on critical opinion of Tolkien's work, promoting the idea that his Middle-earth is a childish world of absolutes, of moral black and white, of right and wrong without shades of grey and with no nuances to modify the polarity of its values.

That grown-up people whose job it is to read and evaluate books could be so naïve is perturbing and bodes ill for the future of imaginative literature. To correct their error and defend the value of fantasy against realism as a medium for authenticity, I will offer four examples of Tolkien's moral complexity and ambiguity, one from a little-known minor work, *The Notion Club Papers*, and three from the better-known *Lord of the Rings*. *The Notion Club Papers*, his unfinished time-travel story, was meant to connect his legendarium to the modern world. It will serve as an introduction to Tolkien's fondness for interrogating standards of morality, a predeliction further developed in the other examples. I will begin with an episode from *The Notion Club Papers,* an episode entirely unrelated to the plot or theme of the story. Why, then, is it there? I suggest that it offered Tolkien a way to examine nuances of morality that obviously resonated with him. It engages Tolkien's private interests and professional standards, as well as his ideas of right and wrong.

In part 1 of the *Papers,* a member of the Notion Club, Michael Ramer, tells of a waking dream he has had in which he sees a man looking at an open book. The man *"turns a leaf of the book—and sees a new light, makes a discovery"* (*SD* 191). According to Ramer, the emotions associated with this dream scene are *"worry"* and a "dull sense of loss, as . . . when something precious [is] broken or lost" (*SD* 191). The explanation is not far to seek and introduces a dilemma in which the conventional values of right and wrong are deliberately called into question. The man in the dream, a librarian at a small university, is cataloging a "splendid book-collection" left to the university by a deceased donor. The "new light," the "discovery," is of two documents in the book being examined, one a "unique fragment of a MS. in very early Welsh, before Geoffrey, about the death of Arthur" (*SD* 192), the other is a loose leaf containing a will that postdates the bequest to the university. It directs that the book collection be sold and the proceeds used to found a Chair of Basic English. What will be "broken" is the book collection; what will be "lost" is the unique Arthurian fragment. To report the discovery will lead to sale of the books, risking the loss to future scholars of that "unique fragment" that might change literary history. It would be a "serious temptation," even in Edmund Wilson's eyes, to suppress the will, thus preserving the manuscript fragment and allowing the books to stay in the university—and this temptation is the point of the dream scene.

Not only is this a conflicted situation, it is one calculated to drive an academic to tears. Ramer and his audience, the Notion Club, are academics very like Tolkien. Like Tolkien, they are book-lovers, philologists, and students of myth and legend. So the dispersal of a book collection, and the promotion of Basic English, and the possible loss of a unique Arthurian fragment, all consequent on the sale of the collection, would have caused them—as it obviously caused him—great distress. Tolkien confronts his librarian with a choice not just between right and wrong—that would be too easy—but between a legal duty and a professional obligation, between his commitment to the law and his responsibility to history and scholarship. It would be wrong to suppress the will. But would it be right to disperse the book collection to various buyers, thus depriving the library and its users of access to the books and risking the loss to history and scholarship of that unique Arthurian fragment? The librarian's problem is how to do the right thing in a situation where two different right things are in conflict with one another. I am sorry to tell you that there is no outcome to this particular dilemma. Having given his fictive librarian this wrenching choice between his duty and his vocation, Tolkien leaves him—and the reader—hanging. The story is unfinished and the dilemma unresolved.

But the story illustrates Tolkien's fondness for inventing (and leaving unresolved) such dilemmas, which he does again and again in *The Lord of the Rings*. Muir's dictum that the good people are good and the bad people are bad and Wilson's assertion that the confrontation of good and evil is "simple" are so off the mark that Tolkien felt moved to address the question., In a letter to Naomi Mitchison in September 1954 he wrote that, "Some reviewers have called the whole thing simple-minded, just a plain fight between Good and Evil, with all the good just good, and the bad just bad." He conceded that this judgment was "[p]ardonable, perhaps (though at least Boromir has been overlooked)" (*Letters* 197).

Tolkien was being generous. To overlook Boromir is not "pardonable"; it is shallow, simplistic, and slipshod, for Boromir is the most obvious refutation of Muir and Wilson and their reading of Tolkien's work. Boromir is neither "consistently good" nor "immutably evil" in Muir's terms. He is a mixture of both. He is good when he rescues the hobbits from the snow and clears a way through the drifts for the Fellowship, acting on behalf of his fellows and using his strength to good purpose. But he is not "consistently" good. He is not only evil, he is criminal when he attempts to take the Ring by force. He persuades himself that he has a good—that is to say, moral—reason, to save his country from destruction, and makes the conventional excuse that the end justifies the means. But he is not "immutably" evil, for he recognizes his error and tries to make amends.

In this respect, Boromir, for all his ambiguity, is a fairly straightforward character. He knows what is right and what is wrong; he is tempted and falls into error, but repents, atones by defending the hobbits, and is absolved by Aragorn. As the story progresses, however, Tolkien creates more complex situations where it is becomes increasingly hard to distinguish good from evil and right from wrong, where characters wrestle with morally ambiguous questions and get no absolution, and the reader gets no clear resolution of the good-bad dichotomy. These situations clearly demonstrate that Tolkien, raising questions about what are conventionally seen as absolutes and calling their meaning into question, preferred moral complexity to moral simplicity. My examples from *The Lord of the Rings* include Sam at the pass of Cirith Ungol, Frodo at the Forbidden Pool, and Gandalf and Aragorn at the Black Gate.

Let us start with Sam Gamgee. It is no accident that Tolkien has placed him in the most emotionally complex situation in the story, a situation that starts with raw emotion and works its way to concepts of right and wrong. Sam's name, *Samwise,* comes from an Anglo-Saxon word compound *sámwís,* meaning "half-wise," and Tolkien does, indeed, translate *Samwise* into Westron as "half-wise" or "simple." Given Sam's uncompromising nature, I take "simple" to mean not "simple-minded" but "unmixed, uncomplex, having no divisions." Not for nothing does Frodo tell him, at the end of the story, "you were meant to be solid and whole, and you will be" (*RK* VI, ix, 306). Unlike Saruman or Denethor, who are both divided, both complicated mixtures of pride, ambition, and knowledge, Sam is "simple." He has no pride, his only ambition is to take care of Frodo, and his intellect is not vexed by subtle distinctions, such as "the end justifies the means." Tolkien deliberately places this uncomplicated hobbit in a complicated situation in which he is forced to make a choice among difficult options without any clear guide, and without, moreover, having enough information by which to judge.

As the scene opens, Sam's options are multiple, and his winding road to final action is not paved with clear intentions but follows a circuitous route along degrees of personal preference. Sam's choices, some only briefly considered, are:

1) retreat—to go back to the Shire leaving Frodo dead and the mission unfulfilled;
2) retribution—to kill Gollum;
3) suicide—to kill himself;
4) duty—to take the Ring to the Cracks of Doom.

Note that right and wrong, good and bad, are not uppermost in his mind. He does not think in terms of principles but of possibilities. Sam has no one to advise him and no one to judge him. His first option, retreat, is the weakest, going against his conscience and his loyalty: "leave Mr. Frodo dead, unburied on the top of the mountain, and go home?" That would not be right. It would also be impractical, since home is a long way away.

Almost immediately, Sam rejects this option in favor of its opposite. "Go on? Is that what I've got to do? And leave him?" (*TT* IV, x, 340). This would force Sam to violate his own moral code and abandon Frodo. It is also impractical, since Sam doesn't know where "on" is. And in spite of saying farewell, arranging Frodo's body and taking his sword and the star-glass, Sam does not "go on." Instead, Tolkien has him consider other options. Next on the list is revenge, as Sam tries "to find strength to tear himself away and go on a lonely journey—for vengeance. If once he could go, his anger would bear him down all the roads of the world, pursuing, until he had him at last: Gollum. Then Gollum would die in a corner" (341). I don't know about Edmund Wilson, but I would call this a "serious temptation." But Sam rejects this as well, not because it is not right—that is not yet an issue—but because "[i]t would not be worth while to leave his master for that. It would not bring him back. Nothing would" (341).

The realization that nothing will bring Frodo back brings Sam directly to his next option: suicide. Since Frodo is lost, "[t]hey had better both be dead together. And that, too, would be a lonely journey" (341). For Tolkien, a Catholic, suicide is not just wrong, it is sinful, yet Tolkien describes Sam as tempted (at least momentarily) by the sin. "[Sam] looked on the bright point of the sword. He thought of the places behind where there was a black brink and an empty fall into nothingness. There was no escape that way. That was to do nothing, not even to grieve" (341). Of all his options, this is at once the most tempting and the least effective.

Sam's last choice, the one he selects, is guided by duty, not morality. It is his duty to "*see it through*. Another lonely journey, and the worst" (341). This is a public rather than a private choice, putting Sam's obligation to the quest ahead of his loyalty to Frodo, and though it is hardly practical, since he doesn't know the way, this is the option that Sam chooses. And then Tolkien engineers an abrupt about-face, pulling a total surprise on the reader, who by this time is with Sam, mourning for the dead Frodo. With no narrative warning either to him or the reader, Sam finds out from overhearing the orc soldiers that Frodo is alive. This changes his whole outlook, introducing for the first time the terms *right* and *wrong*, and causing him to completely reverse his judgment.

"'I got it all wrong!' he cried. 'I knew I would.'" Sam's use of the word here is not moral, it is practical. He is not so much guilty of wrongdoing as of having made a mistake, committed a blunder. He goes on. "'Now they've got him, the devils! the filth! Never leave your master, never, never: that was my right rule. And I knew it in my heart. May I be forgiven!'" (*TT* IV, x, 351). The word "right" is introduced here, to companion "wrong," but Sam's "right" is more moral than his "wrong." He now asks for forgiveness because in his own eyes he has committed a sin. He has violated his "right rule," his own standard of morality. Having made the mistake of leaving Frodo, his "right rule" tells him to do the right thing and go back to Frodo.

But he cannot go back to Frodo: Tolkien makes sure he is physically shut out as the gate is closed and barred against him. And here is where ambiguity really takes hold, setting conventional standards of right and wrong topsy-turvy. By "getting it all wrong" Sam has inadvertently gotten it all right. By choosing duty over loyalty, revenge, and suicide, he has done the right thing for the wrong reason. Following public duty rather than private morality, he has saved the Ring from the orcs and thus from Sauron. Tolkien's intentional and ironic twists and turns in this situation leave simple good and bad far behind and stand traditional morality on its head. (I am aware that Tolkien also implies that a greater—some would say spiritual—purpose is being served than Sam is aware of, but that is not part of this paper, which is concerned only with earthly standards of behavior.)

Leaving Sam in Cirith Ungol to cope with his situation, let us look at another character, Frodo. Unlike Sam, Frodo is not "simple." He has knowingly taken on a suicidal mission and made his peace with the fact that it will probably fail. He can accept help from Gollum, whom he knows to be evil, and can even pity his condition, whereas Sam hates Gollum on sight and would willingly kill him. Frodo knows how to adjust right and wrong to the realities of a situation until he comes to the pool of Henneth Annûn. Here, Tolkien puts Frodo in an even worse double bind than Sam's, giving him not too many choices, but only one impossible one—not between shades of right but between bad and worse. Tolkien invents a no-win situation in which Frodo's only viable choice violates all notions of right and wrong and morality. Told that Gollum faces execution by Faramir for having found the Forbidden Pool, Frodo can only save Gollum's life by lying to him, betraying his trust, and luring him unsuspecting into a trap. "[Frodo's] heart sank. This was too much like trickery. . . . certainly what Frodo did would seem a treachery to the poor treacherous creature. It would probably be impossible ever to make him understand or believe that Frodo had saved his life in the only way he could. What else could he do?—to keep faith, as near as might be, with both sides" (*TT* IV, vi, 297). Trying to keep faith with both sides, Frodo must break faith both with Gollum and with himself. Note that it worries Frodo that Gollum will not understand, that his actions will be misconstrued. I would call this a "serious" problem, in Wilson's terms.

We can contrast Frodo's dilemma with Sam's. Unlike Sam, who must choose among degrees of right, Frodo must choose between two wrongs. Sam wound up doing the wrong thing—leaving Frodo—for the right reason—to continue the quest—which turned out to be the right thing for a reason he never thought of—to save the Ring from Sauron. Frodo is forced to do the wrong thing—to lie and betray—for what he knows is the right reason—to save Gollum's life. The lesser immorality will prevent the greater. But that doesn't make it easy. Sam's multiple choices were a deliberate spectrum of motives, actions, and outcomes. Frodo's choice is stark and unambiguous, and its morality is situational and contingent. Tolkien has arranged the situation so that both the reader and Frodo must acknowledge that the end justifies the means.

Frodo certainly does not consider himself "good" in doing what he does. Indeed, he feels "very wretched" and "hates the whole business" (297). Nor does Faramir consider himself "bad" for forcing Frodo to protect the secrecy of his stronghold against Gollum. Who is right and who is wrong? Whose side does Tolkien want the reader to be on, Faramir's or Frodo's? Whose side should Frodo be on? He owes his life to Gollum, who may be a villain in other circumstances but in this particular situation is completely innocent. He's not spying, he is doing no harm, he just wants fish. Here is a situation to confound Edwin Muir, in which a good person—that is, Frodo—is not "consistently good," and an evil figure—that is, Gollum—is not "immutably evil." The good guy is bad and the bad guy is, if not good, at least neutral, pathetic, and strangely appealing. Listen to him:

"Poor Smeágol, all alone." "Fissh, nice fissh." "Not nice Master. Leaves poor Smeágol and goes with new friends." When Frodo voices the catchword of all cheats and deceivers, "trust me," Gollum is understandably suspicious. "We must trust Master? Why? . . . Where is the cross, rude hobbit?" And when Gollum sees the trap, he accuses Frodo of being "Wicked! Tricksy! False!" (297). He's right, and Frodo knows it. And when Frodo says again, "Trust Master," Gollum spits at him. With good reason, since Frodo is delivering him into the hands of enemies who have no understanding of him. Faramir calls Frodo's protection of Gollum "unwise." Yet even Faramir recognizes the ambiguity of the situation, admitting to Frodo that "it seems less evil to counsel another man to break troth than to do so oneself" (301). It is easier to tell someone else to be bad than to do it oneself. There is no right choice here, only a choice between two wrongs.

Why has Tolkien created this episode? I propose two reasons. The first is because he knows the way of the world and is trying to portray it faithfully. Seldom in real life do we get to choose between good and bad. More often we are forced to choose, like Frodo, between bad and worse, a decision that requires far more nuance in analysis and action than choosing between simple good and bad. My second reason is more structural. I propose that Tolkien invented Frodo's dilemma at least in part to match it against a similar dilemma experienced later on by Gollum. Critics have noted the symmetry between Frodo and Gollum—both are hobbits, both are Ring-bearers, both are captured by the spell of the Ring, each embodies what the other is or could have been. I want to suggest a deeper symmetry of motive and action—and choice. Frodo's betrayal of Gollum at the Forbidden Pool foreshadows Gollum's betrayal of Frodo at the Pass of Cirith Ungol, although only in hindsight can we see the latter as a tragic parody of the former.

Frodo's moral dilemma is clear, and when he is driven into betrayal, we understand and sympathize. Gollum's moral dilemma is also clear. Returning from his desertion of Sam and Frodo at the Stairs of Cirith Ungol, Gollum approaches the two sleeping hobbits. In a scene unrivaled in the book for its poignance, Tolkien makes the reader see Gollum as "an old, weary hobbit," who looks back toward the pass, "shaking his head as if in some interior debate." Then he reaches out to touch Frodo in what is "almost a caress," only to be abused by Sam for "'pawing at Master'" (*TT* IV, viii, 324). Sam's insensitivity, his crass misreading of Gollum's motive, drives Gollum over the edge, and the "fleeting moment" passes beyond recall. However fleeting, I want to define this moment as a "serious temptation" in Wilson's terms. Though I doubt Wilson was capable of seeing virtue as a temptation, Tolkien is, and it is clear that at this moment Gollum is tempted by good. At this crux, he is not "immutably evil," but both good and evil, divided in "interior debate"—a "Slinker and Stinker" moment beyond Sam's capacity to understand. Tolkien gives Gollum a choice and allows him to almost make the right one. It is typical of Tolkien's paradoxical treatment of good and evil that Gollum is pushed into evil by the involuntary evil of the most unequivocally good person in the book.

From C. S. Lewis on, readers have noted the "irony" that it is Sam, whose love and loyalty for Frodo are the purest emotion in the book, who pushes Gollum over the edge and thus is instrumentally responsible for Frodo's later entrapment by Shelob. Few, however, have remarked that it is Tolkien who has engineered this moral tangle, Tolkien who, yet again, has contrived to have a "bad" person, Gollum, almost do a good thing by refraining from doing a bad one, and to have a good person, Sam, involuntarily do a bad thing without even thinking about it. Of the two, Gollum and Sam, whose is the greater immorality? Gollum has a reason for his betrayal of Frodo, though it is a bad motive. Sam has no reason at all: he just reacts, out of hatred and (I suggest) jealousy. I propose that Tolkien is making a point here, that this whole elaborate interlace of actions, motives, and reasons for choice is illustration of the complexities of real life, where actions are seldom easily defined and even more seldom easily understood.

While we are on the subject of Gollum, let us note that his behavior throughout the book conforms to his own standards of right and wrong. Gollum keeps his promises, though his interpretation of their import may not be everyone's. His first promise, sworn by the Precious, is to be "very, very good" and to "serve the Master of the Precious" (*TT* IV, I, 225). And until they reach Cirith Ungol he is "very good." He navigates Frodo and Sam through the Dead Marshes, he finds rabbits for Sam to cook, he helps the two hobbits avoid orcs. Even in the Slinker-Stinker dialogue with himself that Sam overhears, his rationale for getting the Precious, though it is based on the wording of the oath, still abides by that wording. He has sworn to protect the Master of the Precious and if he has the Ring he will be the Master. Casuistic though it is, and not unlike Boromir—and Saruman and Denethor—this is, in Gollum's own mind, a right choice.

My last example from *The Lord of the Rings* concerns the morality of the choice made by Gandalf and Aragorn at the Black Gate. Without much hope, Aragorn and Gandalf mount a last-ditch effort to distract Sauron from Frodo and Sam's errand, wherever they are, by leading a small army to the Gates of Mordor. Here they are met by the lieutenant of the tower, who displays to them a short sword, an elven cloak and brooch, and Frodo's mail coat. The implication is unmistakable that these tokens have been taken from a captured Frodo. The lieutenant taunts Gandalf and Aragorn that "now he shall endure the slow torment of years, as long and slow as our arts in the Great Tower can contrive, and never be released, unless maybe when he is changed and broken, so that he may come to you, and you shall see what you have done. This shall surely be—unless you accept my Lord's terms" (*RK* V, x, 167).

Frodo's safety and his sanity are hostage to their surrender. For the captains of the West to surrender to Sauron without a fight would be disastrous; their job is to preserve Middle-earth from his tyranny, and their moral code requires them to resist evil as long as they can. But it is morally wrong by any standard to knowingly condemn an innocent person to torture. And yet readers concur with Gandalf and Aragorn's choice not to accept Sauron's terms but to fight. Nobody closes the book at that point and says, "This is an immoral story." As readers, we know that Frodo is not a prisoner, and the display of the recovered items is a subterfuge and a trick. But Gandalf and Aragorn do not know that. Pippin, at least, is "crushed with horror" at Gandalf's rejection of Sauron's terms, so horrified that he looks forward to his own death, thinking to himself, "Well, well, now at any rate I understand poor Denethor a little better. We might die together, Merry and I, and since die we must, why not?" (*RK* V, x, 168). This insight by the most light-hearted of the hobbits, who, pages earlier, had thought Denethor out of his mind to take Faramir into death with him, is evidence of Tolkien's acceptance of the dark side of the human psyche.

But accepting one's own death and allowing another person to die are two different things. How moral is Gandalf's and Aragorn's abandonment of

Frodo? They take the tokens "in memory" of Frodo and accept the necessity of his sacrifice—one life for many. In modern terms, they crunch the numbers. This is a statistical calculation. But is this a moral choice? Does the end—saving Middle-earth—justify the means—sacrificing an innocent person? Is sacrifice even a moral issue? The whole idea of sacrifice is that it is practiced on the undeserving, whether it be a goat, a bull, or Isaac, son of Abraham. It is an idea which, if you accede to it, either negates or transcends morality.

This is not the only appearance of such situations. *The Lord of the Rings* has a number of instances in which "good" characters perform actions usually deemed immoral or unethical. As Bruce Charlton points out in his blog, Bruce Charlton's Notions, and as others have observed as well, Gandalf, Aragorn, and Frodo all mistreat Gollum in the service of a higher goal. Gandalf puts "the fear of fire" into Gollum in order to wring the true story out of him (*FR* I, ii, 66). Aragorn is "not gentle" in his similar handling of Gollum, tying him with a halter and "taming" him by starvation (*FR* II, ii, 266–67), and Frodo ties him with an elven rope that makes him scream with pain. Are these actions moral or immoral? As readers, we recognize that all three characters are acting in the service of a higher good—saving Middle-earth. But do we grant the same latitude to the librarian with the unique Arthurian fragment?

And how much latitude should we give Gollum, who so carefully guides and counsels Sam and Frodo on the first stage of their journey to Mordor, telling them where and when and how to hide and bringing Sam the makings of rabbit stew, all the while being patronized, abused, and insulted for his efforts. While it can be argued that Gollum does what he does in the service of his own "high" goal, recovering the Ring, we must also recognize that, as with the librarian, Tolkien would seem to have loaded the dice in favor of Sam. I say "would seem," because a closer look reveals that Tolkien has a deeper understanding of and sympathy for Gollum than first appears, not only giving him that moment with the sleeping Frodo but going so far as to have Sam wonder if Gollum sees himself as the hero of the story in which to Sam he is a villain. "Why, even Gollum might be good in a tale . . . I wonder if he thinks he's the hero or the villain? 'Gollum . . . Would you like to be the hero?'" (*TT* IV, viii, 322).

This apparently idle speculation by Sam shows the other side of Tolkien, and may well have been a spur for another twentieth-century writer, John Gardner, whose postmodern novel *Grendel* reverses the situation of *Beowulf* and makes its villain, Grendel, the hero and point of view character in his own tale. Is morality relative? Does it depend on who's talking? Does the magnitude of the situation determine the level of right and wrong? Tolkien appears—at least in his fiction—to be endorsing situation ethics, a code in which the exigencies of the situation can override accepted criteria of right and wrong and establish a more flexible standard.

I have spoken at some length about morality. But what about fantasy, the literary genre that led the critics astray to begin with? Here is where fantasy overtakes and even reshapes morality. In a fantasy, in an imaginary world, Tolkien seems to have felt free to interrogate or undermine principles that in ordinary life he undoubtedly would have upheld. His Catholic faith required him to abjure sin, to obey his conscience, to follow Christ and the Ten Commandments. It is a code of clearly defined right and wrong and has no room for situation ethics. But as we have seen, his secondary world of Middle-earth is filled with situations where right and wrong are often difficult to define and also often difficult to distinguish from one another. It was, apparently, fantasy that gave Tolkien in middle age the distance to write at length about the horrors of a war he had seen close up in his youth. The war poets of his own generation, like Wilfrid Owen and Siegfried Sassoon, had written explicitly and with grim realism about the war they had experienced. Not so Tolkien. Just as he needed the framework of an imaginary world before he could confront in writing a swamp filled with dead bodies, or a battlefield where soldiers are sprayed with liquid fire, or a world where counselors betray their leaders, so he may have found it easier to create an imaginary world where good and evil are confused, where situations arise in which right and wrong could be not just confused but even mistaken for one another, than to depict such confusion taking place in a real world.

It may be unsurprising in a fantasy world to have one character can say to another, as does Aragorn to Éomer, "good and ill have not changed since yesteryear, nor are they one thing among Elves and Dwarves and another among Men" (*TT* III, ii, 41), and, several chapters later, to have another say, as does Faramir to Frodo, "it seems less evil to counsel another man to break troth than to do so oneself (*TT* IV, vi, 301). It might be somewhat surprising to have both characters be right. But then to go on to have other character, Frodo, break troth in full awareness of the fact that it is wrong to do so, and have the reader approve of his action, bespeaks a psychological complexity closer to the world of Dostoyevsky than to that of fairy tale. The problem is that few critics look for Dostoyevskyan depth in a fantasy novel, and so they are not prepared to find it even when it is there. If the hero is only three feet tall and has furry feet, the story cannot have any kind of philosophical sophistication. The very fact that this is an invented world peopled by Elves and Dwarves and Hobbits has led the nay-sayers to pigeonhole the story as an unrealistic fairy tale. This has allowed them their simplistic, shallow, and stubbornly naïve categorization of this far from simple, philosophically profound, and sophisticated narrative.

To conclude, Tolkien's view of morality is more complex and his presentation of right and wrong in his fiction more nuanced and ambiguous than his critics have given him credit for. In the situations discussed above, it is clear that he acknowledges extenuating circumstances and understands the perplexity of difficult choices. Far from presenting "a simple confrontation . . . of the Forces of Evil with the Forces of Good" (Wilson 313), he goes out of his way to invent complex situations and ambiguous circumstances through which to explore the hidden recesses of human motivation and the power of immediate pressure to affect both public and personal distinctions between right and wrong.

PART THREE

"Arresting Strangeness"

Making It Different

> Fantasy, of course, starts out with an advantage: arresting strangeness.
> —J. R. R. Tolkien, "On Fairy-stories"

This section explores the practical but not uniformly successful ways in which Tolkien tried to create what he called the "arresting strangeness" of fantasy (*MC* 139), the element that gives fantasy the advantage over more realistic texts, that at the same time alienates and captures the attention of the reader. He called such an element a "green sun" (*MC* 140) and applauded its paradoxical ability to build a strange new world that readers could accept on its own terms.

Two essays deal with his ability to bestow, or perhaps reveal, arresting strangeness in the natural world. "The Forests and the Trees: Sal and Ian in Faërie" explores Tolkien's creation of a supernatural landscape of mountains and forests, rocks and rivers, without sacrificing their natural qualities or appearances. A related essay, "How Trees Behave—Or Do They?" focuses on the verisimilitude (or lack thereof) of Tolkien's presentation of trees, from the evocative mystery of Old Man Willow to the outright fantasy of Treebeard and the Ents to his over-the-top treatment of the Huorns.

Of the other two essays, one addresses the vexed question of overt Christianity in his major fiction, and one considers his use of pagan folklore. "Myth and Truth in Tolkien's Legendarium" draws on Tolkien's letters, the narrative of Númenor, and a late (c. 1959) dialogue debate, "Athrabeth Finrod Ah Andreth," contrasting narrative points of view between an elf and a human on mortality. This essay examines his views on and uses of Christianity and Christian reference in the construction of his mythology. "Fays, Corrigans, Elves, and More: Tolkien's Dark Ladies," written for this volume, examines the mysterious figure of the fay in Tolkien fiction, from the shadowy blue-robed Lady of the Forest in his earliest short fiction, *The Story of Kullervo*, to his Breton-derived *The Lay of Aotrou and Itroun* to his atypical Guinever in *The Fall of Arthur* to the elven queen Galadriel in *The Lord of the Rings*.

The Forests and the Trees

Sal and Ian in Faërie

Back in the 1970s, it was almost de rigueur for a book about (as opposed to by) Tolkien to display on its jacket a photograph of the professor standing by, sitting near, leaning against, or simply looking at a tree, preferably a venerable and gnarled one. Sometimes there was just the photograph of the tree, with Tolkien's invisible but implicit presence hovering just out of sight. It seemed clear that the photographer (or more probably the publisher) knew the tree image was iconic and would sell whatever was the book in question. And that was before *The Silmarillion*, before we knew about Telperion and Laurelin, about the forests of Neldoreth and Doriath and Taur-nu-Fuin and Nan Elmoth. We didn't really need them. *The Lord of the Rings* gave us more than enough trees on which to confer icon status. There was Bilbo's Party Tree, the mallorns of Lóthlorien, the trees planted by Sam after the Scouring of the Shire. There was Treebeard, the lovable old ent who befriends Merry and Pippin. But maybe it was just our romantic perception of Tolkien and trees. We seldom associated the jacket photos with the dark enchantment of the Old Forest and the malevolence of Old Man Willow, or with the mysterious Huorns, whose revenge on Saruman blurs the line between vegetable and human. Tolkien's trees, the most memorable ones, seem to be sentient beings, alive and aware in a world that is equally aware of them.

In Alan Garner's 2003 fantasy novel *Thursbitch*, Ian, a highly rational priest, and Sal, a deeply imaginative geologist, express opposing views of a stony outcrop on a ridge in rural Cheshire. "It knows we're here," Sal tells Ian. "And we are being watched" (Garner 40). In a later scene she adds, "Most geologists agree about sentient landscape" (87). What Sal means by *sentient landscape* is what Tolkien tried to create in his trees, beings with awareness and intent and memory. "Some places," Sal tells Ian, "have to be treated with respect" (87). Skeptical Ian disagrees, countering that, "what I accept as appearing to be a strong atmosphere is no more than the projection of our own experience and emotion onto a circumscribed place" (87). For Sal, the natural world is animate and aware of human beings. For Ian, those qualities are subjectively imposed on indifferent nature by human psychology.

I've chosen Ian and Sal to open this essay about J. R. R. Tolkien because although Garner's fantasy is different from Tolkien's, it is the mark of both authors' skill to use the dichotomy between subjective and objective reality exemplified by Sal's and Ian's perspectives to create the atmosphere of the invented world. Tolkien's imaginary Middle-earth is a landscape in which mountains, rocks, forests, even individual trees seem sentient, possessing awareness, memory, and intent. An early example can be found when the Fellowship is in Hollin, where Legolas says he can hear the stones mourn the passing of the Elves: *"deep they delved us, fair they wrought us, high they builded us; but they are gone" (FR* II, iii, 297). Not just inanimate chunks of rock, to him the stones have awareness and memory, and can feel loss. Hollin is a fairly rare instance (Lórien is another) where the relationship between nature and the peoples of Middle-earth (Elves, Dwarves, Hobbits) is presented as amicable; far more often, as we will see, it is shown to be hostile and antithetical. In either circumstance, Sal would understand completely. Ian would call it projection.

The word Tolkien used to encompass such sentient landscape was *Faërie*, from Old French *fée, fae* plus the agentive suffix *-erie*. It meant "enchantment"—both the act of enchanting (the casting of a spell) and the condition thus produced. Tolkien referred to it as a "realm," as if it were a territory or landscape but also an altered state of perception, a territory of the mind whose borders are those of the human imagination. In a word, fantasy. In the "Fantasy" section of his essay "On Fairy-stories," Tolkien concedes that such Faërie is difficult to make believable. An oft-quoted passage from that essay points out that while it takes little effort to say "the green sun" or even to imagine it, it takes a special skill to create a secondary world in which a green sun will be credible. His term for such credibility is "inner consistency." (*MC* 138), and the special skill to create it he names "elvish craft," "sub-creation," or at its most persuasive, "Faërian drama," about which more in a moment (*MC* 139–42).

That he chose forests as his chief locations of Faërie is in part because of their obvious nature as untamed in a landscape otherwise habitable by humanity. Forests are by their nature dark, often impenetrable, and, while not necessarily hostile to human beings, wild; they must be to some extent tamed in order for people to live in them. Moreover, as a scholar of Old and Middle English, Tolkien knew perfectly well that the Old English word for "mad," *wód* (Middle English *wode* or *wood*, denoting an altered state of consciousness), was also the word for a forest or woodland. He made good use of the connection, and I hope to follow his example. The forests and trees I will discuss as green suns and evaluate for their inner consistency are four in number—the Old Forest; its chief denizen, Old Man Willow; the mysterious Huorns of Fangorn Forest; and, at a slight tangent from the others, the birch tree in Tolkien's last short story, *Smith of Wootton Major*. I will examine Tolkien's elvish craft in investing each of these natural phenomena with consciousness and making the reader accept that imaginary consciousness as a real dynamic in his secondary world of Faërie. His craft improved as he learned to negotiate between objective reality and subjective experience—between Ian and Sal. Before I focus on forests and trees, I will set the stage for further discussion with two examples, contrasting sub-creation in *The Hobbit* with elvish skill in *The Lord of the Rings* to dramatically illustrate the steepness of Tolkien's learning curve.

Stone Giants and Cruel Caradhras

In *The Hobbit*, Bilbo and the dwarves are caught in a mountain storm initially described as a "thunder-battle" in which "storms come up from East and West and make war" and "lightning splinters on the peaks, and rocks shiver, and great crashes split the air and go rolling and tumbling into every cave and hollow" (*H* 55). So far, so good. Ian would approve. The storm, while compared to battle and war, is still within the realm of natural occurrence— wind, lightning, thunder. In the next paragraph, however, what started out as violent but realistic weather changes without notice into "stone giants" who are "hurling rocks at one another for a game, and catching them, and tossing them down into the darkness where they smashed among the trees" (*H* 55). The party can "hear the giants guffawing and shouting all over the mountain" (*H* 55). Thorin Oakenshield predicts that "if we don't get blown off, or drowned, or struck by lightning we shall be picked up by some giant and kicked sky-high for a football" (*H* 56–57). This is over the top, and even Sal would have to be skeptical. It is hard not to read stone giants and footballs as metaphors, rather than the reality we are told Bilbo and the dwarves experience, and the disconnect between the two violates Tolkien's own principle of inner consistency. It might do for the bedtime story *The Hobbit* originally was, but it is bad fantasy by the standards of Tolkien's essay, written after *The Hobbit* and therefore, we may presume, influenced by it. The stone giants lack inner consistency, and their ball game smacks more of a nursery game of "let's pretend" than serious sub-creation and elvish skill.

By the time Tolkien wrote his next mountain storm some years later, the one on Caradhras that drives the Fellowship off the mountain—tentatively dated by Christopher Tolkien to 1939 (*RS* 309)—his elvish craft had materially improved. There is the same situation—travelers caught by weather in the mountains. There are the same phenomena—shrill cries, wild howls on the wind, stones and boulders falling all around, hostile environment, plus snow. Yet, without ever saying so, Tolkien creates this storm not as stone giants but as the intentional activity of the mountain itself. While the party is stopped, the snow and wind die down, but as soon as they start forward again, the storm returns "with fresh fury. The wind whistled and the snow became a blinding blizzard" (*FR* II, iii, 302). The Company hears "eerie noises in the darkness" which may only be "a trick of the wind" but which have the sound of "shrill cries, and wild howls of laughter." Stones and boulders begin to fall all around them. "Let those call it the wind who will," says Boromir, "there are fell voices on the air; and these stones are aimed at us." Aragorn replies, "I do call it the wind . . . But that does not make what you say untrue" (302). In Tolkien's 1939 draft, these lines are given to Trotter and Gandalf, but their message is the same (*RS* 424).

The line between objective and subjective has been both drawn and crossed. Aragorn's double negative, "not untrue," suggests a positive. What Boromir hears can be both the wind *and* fell voices, the stones can fall and still have been aimed. Aragorn suggests a motive: there are "things in the world that have little love for those that go on two legs," and the world is divided not between man and nature but between two legs and no legs. When the Company's forward progress is stopped, and they are forced to spend a cold and snowy night on the mountain, Gimli's wry comment is that "Caradhras has not forgiven us. . . . He has more snow to fling at us, if we go on" (*FR* II, iii, 305).[1] Gimli is correct, for when the Fellowship gives up and retreats down the mountain, they have hardly passed the beaten track when "with a deep rumble there rolled down a fall of stones and slithering snow," and when the air clears they see that the path behind them is completely blocked. And with that last stroke, the narrator tells us, "the malice of the mountain seemed to be expended, as if Caradhras was satisfied" (307).

Sal would say the mountain was aware that the Fellowship was there, was watching them, and contrived the storm as a way to drive them back. Ian would point to Tolkien's qualifiers, *seemed* and *as if,* and argue that all we know about the storm is the projection of the Fellowship's "own experience and emotion." As readers, we can take our choice. But that there is a choice at all represents a substantial improvement over the disconnect between metaphor and actuality that was the case with the storm in *The Hobbit*. On Caradhras, there are no stone giants, no ballgame. There is just the mountain being internally consistent with itself, behaving like a mountain, yet creating in the Fellowship subjective responses that invite the reader to join them in perceiving intent behind the storm.

Faërian Drama

The question of intent brings up the term *Faërian Drama* from "On Fairy-stories," which I mentioned above and which Tolkien describes as

> those plays which according to abundant records the elves have often presented to men [and which] can produce Fantasy with a realism and immediacy beyond the compass of any human mechanism. As a result, their usual effect (upon a man) is to go beyond Secondary Belief. If you are present at a Faërian drama, you yourself are, or think that you are, bodily inside its Secondary World. The experience may be very similar to Dreaming, and has (it would seem) sometimes (by men) been confounded with it. But in Faërian drama you are in a dream that some other mind is weaving, and the knowledge of that alarming fact may slip from your grasp. To experience *directly* a Secondary World: the potion is too strong, and you give to it Primary Belief, however marvellous the events. (*MC* 142)

Since this describes the effect of Faërian Drama, but does not define it, efforts to interpret what the passage, or even the phrase, might mean are at best educated guesses. Here is mine, and it hinges on the altered state of mind created by fae-erie. Faërian Drama is intensification of this altered state to the point of what Tolkien calls "Primary Belief," acceptance as real of what is imagined. Faërian Drama enchants, it casts a spell; but it enchants to a degree more extreme than most imaginative experience and casts a spell more compelling than human imagination can produce on its own. It becomes direct experience so convincing that it seems to be really happening.

The key words are "a dream that some other mind is weaving." The phrase is provocative, inviting speculation as to what Tolkien really believed about Elves. Avoiding interpretation, I shall stick to explanation on a more mundane level. I take his words to describe a spell that transcends one's own conscious imagination to make the enchantment appear to interact purposefully with the observer. At the level of Faërian Drama, observers are so enchanted, so under the spell of the secondary world, that they accept the enchantment as reality. In these terms, it would not be unreasonable to imagine that Tolkien intended the mountain storm in *The Lord of the Rings* to be a sort of Faërian Drama in which the mountain itself cast a spell, that he intended the Fellowship to be caught in a dream that Caradhras was weaving. Sal would have no problem with this, but Ian would not allow it.

The Forest and the Willow

Now let's get on to forests and trees and see how Tolkien's enchantment gives these green suns inner consistency. The first occasion for this comes in the Old Forest. Merry Brandybuck describes the Old Forest as "very much more alive, more aware of what is going on, so to speak, than things are in the Shire" (*FR* I, vi, 121). "Aware" is the key word here. As a collective entity, the Old Forest is made to seem aware, sentient, responding to the hobbits' entry into its territory. The trees "do not like strangers," says Merry. "They watch you." He goes on: "They are usually content merely to watch you. . . . Occasionally the most unfriendly ones may drop a branch, or stick a root out. . . . But at night things can be most alarming, or so I am told. I have only once or twice been in here after dark, and then . . . I thought all the trees were whispering to each other, passing news and plots along in an unintelligible language; and the branches swayed and groped without any wind" (121). This sounds very much like Sal, yet we can recognise with Ian the subjectivity of Merry's description. His qualifiers, "so I am told," and "I thought," keep the description to hearsay or personal experience.

In her article "The Unique Representation of Trees in *The Lord of the Rings,*" Cynthia Cohen points out that the trees of the Old Forest never (with the exception of Old Man Willow) behave other than as trees (91–126). Yet their "tree" behavior—shifting paths, dropping limbs, snagging branches—is interpreted by the hobbits as hostility as they pick their way among the trees, getting "an uncomfortable feeling that they were being watched with disapproval, deepening to dislike and even enmity" (*FR* I, vi, 122). Pippin reacts to the forest, shouting, "Just let me pass through, will you!" (122). There is no echo or answer, but the wood *seems*—how often Tolkien uses that word!— to be more crowded and more watchful. Frodo tries a song to cheer them up, but it falls flat, and just as he gets to "*east or west all woods must fail,*" a large branch falls onto the path.

Now, as Cohen points out, and as Ian would agree, tree branches do fall from natural causes. What makes this particular falling branch ominous is the timing, as if in response to Frodo's threat. Merry reinforces this impression of intention by remarking, "They do not like all that about ending and failing" (*FR* I, vi, 123), as if the trees had ears and could take offense at what they heard. Is the forest sentient? Or is Merry projecting his own emotion? We are not told. To the hobbits, the Old Forest may *seem* ominous, fearsome, even hostile, but the narrator carefully stops short of ascribing intent. That will come later, after the threatening atmosphere of the Old Forest has prepared the way. A forest whose trees grow across paths, drop branches, and trip travelers with their roots is still just a forest, whatever anxiety the hobbits may project. Yet the apparent threat intensifies as the hobbits penetrate deeper into the forest. They find their progress unaccountably blocked by "deep folds in the ground," and "thick bushes" that block passage to the left, forcing them always to the right and downward. Lurking behind the apparent natural phenomena is the spectre of intent.

What "other mind" might be dreaming this drama? We do not learn until the hobbits have escaped his clutches that it might be Old Man Willow, whose "grey thirsty spirit drew power out of the earth and spread like fine root-threads in the ground, and invisible twig-fingers in the air, till it had under its dominion nearly all the trees of the Forest" (*FR* I, vii, 141). Even Ian would agree that a tree that tries to devour hobbits is more than an emotional projection, that it is acting/dreaming independent of hobbit experience. Old Man Willow's capture of Merry and Pippin is a combination of tree attributes (cracks in the trunk) and human behavior (entrapping the hobbits). It is both a Faërian Drama and a green sun, and might, if Tolkien were not so skillful, strain the inner consistency of reality. But Tolkien is skillful, and the inner consistency does not break: the Faërian Drama plays out, the green sun retains credibility. Here's how.

Overtaken by sleep in the Withywindle Valley, the hobbits give themselves up to the "spell"—and by *spell* I suggest that Tolkien means the enchantment of Faërian Drama. By this time, both the hobbits and the reader have accepted the spell of the forest, though neither is yet persuaded that it is a dream that some other mind—in this case, Old Man Willow's—is dreaming. Tolkien's elvish skill is evident in his gradual anthropomorphizing of the tree, from "a huge willow-tree with branches "*like* reaching arms with many long-fingered hands" (*FR* I, vi, 127; my emphasis) to Tom Bombadil's recognition of "Old Man Willow" and "Old grey willow-man!" who "should not be waking" (131), as if the somnolence of the tree is all that restrains it from action. Keeping his description in the realm of hobbit experience—heat, sun, buzzing flies, mid-afternoon sleepiness—rather than narrative fact, Tolkien gradually introduces enchantment, although at this stage, as with Caradhras, it is all conveyed from the perspective (Ian would say the projection) of those who are enchanted: that is to say, Frodo, Sam, Merry, and Pippin.

The hobbits *feel* hot; sleepiness *seems* to creep up their legs and fall upon their eyes; leaves flutter *on the edge of hearing;* they rustle *like* laughter; they *seem* to hiss in pain and anger; Merry and Pippin can *almost* hear words. Sam says, "I don't trust [this tree]. Hark at it singing about sleep now!" (*FR* I, vi, 128). But while Sam hears singing, the reader does not. Sam also hears a splash and the snick of a lock closing, more explicit sounds whose meaning is not immediately revealed. When Sam sees Frodo in the water, a great tree-root "seems" to be holding him under. This explains the splash, but not its agency. Frodo tells Sam that he *felt* the tree throw him in, but Sam advises him not to sit in such a precarious place if he *feels* sleepy. Two conflicting perceptions are in force here, and the reader is not yet told which to credit.

The stakes are raised when Sam and Frodo discover that Pippin has vanished within the tree and Merry is pinched in a tree crack. This explains the snick of the lock, a more ominous sound than the splash, and moves the tree away from the pathetic fallacy and toward Faërian Drama, from qualities projected onto the tree to its own full awareness and intent. With more truth than he realizes, Sam tells Frodo that he must have been "dreaming." So he was, but the dream was woven by "some other mind," as we are starting to learn. The first explicit transition from inactive plant to sentient creature, from "it" to "he," comes secondhand from Merry, who both speaks for and personifies the tree by saying, "He'll squeeze me in two.... He says so!" (*FR* I, vi, 129). But "he" does not speak and is yet unnamed. It is Tom, not Merry, who transforms the tree from a plant to a personality, and because Tom accepts him, the reader accepts him as well. Most important, Tom gives him a proper name. When Frodo tells Tom, "My friends are caught in the willow-tree" (referring to a plant), Tom replies with personification. "Old Man Willow?... I know the tune for him. Old grey Willow-man!" (131).

But what's in a name? "Old Man Willow" sounds like the sort of affectionate nickname that might be given to a local landmark, like the Old Man of the Mountain. "Old grey Willow-man," however, is something else, and even Ian would have trouble calling him a projection. The shift of language from Old Man to Willow-man and the addition of the hyphen create a hybrid who is both a tree and a man, a vegetable monster out of science fiction or horror. Tom's later description fits this paradigm: "Tom's words laid bare the hearts of trees and their thoughts, which were often dark and strange. . . . But none were more dangerous than the Great Willow: his heart was rotten but his strength was green; and he was cunning, and a master of winds, and his song and thought ran through the woods on both sides of the river" (*FR* I, vii, 141). And yet, if we are to take Tolkien at his word, such villainy is inconsistent with his view of trees.

"In all my works," wrote Tolkien in 1972, "I take the part of trees as against all their enemies" (*Letters* 419–20). Fine words, but the reality is somewhat different. Tolkien describes Old Man Willow from his enemies' (that is, the hobbits') point of view as dangerous, cunning, and rotten at the heart, the captor of the hobbits and the haunter of Pippin's and Merry's dream in the house of Tom Bombadil. Never does he explicitly take the part of the Old Forest against the hobbits. Granted, he does supply a rationale for its apparent hostility, both in the above description and in Merry's account of how the hobbits chopped down "hundreds" of trees and burned them to keep the Old Forest out of the Shire. Yet this stops short of taking the part of trees.

One of Tolkien's most unforgettable characters, Treebeard, does take the part of trees, and in doing so reflects his creator. However, his condemnation of the tree-cutting orcs, his characterization of Saruman as having a mind of "metal and wheels" (read "industrialization"), and his lament for "creatures I had known from nut and acorn," whose voices are "lost forever now" and for "wastes of stump and bramble where once there were singing groves" (*TT* III, iv, 77) is not so much elvish craft as polemic. This is rhetoric, not enchantment. Treebeard does not qualify as sentient nature in the same sense as Caradhras or the Old Forest. He is not landscape but rather a distinct species, like Hobbits. He is not a tree but an Ent.

Moving Towers of Shadow

Evidence for sentient nature in Fangorn is ambiguous and contradictory from the very first view we get of it. Sheltering under the eaves of the wood, Aragorn advises Legolas and Gimli that "it is perilous to touch the trees" and warns them to "cut no living wood" to make their campfire. Yet when the fire is blazing, Legolas observes that "[t]he tree is glad of the fire." The boughs appear to bend so as to come near the flames, while the brown leaves rub together like "cold cracked hands taking comfort in the warmth," though the narrative cautions that, "It may have been that the dancing shadows tricked their eyes" (*TT* III, ii, 44). Predictable words and phrases—"appear," "may have been," leaves "like . . . hands"—work to qualify this image, and we may suppose that Tolkien has inserted this vignette to create the impression of Fangorn Forest as a sentient phenomenon. How well it works is open to question.

Charming though this picture may be of a tree rubbing its hands and warming itself at the fire, the idea of something made of wood actually reaching out to fire is hard to believe, and sorts ill with Aragorn's advice about living wood. It strains inner consistency to the breaking point, especially in light of the subsequent death at Isengard of Beechbone, an ent destroyed by Saruman's "liquid fire." The most obvious candidates for sentient nature in this portion of the book would be the Huorns, the dark, mysterious denizens of the deepest parts of Fangorn Forest, creatures of indeterminate nature with an abiding hatred of Orcs. As Tolkien presents them, however, they, like the tree rubbing its hands at the fire, stretch sentient landscape to the very brink of the fantastic and over the edge. They tax secondary belief beyond its capacity, and it is clear that Tolkien struggled with what exactly they should be and how they would fit into his secondary world. An early draft has Merry remark, "I cannot make out whether they [Huorns] are trees that have become Entish, or Ents that have become tree-like, or both" (*WR* 56). The reader may well agree. Merry's remark echoes Treebeard's nonexplanation that "[s]ome of us are still true Ents, and lively enough in our fashion, but many are growing sleepy, going tree-ish, as you might say. Most of the trees are just trees, of course, but many are half awake. Some are quite wide awake, and a few are, well, ah, well getting *Entish*. That is going on all the time (*TT* III, iv, 71). The terms *tree-ish* and *Entish* are not precise,[2] and the place of hybrids along the *-ish* spectrum is never precisely located. Trying to make sense of this ambivalence, Paul Kocher posits a kind of asexual life cycle in which "some (not all) trees grow into enthood while some (not all) ents decline into treehood" (Kocher 71). Kocher defines the Huorns as a kind of mixed breed, "half-tree, half-ent" (112). None of this is much help to the reader trying to get a handle on how trees can march in a body and turn a hill into a forest overnight. Ents are a new species, and because Tolkien tells us they are, we believe him and accept them as such, but the Huorns are trees, and their untreelike behavior is more puzzling than mysterious, giving rise less to enchantment than to perplexity.

Avoiding explanation, Tolkien surrounds them with special effects. Legolas sees "[e]yes looking out from the shadows of the boughs" (*TT* III, viii, 154). The destruction of the orcs at Helm's Deep is accompanied by creeping darkness "blacker than night," "moving towers of shadow," and "whisperings and groanings and an endless rustling sigh." The earth shakes, the ground trembles, and in the morning the orcs and the trees are gone. Cynthia Cohen suggests that the Huorns are "imagined with particular care not to rupture 'the inner consistency of reality'" (116). Much as I admire her essay in all other respects, I must disagree here. Tolkien certainly worked hard to invest the Huorns with believability, but he succeeded only in part. If there is a spell here, it is as likely to bewilder as to enchant.

Malevolent mountains, hostile forests, even three-foot-high human beings have some counterparts in the phenomena of the real world. Trees that travel under their own steam do not, and here the secondary world that keeps the reader under its spell is broken. Like Caradhras and the Old Forest, the Huorns appear to have consciousness, memory, and intent, but unlike Caradhras, which conforms to mountain behavior, or the Old Forest, which conforms to the nature of woodlands, the Huorns' behavior does not conform to what should be their nature as trees. Nor does it fully convince as something more than trees. Huorns are not a separate species like Ents, yet they move and act beyond the capacity of trees. They violate Tolkien's own principle of the inner consistency of reality.

Cynthia Cohen's discussion of Tolkien's draft attempts to make the Huorns both treelike and ambulatory (they have split trunks, they have been trained by the Ents, they are half-entish) shows him considering and then discarding a variety of approaches (116–17). Finally, he seems to have given them all up as unworkable and simply left the Huorns unexplained. "I do not understand all that goes on," Treebeard tells Merry and Pippin, "so I cannot explain it to you" (*TT* III, iv, 71). This reverses the dynamic of Tom Bombadil and Old Man Willow. Because Tom accepts the Willow Man, the reader does also, but if Treebeard doesn't understand the Huorns, the reader has little hope of doing so. Yet if Treebeard doesn't understand the Huorns, who does? The spell is imperfectly cast, and the Faërian Drama fails to sustain secondary belief. For all his complaints about Shakespeare's handling of Birnam Wood—"I longed to devise a setting in which the trees might really march to war" (*Letters* 212)—Tolkien doesn't do much better.

In sum, Tolkien so far is scoring three to one. The Old Forest, Old Man Willow, and Treebeard are green suns whose inner consistency and careful integration into Tolkien's sub-created world allow the reader to accept them as sentient. The Huorns are one green sun too many.

"Go away and never return"

As puzzling in its own way as the Huorns is the least explicable tree in all of Tolkien's fiction, the birch in his short work *Smith of Wootton Major*. In its negative response to Smith's human incursion into Faery, the birch tree echoes the response of the Old Forest and Old Man Willow. In his refusal to explain the phenomenon, Tolkien gives his best example yet of Faërian Drama. Smith has a passport into the realm of enchantment, the magic star which came to him in the Great Cake at the Twenty-four Feast. With the star on his brow, Smith can wander freely in Faery and observe its mysteries. This does not mean that those mysteries are explained, just that he is permitted to see them up close. For the entirety of his excursions into Faery, Smith is in a Faërian Drama, a dream that some other mind is weaving. It is a sentient landscape, but Tolkien gives us no Caradhras or Old Man Willow to whom to ascribe the dream. Smith's experience is left to stand on its own as Tolkien's most uncompromising presentation of the power of the imagination. The severity of his vision is most manifest in the episode of the birch tree. Wandering in Faery, Smith inadvertently trespasses by setting foot on the lake of tears. It is not water, but some hard substance which, when he falls onto it, responds with a reverberant boom that awakens the wind. The wind in turn drives Smith back from the lake and whirls him onto the shore "like a dead leaf" (*SMW* 29). To save himself, Smith clings to a young birch tree which is first bent double by the blast and then stripped of its leaves.

The similarity here to the wind that spreads from Old Man Willow "outward to the branches of all the other trees roundabout" is difficult not to notice (*FR* I, vi, 129). When the wind dies down, the naked birch tree weeps, and the implication is that its tears are in response to the wind's ravages. Wanting to thank the birch, Smith "set his hand upon its white bark," asking what he can do "to make amends" for what his trespass has cost it. Without spoken words, he *feels* the reply of the tree "pass up from his hand." "Nothing," it tells him. "Go away! The wind is hunting you. You do not belong here. Go away and never return!" (*SWM* 30). What would Ian make of this? That it is projection? Sal would say the tree is sentient, watchful. This exchange is significant for what it reveals about Tolkien's negotiation of the line between the objective and subjective, between the human Smith and the nonhuman tree, and within the tree itself between animate and inanimate. The tree does not speak and Smith does not hear, yet emotion and opinion pass from the tree to Smith and his question is answered.

The closest episode to this in Tolkien's fiction, yet with a markedly different ethos, comes in *The Lord of the Rings* when Frodo, newly arrived in Lórien, lays his hand upon a tree: "[N]ever before had he been so suddenly and so keenly aware of the feel and texture of a tree's skin [not bark] and of the life within it. He felt a delight in wood and the touch of it, neither as forester not as carpenter; it was the delight of the living tree itself" (*FR* II, vi, 366).

In parallel passages from two different works, Tolkien has contrived a kind of telepathic communication between tree and human that crosses the line between observer and observed. Yet the transaction in each is altogether interior, confined to what the recipients—Smith and Frodo—feel, and is presented entirely from their human sensory point of view. Frodo feels delight, yet the delight is not his own: not delight *in* the tree but the delight *of* the tree itself, its own emotion communicated to him. Similarly, Smith feels the tears of the birch trickle down his face, and the taste is "bitter on his lips" (*SWM* 30). Like the feel of the tree under Frodo's hand, the sensation is explicit, yet the source of the bitter taste on Smith's lips is left uncertain. Is it the taste of the tears themselves, telling him (and us) us something about the tree? Or is it Smith's own bitterness at the news that he does not belong in Faery? Is this Sal's sentient landscape or Ian's projection of emotion?

Standing out from the rest of Smith's adventures in Faery both for its violence and its mystery, the birch-tree episode invites interpretation but provides no key. No explanation is ever given Smith for why the lake resounds at his touch or why the wind is hunting him, except the birch tree's warning that he does not belong there. But how does the tree know that? Does it represent something beyond itself?[3] Unlike Old Man Willow and the trees of the Old Forest, the birch has no expressed antipathy for things that "go free upon the earth." When it tells Smith he does not belong there, it is not speaking for itself but for its world of Faery. And what, exactly, is this particular Faery world as Tolkien understands it? For an answer, we must go to Tolkien's profession and academic life-work, philology.

Part of the Proto-Indo-European language theory as it was understood in Tolkien's time hinged on a small cluster of words—*salmon, beech, birch, turtle*—which were found to occur in some form in all I-E languages, regardless of whether these species themselves were native to the region. The conclusion was that these were among the oldest words, carried and passed along and down through migration, and their continuance might point back to their place of origin, the first homeland of Indo-European speakers. It is not unreasonable to conjecture that Tolkien, who had twice tried to write about time travel and the human desire to visit that other country which is the past,[4] might have wanted to locate his Faery in another time as well as another space; so that he sent his Smith, like Frodo in Lórien, wandering into a lost past, a "vanished world," "a timeless land that did not fade or change or fall into forgetfulness" (*FR* II, vi, 365–66). Coincidentally, it is in this passage in *The Lord of the Rings* that Frodo, like Smith, feels the emotion of the tree under his hand. If there is a message here, it may be a double one—first, that we cannot live wholly in the world of imagination, and second, that we cannot recover the past, a lost country that now exists only in the imagination. Living perforce in the present, we, like Smith, "do not belong" there.

Perhaps because of its ancient origin, the birch was a sacred tree for many native populations in the northern hemisphere, among them Siberian, Celtic, and Norse. Among the Finns, the birch was thought to have a tree spirit which dwelt within it.[5] The birch occurs in Scottish folk poetry, like the poem "The Wife of Usher's Well," where the birch grows at the gates of paradise and thus is a marker of the otherworld. Tolkien himself wrote two "birch" poems in Gothic for *Songs for the Philologists* when he was at Leeds in the early 1920s (see note 3). A personified weeping birch is featured in Runo 44 of *Kalevala*, the Finnish folk-epic that so impressed Tolkien when he first read it as a schoolboy at King Edward's School in Birmingham. The language of the verses is strikingly similar to Tolkien's description of the weeping birch in *Smith of Wootton Major*.

> And I weep my utter weakness,
> And my worthlessness lament for,
> * * * * *
> And the wind brought ills upon me,
> And the frost brought bitter sorrows;
> Tore the wind my green cloak from me,
> Frost my pretty dress from off me.
> Thus am I of all the poorest,
> And a most unhappy birch-tree,
> Standing stripped of all my clothing,
> As a naked trunk I stand here,
> And in cold I shake and tremble,
> And in frost I stand lamenting. (*The Kalevala*, tr. Kirby, Runo 44, ll. 149–58)

The wind tearing its green dress, the birch stripped to a naked trunk: these similarities notwithstanding, the two birch episodes are different in context and in resolution. The naked *Kalevala* birch-tree is "stripped of all [its] clothing" through the natural actions of wind and frost in a northern climate. Moreover, its plight is solved by Väinämöinen, the epic's "eternal singer," who uses its wood to make a *kantele*, a Finnish harp, with which, Orpheus-like, he enchants the land with his music.

Smith's birch-tree, in contrast, suffers explicitly because he has roused the wild wind, not a natural occurrence but a direct and supernatural response to his presence in Faery, and Tolkien gives the tree no savior, musical or otherwise. The wind is hunting Smith because he does not belong there. Enchantment has its dark side, as Tolkien clearly knew. Although the birch tree is not part of a forest and appears to be standing alone on the lake shore, it is hard not to equate this whole episode—Smith's encounter with the lake, the wind, and the birch tree—with the hobbits' encounter with Old Forest and Old Man Willow. Both conform to Tolkien's concept of a perilous realm—in *Smith*, it is explicitly called *Faery*—where pitfalls await unwary travelers, among whom, in addition to the hobbits, we must surely include Smith.

We must just as surely include Tolkien, who called *Smith of Wootton Major* a book "already weighted with the presage of bereavement" (*Letters* 389), a statement interpreted by Humphrey Carpenter as containing Tolkien's awareness "that he would soon have to surrender his own star, his imagination" (*Tolkien* 243). No longer in touch with Faërie, no longer the participant in Faërian Drama, Tolkien would have to awaken from the "dream that some other mind was weaving" and, like Smith, "come back to hammer and tongs" (*SWM* 52) and everyday life. It is not by accident that Smith's craft is that of blacksmith. In the ancient (that is, pre-Christian) world, the smith's power over fire and iron put him on a level with or just below the gods and gave him a special place in Western European mythologies. Smith's exchange of Faery for the tools of smithing has in it the echo of an old English folk belief that "cold iron" (that is, iron worked into tools and weapons) is anathema to fairies, who retreat from its touch.

The corollary historical notion is that the advent of the Iron Age was in Western Europe roughly coincident with the advent of Christianity and that both were factors in driving out (or underground) indigenous belief in the pagan supernatural: in fairies, elves, and the like. The poem "Farewell Rewards and Fairies," by seventeenth-century writer Richard Corbet (an influence on both Rudyard Kipling and Tolkien) summed up this idea, declaring, "now, alas, they all are dead; / Or gone beyond the seas." Kipling's response was to make Corbet's phrase "Rewards and Fairies" the title of his sequel to Puck of Pook's Hill, two volumes of short tales about England's storied mythic and early historical past (and a little noticed but clearly traceable influence on Tolkien). Tolkien's response was his "mythology for England" (which includes *The Lord of the Rings*), with its lingering image of Elves leaving Middle-earth and going westward to Valinor. This was, among other things, his way of accounting for the loss of enchantment in modern life because of the disappearance of elves and fairies from the British landscape and from British belief, surviving now only as folklore documented by collectors and published as either scholarly tomes or books for children.

If Smith's return to hammer and tongs signals his farewell to Faery, cold iron may be Tolkien's reluctant farewell to his own "rewards and fairies," to the powerful enchantment that he knew and did in part believe, and certainly wrote about as Faërian Drama. Tolkien's subsequent writings, as published by Christopher Tolkien in The History of Middle-earth (see particularly "Quendi and Eldar," the latter part of volume 11, *The War of the Jewels*, and the "Late Writings" section of volume 12, *The Peoples of Middle-earth*), are discursive, expository, and philosophical (as opposed to creative) in their effort to provide a rational framework for the essentially nonrational kind of story that is myth. While these writings are deeply interesting to scholars, they have little to give to lovers of his fantasy and his secondary world. Tolkien spent the last years of his life demythologizing his mythology, replacing its poetry with astronomy, theology, genetics, and linguistic and social customs. His later writing analyzes and explains a secondary world rather than creating one, leaving little room for enchantment. It seems clear that the deep-running mystical strain in his nature that was the wellspring for his imagination, the strain that gave him license to believe in fairies and ascribe sentience to trees (see note 5 on the tree-fairy), either faded or fell dormant. *Smith of Wootton Major* is his purest faërie tale and his strongest statement about Faërian Drama. It is also the last fairy story he ever wrote. It may be no accident that he conveyed his farewell in a Faërian Drama and through the agency of a tree.

How Trees Behave—Or Do They?

On 8 March 1939, J. R. R. Tolkien gave a lecture, "Fairy-stories," at the University of St. Andrews, Scotland. Some four years later, probably sometime in 1943, he revised his talk for publication in *Essays Presented to Charles Williams*, drafting new material to add to the original lecture and titling it "On Fairy-stories." Among the drafts was a lengthy discussion on the possibility that fairies (which he conflates with elves) are real beings. It includes the following passage, introduced by a phrase that comes up more then once in the essay, "If Fairies exist" (*TOFS* 254), a conditional followed by the implicative conjunction "then." In logic, this is called the "if-then" construction, a hypothesis followed by a deduction and its consequences. For Tolkien, the consequence in this case was that fairies "are a quite separate creation living in another mode." He went on to say, "They appear to us in human form (with hands, faces, voices and language similar to our own). . . . For lack of a better word they may be called spirits, *daemons* . . . subject to Moral Law, capable of good and evil, and possibly (in this fallen world) actually sometimes evil" (254–55). He then gave an example:

> Thus a tree-fairy (or dryad) is, or was, a minor spirit in the process of creation who aided . . . in the making effective of the divine Tree-idea or some part of it, or of even of some one particular example: some tree. He is therefore now bound by use and love to Trees (or a tree), immortal while the world (and trees) last—never to escape, until the End. It is a dreadful Doom . . . in exchange for a splendid power. What fate awaits him beyond the Confines of the World, we cannot know. It is likely that the Fairy does not know

himself. It is possible that nothing awaits him—outside the World and the Cycle of Story and of Time. (*TOFS* 254–55)

This is an arresting passage for several reasons. First, few people today believe in fairies, yet Tolkien writes as if he did. Starting in the conditional mode with "if," Tolkien moves almost immediately to the declarative, assuming the reality of what is for most people the stuff of myth and fable. Second, he picks a specific kind of fairy, a dryad, to illustrate his hypothesis. In Greek mythology, the dryad was a spirit in the form of a young maiden or woman. While Tolkien uses the Greek word to support the English phrase, his interest in folklore would almost certainly have made him aware of more Northern European examples, such as those mentioned by the anthropological folklorist Edward Burnet Tyler in *Primitive Culture:* "The peasant folklore of Europe still knows of willows that bleed and weep and speak when hewn, of the fairy maiden that sits within the fir-tree, of that old tree in Rugaard forest that must not be felled, for an elf dwells within, of that old tree on the Heinzenberg near Zell, which uttered its complaint when the woodman cut it down" (qtd. in Dorson, *British Folklorists* 194). Third, Tolkien's discussion appears in a scholarly essay, not a piece of imaginative fiction. Dryads were much beloved of Romantics such as Keats and Coleridge, and of romantic Edwardians such as Arthur Rackham, but they were rather out of fashion in the modern and postmodern criticism of Tolkien's twentieth century. Tolkien, psychologically and spiritually closer to Keats and Coleridge and Rackham, has in his fiction many kinds of fairies, which he called elves. He has Light Elves, Dark Elves, Grey Elves, High Elves, Deep Elves, Wood Elves, even Half-elves. Does he have any tree-fairies? Any dryads?

Given its faërian beauty, we might be tempted to start with Lórien, whose mallorn trees, with their silver bark, gold leaves, and white blossoms, seem obvious candidates, and whose presiding spirit Galadriel could easily pass for a dryad as the term is conventionally understood. But obvious is not always best, and a close look shows more differences from Tolkien's tree-fairy than similarities. Although the Lórien elves are called Galadhrim, "tree-people" or "tree-elves" (which comes close to "tree-fairy"), they do not really fit the type described in the essay. They live in trees, but residentially, in tree-houses, not as inhabiting spirits. The trees themselves, however beautiful, are inanimate in all senses of that word. They have neither awareness nor personality. They have no souls. Tolkien creates no spiritual connection between the elves and the trees. As for Galadriel, she has no special power over, nor any particular affinity with, trees. She reigns but she does not rule. Furthermore, she is female, and although this fits Greek paradigm, where the tree-fairy was a young woman, it doesn't fit Tolkien, who was going against type in making this traditional figure male, using the pronouns *he, him, himself*.

We may have better luck with his other forests—the Old Forest, Fangorn, the mysteriously appearing and disappearing Huorn-wood. Here the trees appear sentient, their inhabiting spirits are a part of their nature, and they are or seem to be male. Though they look more tree than fairy, Tolkien's actual tree-characters, Old Man Willow, and Treebeard, and the mysterious Huorns, fit his description far better than does Galadriel. Like his tree-fairy above, they are "subject to Moral Law, capable of good and evil, and possibly (in this fallen world) actually sometimes evil." They certainly qualify as "minor spirit[s] in the process of creation who aid . . . in the making effective of the divine Tree-idea or some part of it, or of even of some one particular example: some tree" (*TOFS* 255).

Granted, the relationship is not immediately obvious. Tolkien's characters are not sprites; they are actual trees, rooted in the soil of the Old Forest and Fangorn. They are covered in bark, not skin. They are not young and pretty but old and rugged. They do not look or act like spirits. Yet despite these obvious differences, I suggest that there is a reciprocal connection between the fiction and the essay, in which each influenced the creation of the other. Some chronology will clarify the relationship. The tree-fairy is conspicuously absent from the earliest draft of Tolkien's essay, Manuscript A. This was written in March 1939, when *The Lord of the Rings* was in its embryonic stages of conception and the tree-characters were only notes or outlines, if they appeared at all. In contrast, Manuscript B, where the passage appears, was written in 1943, four years later, when these characters were well developed.

Old Man Willow

I will begin with Old Man Willow, the earliest tree-character in the interior chronology of the story as well as in the exterior chronology of composition. His actual introduction into Tolkien's sub-created world came in a 1934 poem, "The Adventures of Tom Bombadil," in which Old Man Willow, already a predatory tree, captures Tom Bombadil and has to be told by Tom to go "back to sleep again." The poem was published as part of the 1962 collection, *The Adventures of Tom Bombadil*. But Old Man Willow can be said to have hit the big-time with Tolkien's early work on *The Lord of the Rings*. In a 1938 note on a draft of chapter 1, Tolkien talks about the hobbits getting "caught by Willowman" (*RS* 42–43), and in further notes has Willowman trap Bingo and Odo (112, 115), who are then rescued by Tom Bombadil (117).

Further notes mention the Willow but do not develop the scene we know from the finished text, where the hobbits are actually captured. A more developed treatment, also from 1938, appears in the second version of the Tom Bombadil chapter, which includes an early version of Tom's description of the Old Forest to the four hobbits.

> Amongst [Tom's] talk there was here and there much said of Old Man Willow, and Merry learned enough to content him . . . though not enough for him to understand how that grey thirsty earth-bound spirit had become imprisoned in the greatest Willow of the Forest. The tree did not die, though its heart went rotten, while the malice of the Old Man drew power out of earth and water, and spread like a net, like fine root-threads in the ground, and invisible twig-fingers in the air, till it had infected or subjugated nearly all the trees on both sides of the valley. (*RS* 120–21)

Here the Willow and the Old Man are not yet the indivisible being they will become as the character develops. Both Manuscript B and the 1938 draft of the chapter associate a tree and a spirit, a "non-incarnate mind" (*TOFS* 255). Both refer to that spirit as being bound to or imprisoned in a particular tree. The notion that the spirit is "subject to moral law" and "capable of good and evil" (*TOFS* 255) is reflected in "the malice of the Old Man" (*RS* 120–21), who apparently turns the Willow's heart rotten, making them both evil. The fact that Merry cannot understand the process by which the "thirsty earth-bound spirit" became "imprisoned" in the willow without any agency, including that of the tree, suggests that at that time Tolkien did not understand the process either. He had the idea but not the mechanism, and solved the problem later on by simply merging them into one entity, making Old Man Willow both tree and spirit.

This seems to have occurred in what Christopher Tolkien calls the "third phase" of revision for these opening chapters, which he conjecturally dates to mid- or late 1939—that is, after Tolkien's lecture and the draft Manuscript A he wrote for it. The published version includes this revision, and uses Tom's authority to add some significant sentences to his description. The revision reads as follows:

> Moving constantly in and out of [Tom's] talk was Old Man Willow, and Frodo learned now enough to content him. . . . Tom's words laid bare the hearts of trees and their thoughts, which were often dark and strange, and filled with a hatred of things that go free upon the earth. . . . none were more

dangerous than the Great Willow: his heart was rotten, but his strength was green, and . . . his song and his thought ran through the woods on both sides of the river. His grey thirsty spirit drew power out of the earth and spread like fine root-threads in the ground, and invisible twig-fingers in the air, till it had under its dominion nearly all the trees of the Forest. (*FR* I, vi, 141)

No longer is the Old Man "imprisoned" in the Willow; their characteristics are now melded. It is the tree itself that has the "grey thirsty spirit," the tree whose roots and twigs draw "power out of earth" and air. Tree and tree-fairy are one entity. At first glance, the willow is only a tree, albeit an impressive one. "Enormous it looked, its sprawling branches going up like reaching arms with many long-fingered hands, its knotted and twisted trunk gaping in wide fissures that creaked faintly as the boughs moved" (*FR* I, vi, 127). The hobbits see "the grey and yellow leaves, moving softly against the light, and singing" (128).

Consonant with Old Man Willow's tree-appearance, the "singing" leaves could be read as metaphor. But Tolkien's choice of *singing* over the more conventional *rustling* for the leaves has an anthropomorphizing—or dryadmorphizing—effect. Tolkien is animating nature by subtly cranking up the level of consciousness in a natural phenomenon, as he does later with Caradhras, not taking it far beyond probability but implying intent in what is usually seen as natural activity. Old Man Willow retains what Tolkien deemed essential for successful fantasy, the "inner consistency of reality" (*MC* 138, 139): the necessity of any particular element to conform to the norms of the secondary world. He is a logical extension of the Old Forest, making actual what the hobbits think they perceive in the trees. His subsequent actions in engulfing Pippin, entrapping Merry, and trying to drown Frodo are malevolent, the dark side of the tree-fairy. Moreover, the reaction of Old Man Willow to Sam and Frodo's attempts to set him on fire—"a tremor" that runs through the whole tree, leaves that seem "to hiss . . . with a sound of pain and anger," and branches that sway violently (129)—recalls Tyler's "willows that bleed and weep and speak when hewn" (qtd. in Dorson, *British Folklorists* 194).

In addition, the trees of the Old Forest, though they never exceed the observed characteristics of trees—dropping branches, sticking up roots—seem to react to the hobbits' presence, giving an impression of motivation and intent that is enhanced by the ominous crowding that herds the hobbits "eastward and southward into the heart of the forest," which is "not at all the direction they wished to take" (*FR* I, vi, 125). They finally arrive where they do not want to go, the Withywindle valley, which is, according to Merry, "the queerest part of the whole wood—the centre from which all the queerness comes, as it were" (*FR* I, vi, 124). Here Frodo sees "leaning over him a huge willow-tree, old and hoary." The implication is that the willow has maneuvered their arrival, and it is not hard to imagine that it has planned the capture (and possible death) of the hobbits. Tom's words about the thoughts of trees, that they are "filled with a hatred of things that go free upon the earth" would be sufficient motive. It is worth noting that in Manuscript B Tolkien never said the fairy was nice, just that he was bound to his tree and responsible for it. In fact, he deliberately raised the possibility that such a being could be evil.

Treebeard

The same progression seen in Old Man Willow—from embryonic concept to fully realized creature blending the natural with the supernatural—also distinguishes my next tree-fairy candidate, Treebeard. In 1956, Tolkien wrote to "Mr. Thompson," "I have no recollection of inventing Ents. I came at last to the point, and wrote the Treebeard chapter without any recollection of previous thought: just as it now is" (*Letters* 231). The creative process was not quite as simple as Tolkien remembered it. Treebeard was a late addition to the story, in what Christopher Tolkien calls the "third phase" of *The Fellowship* in 1939, appearing initially as the "Giant Treebeard" (and thus not a tree at all), who was at first on the side of Sauron and imprisoned Gandalf in Fangorn. An early draft describes him as having a "thick gnarled leg with a rootlike foot," which Frodo at first mistakes for "the stem of a monstrous oaktree" (*RS* 384). Although the tree association is present in embryo with the comparison to a monstrous oak tree, Treebeard was still a giant (*TI* 6). In a subsequent note, Tolkien jotted, "If Treebeard comes in at all—let him be kindly and rather good? About 50 feet high with barky skin. Hair and beard rather like *twigs*. Clothed in dark green like a mail of short shining leaves" (*RS* 410). The "mail of short shining leaves" evokes the folklore figure of the Green Man or Jack in the Green, a vegetation spirit celebrated in fertility rituals, and the twiggy hair and beard recall the foliate heads of medieval sculpture. He is on his way to becoming a tree.

Treebeard is called an "Ent" for the first time in about 1940 (*TI* 250). But since *ent* is an Anglo-Saxon word meaning "giant," his essential character may not yet have changed much. By 1944 (i.e., just prior to the 1945 Manuscript B with the tree-fairy passage), he was as we know him from the published text, a walking talking guardian of trees, in function the closest thing to Tolkien's idea of a tree-fairy without being called one that you can get. Treebeard's looks now seem consciously designed to merge fairy into tree. Described as "Man-like, almost Troll-like" (*TT* III, iv, 66), a reminder of the giant he once was, Treebeard is still far more tree than man or troll, being a "figure, at least fourteen foot high ... with a tall head and hardly any neck.... clad in stuff like green and grey bark," his lower face "covered with a sweeping grey beard, bushy, almost twiggy at the roots, thin and mossy at the ends," and having "large, knob-knuckled" hands. His "large feet," no longer "rootlike," have "seven toes each" (*TT* III, iv, 66). And unlike man or troll, he is certainly, like the tree-fairy, "bound by use and love to trees." While Old Man Willow fits Tolkien's idea of the tree-fairy as an entity with the potential for evil, Treebeard, in his position as shepherd of trees, better fits the tree-fairy's more benevolent role as "'agent' in the making effective of the Tree-idea or some part of it" (*TOFS* 154). As the old ent tells Merry and Pippin, "we do what we can. We keep off strangers and the foolhardy; and we train and we teach, we walk and we weed" (*TT* III, iv, 71).

Treebeard, of course, is a much more fully developed character than Old Man Willow. He has a voice, not mere singing leaves; he has a personality, not just an aura of evil; he has opinions, not just tendencies. Moreover—and this will become more important as the story develops—he wants only to watch and guard, not to dominate, as Old Man Willow, with his grey thirsty roots, quite clearly does. Treebeard has a memory, which gives him a temporal space within the history of Middle-earth, and he has a sense of his own identity and place in the natural scheme of things. He is Tolkien's first fully conscious and self-aware creation from the natural world. Probably Old Man Willow, rooted at the center of the Old Forest and staying closer to the demeanor and appearance of a real tree, is the more realistic sub-creation. But Treebeard, because he demands greater suspension of disbelief—trees do not have hands and feet, and cannot talk or walk, with a gait like "wading herons" (154)—Treebeard, a tree yet not a tree, is paradoxically the more believable one.

The Huorns

Yet without Treebeard and Fangorn Forest we would not have the Huorns, whose dark destructiveness actually seems closer to Old Man Willow than to Treebeard. The Huorns are problematic not only because they seem less like tree-fairies than my other two examples—they are not individuals but a collective, and have no discernible personality—but also because their appearance in the story seems less defined than that of the other two. At first glance, they are just a kind of surreal picture of nature on the rampage. Old

Man Willow is a tree. Treebeard is an Ent. But what exactly is a Huorn? Is there even such a thing as a Huorn (singular), or are they simply an aggregate, a moving mass? They are anticipated in early draft notes by a reference to "Treebeard and his Three Giants" (*TI* 210), suggesting that Treebeard (still a giant at this point) has followers, related beings whom he can summon at need. In the story as published, however, they are neither giants nor Ents (though the latter is debatable, as we will see), and they certainly don't behave like trees. Unlike the trees of the Old Forest, they exceed what trees are known to do, and unlike Old Man Willow, they are not rooted but can move at will and attack in a mysterious way that is never defined. In spite of this, I want to make the case that they are variations of the tree-fairy, neither good (like Treebeard) nor evil (like Old Man Willow), but dark, violent, and revengeful (with good reason), with a past history hinted at but never revealed.

The Huorns first appear in drafts dated by Christopher Tolkien to the winter of 1941–42 (*TI* 379). There is little or no description of them, and they appear only in notes for the Battle of Isengard. At this early stage, they are called first Galbedirs, then Lamorni, then Orónomar/Oroními, all of which have the same meaning, "Talking Trees" (*WR* 47, 50), and are described by Merry as "trees [the Ents] have trained and made half-entish" (*WR* 50). A later draft has him add "though far wilder, of course, and crueller" (*WR* 55). It is here that the word *huorn* first enters the text, along with Merry's uncertainty about their nature. "I cannot make out whether they are trees that have become Entish, or Ents that have become tree-like, or both" (*WR* 56). This is close to the published text, where Merry says, "I think they are Ents that have become almost like trees, at least to look at." He then goes on,

> They stand here and there in the wood or under its eaves, silent, watching endlessly over the trees, but deep in the darkest dales there are hundreds and hundreds of them, I believe. . . . [I]t is difficult to see them moving. But they do. You stand still looking at the weather, maybe, or listening to the rustling of the wind, and then suddenly you find that you are in the middle of a wood with great groping trees all around you. They still have voices, and can speak with the Ents—that is why they are called Huorns, Treebeard says—but they have become queer and wild. Dangerous. I should be terrified of meeting them, if there were no true Ents about to look after them. (*TT* III, ix, 170)

Merry's suggestion that Huorns are Ents that have become "almost like trees" implies a regression from personality to type, from a higher level of consciousness to more instinctive behavior. It would explain their mobility, since Ents are mobile and can move fast. But it raises a mechanical problem, for where Ents have feet to travel on, Huorns have roots, which by their nature are anchors to place. What Merry tells us is opinion based on observation, not fact. Maybe Merry is an unreliable narrator.

Knowing Tolkien's predilection for languages, we might expect some etymology at work, even though these names were abandoned. Tolkien's commentary on his languages, *Words, Phrases and Passages in Various Tongues in* The Lord of the Rings (originally appearing as issue 17 of the journal *Parma Eldalamberon*), glosses *huorn* with a question mark as "tree," which is not much help, and offers *ho* "spirit, shadow," which is not bad, but also *hu* "hound," which is no help at all (*WPP* 86, 198). *Orne* is easy; it's a Sindarin word meaning "(tall) tree" (*WPP* 204). The *hu* element is harder to identify if you don't like "shadow" or hound." In light of the earlier names (Galbedir, Lamorni, etc.), Treebeard's explanation that they are called Huorns because they have voices seems reasonable. All well and good, except that the Huorns do not speak. Maybe Treebeard is an unreliable linguist.[1]

But if, as I want to suggest, the Huorns are a kind of Tolkienian tree-fairy, how do they "make effective the tree-idea"? Through a masterful use of authorial legerdemain. Tolkien's staging of the Huorns is one of the slickest tricks in his sub-creative bag, for they are never clearly defined or explained, as are Old Man Willow and Treebeard. Now you don't see them; now you do. Tolkien builds up an impression largely through other characters' reactions to them, starting with Legolas's intuition before ever the Huorns enter the story by name. When the Three Hunters first come to the eaves of Fangorn, Legolas says, "I catch only the faintest echoes of dark places where the hearts of the trees are black" (*TT* III, v, 94). There is something mysterious about Fangorn Forest, and it is not just the imposing but surprisingly friendly Treebeard, whom the hobbits first encounter. Tolkien intensifies the mystery later with phrases such as "strange trees," "darkness blacker than night," "moving towers of shadow," and "whisperings and groanings and an endless rustling sigh" that shake the earth (*TT* III, viii, 158), describing not the Huorns themselves, but the impression they make on observers.

Treebeard echoes Legolas when he tells Merry and Pippin rather obscurely, "*Taurelilómëa-tumbalemorna Tumbaletaurëa Lómëanor*," which Appendix F under "Ents" translates as "Forestmanyshadowed-deepvalley-black Deepvalleyforested Gloomyland," which according to the appendix means, "more or less: 'there is a black shadow in the deep dales of the forest'" (*RK*, App. F 408). Just what this refers to is uncertain. It seems akin to Legolas's description, and even closer to Treebeard's account of Fangorn as having "trees that are bad right through.... some very dangerous parts.... some very black patches.'" When Merry then asks, "Like the Old Forest away to the north, do you mean?" Treebeard replies, "[A]ye, something like that, but much worse. I do not doubt there is some shadow of the Great Darkness lying there still away north; and bad memories are handed down. But there are hollow dales in this land where the Darkness has never been lifted, and the trees are older than I am" (*TT* III, iv, 70–71).

Are these supposed to be Huorns? We are never told. And then Treebeard himself tells Merry and Pippin, "I do not understand all that goes on, so I cannot explain it to you" (71). If Treebeard, the character who might be expected to know the most about the Huorns, cannot explain "all that goes on," who can?

Apparently not Tolkien, who doesn't even try. In good creative writing fashion, he practices "show" rather than "tell." This is how the Huorns first appear to Théoden and his Company after Helm's Deep: "The land had changed. Where before the green dale had lain, its grassy slopes lapping the ever-mounting hills, there now a forest loomed. Great trees, bare and silent, stood, rank on rank, with tangled bough and hoary head; their twisted roots were buried in the long green grass" (*TT* III, vii, 146).

These newly present trees, having appeared overnight, look like a forest that has stood for many years. In that respect they are trees, and there are references in the drafts to the "Huorn-wood" (*WR* 39, 70). But in their unexplained mobility and ability to move with the speed of wind, they are not trees. They were not at Helm's Deep the day before. They have not grown overnight but have arrived from somewhere else. Where? Those "hollow dales where the Darkness has never been lifted"? We are not told. Leaving Helm's Deep, Gandalf and his companions come to a wood—the same wood? Presumably so, although again we are not told—where the trees "are grey and menacing, and a shadow or mist was about them. The ends of their long sweeping boughs hung down like searching fingers, their roots stood up from the ground like the limbs of strange monsters, and dark caverns opened between them." The company hears "the creaking and groaning of boughs, and far cries, and a rumour of wordless voices murmuring angrily" (*TT* III, vii, 151). The "wordless voices murmuring" implies sound, but stops short of speech. It harks back to the singing of Old Man Willow. The Huorns can vocalize but they cannot talk. They have voices but no words, no language.

So if they're not trees and they're not Ents, what exactly are the Huorns? Gandalf calls them "a thing beyond the counsels of the wise" (*TT* III, viii, 149). They may have been beyond the counsel of Tolkien, which may be why he gives Merry and not the narrator the only explanation of them that we get. The fact is, Tolkien never clearly tells his readers what the Huorns are; he just shows us what they do and tells us why (though not how) they do it, leaving us to fill in this partial outline by connecting the hints that he has given us. Although we cannot truly comprehend them, we can visualize them. Their "tangled boughs," "hoary heads," and "twisted roots" seem straight out of an Arthur Rackham illustration, and indeed Rackham, the premier illustrator of Tolkien's boyhood, may have been one inspiration for their depiction. Nonetheless, the result of Tolkien's reticence is that the Huorns are the most mysterious, most provocative because least explicit, most purely mythological of all the phenomena of his sub-created world. They are tree-fairies as defined by their actions, aiding in the process of creation by making effective (against the Orcs) the divine Tree-idea. How they do it remains their secret.

Smith's tree

A postscript and exception to this discussion is Tolkien's most traditionally dryad-like tree, this one outside the realm of Middle-earth but firmly within the realm of Faërie. This is the "young birch" that shelters Smith of Wootton Major from the wild wind that harries him when he steps on the lake of tears. Of all Tolkien's trees, the birch seems most in line with the conventional image of the dryad. Unlike Old Man Willow and Treebeard (and by implication the Huorns), the birch not only is not male, it has no gender, being referred to consistently with the neuter pronoun *it*. Yet taxonomically the birch produces both flower and fruit; this, coupled with its slender trunk and fluttering, dancing leaves, makes it seem quintessentially, almost stereotypically, female. Moreover, its flexibility—it is "bent down to the ground" by the wind—its white skin, and its vulnerability—it is naked, "stripped of every leaf," and its tears fall like rain—give it a distinctly feminine quality very much in keeping with classical depictions of dryads. Having been created in the years 1964–67, Smith's birch cannot have contributed to Tolkien's 1943 concept of the Tree-fairy, but (gender excepted) may still have derived from it. It is certainly Tolkien's most fairy-like tree, making effective for the reader the "divine Tree-idea," and could easily have been the inspiration for a Rackham illustration. One wishes it had been.

Conclusion

With the possible exception of the birch, it's pretty clear that when Tolkien says "tree-fairy" he is not thinking of a pretty girl in a filmy tunic. He is thinking of something rough and rugged that conveys the height and weight and breadth and durability of a tree, that captures the essence of a tree, that gives a tree its soul. In this respect, the tree-fairy of Manuscript B and the tree-characters of *The Lord of the Rings* are members of the same body of lore, reciprocally connected in time as well as in spirit. A time line of their appearance in his writing will show the relationship.

> 1938. First mention of "Willowman," "Willow of the Forest," "the Old Man."
> March 1939. Manuscript A. No tree-fairy.
> Mid-1939. Old Man Willow fully developed.
> 1940. Treebeard changed from giant to Ent.
> 1941–42. First appearance of Huorns.
> 1943. Manuscript B with tree-fairy passage.
> 1944. Treebeard fully developed.

What I deduce from this is that the idea grew over time, that it was a "tale that grew in the telling," to borrow a phrase. It was Tolkien's creation of and engagement with his fictional tree-characters that led him to the explicit tree-fairy of Manuscript B, and the concept of the tree-fairy as described in Manuscript B that personalized and animated those characters. Neither, I suggest, could have occurred without the other. When we read Old Man Willow and Treebeard and the Huorns as variations on Tolkien's idea of the tree-fairy, we are reaching back to a longer and more profound mythological history than his present Middle-earth. When we understand the term *tree-fairy* in light of Old Man Willow or Treebeard or the Huorns—or even Smith's birch—the phrase, and indeed the whole passage in Manuscript B, take on a gravity and seriousness that the word *dryad* does not suggest and even the compound *tree-fairy* does not by itself invite.

I suggest that this gravity, this seriousness, is what Tolkien felt when he was writing, and what he intended his readers to understand in both his fiction and his scholarship. The two genres are interlocking and interdependent, like the dryad and his tree, and both derive from, as Tolkien said of *Beowulf*, "a past with a deeper and darker past" behind it. What Tolkien was trying to convey was something both supernatural and spiritual that he felt was important for the world to know. His tree-fairy and his tree-characters are archaic yet tenacious, ancient yet curiously vital manifestations of a mythic world of sentient nature. This is a world that is, as he said in his *Beowulf* essay, "alive at once and in all its parts," a world aware of itself and us, not only watching us but interacting with us and affecting us, if we only knew it.

Tolkien knew it.

Myth and Truth in Tolkien's Legendarium

"Of course there . . . is all the Arthurian world, but. . . . it is involved in, and explicitly contains the Christian religion. . . . [T]hat seems to me fatal. Myth and fairy-story must, as all art, reflect and contain in solution elements of moral and religious truth . . . but not explicit, not in the known form of the primary "real" world.
—J. R. R. Tolkien, letter to Milton Waldman, *The Letters of J. R. R. Tolkien*

All myths are true for the people whose myths they are. This does not mean that all myths are factual, but that they express some deeply held belief or world-view that gives meaning to their culture. Thus Beowulf may never have existed, but the northern imagination recognized the truth that a young hero could triumph over Grendel, and an old hero must lose to the dragon. Both Beowulf's victory and his defeat speak to the truth that we all fight and we all die. Oedipus may or may not have lived, but the truth that man cannot outrun his fears was essential to the Greek worldview, and is equally relevant to our own. Yet while these two truths are similar, they are also different, each specific to its own culture. Gandhi declared that absolute truth is a diamond whose multiple facets can never all be seen at once, but all of which reveal partial truths. The stories of Beowulf and Oedipus are facets—different stories illustrating culturally differing values—of a larger truth about the human condition.

What has this to do with Tolkien, a twentieth-century Englishman who wrote a fictional "mythology for England" to express what he felt were some deeply held truths and beliefs about his culture? How "true" is his mythology? On 14 October 1958, just two years after the publication of *The Lord of the Rings*, he wrote to Rhona Beare that "it must be remembered that mythically these tales are Elf-centred, not anthropocentric" (*Letters* 285). As a commentary on the stories that introduced Hobbits (a subspecies of humanity) to the reading public, this is a statement worth noting. And in the same letter to Milton Waldman quoted above, in which Tolkien offered his legendarium as a better mythology for England than the "Arthurian world" with its overt Christianity, Tolkien wrote that "[a]s the high Legends of the beginning are supposed to look at things through Elvish minds, so the middle tale of the Hobbit takes a virtually human point of view—and the last tale blends them" (*Letters* 145).

"Elf-centered," "Elvish minds," "human point of view," the last tale (*The Lord of the Rings*) as a blend of elvish and human: these phrases mean that the various stories of Tolkien's legendarium are facets shaped by point of view, with each facet—elvish, human, and blended—presenting a different angle of vision. But it also means that they are all "true" in terms of those whose myths they are. This has major implications for any interpretation of Tolkien's work. It means that nothing in the legendarium should be taken as absolute. It means that all his narrators, interrogators, translators, scribes, compilers, redactors—Lindo, Rúmil, Eriol/Ælfwine, Pengoloð, Heorrenda, Findagil the Scribe and Daeron the Minstrel, Bilbo with his "memoirs," and Frodo and Sam as their continuators—are each putting their individual spin on the story. The repeated iterations throughout all his mythological texts of phrases such as "it is said," "some say," and "it is told that"—or even, as in the story of Aredhel and Eöl, "it is not said," or, in *The Hobbit*, "Gandalf! If you had heard only a quarter of what I have heard about him"—are evidence not just of the origin of the stories in oral tradition but also of the idea that none has preeminent authority.

Tolkien's many versions of the title page of the Red Book of Westmarch further demonstrate his concern for perspective. Here are samples.

Memoirs of an Amateur Burglar
My Unexpected Journey
There and Back Again and What Happened After
Adventures of Five Hobbits
The Case of the Great Ring (compiled from the records and notes of B. Baggins and others)
What the Bagginses Did in the War of the Ring
The Downfall of The Lord of the Rings and The Return of the King
(as seen by B. and F. Baggins, S. Gamgee, M. Brandybuck, P. Took, supplemented by information provided by the Wise.) (*SD* 111)

Tolkien knew that myths are made by ordinary human beings, not by the heroes and gods and monsters those myths picture, and he clearly wanted *The Lord of the Rings* to convey a hobbit point of view.

In this respect, Christopher Tolkien's 1977 *The Silmarillion*, which dismantled the narrative framework his father had so carefully erected around his stories and thus removed point of view, was unfaithful to J. R. R. Tolkien's design, and led to misconceptions about Tolkien's work that still operate to this day. *The Silmarillion*'s unequivocal opening statement, "There was Eru," established the very absolutism that, as his letters show, Tolkien had gone to great lengths to destabilize. It is to Christopher's credit that he recognized this, acknowledged it, and set about to rectify the error by reinstalling the frame, thus giving us the invaluable resource that is The History of Middle-earth. Here we can see Tolkien not just creating a mythology for England but trying out a variety of frames, narrators, and narrative devices to effect its transition from oral tale to printed book.

In addition, there is textual evidence for point of view as a consciously imposed narrative element. I will offer two examples, one straightforward and one problematic. The straightforward example is the historically and culturally oriented presentation of the destruction of Númenor in three separate versions dating from 1936 onward. The problematic example is the "Athrabeth Finrod ah Andreth," the debate about death between Finrod, an elf, and Andreth, a human, written in the years between 1955 and 1959 and published as part of *Morgoth's Ring*.

Let us begin with Númenor. A note on an envelope containing texts of "The Drowning of Anadûnê" states that it "[c]ontains very old version (in Adunaic) which is good—in so far as it is just as much different (in inclusion and omission and emphasis) as would be probable in the supposed case:

(a) Mannish tradition
(b) Elvish tradition
(c) Mixed Dúnedanic tradition" (*SD* 406).

The subject of this note is the late (probably circa 1936) entry into Tolkien's mythology of the island of Númenor, which apparently is there chiefly so that it can precipitate the tidal wave that is part of the remaking of Arda. The careful notation of differences in "the supposed case" of "inclusion and omission and emphasis" is evidence that Tolkien intended the story to differ as it is told in the mannish tradition, the elvish tradition, or the mixed Dúnedanic tradition. Three versions of the story exist, and all were written around the time when he was also engaged in writing the "last tale," *The Lord of the Rings*, which blended the elvish and human points of view. The versions are 1) "The Fall of Númenor," written in connection with "The Lost Road" (1936); 2) the later "Akallabêth," which was published as part of *The Silmarillion* (1977); and 3) "The Drowning of Anadûnê," which forms an addendum to *The Notion Club Papers*, composed in early 1944 (although not published until 1992). As a further complication, Tolkien had one of the characters in *The Notion Club Papers*, Edwin Lowdham, make a copy in Old English of a presumed earlier version of the story; which versions were included in the text as Alwyn Lowdham's transcription in Avallonian (elvish) and Adûnaic (mannish), and in Christopher Tolkien's notes.

It is not my purpose here to tease out which of the versions may have been intended to derive from which tradition. Nor do I intend to dissect the extremely complicated history of Tolkien's writing and re-writing of the incident; his habit of repeated revision of competing texts makes it challenging to establish a chronology of composition in real-world time. To the extent that either is possible, it has already been addressed, the first by Christopher Tolkien in The History of Middle-earth, the second by Douglas Kane in his *Arda Reconstructed*. It is sufficient to note Christopher Tolkien's words on the subject in his commentary on "The Drowning of Anadûnê."

> It seems to me likely that by "Elvish tradition" he [Tolkien] meant The Fall of Númenor; and since "Mixed Dúnedanic tradition" presumably means a mixture of Elvish and Númenorean tradition, he was in this surely referring to the Akallabêth, in which both The Fall of Númenor and The Drowning of Anadûnê were used (see pp. 376, 395-96). I conclude, therefore, that the marked differences in the preliminary sketches reflect my father's shifting ideas of what the "Mannish tradition" might be, and how to present it; he was sketching rapidly possible modes in which the memory, and the forgetfulness, of Men in Middle-earth, descendants of the Exiles of Númenor, might have transformed their early history. (*SD* 406–7)

A note dated by Christopher to "1958 or later" seems to confirm this. Here Tolkien wrote:

> It is now clear to me that in any case the Mythology must actually be a "Mannish" affair.... The High Eldar living and being tutored by the demiurgic beings must have known, or at least their writers and loremasters must have known, the "truth" (according to their measure of understanding). What we have in the Silmarillion etc. are traditions... handed on by Men in Númenor and later

in Middle-earth (Arnor and Gondor); but already far back . . . blended and confused with their own Mannish myths and cosmic ideas. (*MR* 370)

He has moved from "mythically these tales are Elf-centred" through a more complex view of "(a) Mannish tradition, (b) Elvish tradition, (c) Mixed Dúnedanic tradition," to the assertion that "the Mythology must actually be a 'Mannish' affair"—in short, to facets of the diamond but not its entirety. This might seem to be the last word on the subject, but in fact it cannot be if two of the facets contradict each other.

Contradiction is the burden of the "Athrabeth," written in the years 1955–59,[1] in which two opposing points of view each claim the last word. We cannot honestly look at Tolkien's treatment of myth and truth without addressing the "Athrabeth," which gives us point of view with a vengeance. The story is largely a dialogue between two characters, Finrod and Andreth, who express diametrically opposite points of view about a single circumstance, the death fate of Men in Tolkien's Middle-earth. Finrod, the elf, maintains (in accordance with Tolkien's elvish creation story the "Ainulindalë") that death is the "gift" of Ilúvatar to Men. Andreth, the human, argues that since Elves do not die, the death of Men must be their punishment for some transgression, though she does not know what that might have been. To support her position, she quotes one Adanel, a wisewoman, whose "Tale," appended to the "Athrabeth," begins with the traditional oral opening "Some say." And what some say is that there was a "Disaster at the beginning of the history of our people" in which Men turned away from a "Voice," which called them "my children" and seemed to be Ilúvatar (*MR* 345), accepting instead a demiurge who is clearly Melkor. In short, there was a Fall. Men are then told by the "Voice" that their lives "shall be shortened" (*MR* 347): that is to say, they will die—not quite the biblical "ye shall surely die" of Genesis, but close. Tolkien then has Adanel project this unsubstantiated past into an as-yet-unrealized future "Great Hope," which is that "Eru will himself enter into Arda and heal Men and all the marring" (*MR* 351).

Christopher Tolkien describes this as "the extension—if only represented as a vision, hope, or prophecy—of the 'theology' of Arda into specifically, and of course centrally, Christian belief" (*MR* 356). Yet in 1953, Tolkien had written to Robert Murray, who had read parts of *The Lord of the Rings* in galley-proof and typescript, that he "had not put in, or had cut out, practically all references to anything like 'religion' . . . For," he said, "the religious element is absorbed into the story and the symbolism" (*Letters* 172). In the "Athrabeth," the "religious element" is the central factor in the story. How are we to read what seems to be a complete about-face?

An answer can be found in two of Tolkien's letters, both written in 1954—that is, just before he wrote "Athrabeth"—both touching on the mortality of Men in his legendarium. The first, to Peter Hastings, written (but not sent) in September 1954, stated that "Men are essentially mortal and must not try to become 'immortal' in the flesh," and further, that "'mortality' is thus represented as a special gift of God . . . and not a punishment" (*Letters* 189). The second, written to Robert Murray in November of that same year,[2] declared that "the view of the myth [of the Downfall of Númenor] is that death—the mere shortness of human life-span—is not a punishment for the fall" (205n). Both letters were written to men who were, in a sense, public representatives of their faith. Hastings was the manager of the (Catholic) Newman Bookshop in Oxford, and Robert Murray, a Jesuit priest.

We may suppose that Tolkien was responding to comments in both letters which had questioned, perhaps criticized, the "theology" of a work its author clearly intended as fiction. This had the effect of forcing Tolkien to defend his imagination.[3] He wrote to Hastings that "[t]he tale is after all in the ultimate analysis a tale, a piece of literature, intended to have literary effect, and not real history" (*Letters* 188). This is an important point. We are talking about fiction here, not about history or religion or philosophy. But if the tale is not "real history," then what justifies "real history" cutting across its boundary? The line Tolkien himself drew between "myth and fairy-story" and explicit religion is not just blurred, it is deliberately crossed.

By reading his fiction as theology—and questioning it—Hastings and Murray were putting extra-literary pressure on what had been for Tolkien a work of imagination. It can be no accident that in the year after his responses to Hastings and Murray he began work on the "Athrabeth," with its emphasis on point of view. Christopher Tolkien is right. The foundations of Christian belief have been "extended" into the theology of Arda. But they have been extended by way of unfounded information reported at second and sometimes third hand. Andreth's "truth," if that is what it is, is no less partial—in fact, more so—than that of Finrod, for Finrod relies largely on the "Ainulindalë" while Andreth relies on rumor and hearsay. Narrative frame and narrator point of view are not just doubled, they are tripled. Andreth cites Adanel, who cites the words of a faceless "some" she cannot even identify. If Tolkien is "extending" the theology of Arda into Christian belief, he is doing so through the voices of at least two, and possibly three, unreliable narrators. Recall Tolkien's statement (quoted above) that, "The High Eldar . . . must have known . . . the 'truth.' . . . What we have in the Silmarillion etc. are traditions . . . handed on by Men . . . blended and confused with their own Mannish myths and cosmic ideas" (*MR* 370).

The Tale of Adanel would fit with later "traditions handed on" but also "blended and confused," while the Eldar's (i.e., Finrod's) information, closer to the source, would have been closer to the "truth." Recall also Tolkien's word "fatal" in the letter to Waldman (*Letters* 144). It suggests that the real-world myth would literally kill the secondary world by breaking its boundary and pulling the reader back into the primary one. That Tolkien was aware of this is shown by a comment included among the "Athrabeth" manuscripts that the story was becoming "too like a parody of Christianity" (*MR* 354). His use of the word *parody* suggests a concern that Christianity's markers appearing in an invented secondary world would be too incongruous to be taken seriously. In that case, the "Athrabeth" and the "Tale of Adanel" are not endorsing Christianity, they are interrogating it. The dialogic structure of the piece pits Finrod's defense of Eru against the limited vision of his second-created beings, and the pitfall for the unwary is to assume that because Andreth and Adanel invoke Christianity they therefore speak for Tolkien.

It is equally possible to assume that they do not, for if Andreth and Adanel are right, Tolkien's invented godhead, Eru, is wrong, the premise of his invented mythology is undermined, and his whole structure is dismantled. In diametric opposition to Tolkien's statement (quoted above) that "'mortality' is thus represented as a special gift of God . . . and not a punishment" (*Letters* 189), Andreth and Adanel redefine the gift as punishment, using the circular argument that death is punishment and Men die, therefore they are being punished. With no history to back it up, a Fall is adduced as the cause for this, using the equally circular argument that since Men are punished, they must have done something to be punished for. It doesn't take Aristotle to detect the fallacy in this logic. Nor does it take a Tolkien critic to see the flaw in the subcreation, the mythology's apparent violation of its own inner consistency.

Fall per se is not the problem here; the difficulty lies in Tolkien's presentation of the Fall and its aftermath. Tolkien wrote to Waldman, "There cannot be any 'story' without a fall—all stories are ultimately about the fall" (*Letters* 147), and his mythos has other falls, notably the primal fall of Melkor in rebelling against Eru's theme and the later fall of the Men of Númenór in setting foot on the Undying Lands. Both Falls are presented by reliable narrators conversant with the mythic tradition from which they come. Thus in Tolkien's earliest conception in *The Book of Lost Tales*, it is "Manwë Súlimo, Lord of Elves and Men" who, in the Elvish tradition, "whispered" the "Ainulindalë" (and thereby the fall) "to the fathers of the father of Rúmil," Tolkien's earliest narrator, whose audience and scribe is Eriol (*BLT* I 52). And when Tolkien temporarily abandons the "Eriol saga" for the "Atlantis story" in *The Lost Road* and *The Notion Club Papers*, the Númenorean Fall and its consequence, the destruction of Númenor, are presented as direct memories inherited by his twentieth-century English protagonists as part of the mannish tradition within the secondary world.

What gives cause for question in the "Athrabeth" is the way in which its particular Fall is presented—as hearsay, and with no concrete information to back it up. An unsubstantiated Fall set in an unremembered past and based on unconfirmed report is open to question—by Finrod, if not by the average reader. But Tolkien has Adanel—with even less support—introduce the Incarnation as a kind of wishful thinking, a "hope" that Eru, who up to now has allowed bad things to happen, will someday enter into Arda in person to fix them. This directly contradicts the "Ainulindalë," wherein Ilúvatar specifically appointed to Men the task of changing the outline of Creation, giving them the capacity to go beyond the Music and have their operation "be, in form and deed, completed, and the world fulfilled unto the last and smallest" (*S* 42). In stretching his invented mythology to encompass a real-world myth, Tolkien was mixing faith and fable, truths not different in degree but in kind.

Since *The Lord of the Rings* was first published in 1954–55, nobody—with the possible exception of Peter Hastings—has been in any serious doubt that its values and ethos were in harmony with Tolkien's own Christianity.[4] In mixing myth and actuality, as Tolkien did in "Athrabeth," he was sailing very near the wind, especially since he was of two minds about how to handle the issue. Tolkien was right the first time, in the statement to Walden that forms the epigraph which begins this essay. His later insertion into the legendarium of explicit Christianity was an error in judgment. Myth and fairy story must, as all art, reflect and contain in solution elements of moral and religious truth (or error), but not explicitly, not in the known form of the primary "real" world. That would be, and this case I suggest that it was, fatal to the truth of Tolkien's myth.

Without further information, it is impossible to know what Tolkien meant in the "Athrabeth," and I do not pretend to know any more about what he intended than anyone else. But I do know what he wrote, and I feel compelled to point out that there is more than one way to read the truth of this most perplexing and problematic of Tolkien's myths.

Fays, Corrigans, Elves, and More: Tolkien's Dark Ladies

álfamær ekki var hún Kristi kær "elf-maid she was not dear to Christ"
—J. R. R. Tolkien, Manuscript B, *Tolkien On Fairy-stories*

In all the debate about how much or how little, or how well or how ill, J. R. R. Tolkien wrote about women, one archetypal female figure has been largely overlooked, though she is as typical of his fiction as are his more conspicuous women, such as Éowyn and Erendis and Haleth and Aredhel. She is the Dark Lady of my title and the *álfamær* (elf-maiden) of my epigraph.[1] She is Tolkien's mysterious supernatural woman, often but not always ominous, frequently a forest-dweller, often associated with water, who encounters the mortal hero at a turning point in his life and the story. In his essay "On Fairy-stories," Tolkien acknowledged the "fear of the beautiful fay that ran through the elder ages" (*MC* 151), and it seems clear that both the beauty and the fear held for him a particular fascination.

Definitions of the terms in my title are called for, as while they are often used interchangeably, each has a different meaning. All refer to a supernatural female being, and are not infrequently used in conjunction with one another, yet each has a separate significance that distinguishes it from the others. All carry primarily negative connotations with regard to interaction with humans. Let us start with *elf*. *The American Heritage Dictionary of the English Language* (1969) defines it as "a kind of small magic-wielding people ... sometimes beneficent and sometimes maleficent to man," and its adjective *elfish*, with alternative spelling *elvish*, as "[s]upernatural; weird." In *Elves in Anglo-Saxon England*, Alaric Hall notes the compound *ælfshot*, referring to illness caused by the invisible wounds of elf-arrows, and defines the related but rarer compound *ælfscyne* as "elf-beautiful," with a subordinate meaning of "elf-bright," possibly related to the Norse *ljósálfar*, "bright-elves" (Hall 7, 92–94).

Fay, an archaic word for modern *fairy*, is late Middle English, from Old French *fae, faie*, from Latin *fata* "the Fates," plural of *fatum*, the past participle of I-E *fari* "to speak," and thus "spoken' or decreed. Its Celtic counterpart, *Corrigan* (sometimes spelled *Korrigan* or *Gorrigan*, with variants *Corrikêt* or *Corriganed*), is interchangeable in common usage with French *fée, fay* "fairy" and is often so translated. *Corrigan* is glossed in James McKillop's *Dictionary of Celtic Mythology* as derived from *korr* "dwarf," and defined as a "[w]anton, impish, sprightly female fairy of Breton folklore who desires sexual union with humans" and is often found "near wells and fountains." In his *Celtic Folklore*, John Rhys cites Breton *korr*, with a feminine *korrez* and a derivative *korrik*, "a dwarf, a fairy, a wee little sorcerer," and *korrigan*, "a she dwarf, a fairy, a fairy woman, a diminutive sorceress" (Rhys 2: 671).

Tolkien portrays at least five examples of this mysterious woman, in works ranging chronologically from his very early *Story of Kullervo* to his poem "Ides Ælfscyne" ("Elf-bright [shining] Lady") in *Songs for the Philologists* to his middle-period *Lay of Aotrou and Itroun* to his late-published but also middle-period *The Fall of Arthur*. The sequence culminates in *The Lord of the Rings*, where the character of Galadriel gathers all the aspects, both light and dark, of the "beautiful fay" into one enigmatic and compelling figure.

Until recently, however, access to all her appearances except in *The Lord of the Rings* has been limited and partial. "The Lay of Aotrou and Itroun," published in *The Welsh Review* in December 1945, was subsequently out of print until its current republication by Tolkien's publisher HarperCollins in 2016 as a stand-alone volume. *The Story of Kullervo*, written in 1912–14, was first published in 2010 in the journal *Tolkien Studies*, and was reissued as a stand-alone volume in 2015. *The Fall of Arthur*, written circa 1934, was not edited and published by Christopher Tolkien until 2013. *Songs for the Philologists*, printed privately in 1936, has the rarity of a phoenix egg, and its contents are seldom included in discussion.[2]

Tolkien's unfinished *Story of Kullervo* introduced this mysterious lady as a shadowy but apparently harmless figure, described simply as the "Blue-robed Lady of the Forest" (*SK* 34). She was nonetheless a portent of things to come in respect of her mysterious appearance and her effect on the story. Some years later, more extensively developed and more carefully drawn, she reappeared as the malevolent Corrigan of Broceliande (also called "witch" and "fay") in *The Lay of Aotrou and Itroun*. A few years later she became the witchy, bitchy, seductive, scheming Guinever in his unfinished epic *The Fall of Arthur*, not a supernatural female per se, but described repeatedly as a "fay-woman" (*FoA* 27) and thus grouped with his other supernaturals. More supernatural but less historically attested, Ides Ælfscyne (translated by Tom Shippey as "Elf-fair Lady" [*Road*, rev. ed. 404]) was the title character of one of Tolkien's contributions to *Songs for the Philologists*. The list of fays does not stop there, but culminates in the enigmatic Galadriel of *The Lord of the Rings*, who is called "net-weaver" and "sorcerer" by Éomer (*TT* III, ii, 35), described by Sam Gamgee as "Hard as di'monds, soft as moonlight. Warm as sunlight, cold as frost in the stars. . . . merry as any lass . . . with daisies in her hair" (*TT* IV, v, 288), and by Boromir, who views her with deep suspicion, as "this Elvish Lady" (*FR* II, vii, 373), a phrase in which *Elvish* is not a compliment.

Of the figures I've listed, four—the Blue-robed Lady, the Corrigan, the Elf-fair Lady, and Galadriel—dwell in and embody the mystery of the forest. The human Guinever, firmly associated with court and chivalry, is the exception. But as we will see, Tolkien took care to surround even this highly civilized figure with forest mystery and association. Each of the characters carries with her some of the mystery, otherworldliness, and distance from humanity that the forest and its inhabiting fays brought to Tolkien.

The Blue-robed Lady of the Forest

The earliest of Tolkien's fays is the vatic Blue-robed Lady of the Forest in *The Story of Kullervo*, his adaptation of a segment of the Finnish *Kalevala*. Her title comes from Tolkien's *Kalevala* source, where the blue of her robe (often interchangeably used to mean both blue and green) is associated with the otherworldly aura of forests and mist-covered, low-lying ground. At the point where the Blue-robed Lady enters the story, the hapless orphan Kullervo has already endured his father's murder, his mother's abduction, his own attempted murder by his uncle Untamo, and, when he is sold into slavery, his sadistic mistreatment by his owner's wife. Only after all this does this unrelenting tale of woe reach its climax in a fate-freighted episode that makes Kullervo the unwitting agent of his own destruction.

Having requited his mistreatment by the smith's wife, and at last taking his life into his own hands, Kullervo sets off to avenge his father's death. It is then that he encounters the Blue-robed Lady. Here is the description of the meeting in the Finnish original and in its English translation by W. F. Kirby, which Tolkien first read in 1911.

Tuli akka vastahansa
siniviitta viian eukko. (*Kalevala*, comp. Lönnrot, runo 34, ll. 7–8)

> Then an old dame came to meet him,
> Blue-robed Lady of the Forest. (*Kalevala*, trans. Kirby 2: runo 34, ll. 7–8)

It is worthy of note that in the original *Kalevala* this figure has no supernatural resonances. She is simply an old woman: *akka* in Finnish. Subsequent translations into English (e.g., by Magoun, Bosley, and Friberg) do not always capitalize her title, being content with "green-robed maid of the thicket" (*Kalevala*, trans. Magoun 242); "blue-cloaked thicket-dame (*Kalevala*, trans. Bosley 471); and "Blue-robed matron of the forest" (*Kalevala*, trans. Friberg 275).

However described, the Blue-robed Lady asks Kullervo where he is going, and when he says he is going to avenge his family, she tells him his family is still alive and gives him directions to find them.

> Through the forest must thou journey,
> By the river thou must travel,
> Thou must march one day, a second,
> And must march upon the third day,
> Then must turn thee to the north-west,
> Till you reach a wooded mountain,
> Then march on beneath the mountain,
> Go the left side of the mountain, . . . (*Kalevala*, trans. Kirby 2: runo 34, ll. 143–50)

Her directions are straightforward, and their result is to reunite the wandering Kullervo with his family.[3] While this both postpones his revenge and sets up the incest with an unrecognized sister that precipitates his suicide, nevertheless none of these events—neither the postponement nor the incest, let alone his final death—is presented in *Kalevala* as foreseen or intended by the Blue-robed Lady. She gives directions, nothing more.

In contrast with the Finnish original and the English translations I have cited, Tolkien's treatment of her appearance is considerably more portentous, for his version, otherwise a close paraphrase of his Finnish source, adds another sentence: "*Fare not towards it* [the mountain] *lest ill find thee*" (*SK* 34–35; my emphasis). This added piece of advice changes the tenor of the story, suggesting that the Blue-robed Lady has foreknowledge of what will happen and is trying to steer Kullervo away from the fate toward which he is rushing headlong.

Of course he disregards her advice, and of course ill does indeed find him. Turning aside from the forest path, he goes up the slope of the mountain, where he encounters a maiden, lost and alone, whom he carries off and violates, only to discover she is his sister. As in *Kalevala*, the episode is the turning point of the story, leading first to the maiden's suicide and then to Kullervo's own when, pausing only long enough to finally carry out his revenge, he kills first the murderous Untamo and then himself. In Tolkien's version, the Blue-robed Lady is the messenger of a portent foreseen but not intended. Her "lest ill find thee" hints at supernatural foreknowledge, underscores Kullervo's disregard of good advice,[4] and turns her from a minor character into a fate figure. Tolkien's addition of this line gives her prime importance and invests the whole episode with a more explicitly supernatural and deliberately ominous tone.

We will see other women more elaborately treated as supernatural fate-figures in subsequent works, as Tolkien developed this character over the course of his later, more mature writing. None, however, will have a greater effect on the life of the hero than has the Blue-robed Lady of the Forest on Kullervo.

THE CORRIGAN

As far as can be known, no comparable fay appears again in Tolkien's work until 1930.[5] A more clearly described, certainly much darker and more sinister, supernatural female plays a key role in his *Lay of Aotrou and Itroun*. While in the poem this figure is variously referred to as "witch," fay," and "Corrigan," I have made *corrigan* the term of choice, as it best conveys her Breton origin.

Particular to Breton folklore, Corrigans were Otherworld figures, often of small stature, known for stealing human babies and substituting their own, and also for attempting to seduce mortal men. James McKillop's *Dictionary of Celtic Mythology* defines *corrigan* as a "Wanton, impish, sprightly female fairy of Breton folklore who desires sexual union with humans," often found "near wells and fountains." John Rhys's *Celtic Folklore* defines *korrigan* as "a she dwarf, a fairy, a fairy woman, a diminutive sorceress" (Rhys 2: 671). Thomas Keightley's *The Fairy Mythology* (1882) says of corrigans that, "Like fairies in general the Korrigan [sic] steal children" (432). A variant on this motif is given in Robert Kirk's seventeenth-century *The Secret Commonwealth of Elves, Fauns and Fairies,* where it is the mother, not the child, who is abducted into Faërie. Kirk wrote in 1691 that "Women are yet alive who tell they were taken away when in Child-bed to nurse Fairie Children, a lingering voracious Image of them being left in their place, (like their Reflexion in a Mirrour)" (Kirk 72). In his commentary in the 1893 edition Andrew Lang notes that, "Fairy girls who make love to young men" are "well-known in the Breton ballad, *Le Sieur Nan*" (Kirk 35). That Tolkien knew of Kirk is evidenced by his reference in a draft of "On Fairy-stories" to the apparently well-known story of Kirk's disappearance.

Aotrou and Itroun tells the story of a childless lord who, desperate to get an heir, abandons hope, takes "counsel cold," and goes to the forest of Broceliande[6] seeking supernatural help.

> A witch there was, who webs could weave
> to snare the heart and wits to reave,
> who span dark spells with spider-craft,
> and as she span she softly laughed;
> a drink she brewed of strength and dread
> to bind the quick and stir the dead (*A&I* ll. 27–32)

This forest-dwelling witch (not at this point called fay or Corrigan) is a "crone" who reads the lord's unstated desire and brews for him a magic philter, which she gives him in a glass phial. The implication is that the potion will aid conception and give him the son he longs for. It does, and to celebrate the birth of twins and his wife's request for "venison of the greenwood deer" the lord pursues a white doe (by color an otherworld animal) deep into the forest, possessed by "a longing strange / for deer that fair and fearless range" (*A&I* ll. 265–66). The poem hints strongly that both Itroun's "foolish wish" for venison, which "comes unsought" (l. 239), and Aotrou's choice to hunt in Broceliande, are the spells of the witch, meant to lure him back to her cave. The "dim laughter" he hears in the wood is almost certainly the laughter of the fay (l. 264), echoed at the end of the poem when she laughs at the deaths of Lord and Lady.

Led by the white doe, Aotrou comes to the grotto of the fay (now so-called), no longer a crone but young, beautiful, and seductive. Only here do we learn that she is a shape-changer, an archetypal figure familiar in medieval myth,[7] who can shift from old and ugly to young and beautiful and back again.[8] Conforming to earlier accounts, she is also now explicitly associated with water.

> The sun was lost, all green was grey.
> There twinkled the fountain of the fay,
> before a cave, on silver sand
> under dark boughs in Broceliande.
> . . . .
> The moonlight falling clear and cold
> her long hair lit; through comb of gold
> she drew each lock, and down it fell
> like the fountain falling in the dell (ll. 283–96)

Her *ælflocks* may not be knotted, but their purpose, like that of the corrigans described by Keightley and Kirk, seems clearly to be seduction of the lord.

> "Aotrou! Lo! Thou hast returned—
> perchance some kindness I have earned?
> What hast thou, lord, to give to me
> whom thou hast come so far to see?" (ll. 307–8)

His reply is unambiguous.

> *I know thee not, I know thee not,*
> *nor ever saw thy darkling grot.*
> *O Corrigan! 'twas not for thee*
> *I hither came a-hunting free!* (ll. 309-12)

She demands as her fee for the potion that he wed her. When he refuses, she turns from seductive to vengeful, threatening that if he does not "wed" her he will die in three days. Her prediction comes true. The Lord dies of a mysterious illness, as if struck by *ælfshot*, and his wife dies of grief.

Like *The Story of Kullervo*, *The Lay of Aotrou and Itroun* comes from the dark side of Tolkien's creative nature. A bleak tale of a Christian lord's recourse to pagan magic to get his desire, with the consequent loss of his life, it seems in sharp contrast to his better-known works, such as *The Hobbit* and *The Lord of the Rings*, where redemption, if not actuated, is at least held out as a possibility. The contrast is useful, however, for its points up the dark issues also present in these more famous works and reminds us that Tolkien was used to building, as he phrased it in the poem "Mythopoeia," "gods and their houses out of dark and light" (*T&L* 99). The "Lay" is a good example, for while the poem closes with a conventionally Christian prayer,

> God keep us all in hope and prayer
> from evil rede and from despair,
> by the waters blest of Christendom
> to dwell, until at last we come
> to joy of heaven where is queen
> the maiden Mary pure and clean (ll. 501–6)

Tolkien nevertheless has given the Corrigan the last laugh (ll. 479–86).

> At morn there rang the sacring knell
> and far men heard a single bell
> toll, while the sun lay on the land:
> while deep in dim Broceliande
> a silver fountain flowed and fell

within a darkly woven dell,
and in the homeless hills a dale
was filled with laughter cold and pale. (ll. 479–86)[9]

Guinever

It is as a fay that we look next at Tolkien's Guinever in *The Fall of Arthur* (1934), a figure stereotyped as fallen woman and faithless queen in literature from the Welsh Triads to T. H. White's *The Once and Future King*, a figure staled by familiarity but reimagined in a supernatural context by Tolkien.

In emphasizing the otherworld aspects of Arthur's queen, Tolkien may have taken his cue from the etymology of her name. His immediate Middle English sources, the *Stanzaic Morte Arthur* and the *Alliterative Morte Arthure*, call her respectively Gaynor and Gaynor/Waynor. However, the earlier and more complex Welsh form, *Gwenhwyfar*, from which these derive has as its first element the feminine form of Welsh *gwyn* "white," from Proto-Celtic **Windos* "the white one," from the Indo-European root **syeidh-* "to shine" (cp, Irish *finn*, "fair"),[10] coupled with the second element, which is cognate with Irish *síabáir* "phantom, spirit, fairy" (Bromwich 380–81). Compare the Irish name *Findabair*, daughter of Queen Mab in the Ulster epic *Táin Bó Cúailnge*. Gwenhwyfar/Guinever can thus be translated as "The White Enchantress" or "The White Fay/Ghost/Phantom."

Thus in this context, Tolkien's repeated phrase "fair as fay-woman" becomes not just a simile, but a character-marker, a demonic epithet. The phrase (part of a poetic formula, "fair as fay-woman / in the world walking / for the woe of men") occurs four times in the poem. It is used three times by the narrator: first to describe her effect on Mordred (*FoA* II, p. 27, l. 28), then on Lancelot, (III, p. 37, l. 55), and once editorially: "with cruel justice / fair as fay-woman / they to fire doomed her" (III, p. 38, ll. 74–75). The phrase is used once in direct address to Mordred by his squire Ivor, in whose mouth it becomes an epithet of scorn and hatred: "Fear her no longer, / the fay-woman!" (IV, p. 48, l. 71).

The word *fay* thus repeated cannot but associate Tolkien's Guinever with that other Arthurian fay, Morgan le Fay—queen, sorceress, Arthur's sister, nemesis, and (paradoxically) healer and refuge until his predicted return, described by Sir Thomas Malory as "a grete clerk of nygromancye" (Malory 5). In Tolkien's unfinished epic, Guinever replaces Morgan as fay-woman, and adds the only touch of the supernatural to that poem. Tolkien's poem omits Morgan—and indeed, most of Arthur's family—altogether, and allows the magical otherworld associations to be borne by the "gleaming limbs" of Guinever (*FoA* II, p. 27, l. 28).[11] The effect is at once ambiguous and compelling, situating

Tolkien's Guinever between two identities. She is both the adulterous human queen and the otherworld enchantress whose seduction of Lancelot displaces the legend of Morgan's attempt at the same thing. Tolkien's emphasis on her sexuality—Mordred is "lust-tormented," with "black phantoms of desire unsated" (II, p. 27–28, ll. 26, 39–40)—makes his Guinever sister under the skin to the seductive corrigans of Breton folklore, and certainly to the Corrigan of Tolkien's own neo-Breton lay. Moreover, the phrase "black phantoms" used to characterize Mordred's desire evokes the "white phantom" etymology of her name, thus combining her sexuality with her supernatural aspect.

Guinever is too well known a figure, and too closely associated with knights and Camelot to be a ready candidate for Forest-lady, blue-robed or grotto-dwelling, so Tolkien has chosen to surround her with imagery rather than scenery and to evoke rather than describe her forest connections. As she flees Mordred, "the lights of Camelot lessened and faded; / before lay forest. . . . Wolf had wakened in the woods stalking / and the hind hardly from hiding driven . . . once queen of herds for whom harts majestic in horned combat / had fought fiercely. . . . Guinever the fair in grey mantled / cloaked in darkness" (II, p. 33–34, ll. 185–93). Announcing her escape, Mordred's squire Ivor tells him, "Her trail faded in the trackless stones / hound and hunter in the hills faltered" (IV, p.48, ll. 65–66). Fay, phantom, hunted deer: such carefully chosen images are bound to recall the shape-changing white doe /seductive fay of *Aotrou and Itroun* and the dark forest of Broceliande.

In this Guinever Tolkien gives us the darkest of all literary portraits of that fated but not necessarily fatal queen. In fact, his is the odd woman out in an otherwise fairly conventional lineup of Guineveres. Ranged against the unfaithful queens in *The History of the Kings of Britain,* by Arthur's earliest chronicler, Geoffrey of Monmouth, in the Alliterative and Stanzaic *Mortes,* the "Faithless Wives" of the Welsh *Triads* and the tempestuous, emotionally unstable woman in Sir Thomas Malory's *Le Morte d'Arthur,* Tolkien's Guinever is a cut below, a woman possessed more by self-serving ambition than uncontrolled passion. But grouped with the Blue-robed Lady who speaks for fate, and with the Corrigan, alluring and malevolent, shadowy, and scheming, she finds her proper company among Tolkien's Dark Ladies.

Elf-fair Lady

A fourth addition to that company is Ides Ælfscyne, translated by Tom Shippey as "Elf-fair Lady" (*Road,* rev. ed. 404). She is the title character[12] in one of what Shippey calls Tolkien's "trapped mortal" poems (403), part of his contribution to *Songs for the Philologists.* This is the rarest of all his published works, one reason why Ides Ælfscyne is often overlooked among Tolkien's women. Not only are the *Songs* out of print but they also had a small pressrun to begin with. Adding to their rarity is the fact that many copies were destroyed in a fire. The few remaining copies (perhaps a few as fourteen) are almost all in libraries or private collections; at the time of writing, a single copy posted for sale on the internet was being offered at something close to $25,000. For ease of access, I will use Shippey's transcription and translation (*Road,* rev. ed. 399, 403–5) rather than the inaccessible original. Hard to find though she is, the Elf-fair Lady clearly belongs with the Blue-robed Lady, Guinever, and the Corrigan as one of Tolkien's fays and fatal women.[13]

The speaker in the poem is the bewitched mortal, who narrates how he "came into danger" meeting a maiden, a "fair elf-lady" (see the connotations of *ælfscyne* above) who kissed him, embraced him, and bound him "in her grasp" (Shippey, *Road,* rev. ed. 404–5). She took him "under the gloom" where shadows "flickered" (which I read as forest) and "over the ocean," arriving at last at a green land otherworld where time evidently passed unnoticed, for the speaker returns from his "exile . . . [f]ifty years later" to find those who had known him dead and "in the mould" (405). Tolkien is here using the fairy-tale motif—best known to Americans in Washington Irving's story of Rip van Winkle—of the mortal, trapped in a faërian timewarp where years pass like minutes, who returns to a world that has passed him by. But behind this motif is the less familiar but equally ominous notion of the seduction/abduction of a mortal by a fairy lover. Tolkien's Ælfscyne, his Corrigan, and his Guinever are sisters under the skin.

After that, this enigmatic figure disappears for a while from Tolkien's work, to reappear in a one-line cameo as the rumored "fairy wife" of Bilbo Baggins's distant Took ancestor. John Rateliff notes that in the Bladorthin Typescript the reference is to marriage into "a fairy family (goblin family said severer critics)" rather than the more specific "fairy wife" (29). The parenthetical "goblin" adds a demonic note suggestive of the darker Breton aspects of *corrigan* and *nain,* this last a creature defined by James McKillop as a "fearsome, demon-like creature of Breton Folklore. . . . black and menacing" (302). Evans-Wentz cites Villemarqué on the subject of *corrigans* as *nains,* described as being "dark or even black" and "believed to be evil spirits or demons" (Evans-Wentz 211–12).

Galadriel

The mysterious fay makes her triumphant final appearance in Tolkien's works as the Lady of the Golden Wood, Galadriel, in *The Lord of the Rings.* Galadriel is the Corrigan reimagined,[14] with all that forest lady's attributes transmuted from dark to light. Comparing elven queen with Breton witch, one can see two sides of the same coin composed of the same metals: perilous beauty, a forest dwelling, a fountain, a phial with potent content, even the reading of unstated desires, as when, upon their first meeting, Galadriel silently interrogates each member of the Fellowship in turn, as the Corrigan does the lord.

It should not be overlooked that in spite of the praise lavished on her by Aragorn and Gandalf, Tolkien takes care to surround Galadriel with suspicion before we meet her. Boromir is deeply mistrustful of her, and their meeting in Caras Galadon does nothing to dispel his doubts. Éomer and the Rider of Rohan (having only heard of her but not met her) put her in a class with "sorcerers and net-weavers" (*TT* III, ii, 35). Later in the story, Wormtongue refers to her as "the Sorceress of the Golden Wood" and to Lórien as "Dwimordene" (Vale of Illusion), and accuses her of weaving "webs of deceit" (*TT* III, vi, 118). The conventional reading judges these men for their hearsay evaluation of her and compares their opinions unfavorably to that of Aragorn for whom there is in her "no evil, unless a man bring it hither himself" (*FR* II, vii, 373). Readers tend to side with Aragorn, though even the elfophile Sam Gamgee sees the competing and contradictory sides of her nature. To him she is "[h]ard as di'monds, soft as moonlight. Warm as sunlight, cold as frost in the stars, merry as any lass . . . with daisies in her hair" (*TT* IV, v, 288). Both assessments are valid, both comparisons defensible. Tolkien's Galadriel is a cluster of contradictions, half of which, the negative ones, show her kinship with the Corrigan.

Even without her retroactively supplied backstory as rebel and protest leader, Galadriel is a more complex character than many readers are willing to see. Christopher Tolkien's commentary in the "Galadriel" chapter of *The Treason of Isengard* shows how Tolkien's revisions of the episode in which she refuses Frodo's offer of the Ring move uneasily between light and dark. First "Frodo offers Galadriel the Ring. She *laughs*. . . . she will only retain the unsullied [i.e., elven] Ring" (*TI* 254). Next Christopher Tolkien gives "Galadriel's assertion [that] *nothing* that was Sauron's can be made use of" (254). Following this, he comments that "[a] page found wholly isolated from other manuscripts of *The Lord of the Rings* carries more developed drafting for Galadriel's refusal of the Ring" (254–55), leading to Christopher's conclusion that these "show him [Tolkien] revolving the mode by which he should withdraw the Three Rings of the Elves from inherent evil" (256). Lastly and somewhat perplexingly, Christopher describes a later typescript where, in response to Frodo's offer, "Galadriel laughed 'with a sudden clear laugh of pure merriment': pure was struck out early, and afterwards 'of merriment'. And as my father first wrote her words she said 'And now at last it comes, the final probe'" (260). The cancellations are significant. Galadriel's laugh, bereft of its qualifications of "pure" and "of merriment," now stands simply as "clear" and seems an odd response to Frodo's offer, reminiscent of the laughter of the fay in *Aotrou and Itroun*. Christopher then mentions "a further text of this chapter" in which Galadriel "still laughs 'with a sudden clear laugh of merriment'" (261), but here Tolkien's concern is clearly the Rings themselves and only concomitantly the psychology of Galadriel's reaction to Frodo's offer.

Yet while Tolkien was clearly of two minds about Galadriel's character, he nevertheless, in his final, published version of this episode, chose to present her refusal as a study of character rather than use it to define the nature of the Elven Rings. The shock to the first-time reader of Galadriel's transformation when Frodo offers her the Ring is surely intentional on Tolkien's part, and has its seeds in his earlier cancellation of "pure" and "merriment" followed by "at last it comes, the final probe" (260). Mark how he builds on his earlier treatment, expanding the word *probe* into Galadriel's litany of beauty and terror: "'And now at last it comes. You will give me the Ring freely! In place of the Dark Lord you will set up a Queen. And I shall not be dark, but beautiful and terrible as the Morning and the Night! Fair as the Sea and the Sun and the Snow upon the Mountain! Dreadful as the Storm and the Lightning! Stronger than the foundations of the earth. All shall love me and despair!'" (*FR* II, 7, 381).

All shall love me and despair. Coming from the stately, white-robed, golden-haired queen of Caras Galadon, this is an astonishing sentence. And her subsequent lightning transformation from bright to dark and back again when offered the Ring out-corrigans the Corrigan. It is a psychological shape-change more terrifying than the Corrigan's alteration in *Aotrou and Itroun* from beautiful fay to hideous crone, for the reason that Galadriel's Jekyll-Hyde transformation takes place not over the course of two separate episodes but all in a moment and before Frodo and Sam, through whose eyes we see her stature increased, her beauty heightened, her attraction intensified, all to a supernatural level.

But this transformation is not out of character, not if you have listened to Sam Gamgee and Boromir and Éomer and Wormtongue. And they are not alone; their recognition of the dichotomy of Galadriel's nature is here shared by Galadriel herself. In that moment Galadriel sees herself as the Corrigan, as Ides Ælfscyne,[15] as La Belle Dame Sans Merci—the fatal woman who has for millennia lured men to destruction. That she then voluntarily relinquishes her particular power is her salvation. "I pass the test. . . . I will diminish, and go into the West, and remain Galadriel" (*FR* II, 7, 381). There is magic here, but magic of a particularly insidious kind because it is appears to us indirectly, seen through other eyes, not just Frodo's and Sam's but also, in that moment, Éomer's and Wormtongue's and Boromir's. All their eyes are focused on the same image and all convey to the reader the same emotion, the fear of the beautiful fay.

Conclusion

In sum, this quintet of ominous, powerful female figures, the Blue-robed Lady, the Corrigan, the fay-like Guinever, the Elf-fair Lady, and the elven queen Galadriel, are drawn with the same brush and all derive from the dark side of Tolkien's perilous realm of Faërie. They balance and round out his gallery of female portrayals and are fit to stand alongside Éowyn and Erendis and Haleth and Aredhel and Lúthien. Tolkien was no misogynist, either in life or in art, but he recognized and respected the double-sided nature of beauty, the lure of mystery, and the danger of underestimating the power of a woman.

PART FOUR

Boiling Bones; Serving Soup

> By "the soup" I mean the story as it is served up by its author or teller, and by "the bones" its sources or material . . .
> —J. R. R. Tolkien, "On Fairy-stories"

A central section in "On Fairy-stories" introduces what Tolkien called the "Pot of Soup" or the "Cauldron of Story." The image is the homely one of the big iron pot on the back of the stove, a broth perpetually on the boil with the bones and meat scraps, vegetable bits and leftovers the thrifty cook is too frugal to throw away. There they simmer all together until, as Huck Finn says, "things get mixed up and the juice kind of swaps around" (Twain 14). The dominant bones in Tolkien's cauldron have long been identified as elements of Germanic and Arthurian myth and legend. Here I look at how some of the less-studied elements in the broth, the bits of real-world mythology such as Finnish and Celtic and even French, also swap around in Tolkien's soup and add their flavor to the great fictive mythos he wished to dedicate "to England" (*Letters* 144).

"Tolkien, *Kalevala*, and Middle-earth," written for this volume, looks at the ways in which one of Tolkien's earliest mythic enthusiasms, the Finnish *Kalevala*, influenced his epic "Children of Húrin" as well as his most enigmatic character, Tom Bombadil. "Tolkien's Celtic Connection" explores the influence of insular Welsh and Irish myth and legend on Tolkien's own legendarium. "Tolkien's French Connection" looks at the elements of medieval French romance in *The Hobbit*. "Drowned Lands" explores the connections between Tolkien's Fall of Númenor and real-world accounts of inundations and lost lands, including Lyonesse, the Kingdom of Ys, and Atlantis. "Voyaging About: Tolkien and Celtic *Navigatio*" examines the influence of medieval Celtic *imramma* (or voyage stories), such as those of Bran, Brendan, and Mael Duine, on Tolkien's own "Imram" and the related voyages in his two unfinished time-travel stories, *The Lost Road* and *The Notion Club Papers*.

Tolkien, *Kalevala*, and Middle-earth

That the Finnish *Kalevala* was an early and seminal influence on Tolkien's legendarium is by now an established fact.[1] Nevertheless, there is always something more to say. *The Story of Kullervo*, Tolkien's earliest attempt at serious fiction (unpublished until 2010 and first appearing in book form only in 2015) reinforces what we know of his debt to *Kalevala* and adds essential and hitherto missing pieces to the growing mosaic of what he came to call his secondary world.

First, *The Story of Kullervo* broadens our understanding of the nature of sub-creation and its relationship to the specific process of language and the importance of names. Second, it gives us Tolkien at his darkest, and thus is a portent of things to come. As tragedy, it foreshadows and throws into sharp relief the dark thread followed by others in the greater story—by Frodo, Boromir, Denethor, Saruman, even Beechbone the Ent—a strand often overridden by the brighter threads of his work. *Kullervo* deepens our understanding of Tolkien's other tragic hero, Túrin Turambar. On a more mythological level, *The Story of Kullervo* animates the landscape of Tolkien's story by peopling it with his own invented gods, demigods, and nature spirits. Lastly, a deepened understanding of Tolkien's debt to *Kalevala* strengthens our perception of the connection between Tolkien's enigmatic Tom Bombadil and *Kalevala*'s ancient sage Väinämöinen, a connection often noted but seldom explored in any depth. All of these aspects of his work deserve careful consideration, which should begin where Tolkien began, with his treatment of Kullervo.

The Story of Kullervo

This sorry tale of bad luck, bad treatment, and bad behavior is soon told. Two brothers quarrel over property. One brother murders the other and takes his land, his wife, and his son. The son vows to avenge his father's death but soon begins behaving oddly. Seeing him as a growing threat, the uncle first tries to kill the boy and failing at that, sends him to another land where, unhappy, mistreated, and misunderstood, the son questions his fate and wonders why he was born. At length he escapes enslavement by arranging the death of one of his captors. On his return home to carry out his vow of vengeance, he becomes involved with a young woman whose suicidal death by drowning provokes him to the point of hysteria. In a final debacle, he makes good his vow to avenge his father, killing his uncle and setting fire to the hall, after which he is himself killed with his own sword.

That, in brief is the plot of Tolkien's first short story, written when he was twenty-two and an undergraduate at Exeter College, Oxford. You will have recognized that it is also the plot of Shakespeare's *Hamlet*, and you may know as well that it is in fact only one more variant of a story widespread in early medieval Europe, with versions in Danish, Irish, and Icelandic,[2] as well as in the Finnish *Kalevala*. Reading *Kalevala* as a student at King Edward's School in Birmingham, Tolkien discovered not just another mythology to add to the known body of Greek, Roman, Celtic, and subcontinental Indian mythologies then being studied but a whole new world, complete with flora, fauna, and a brand new set of gods—a world to which he was so powerfully attracted that when he went up to Oxford in 1911, he checked out C. N. Eliot's *Finnish Grammar* in the hope that he could teach himself enough of the language to read it in the original. He couldn't. But he learned enough to go on with.

In his talk "On the 'Kalevala,'" given to an Oxford undergraduate society in 1915, Tolkien translated the title into English as "Land of Heroes," Kaleva being the mythic eponymous ancestor of the work, and the locative suffix *-la* indicating place or region. Building on the notion that *Kalevala* was not just a new story but a new world, he compared the experience of the first-time reader (i.e., Tolkien himself) to that of "Columbus on a new continent or Thorfinn in Vinland," reveling in "an amazing new excitement" (*SK* 68), an "almost indefinable sense of newness and strangeness" (69), a world of "strange people" with "a wealth of mythology" (69, 81), of "forgotten tongues and memories of an elder day" (69). And he cautioned his hearers that "you may feel you do not want to go back home for a long while if at all" (69). He was surely speaking of himself, for in a very real sense he never did go back home, but went on for the rest of his creative life to explore the strange people, the forgotten tongues and memories of an elder day that comprised his own mythology.

He was just beginning that exploration when he wrote *The Story of Kullervo* in 1914 or thereabouts. Decades later, in his essay "On Fairy-stories," he articulated the concept behind the process he had already put into practice, declaring that "the story-maker proves a successful 'sub-creator.' He makes a Secondary World which your mind can enter. Inside it, what he relates is 'true'; it accords with the laws of that world" (*MC* 132). Practice, however, came first, and The *Story of Kullervo* was Tolkien's earliest attempt at sub-creation, employing what he learned from *Kalevala* about the nuts and bolts of making a secondary world.

Tolkien Sub-creator

The first manuscript page of *The Story of Kullervo* is a graphic example of the world-making process in action. It is filled with emendations and corrections, not all of which are stylistic or editorial. The most significant show the fledgling author first writing the *Kalevala*'s original place and personal names but almost immediately changing his mind, crossing out or marking with asterisks the Finnish names and writing in above them or in the margin names of his own invention. Thus initial *Suomi* was changed to *Sutse;* initial *Karelja* was changed to *Telea;* initial *Russia* became *Keme/Kemenume,* glossed in an appended list of names as "The Great Land."[3] Tolkien was at once discovering, creating, and claiming this world, not as *Kalevala*'s primary world, however new and strange, but as his own sub-created secondary one.

One of the great charms of the Finnish mythological world is its exuberant proliferation of gods, demigods, and nature spirits, who seem to pop up whenever and wherever they are needed, from Pellervoinen ("spirit of the field" or "son of the soil"), who sows vegetation on the newly formed land, to Tapio ("God of the Forest") and his spouse Mielikki, to Ahto and Vellamo, god and goddess of the sea and waters, to Ukko in the heavens and Tuoni in the underworld. These and a host of other spirits, great and small, people the world of *Kalevala* and give to the world of this myth what Tolkien admired as its "luxuriant animism" (*SK* 80).

While Tolkien's adaptation retained the Finnish names of the main characters—Kullervo, Untamo, and Kalervo—many other names, according to the Finnish philologist Leena Kahlas-Tarkka, have "no correspondence in the *Kalevala*" but are "of Tolkien's invention" (qtd. in Lee 265). Kahlas-Tarkka supplies a list of such names—Palikki, Telenda, Kaltuse, Pulu, Kuru—the names of demigods and nature spirits, to which list I would add Ilu, Ilwinti, Manoine, Malolo Tanto, Lempo, Samyan, Nyeli, Amuntu, Terenye, Asemo, and Lumya. These names and their bearers give to Tolkien's story the "luxuriant animism"

(*SK* 80) that he said he found in the world of *Kalevala*. Phonologically modeled on Finnish, the names are clear precursors of Qenya, the earliest of his invented languages, while the characters so named foreshadow the minor deities and nature-spirits in Tolkien's own legendarium whose names, in both later Quenya and Sindarin, contribute so much to the texture of Tolkien's secondary world. Many years later Tolkien declared in a letter to a reader, "It was just as the 1914 war burst on me [note the congruence with his writing of *The Story of Kullervo*] that I made the discovery that 'legends' depend on the language to which they belong; but a living language depends equally on the 'legends' which it conveys by tradition" (*Letters* 231). His own languages and legends are the best evidence of this, but it was his work with *Kalevala* that taught him.

In 1914, Tolkien wrote to his fiancé, Edith Bratt, that he intended to include "chunks of poetry" in his adaptation (*Letters* 7), and indeed the central portion of *The Story of Kullervo* is a long, metric cattle charm in verse, borrowed with little modification from a corresponding charm in Kirby's *Kalevala* translation. It is an example in miniature, the part for the whole, of Tolkien's adaptive and sub-creative process. When in *Kalevala* the wife of the smith Ilmarinen sends Kullervo out to herd the cattle, she calls on the spirits of the countryside to keep them safe, and her chant peoples the text with a host of names, from the most lofty to the most earthy, that bring the countryside alive.

> Watch them, Jumala most gracious,
> . . . .
> Send the Daughters of Creation,
> That they may protect my cattle,
> And the whole herd may look after.
> . . . .
> "Suvetar [Summer], the best of women,
> Entelätär [South Wind], Nature's old one,
> Hongatar [Fir Tree], the noble mistress,
> Katajatar [Juniper], maiden fairest,
> Pihlajatar [Rowan], little damsel,
> Tuometar [Cherry Tree], Tapio's daughter, (*Kalevala*, trans. Kirby 2: ll. 79–80)

Compare this with Tolkien's version, in which the wife of the smith Āsemo calls on nature spirits (whose names echo those in *Kalevala* but are of Tolkien's own invention) to protect her cattle.

> Guard my kine O gracious Ilu
> . . . .

Send the daughters of Ilwinti
. . . .
Come thou children of Malōlo
At Ilukko's mighty bidding
O [Uorlen?] most wise one
. . . .
O thou Sampia most lovely
. . . .
O Palikki's little damsel
And Telenda thy companion
. . . .
O Terenye maid of Samyan (*SK* 22–24)

The likeness is obvious, but the greater significance of this passage is its clear evidence, as on that first manuscript page, of Tolkien's move from adaptation to sub-creation. He is practicing the building of a secondary world out of names, and the names in both his source and his own story are largely those of natural phenomena—of weather, seasons, tree-spirits, dryads. The entities named in this "chunk of poetry"—Ilwinti, Malōlo, Sampia, Uorlen, Palikki, Telenda, Terenye—enrich and augment his world, peopling it with spirits of nature who will eventually reemerge in his own mythology as Ilu[vatar], Manwë, Melian, Yavanna, and a host of other Valar and Maiar, all of whom owe a debt to *The Story of Kullervo* and the process of naming that Tolkien began there.

Many years later, in a draft of his essay on fairy stories, Tolkien gave evidence of how seriously he took the concept, writing of

> spirits, *daemons:* inherent powers of the created world, deriving more directly and "earlier" (in terrestrial history) from the creating will of God, but nonetheless created . . . in fact non-incarnate minds (or souls) of a stature and even nature more near to that of Man (in some cases possibly less, in many maybe greater) that any other rational creatures . . . Thus a tree-fairy (or a dryad) is, or was, a minor spirit in the process of creation who aided as "agent" in the making effective of the divine Tree-idea or some part of it, or of even of some one particular example: some tree." (*TOFS* 254–55)

Where did he get this idea but from *Kalevala*? And where did he take his first steps in re-creating it but in *The Story of Kullervo*?

Tolkien Dark

It was in writing *The Story of Kullervo* also that Tolkien learned the narrative power of tragedy. There is more to his debt to *Kalevala* than simple borrowing, or first steps in sub-creation. *The Story of Kullervo* in itself is a signpost to Tolkien's future work, foreshadowing the darkness that hangs over Middle-earth. It is epic tragedy in the Aristotelian sense, the downfall of a hero through his own *hamartia,* his fatal mistake. In this regard, Kullervo, son of Kalervo, has a claim to being the most tragic character Tolkien ever created.[4] His personality matches his downward path, for he is also the most unattractive, hell-bent character Tolkien ever created, inspiring such adjectives as *resentful, morose, violent, ill-favoured, bitter, crooked, broad, ungainly, illknit, knotty, unrestrained,* and *unsoftened* (*SK* 12, 20). I would add *angry, grudge-holding, stubborn,* and *vengeful.* Tolkien's Kullervo knows the world is against him, and he returns the sentiment. What is there to like about him? Only the fact that the cards are so obviously stacked against him that the reader begins to feel a perverse sympathy for the guy. Nothing ever goes right for Kullervo. He lurches from disaster to disaster, never giving up but never fitting in, wondering all the while why he was ever created and roundly rebuking whoever was responsible for making such a bad job of him. He makes Job look like Pollyanna.

The excesses of *The Story of Kullervo,* its headlong rush from disaster to disaster, its piling of one catastrophe on top of another, its unrelenting gloom and doom, are the hallmarks of a young author at once in emotional crisis and also (perhaps therefore) stretching his creative wings. Tolkien was only twenty-two when he wrote this story, scarcely more than a boy. But the boy is father to the man, and we can see in the young Tolkien who wrote this story of fratricide, child abuse, incest, murder, arson, and suicide the same man who led Boromir to succumb to the power of the Ring, who sent Frodo to the soul-imperiling agony of Mordor, who had Denethor set himself on fire, who had Pippin at the point of death reflect on "the bitter story of his life" (*RK* V, x, 168), who had Wormtongue eat Lotho and murder Saruman, and who at the end of his story denied Frodo the happy ending he gave the Shire, sending him traumatized, wounded, sick, and bereft into an unknown future.

The seeds of darkness were there all along, germinating in Tolkien's first serious narrative effort. It seems to have been the unrelenting gloom and doom of the story of Kullervo that so powerfully drew the young Tolkien at this particular time in his life, the headlong downward trajectory ending in despair and suicide. Now, it is true that all these elements are also present in Tolkien's source, the Kullervo *runos* in *Kalevala.* But it is that very fact, I think, that makes my case. Out of all the stories in *Kalevala*, this is the one Tolkien chose to work with most deeply, and we should look not just at what the story drew out of him, but at what in him resonated with the story.

At the time of its composition in 1914, Tolkien and his chosen subject had things in common. Aside from his obviously temporary college rooms—he was an undergraduate at Exeter College—he, like Kullervo, had no fixed home. He, like Kullervo, was estranged from his extended family, who as staunch Protestants disapproved of his mother's conversion to Catholicism after the death of her husband and cut her off financially and emotionally (Carpenter, *Tolkien* 24). He, like Kullervo, had lost his parents, his father dying when he was not quite four and his mother when he was twelve. There is no good time to lose parents, but twelve is a particularly vulnerable and confusing age, on the cusp of adolescence, just when the world is or should be opening up. Tolkien later referred to it as "really a sad and troubled time," and there is no reason not to take him at his word. The sadness and trouble are reflected in the story he plucked out of *Kalevala* to shape to his own ends, a story of a young man bereft of his family and driven to extremity by circumstances outside his control. There is no margin for error in this cruel, doom-laden world, and there are no redeeming features in the story that is Tolkien's first serious attempt at fiction.

To readers who have met Tolkien in *The Hobbit* and even *The Lord of the Rings*, this doesn't seem like typical Tolkien—until, that is, you look closely at these other works, for equally dark ingredients flavor Tolkien's later fiction. The world in which Kullervo lives is the shadow side of Middle-earth, as if the Old Forest had taken over not just the Shire but Gondor and Rohan and Lórien as well. It is a world of uncompromising cruelty and dark magic, peopled by sorcerers and witches and presided over by a few distant sky-gods, a host of nature spirits who must be wooed to make them kind, and wolves and bears that must be placated to keep them harmless but whose ferocity can also be harnessed as the instrument of vengeance.

The Hobbit starts as a parodic fairy tale aimed at children but ends as a tale of obsession, greed, theft, moral ambiguity, realpolitik, and world war. The first chapter of *The Lord of the Rings*, with its hobbit jollity, feasting, dancing, and comic speeches, can fool you into thinking it's another children's story, but by chapter 2 we are up to our ears in fratricide, addiction, corruption, moral relativism, betrayal, sacrifice, and the onset of another world war. The same tone pervades its parent mythology, the Silmarillion, which is the epic story of a world gone wrong from the beginning, a world bogged down in an unwinnable war fought for the wrong reasons. While Tolkien's own war experience is generally acknowledged as the most immediate impetus of these stories, we cannot overlook *The Story of Kullervo* as their ancestor, or *Kalevala* as the godfather of Middle-earth.

Túrin Turambar

Although I have written elsewhere about the relationship between Tolkien's Kullervo and his Túrin Turambar,[5] Túrin is too important to be wholly overlooked in the present context. All the chief ingredients of Kullervo's story reoccur in the story of Túrin—absent father, lost sister, incestuous encounter, double suicide. And all the negative traits of Kullervo—stubbornness, resentment, insecurity—are to be found in Túrin. The thread of Túrin leads from *Kalevala* through *The Story of Kullervo* to be interwoven into the fabric of Tolkien's mythology so that all the mishaps of Kullervo's life now occur within a larger context, with the unmotivated cruelty of his world replaced by the catastrophes that befall Túrin, framed by Curse of Melko (compare with the curse of the smith's wife) and the malice of the dragon, but also the result of his own bad choices and those of the people around him, from Húrin to Beleg to Morwen to Nienor. Tolkien never finished *The Story of Kullervo*. But elements of it reappear in his future work—its dark vision, its bad decisions, its fated encounters, its heroes pursuing their stubborn way to disaster. The ghost of Kullervo walks the roads of Tolkien's fictive world.

Tom Bombadil and Väinämöinen: Words and Music

In addition to tragedy, *Kalevala* gave Tolkien's story mystery as well, for it is in the Land of Heroes that one must search for the source of Tolkien's most idiosyncratic, enigmatic, and perplexing creation, Tom Bombadil. Tom is a problematic character to many readers, standing both literally and figuratively outside the margin of the folksy, hobbity Shire, and entirely removed from the more pragmatic realism of the Breeland, let alone the cultural sophistication of Gondor. Some readers are put off by what they find to be cloying whimsy in Tolkien's treatment of Tom, and many see him as a loose end in the otherwise tightly woven fabric of Middle-earth. But Tolkien deserves more trust. He doesn't people his world with random figures, and Tom is there for a reason: not just to rescue the hobbits (twice) but to connect them—and the reader—through his recollections to the ancient history of the Silmarillion.

"Who is Tom Bombadil?" That is the mystery to which no satisfactory solution is provided in the story. Goldberry's cryptic "He is, as you have seen him" (*FR* I, vii, 135) is not much help, for it comes down to "he is what he is," a tautology that simply sidesteps the question. Tolkien himself answered the question by saying that Tom was "the spirit of the (vanishing) Oxford and Berkshire countryside" (*Letters* 26), which is as close to "luxuriant animism" as you can get without saying it, and leads us from Middle-earth straight back to Finland and *The Story of Kullervo*.

Tom is a nature spirit like *Kalevala*'s Tapio and Mielikki and Tellervo, and like Tolkien's own Ilwinti and Manoine and Samyan and Terenye. And he is something more. Just as Tolkien drew on Kullervo for Túrin Turambar, so he drew even more directly on another of *Kalevala*'s major characters and its most mythic figure, Väinämöinen, for Tom Bombadil. This is not a new comparison; others have pointed out the resemblance (see this chapter's note 1). Nevertheless, Tom's connection to one particular aspect of Väinämöinen is worth a closer look. That aspect is the integral connection between memory, and magic, and song.

"Mythology is language and language is mythology"

This dictum from a draft of "On Fairy-stories" restates Tolkien's assertion, quoted several pages ago, that "'legends' depend on the language to which they belong; but a living language depends equally on the 'legends' which it conveys by tradition" (*Letters* 231). This is the cornerstone of his creative principle, and he learned it from *Kalevala*.

In one of the first and still one of the best studies of *Kalevala*, the Italian scholar Domenico Comparetti went out of his way to call attention to the importance in Finnish mythology of the "equivalence of the words wizard, poet, wise man (*loitsijä, laulajä* or *runoja, tietäjä*) and the mysterious character of the word *runo*, which signifies poetry" (Comparetti 187). This is a potent vocabulary. The words he cites—*loitsijä, laulajä. tietäjä, runojä*—are all, at one or another time in *Kalevala*, used of Väinämöinen. *Loitsijä*, "wizard," spell-doer," comes from *loitsia*, "cast a spell," 'enchant." *Laulajä* "enact or perform singing," comes from *laulaa* "to sing." *Tietäjä*, from *tietää*, "know," signifies "knower," "one who knows," "sage," "wise man," meaning not just one who possesses knowledge, but one who enacts knowing. The suffix *-jä* appended to each word has a function like *-er/-or* in English, bestowing a performative aspect on a word, as in sing*er*, danc*er*, or act*or*. The equivalence to each other of the words Comparetti cites, and his equation of all of them with the "mysterious" *runo* transforms the simple act of singing into incantation, the power to affect the world with words.

Runo 1 of *Kalevala* concludes with lines 341–42, "Se oli synty Väinämöinen, / rotu rohkean runojan," translated by Kirby as "Thus was ancient Väinämöinen, / He, the ever famous minstrel" (*Kalevala*, trans. Kirby 1: l). The word *runojan*, translated by Kirby as "minstrel," is translated by Magoun as "singer" (Magoun 7), by Friberg as "poet" (Friberg 46), and by Bosley as "bard" (Bosley 10).

John Crawford, who first put *Kalevala* into English, drew not directly from the Finnish but from the 1846–52 dual-language Finnish-German edition of Franz Anton Schiefner, who translated *runojan* into German as *Zaubersprecher*, "magic-speaker" or "spell-speaker" (5). Crawford Englished this as "enchanter" (*Kalevala*, trans. Crawford 13), and it seems plain that for Schiefner and Crawford, as for Comparetti, what is meant is the palpable, kinetic power inherent in words when they are spoken or sung, clearly related to *loitsijä, laulajä*, and *tietäjä*, "wizard" and "singer" and "knower."

To Comparetti's list I will add one more word of great significance, *muistaa*, "remember." This occurs without the suffix in Runo 3: The Singing Contest, and describes Väinämöinen—*muinaisia muisteloita*—in various translations as singing "the songs of bygone ages," (*Kalevala*, trans. Kirby 1: l. 20), "recited recollections of ancient times" (trans. Magoun 16), "recited ancient memories" (trans. Bosley 22), and as "recalling and rehearsing memories of bygone ages" (trans. Friberg 54). This conforms to all we know of the tradition of oral history, from Irish *filidh* and Jugoslavian *guslars* to the West African *griots*. In *Kalevala Mythology*, the Finnish scholar Juha Pentikäinen emphasizes the importance among illiterate northern peoples of the verbal preservation of archaic traditions and cultures (Pentikäinen 123).

Väinämöinen, born from the union of Ilmatar, Daughter of the Air, with the waters of the ocean, is the first and oldest created being in *Kalevala*. He is the "eternal singer" whose knowledge of ancient songs and the origins of the world and of history gives him power over nature. Tolkien's Tom Bombadil is his Middle-earth counterpart. As Tom tells the hobbits, "you are young and I am old. Eldest, that's what I am. Tom was here before the river and the trees. Tom *remembers* the first raindrop and the first acorn. He made paths before the Big People, and saw the Little People arriving. He was here before the Kings and the graves and the Barrow-wights. . . . before the seas were bent. He knew the dark under the stars when it was fearless" (*FR* I, vii, 142; my emphasis). At the Council in Rivendell, Elrond calls Tom, "oldest and fatherless" (*FR* II, I, 278). The other names given to him throughout the book—Iarwain Ben-Adar ("oldest fatherless"), *Orald* ("very ancient"), and *Forn* ("belonging to ancient days")—are all variants of the same concept, like Väinämöinen capable of recollecting ancient times.

Tom remembers and can tell the four hobbits the history of Middle-earth. He has knowledge of woods and waterfalls and downs; he remembers the barrows and the "'little kingdoms" and "strange regions beyond *their memory and beyond their waking thought*" (*FR* I, vii, 141–42; my emphasis). Tom can go "into times when the world was wider, and the seas flowed straight to the western Shore; and still on and back Tom went *singing* out into ancient starlight, when only the Elf-sires were awake" (142; my emphasis). The hobbits are "enchanted" by the "spell" of Tom's words (142). Tom's memory comes into play again later, at the barrow, in the little passage about the brooch from treasure-hoard. "He chose for himself from the pile a brooch set with blue stones, many-shaded like flax-flowers or the wings of blue butterflies. He looked long at it, *as if stirred by some memory,* shaking his head and saying at last: 'Here is a pretty toy for Tom and for his lady! Fair was she who long ago wore this on her shoulder. Goldberry shall wear it now, and we will not forget her!'" (*FR* I, viii, 156–57; my emphasis). Like Väinämöinen, Tom is *loitsijän, laulajän, tietajän, runojän. muinaisia muisteloita,* he possesses ancient memories, remembers ancient times, and sings of bygone ages.

He is an enchanter, a singer who can say of Old Man Willow, "I *know* the tune for him. . . . I'll *sing* his roots off. I'll *sing* a wind up and blow leaf and branch away," and promptly put his words into action (*FR* I, vi, 131; my emphases). Escorting the four hobbits out of his country, he teaches them a charm in verse to summon him in time of trouble, and when that charm is invoked and Tom appears, he can banish the barrow-wight because "[*h*]*is songs are stronger songs*" (*FR* I, viii, 153).

These characteristics are borrowed not just from Väinämöinen but also from those who created and transmitted his stories, the unlettered rune-singers of Finland whose songs Elias Lönnrot collected into *Kalevala*, singers whom Tolkien admired, whom he called "Finnish minstrels" (*SK* 113), "hard-worked uneducated men at the fireside" (112). Väinämöinen is their prototype, and it seems clear that Tolkien intended Tom to be his avatar, a kind of Middle-earth rune-singer, inheritor of its magic, custodian and transmitter of its history and tradition.

Tolkien Runojan

But Tolkien was not just imitating a world, he was also creating one. Tom not only sings runes, he talks them as well. All of his speech, not just his verses but his whole speech pattern, is in a loose approximation of *Kalevala* meter, itself a loose adaptation of Finnish pronunciation and speech rhythm whose primary emphasis is on the first syllable in every word. Though not as strict as the Kirby translation Tolkien first encountered, *Kalevala* poetry in Finnish is unrhymed, nonstrophic trochaic tetrameter, generally a line of four trochees, one long followed by one short syllable.[6] Tolkien modifies this to trimeter but keeps the rhythm. Here is a sample, in both the original Finnish and in Kirby's translation, of a stock poetic formula used for Väinämöinen:

Váka váhna Váinämóinen
Óld and stéadfast Váinämóinen

In the section on language and meter in his *Kalevala* essay, Tolkien gives his own examples of the meter of *Kalevala,* showing how attuned he was to its cadence:

Énkä lähe Inkerelle
Penkerelle Pänkerelle

or

Ihveniä ahvenia
Tuimenia Taimenia (*SK* 77)

And here, from Tolkien's own legendarium, is Tom Bombadil at his first meeting with Frodo and Sam in the Old Forest: "'Whóa! Whóa! Stéady there! . . . Nów my líttle féllows, whére be you a-góing to, púffing líke a béllows? Whát's the mátter hére then? Dó you knów who Í am? Í'm Tom Bómbadil. Téll me whát's your tróuble!'" (*FR* I, vi, 131). Only the typography keeps this from being verse, as reading it aloud makes plain. Short only by one foot of *Kalevala* tetrameter, it has merely to be reset with line breaks to immediately reveal its rhythmic nature.

"Whóa! Whóa! Stéady there!
Nów my líttle féllows,
whére be yóu a-góing to,
púffing líke a béllows?
Whát's the mátter hére then?
Dó you knów who Í am?
Í'm Tom Bómbadil.
Téll me whát's your tróuble!"

Tom's perpetual singing is not just a whimsical idiosyncrasy, as readers of *The Lord of the Rings* sometimes suppose when they encounter him for the first time. Rather, it is an integral part of his nature, directly connected to his power. It's not just the way he talks; it's the way he is. We must see Tom's singing as *runojä* in his scenes with Old Man Willow and at the Barrow, in order to understand its true nature, and his.

Conclusion

None of this breaks new ground, but it is my hope that it enlarges some earlier excavations and digs a deeper foundation for Tolkien's debt to *Kalevala*, the earliest, and in many ways the most formative, of his mythic influences. His fascination with *Kalevala* may have "nearly ruined" his Honor Mods," as he admitted to his son Christopher (*Letters* 87) and to W. H. Auden (214–15), but it gave him the right push in the right direction at the right time. It started his own lifelong process as *loitsijä, laulajä, tietajä, runojä,* of being wizard, poet, wise man, magician, one whose *muinaisia muisteloita,* reinventions of bygone ages, made him his own Tom Bombadil, one whose singing gave the world the Silmarillion and *The Lord of the Rings.*

Tolkien's Celtic Connection

In 1937, Edward Crankshaw, a reader for Allen and Unwin, commended Tolkien's then-unpublished Quenta Silmarillion for having that "mad, bright-eyed beauty that perplexes all Anglo-Saxons in the face of Celtic art," but remarked also that he disliked its "eye-splitting Celtic names." These comments provoked the following rejoinder from Tolkien: "I am sorry the names split his eyes—personally I believe . . . they are good, and a large part of the effect. . . . Needless to say they are not Celtic! Neither are the tales. I do know Celtic things (many in their original languages Irish and Welsh) and feel for them a certain distaste: largely for their fundamental unreason. They have bright colour, but are like a broken stained glass window reassembled without design. They are in fact 'mad' as your reader says—but I don't believe I am" (*Letters* 26).

Understandably nettled at the implication that any part of his invention was derivative, Tolkien was at pains to reject the Celtic connection. Elsewhere and later, he elaborated on this, particularly emphasizing his aesthetic distance from things Irish. He wrote to one correspondent, "I find both Gaelic and the air of Ireland wholly alien" (*Letters* 219) and to another, "the Irish language I find wholly unattractive" (289).

Taking Tolkien's words at face value, readers might well be discouraged from looking for any Celtic elements in his fiction, and indeed most critical commentary has focused instead on his use of Germanic and Norse. But there are words and words, and Tolkien, like the rest of the human race, was not a model of consistency. And some of his own words—especially his invented ones—give a different picture. Many of the names in *The Lord of the Rings*, as he told the audience for his O'Donnell lecture, "English and Welsh," were "composed on pattern deliberately modelled on those of Welsh" (*MC* 197). He wrote to Houghton Mifflin that "'Sindarin' . . . is in fact constructed deliberately to resemble Welsh phonologically" (*Letters* 219).

He willingly admitted Wales to his invented world—at least linguistically—but what about the other Celts? Was he quite so strict in his distaste for things Celtic as he would have his readers believe? The answer is no. *The Lay of Aotrou and Itroun*, one of his early poems, is modeled on the Breton *lai* and was inspired by Breton legend. "Imram" is his retelling of the Irish *Navigatio Sancti Brendani* (The Voyage of St. Brendan), and includes elements from the earlier and even more Irish voyage of Bran. His scholarly essay "The Name 'Nodens'" traces the descent of Nodens from god to Irish hero (Núadu) to Welsh hero (Llud Llaw Ereint) and finally to Shakespearean hero—King Lear. Moreover, a close look at his later fiction—*The Lord of the Rings*, the Silmarillion in all its versions, his two unfinished time-travel stories, and *Smith of Wootton Major*—reveals in all of these significant elements that are unmistakably Celtic and more often Irish than Welsh.

These elements divide into two categories: general pervading concepts and specific, concrete references. In the general category, I offer two examples. The first example is that of the Elves, the central people in Tolkien's mythology. It is true that the word *elf* comes from Germanic *alf*, true also that the main tribal division of the Eldar into Light Elves and Dark Elves comes out of Snorri's *Edda*, and true that the name Ælfwine and its epithet Elf-friend are clearly Germanic. Nevertheless, the Germanic element ends here. The Elves are Germanic in name only; in character and appearance they are clearly Celtic, bearing a marked resemblance to the Irish so-called "fairies," more correctly known as the *sídh*, or the Tuatha Dé Danann. According to Alwyn and Brinley Rees, they are "the most handsome and delightful company, the fairest of form, the most distinguished in their equipment and apparel, and their skill in music and playing, the most gifted in mind and temperament that ever came to Ireland. . . . the Tuatha Dé excelled all the peoples of the world in their proficiency in every art" (Rees and Rees 30).

Compare this with Tolkien's descriptions of the first Children of Ilúvatar. First, in *The Book of Lost Tales*, where they are called "fairies" or "Gnomes," he notes: "But when the Eldar come they will be the fairest and most lovely of all things by far" (*BLT* I 59). Then, in *The Silmarillion*, he describes them thus: "The Quendi shall be the fairest of all earthly creatures, and they shall have and conceive and bring forth more beauty than all my children; and they shall have the greater bliss in this world" (*S* 41). In addition, he says of the Noldor: "Great became their knowledge and skill. . . . they had great love of words, and sought ever to find names more fit for all things that they knew or imagined. . . . and they devised tools for cutting and shaping of gems, and carved them freely in many forms" (*S* 60). It seems clear that from their earliest conception—when they were even called "fairies" (a term that, like Celticism itself, Tolkien would later reject)—the Elves derived from a specifically Irish model.

The second example in the general category is the whole concept of Faërie, an even more crucial element in Tolkien's work. His essay "On Fairy-stories" describes Faërie as "wide and deep and high and filled with many things; all manner of beasts and birds are found there; shoreless seas and stars uncounted; beauty that is an enchantment, and an ever-present peril, both joy and sorrow as sharp as swords" (*MC* 109). The similarity between this and accounts of the Celtic otherworlds is worth noting. According to Proinsias MacCana, the otherworld of the Irish and Welsh was conceived as being "filled with enchanting music from bright-plumaged birds, from the swaying branches of the otherworld tree, from instruments which sound without being played, and from the very stones, . . . 'a marvel of beauty,' 'a wondrous land.' This world transcends the limitations of human time; a mortal returning from a visit may suddenly become aged and decrepit on contact with the material world" (MacCana 124). The otherworld has many names—Tír na nÓg, Annwvn, Mag Mell, Tír Tairngiri, Tír inna mBeo. It is called The Land of Promise, The Land of the Ever Young, The Land of the Living, The Plain of Delights, The Land Under Wave. According to MacCana, "It also transcends all spatial definition. It may be situated under the ground or under the sea . . . in distant islands or coexistent with the world of reality" (124).

Wherever it is, the otherworld is on special occasions accessible to mortal men, who can enter it almost without knowing. This is precisely what happens to Pwyll, Prince of Dyfed, the hero of the First Branch of the Welsh *Mabinogion*. He enters the otherworld quite by accident, while out hunting in a wood. Separated from his companions, he sees a pack of dogs overtaking the same stag his dogs are pursuing. And these are unusual dogs, as he immediately observes, for "of all the hounds he had seen in the world he had seen no dogs the same colour as these. The colour that was on them was a brilliant shining white, and their ears red; and as the exceeding whiteness of the dogs glittered, so glittered the exceeding redness of their ears" (*MC* 172–73).

The dogs' colors are the giveaway; they are otherworld colors, and these are otherworld dogs. Pwyll has unwittingly crossed the invisible barrier, and is now in the otherworld kingdom of Arawn, Lord of Annwvn. This passage, by the way, is taken from the translation of the *Mabinogion* by Gwyn Jones and Thomas Jones (standard in Tolkien's day), as quoted in Tolkien's "English and Welsh" lecture, where he cited it as an example of Celtic descriptiveness. Further evidence that he was well acquainted with the *Mabinogion* is the existence of his partial transcription and translation of the opening episode of "Pwyll Prince of Dyfed," from volume 1 of The Red Book of Hergest, included among his papers in the Bodleian.

Tolkien also undoubtedly knew of the many similar episodes in Irish myth—of Connla, son of Conn of the Hundred Battles, who was lured by an otherworld woman to spend what he thought was a day in the Land of the Ever Young but, when he returned to the world of mortal men, found to be a hundred years; of Oisin, son of Fionn, who had much the same kind of adventure, as did Art, son of Conn, as did the Bran whose voyage to the otherworld became the *Navigatio* of St. Brendan. All of them include a journey to a magic land, a sojourn encompassing some kind of temporal disjuncture, and a perceptible spatial displacement—typical Celtic magic.

The same spatial displacement and temporal disjuncture are part of the operation of Tolkien's versions of the otherworld, of which the best-known are Lórien in *The Lord of the Rings* and Faery in *Smith of Wootton Major*. Crossing over the Silverlode into Lórien, Frodo feels as if he has crossed "over a bridge of time" and is now "in a corner of the Elder Days," a world wherein "all about the green hillsides [is] . . . grass studded with small golden flowers shaped like stars" where "the sky [is] blue and the sun of afternoon [glows] upon the hill" (*FR* II, vi, 364–65). Smith of Wootton Major takes long walks in the evening, and though he returns the same night, his time in Faery can last a week. While his Faery is more varied than Lórien, one of his most memorable visits takes him to a place remarkably like it, "a Vale with Elven voices singing," where "on a lawn beside a river bright with lilies he [comes] upon many maidens dancing" (*SMW* 35). These descriptions echo what is told of the Celtic otherworlds, but Tolkien supported them by a lengthy discussion of the whole concept in an essay he wrote to accompany *Smith of Wootton Major*:

> The geographical relation of [the world] and Faery are inevitably, but also intentionally left vague. . . . there must be some way or ways of access from and to Faery. . . . But it is also necessary that Faery and the world (of Men), though in contact, should occupy different time and space, or occupy them in different modes. . . . an absence from home of, say, a week is sufficient for exploration and experiences in Faery equivalent to months or even years. . . . Entry into the "geographical" bounds of Faery also involves entry into Faery time. How does a mortal "enter" the geographical realm of Faery? . . . It is common in fairy tales for the entrance to the fairy world to be presented as a journey underground, into a hill or mountain or the like. . . . My symbol is . . . the Forest: the regions still immune from human activities. . . . If Faery

time is at points contiguous with ours, the contiguity will occur in related points in space—or that is the theory for purposes of the story. At certain points just within the Forest borders a human person may come across these contiguous points and there enter F. time and space. (*SMW* 86–87)

Both Frodo's Lórien and Smith's Faery are plainly and intentionally situated at just such a contiguous point—adjacent to the human world but definitely part of Faery time and space. Frodo's entry into Lórien and Smith's entry into Faery, like Pwyll's entry into Annwvn, occur through a wood. Both Frodo's and Smith's journeys take them out of mortal time. Smith is often back by evening, though he has spent days and even weeks in Faery. As for Frodo, as I have pointed out elsewhere, his crossing of the Silverlode constitutes a transition into another mode of time, and the return to the Great River, a return to mortal time. The similarities among Smith's Faery, Frodo's Lórien, and the Welsh and Irish otherworlds are too close to be accidental.

So much for the general instances of Tolkien's Celticism. There are more specific examples. One is a note appended to a draft for *The Lost Road* that reads "See Lit. Celt. p. 137." Lit. Celt. is Magnus MacLean's *Literature of the Celts*, published in 1906. Page 137 of that work, quoted by Christopher Tolkien, is an account of the invasions of Ireland, commencing with Cæsair and her husband Finntann, survivors of Noah's Flood, and ending with the Tuatha Dé Danann (*LR* 1, 82). Finntann, who stayed alive down to the sixth century A.D., was said to have been the oldest man in the world. Elsewhere in Tolkien's notes for *The Lost Road* is a sketch for "the Irish legend of Tuatha-de-Danann—and oldest man in the world" (78), which Tolkien projected for one of the story's time-travel episodes. That he never got around to writing it does not detract from the Irishness of what he would have done.

My other examples come from *The Notion Club Papers*, where, as might be expected, they also involve displacement in space and time. The first example involves the apparently chance remark by the story's hero, Arry Lowdham, that his family lived in Pembrokeshire. The choice of place is no accident. It was from Pembrokeshire that Lowdham's father, old Edwin Lowdham, embarked on what would be his last voyage, the journey from which he never returned, with no traces of him or his ship ever found. Pembrokeshire, in southwest Wales, was medieval Dyfed, where Pwyll started out in a wood and wound up in the otherworld. While Tolkien has substituted sea for wood, it seems not unlikely that he intended his Pembrokeshire/Dyfed to have something of the same otherworld overlap.

Several Celtic associations converge here. First, as Peter Berresford Ellis points out in *Celt and Saxon*, Dyfed was settled in the third century AD by

Irish immigrants expelled by Cormac Mac Art. "The Irish kingdom of Demetia (Dyfed)" says Ellis, "prospered and was accepted by the British Celts. Eventually it became absorbed into a British cultural ethos" (Ellis 56), though it seems to have retained its Irish identity for many centuries. Thus there may be Irish as well as Welsh influence in the possible otherworld overlap involving Pembrokeshire and Dyfed. Second, even without this Irish-Welsh connection, Lowdham's Pembrokeshire would be rich in Celtic associations, for the West of England is King Arthur country, from whence the wounded Arthur was transported by ship to the magical otherworld Isle of Avalon to be healed. It is surely no accident that, at one meeting, Tolkien has his Notion Club discuss the myth of Arthur, calling it one of the great "explosive" myths of Western culture.

The subsequent, and by far the most explicit Irish references in *The Notion Club Papers* occur toward the end of the unfinished text. One is the reading aloud in its entirety of Tolkien's "Imram" poem (here assigned to Philip Frankley) about the otherworld voyage of St. Brendan, whose "bones in Ireland lie" (*SD* 264). Nor is this an idle reference or an opportunity to use early work. It is a conscious setup for the subsequent voyages of Lowdham and Jeremy, whose travels through time and space, triggered by the great storm, take them both actually and mythologically to Ireland. Following their dreams, the two men journey up and down the western coasts of England, Scotland, and Ireland. "A good many dreams came," Jeremy reports, "especially in Ireland, but they were very slippery; we couldn't catch them" (*SD* 268). The dreams and flashbacks that constitute Tolkien's method of time-travel are more vivid in Ireland than anywhere else, evidence of the increasingly specific Irish component that Tolkien was adding to his story. Jeremy continues: "The great storm had left more traces there than anywhere. We both heard many tales of the huge waves 'high as hills' coming in on the Black Night. And curiously enough, many of the tale-tellers agreed that the greatest waves were like phantoms, or only half-real: 'like shadows of mountains of dark black wicked water.' Some rolled far inland and yet did little damage before, well, disappearing, melting away. We were told of one that had rolled clean over the Aran Isles" (*SD* 267).

The "Great Wave" is, of course, part of Tolkien's personal mythology, what he called his "Atlantis-haunting" (*Letters* 347), his recurrent dream of a huge wave looming over him and crashing down. It is the germ of "The Fall of Númenor," his own Atlantis story, and the centerpiece of his legendarium. But the same incident is also a pervasive motif in Celtic myth and legend. The best-known example is probably the Arthurian-related lost land of Lyonesse, supposed to lie sunk between the coast of Cornwall and the Scilly Isles. There is as well the parallel Breton story of the overwhelming of the city of Ys. And there is an Irish version. Recurring accounts in Irish legend tell of a storm or a wave that roared in off the Atlantic and rolled far inland, inundating the land, sweeping away a good part of it, and drowning the rest. This drowned land, of which the Aran Islands are said to be the last remnant, is by some equated with the Atlantis myth, and Tolkien goes out of his way to link them both with Númenor. One Irish incident remembered by Jeremy specifically connects present Ireland with the past of Tolkien's own legendarium:

> And we came across one old man, a queer old fellow whose English was hardly intelligible, on the road not far from Loughrea. He was wild and ragged, but tall and rather impressive. He kept pointing westward and saying, as far as we could gather: 'It was out of the Sea they came, as they came in the days before the days.' He said that he had seen a tall black ship high on the crest of the great wave, with its masts down and the rags of black and yellow sails flapping on the deck, and great tall men standing on the high poop and wailing, like the ghosts they were; and they were borne far inland, and came, well, not a soul knows where they came. (*SD* 267)

It is worth noting that in the version of the Ælfwine story included in his notes for *The Notion Club Papers*, Tolkien's mariner Ælfwine was shipwrecked "on the West shores of Erin."

These references make it clear that Tolkien intended to establish a specifically Irish connection for his own Atlantis of Númenor, and that he sent Lowdham and Jeremy to Ireland precisely to connect them with its downfall. It is possible also that this episode was to have become a part of the increasingly complex Ælfwine-Eriol saga, which Tolkien had originally intended as the frame for his "mythology dedicated to England," a concept that he began to develop back in *The Book of Lost Tales*.

That he either did not or could not complete his vision should not keep his readers from exploring the ramifications of what he did do, nor from recognizing the marked, explicit Celtic direction in which his mythology was headed at that time. Middle-earth, its legends, and its languages went through many revisions and reworkings over the course of composition. But the "Celtic things" remained. They were neither eye-splitting nor mad and bright-eyed, as Tolkien maintained, but Edward Crankshaw was on the right track in recognizing that they were there.

Tolkien's French Connection

It may surprise some of Tolkien's readers (and it would certainly have surprised Bilbo) to learn that the original hobbit, fat, bumbling, suburban in outlook, and slightingly compared by Gloin to a grocer, should actually be more respectfully compared to a knight in the tradition of medieval French romance. There is a reason for this surprise. Ever since the publication of Humphrey Carpenter's biography, conventional wisdom has held that J. R. R. Tolkien was averse to all things French. He unequivocally stated his distaste for the French language, saying flat out, "I dislike French" (*Letters* 288), while as for French cuisine, Carpenter noted his dislike of "tiresome French cooking" and its "pernicious influence" in England (*Tolkien* 119, 129). Also according to Carpenter, Tolkien deplored the Norman Conquest (*Tolkien* 129) and promoted a return to "English goodliness of speechcraft," by which, says another biographer, John Garth, he meant "a language purged of . . . French derivatives" (52). And then there is Tolkien's sniffy comment in "On Fairy-stories" that in France the fairy tale "went to court and put on powder and diamonds" (*MC* 111). Although this is not a scathing criticism, it does not sound like a compliment, while in an early draft he went farther, declaring that French fairy stories are "not to [his] taste" and that he "never had much affection" for "these French things" (*TOFS* 214). Carpenter lumped all this together as Tolkien's "Gallophobia" (*Tolkien* 67), and conventional wisdom has embraced the term ever since.

But dislike does not preclude influence—indeed, it can sometimes foster it—and an author is not always the most reliable authority on his own work. Neither conventional wisdom nor Carpenter, let alone Tolkien himself, should be taken as the last word on Tolkien's relations with France and things French. Two of his early poems," The Lay of Leithian" and *The Lay of Aotrou and Itroun,* derive from France. *Lay* itself is a loan-word from Old French *lai* "a long narrative in verse." And while *leithian* is Tolkien's own Elvish term, meaning "release" (*LR* 368), the words *aotrou* and *itroun,* meaning "lord" and "lady," are Breton, as is the poem "Aotrou Nann Hag Ar Gorrigan," on which Tolkien modeled his own. It can be argued that these last terms and Tolkien's source for them are Celtic and thus not strictly French, but while this is correct, it is not the whole picture. "Aotrou Nann Hag Ar Gorrigan" was first published in France in a dual-language French and Breton anthology of folklore, an edition of which Tolkien bought and inscribed in 1922. The anthology was the work of a French folklorist of Breton descent and ties in well with Tolkien's interest in the mythic and folkloric substrates of European cultures—all of which brings it a lot closer to France than to Tolkien's more recognized influences in Germany, Scandinavia, and Anglo-Saxon England.

And if we turn from poetry to prose, we will find some important and notably French-derived terms in Tolkien's essay "On Fairy-stories" (*Letters* 118). In one memorable paragraph he used two such terms, declaring that fairy-stories are about "the *aventures* of men in the Perilous Realm," which he called "*Faërie*" (*MC* 113). Thus the same essay in which he looks down his nose at French powder and diamonds shows him turning to French vocabulary when he needed the precise word to convey a particular meaning. Moreover, these words are not merely precise and apt, they are essential to his critical and creative vocabulary, recurring significantly, as we shall see.

Nevertheless, *aventures* is so unlikely a word for a presumed Gallophobe to use that the copy editor for *The Tolkien Reader* thought it was a typo and inserted a *d,* correcting it to *adventures.* In fact, *adventures* is the typo, and *aventures* is Tolkien's correct spelling and usage. The editorial mistake is pardonable, however, as *aventure* is not a word in common parlance—not, at least, in English. It is part of the specialized vocabulary of French romance, where it denotes the exploits of knights errant in a magical otherworld often called "the forest of *aventure.*" The Celtic equivalent is Old Irish *echtra, echtrae, ectra, echtrai,* usually translated "adventure," an Irish tale type involving the hero's journey to the otherworld, of which there are numerous examples (MacKillop 148), and to which the medieval French stories clearly have some relationship. There is an equivalent Welsh tale type, exemplified in the *Mabinogion* by the adventure of Pwyll, prince of Dyfed in Annwvyn (from *an* "in, inside" + *dwuyn* "deep") (*Pwyll* 26). The modern Breton equivalent of the word is *Anaon,* signifying the world of the dead. I have been unable to find an equivalent Welsh or Breton term for the tale-type *echtrae,* but the tales themselves certainly exist. Tolkien would have been aware of all these examples (he made his own translation of *Pwyll Pendeuic Dyuet*) and their relationship through shared Celtic heritage with the medieval French romances, but the closest parallels to Bilbo's adventures are in the French rather than the more strictly Celtic stories.

Adventure comes from the French into Middle English as *auentur(e) / aunter*, which Tolkien's *Middle English Vocabulary* glosses as "chance, (notable) occurrence, feat, risk" (*Vocabulary* [np]). But even here it means more than just "escapade." It suggests the kind of danger embodied in the *echtrae*, implying entry into the otherworld, encounter with the unexpected, the unexplained, even the supernatural, as in the Middle English *The Awnters off Arthure at the Terne Wathelyne*, in which Arthur encounters a ghost at a haunted tarn or lake. In the French romances, the word was sometimes spelled *avanture*, suggesting *avant*, "forward,"[1] and connoting "what's coming," meaning the unknown and by implication the mysterious future. When Tolkien talked about "the *aventures* of men in the Perilous Realm," he meant all of this.

The same is true of his other notable French derivative, *Faërie*, meaning the perilous realm. *Faërie*, like *aventure*, means more than its modern counterpart. It does not refer to fairies, but to Faërie, described by Tolkien as "the realm or state in which fairies have their being" (*MC* 113). The agentive suffix *-erie* denotes both a process and a condition, as in *cook-ery, witch-ery, slave-ery*. Thus *faë-erie* is both the process of enchantment and the condition of being enchanted, the altered state produced by fairy stories. The word derives from Old French *fae* or *fée*, from Latin *fata/fatum* "Fate," the past participle of *fari* "to speak," hence a word spoken, a spell cast, or a story told. The connection to *Fate* as that which is spoken suggests the reason Tolkien called *Faërie* "the Perilous Realm" (*MC* 113), and French romance called it "the forest of *aventure*." "Small wonder," said Tolkien in the essay, "that *spell* means both a story told, and a formula of power over living men" (*EPCW* 56, *MC* 128).

But what has this to do with *The Hobbit*? Or, to put it more bluntly, "so what?" French words in a poem and an essay do not necessarily translate to French influence in a children's story. Moreover, *The Hobbit* has been getting on very well for seventy years without recourse to French influence. I suggest a couple of "so whats." First, recognition of French influence expands *The Hobbit* from children's fairy tale to the more "literary" genre of romance. With one notable anomaly, which I will address in due course, the narrative structure of the first half of *The Hobbit* replicates the narrative structure of medieval French romance.[2] The romance structure goes like this. A hero—usually a knight—leaves home—usually King Arthur's court—on errantry (from Fr. *errer* "to wander"). He undergoes trials in battles against extraordinary opponents, after which he returns to home base.

The pattern is a recognizable subset of the Hero Path, the master paradigm described by Joseph Campbell as *"separation—initiation—return"* (23). But instead of Campbell's one decisive encounter with a single foe, medieval romance gives its heroes a series of random encounters with a succession of foes—other knights, giants, robbers, lions, wild men, serpents. It is easy to see Bilbo's path in *The Hobbit*—leaving Bag End to wander from trolls to wolves to goblins to Gollum to wood-elves—as a clear parallel. His comically named sword, Sting, has an ancestor in Arthur's Excalibur and Roland's Durendal. Even in the story's second half, Thorin Oakenshield's exhortation in the dragon's cave that Bilbo "[c]ast off [his] old coat and put on" the *mithril* mail-coat, belt, and helmet (*H* 203) carries out the dictum that "clothes make the man" (or the hobbit) and effectively transforms Bilbo from amateur burglar to medieval knight, while Bard the Bowman's later comment that he is "worthy to wear the armour of elf-princes" confirms his new status (*H* 230).

Second and more specifically, the French connection invites a rereading of the opening conversation between Gandalf and Bilbo that directly counters conventional wisdom regarding French influence, Carpenter's "Gallophobic" appellation, and Tolkien's own statements about taste. In the first five pages of *The Hobbit,* the word *adventure* occurs a total of twelve times— a little more than twice on every page. That's a pretty high average, and it is conscious repetition, not careless writing. I hope to persuade you that when Tolkien said *adventure* in *The Hobbit* he meant *aventure* as in his essay. Here are the relevant occurances:

1. p. 11, the narrator: The Bagginses "never had any adventures."
2. p. 11, the narrator: "This is a story of how a Baggins had an adventure."
3. p. 12, the narrator: "[O]nce in a while members of the Took-clan would go and have adventures."
4. p. 12, the narrator: "Not that Belladonna Took ever had any adventures."
5. p. 13, the narrator: "[T]ales and adventures sprouted up all over the place wherever [Gandalf] went,"
6. p. 13, Gandalf to Bilbo: "I am looking for someone to share in an adventure."
7. p. 13, Bilbo to Gandalf: "We are plain quiet folk and have no use for adventures. . . . !"
8. p. 14, Bilbo to Gandalf: "We don't want any adventures here."
9. p. 14, Bilbo to Gandalf: "Not the Gandalf who was responsible for so many quiet lads and lasses going off into the Blue for mad adventures?"
10. p. 15, Gandalf to Bilbo: "I will . . . send you on this adventure."
11. p. 15, Bilbo to Gandalf: "I don't want any adventures."

12. p. 15, the narrator: "Bilbo . . . was beginning to think he had escaped adventures very well."

Like a leit-motif in music, this recurrence is cumulative, echoing and re-echoing until the word spoken becomes "a spell cast, a formula of power," and finally "a story told." I do not suggest that the copy editor of *The Tolkien Reader* emended *The Hobbit*, but I do suggest that Tolkien's intention is best served if we remove that *d*. I also suggest that when Bilbo said "into the Blue" in *The Hobbit*, he meant Faërie, as in Tolkien's essay "On Fairy-stories."

But even if the words and the concepts behind them are French-derived, does that necessarily make *The Hobbit* a French romance? Not by itself, no—but it helps. Supporting evidence comes from actual French romances. If we look at *The Hobbit* in the context of three actual romances, two by the French poet Chrétien de Troyes, and one adapted from the French by Sir Thomas Malory in *Le Morte D'Arthur*, we will see sufficient similarity to support my argument. I want to emphasize that I am not analyzing plot here, merely tallying *aventures* as they occur in the episodic world of French romance. I also want to emphasize that the humor of these stories, like that in *The Hobbit*, undermines their subject matter. All three are spoofs, seeming to extol *aventure* while actually poking sly fun at it, as when Chrétien's hero Yvain, asked to fight some giants, hopes they will be on time so he won't be late for his date to rescue a maiden from burning at the stake. Malory, too, plays for laughs, having that paragon of knighthood, Launcelot, so lost in a dream of Guinevere that he forgets where he is and falls ingloriously off his horse. Tolkien's burglarious hobbit hero starts out as equally incompetent, trying to steal a talking purse whose unexpected vocal ability betrays him to the trolls. Like the character in *Monty Python*, he gets better, but it takes time.

In Chrétien's *Erec and Enide*, the young knight Erec gets lost in the *"forest of aventure,"* where he is insulted by an arrogant knight. He pursues him through the forest, defeats him in a tournament, and brings home the beautiful Enide as a bride. When after their wedding he overhears her incautious lament that spending too much time with her has damaged his knightly reputation, he forces her to go on errantry with him so that he can prove his prowess. The satire here is edged and cutting. One of Arthur's knights puts his lady at risk by using her as sexual bait to attract highway thugs, predatory seducers, and potential rapists, yet when she tries to warn him what's coming, he commands her to keep her mouth shut. Unlike Bilbo and Launcelot, Erec is not incompetent; he is just bullying and tyrannical and criminally irresponsible. His *aventures*, which he intends to present him in a heroic role, are cumulatively ironic as he is wounded by one attacker, knocked unconscious by another, and finally apparently killed by a third. While in each of these episodes, it is Erec who seeks *aventure*, it is the long-suffering Enide who finds it, repeatedly having to save him from her attackers. The final episode, "The Joy of the Court" (explicitly called an *aventure*), occurs in an orchard (not quite a *forêt*, but close enough), and in it Erec at last defeats another knight, Maboagrain, who is also fighting to impress his sweetheart. Both pairs of lovers are reconciled by means of this senseless mayhem, and all four live happily ever after.

In Chrétien's next romance, *Yvain*, the eponymous hero leaves Arthur's court to go "adventuring" (*Yvain* l. 167) in *la forêt aventureuse* of Broceliande, a notoriously otherworld locality. Here he encounters a wild man, unwittingly provokes a tempest, kills the magical Knight of the Storm, marries the knight's widow, but leaves her for a year to fight in tournaments, after which he defends a lady from attack by a wicked seneschal, saves a lion from a serpent, kills the aforementioned giants—who fortunately show up on time to be killed—and rescues the maiden. It is important to note that in each of these episodes, the *aventure* is there simply for its own sake, with no larger unifying purpose or plot. Like Erec, Yvain is looking for *aventure* and he finds it. After fighting incognito as "the knight with the lion" (compare the epithets Bilbo assumes with the dragon), he returns to his abandoned wife and they live happily ever after.

I hope you have seen some parallels with *The Hobbit* here, but I hope you have also noticed the glaring difference I mentioned in my first paragraph. Unlike the romances it parodies, Tolkien's story has no love interest. It strains imagination to picture Bilbo Baggins as a lover or a husband. Indeed, Tolkien himself, planning the sequel that became *The Lord of the Rings*, considered but dismissed as unworkable the notion that Bilbo could marry and have children. However, while a love interest is a standard trope in medieval romance, it is not a requirement, and Bilbo's other attributes qualify him.

Malory's "Noble Tale of Sir Launcelot Du Lake," adapted from the French prose *Lancelot*, also plays down the love interest while otherwise following the pattern. Like Erec and Yvain, Launcelot rides away from Arthur's court to "preve" himself in "straunge [that is, "marvelous"] adventures." He tells his nephew, Sir Lyonel, that, "we must go seke adventures" (Malory 149). Why "must" they? Because that is what knights do, and Malory provides plenty of comedic *aventures* to keep his knight errant busy. Launcelot is kidnapped for illicit purposes by Morgan le Fay, hit on by another women (he turns them both down out of love for Guinevere), climbs a tree in his underwear to rescue a hawk, defends himself with a tree branch against a fully armed knight, and fails to prevent another knight from beheading his own wife.

Launcelot finally gets his payback by trading armor with Sir Kay, the biggest wimp in Arthur's court, thus making Kay unattackable while himself beating the pants off all the knights who think he's an easy mark. At the end of his *aventures,* Launcelot returns to Arthur's court with "the grettyste name of ony knight of the world" (173). It makes you wonder just what "greatest" means in this upside-down romance world.

All three of these figures trace a narrative arc that we can see also in *The Hobbit.* Departure from home and entry into Faërie followed by an escalating series of *aventures,* culminating in a final battle and a return to home base and happy ever after. The word used for Erec's and Yvain's and Launcelot's deeds—*aventure*—is deliberately echoed in Bilbo's opening conversation with Gandalf. Tolkien's hero is a parodic romance knight, a bumbling, suburban householder pitched without warning into a series of knightly *aventures* for which he seems ludicrously unfitted. Bilbo does not "seke" a "grete name." He does not kill a giant, win a wife, rescue a maiden, or make friends with a lion. But he does get captured by trolls, ambushed by goblins, surrounded by wolves, rescued by eagles, lost in Mirkwood (a *forêt aventureuse* if ever there was one), attacked by spiders, and detained by elves. In his final encounter, the Battle of Five Armies, he, like Erec, is knocked unconscious.

As is the case with Erec, Yvain, and Launcelot, no plot connects Bilbo's *aventures* to one another. They are episodic and unrelated, each *aventure* self-contained and discrete. In *Master of Middle-earth,* Paul Kocher points out that unlike Frodo, "Bilbo's enemies are serial, not united under any paragon of evil as is to happen [in *The Lord of the Rings*]. *The Hobbit*'s trolls, goblins (orcs), spiders, and dragon know nothing of one another, and all are acting on their own" (Kocher 30). At the end of his adventure, Bilbo returns home, leaving in his wake peace and prosperity and bringing with him treasure, plus Gandalf's comment that he is "not the hobbit" that he was when he set out (*H* 253). Like Erec and Yvain, he has been changed by his *aventures,* although (also like Erec and Yvain) that was not his reason for seeking them.

Retrospective references in *The Fellowship of the Ring* to Bilbo's journey in *The Hobbit* deliberately repeat the key word and tend to support the idea of adventure for its own sake, as was the case in *Erec* and *Yvain*. In chapter 1 of *The Lord of the Rings,* Bilbo, like Erec and Yvain and Launcelot, leaves Bag End as he did in *The Hobbit* with no goal in mind but the need for a "holiday" (*FR* I, i, 40). At the Council of Elrond, he whispers to Frodo, "I almost wish that my adventures were not over" (*FR* II, ii, 261), and the narrative points out that Frodo's fiftieth birthday marks the age at which "adventure had suddenly befallen Bilbo" (*FR* I, ii, 52). I believe we may safely confer a French pronunciation on this apparently English word.

Comparison of *The Hobbit* with *The Lord of the Rings* is inevitable, but reveals more differences than similarities. In the most general sense, both follow the traditional romance trajectory—a hero's journey and return. Within that, however, are substantial subgenre distinctions—what Paul Kocher calls "polarities in tone and scope between *The Hobbit* and its successor" (30)— that make *The Hobbit* and *The Lord of the Rings* "so unalike fundamentally as to be different in kind" (19). In spite of surface similarities—journey plots, hobbit heroes, multicultural elves, dwarves, orcs, and wizards—the two are not just different books, they are, as Kocher says, different *kinds* of books. One is a fairy-tale romance for children, the other, a bigger and darker story closer to epic than romance. Each kind is signaled by its key word: *aventure* for *The Hobbit*, *quest* for *The Lord of the Rings*.

Like *aventure* and *faërie*, the word *quest* is French in origin, coming into Middle English through Old French *queste* "to seek or search for," from Latin *quaerere* "pursuit or search," from earlier Latin *quaerere* "to seek." The nature of Frodo's quest, in contrast to Bilbo's adventure, imposes a more unified structure on his story. That Tolkien was well aware of the distinction is shown by his post–*Lord of the Rings* recasting of the events of *The Hobbit* from Gandalf's perspective as "The Quest of Erebor," which takes all the *aventure* out of the story—and all of the fun as well.

In the second chapter of *The Lord of the Rings*, Frodo—and Tolkien—make a clear distinction between Bilbo's journey as "a series of *adventures* ... ending in peace" (*FR* I, ii, 72) and Frodo's journey with the Ring as a "perilous *quest*" (*FR* I, xi, 70). Elrond twice refers to a quest, telling the Council that "the quest may be attempted by the weak with as much hope as the strong" (*FR* II, ii, 283), and, when the Company sets out, actually giving it a title: the "Quest of Mount Doom" (*FR* II, ii, 294). Galadriel also refers to the "quest," telling Frodo, "Your quest is known to us" and warning that "your Quest stands upon the edge of a knife" (*FR* II, vii, 372), as does Celeborn, who tells the Company that the time has come when "those who wish to continue the Quest must harden their hearts to leave this land (*FR* II, viii, 383). At Mount Doom, Frodo tells Sam that but for Gollum "the Quest would have been in vain." "So let us forgive him," he counsels, "[f]or the Quest is achieved" (*RK* VI, iii, 225).

Frodo's journey is in a different key from Bilbo's, not only because Tolkien spent more time and care on developing *The Lord of the Rings* than he did on *The Hobbit* but also because he was conscious of a different authorial purpose. Bilbo had *aventures*—dangerous escapades exciting for their own sake, ending in peace and prosperity for Elves, Men, and Dwarves, and for Bilbo himself. Frodo goes on a *quest*—a journey as perilous for soul as for body— with a fixed purpose, a goal beyond itself. And while Frodo's quest, like Bilbo's adventure, ends in peace, the peace will not include him, for his quest has left him unable to enjoy it. Unlike Erec, Yvain, and Bilbo, Frodo gets no happy ever after.

In its emphasis on quest, *The Lord of the Rings* has less relationship to *The Hobbit* and to romance than to the spiritual and psychological "Tale of the Sankgreal" from *Le Morte D'Arthur*. We might say that *The Lord of the Rings* is to the "Tale of the Sankgreal" as *The Hobbit* is to "The Tale of Launcelot." Built on a century's worth of literature about the Quest for the Holy Grail, Malory's "Sankgreal" is the apogee of the quest narrative, whose goal is the highest in Christian European literature—the Cup symbolizing Christ's sacrifice for humanity. Frodo's quest likewise involves sacrifice, but here the values are reversed, for his goal is not achievement but destruction, and the sacrifice is the result of the quest, not its highest vision. Yet each object stands in its particular work as a test of the major characters. Malory's portrayal of the various effects of the quest on a selection of Arthur's knights—Gawain, Bors, Lyonel, Perceval, and Launcelot—is designed to show the levels of spirituality at Arthur's court from lowest to highest. Consider the following quote about Gawain: "Whan sir Gawayne was departed from his felyship he rode longe withoute ony adventure, for he founde nat the tenth parte of aventures as they were wont to have. For sir Gawayne rode from Whytsuntyde tylle Mychaelllmasse, and found never adventure that pleased him" (Malory 558). Malory's repetition of the word is not unlike Tolkien's in the opening of *The Hobbit*, but here it is a sure sign that Gawain is on the wrong track. He has no spiritual goal. He doesn't want *quest*, he wants *aventure*. He's just looking for fun. The fact that he does not find it suggests that he's not only on the wrong track, he doesn't even know it.

The contrast to Gawain is his close friend, Launcelot, who is on the right track but—like Gawain though for different reasons—also will not find what he seeks. On his return to Arthur's court, Launcelot tells Guinevere, "I was but late in the quest of the Sankgreall, and . . . I saw in that my queste as much as ever saw ony synfull man lyvynge" (Malory 611). The difference in the two men's terminology will not have escaped your notice. Like the difference between *The Hobbit* and *The Lord of the Rings*, the difference between *aventure* and *quest* is the measure of the difference between Bilbo and Frodo, Gawain and Launcelot, and in the outcome for each.

As the Grail is a test, so is the Ring. In Launcelot's struggle between God and Guinevere, we can see a parallel with the struggle of Frodo to resist the Ring. There is no comedy here, as there is in the romances, only irony. Both Frodo and Launcelot fail in their struggle and consequently in their quest. Both are irrevocably marked by their failure, and come to painful self-knowledge as a result. In both cases, the drama and irony of the stories rely on the paradox that although the heroes fail, it is through their failures that the quests are achieved. Where Launcelot fails, his son Galahad achieves the quest and finds the Grail. But without Launcelot, there would have been no Galahad. When Frodo fails by putting on the Ring instead of throwing it into the fire, he makes it possible for Gollum to take the Ring and himself fall into the fire. Without Frodo's failure, the quest would not have succeeded.

Both heroes have to live with the knowledge of their failures. Returned to court, Launcelot tells Guinevere, "if that I had nat had my prevy thoughts to return to youre love agayne as I do, I had sene as grete mysteryes as ever saw my sunne Sir Galahad" (Malory 611). Returned to Bag End, Frodo cannot reintegrate into the community he left behind. Tolkien commented that after Frodo's return to the Shire, he was afflicted by "unreasoning self-reproach: he saw himself and all that he had done as a broken failure. 'Though I may come to the Shire, it will not seem the same, for I shall not be the same'" (*Letters* 328). And this is the final, fundamental difference between Bilbo and Frodo and *adventure* and *quest:* not just that one succeeds where the other fails but that such success or failure is built into the nature of each journey and thus into the nature of each book.

Adventure for its own sake is self-contained, with rewards in keeping with the consequences of the adventure. This is not to suggest that Bilbo is Tolkien's Sir Gawain, for that comparison won't hold either in the writing or the reading. Bilbo is a much better person than Malory's Gawain, and, unlike Gawain, he knows the difference between an adventure and a quest. But I will suggest that Frodo comes close to being Tolkien's Launcelot, the honest, honorable, flawed hero of a quest in which he is doomed to fail and in failing show the pathos and poignance of the human condition as Tolkien saw it. "I am a Christian, and indeed a Roman Catholic," he wrote in 1956, "so that I do not expect 'history' to be anything but a long defeat" (*Letters* 255). This is not a hopeful vision. But it fits Frodo's situation. It does not fit Bilbo's, and that is the chief difference between the two books.

Nevertheless, both heroes, each on a different journey but both operating within separate aspects of a well-recognized tradition, show clearly what Carpenter misconstrued, what conventional wisdom has ignored, and what Tolkien tried to downplay, that the vocabulary and mechanisms of French romance left their Gallic stamp on the "English goodliness of speechecraft" in Tolkien's narratives, and on their shape and content as well. Tolkien's French connection was stronger and its influence more formative than either he or the many scholars of his work have wanted to admit.

Drowned Lands

Then Manwë upon the mountain called upon Ilúvatar, and for that time the Valar laid down their government of Arda. But Ilúvatar showed forth his power, and he changed the fashion of the world: and a great chasm opened in the sea between Númenor and the Deathless Lands, and the waters flowed down into it. . . . And Andor, the Land of Gift, Númenor of the Kings, Elenna of the Star of Eärendil, was utterly destroyed. For . . . its foundations were overturned, and it fell and went down into darkness, and is no more. . . . there came a mighty wind and a tumult of the earth, and the sky reeled, and the hills slid, and Númenor went down into the sea, with all its children and its wives and its maidens and its ladies proud; and all its gardens and its halls and its towers, its tombs and its riches, and its jewels and its webs and its things painted and carven, and its laughter and its music, its wisdom and its lore: they vanished for ever [in] the mounting wave, green and cold and plumed with foam. . . . (S 278–79)

This passage describes an event that haunted Tolkien's imagination and his prose. He wrote it in English; he wrote it in Anglo-Saxon; he wrote in Quenya and Sindarin and Adûnaic. It is the climactic scene of a work variously titled the *Akallabêth*, the *Atalantië*, the Drowning of Anadûnê, the Fall of Númenor.

It is the epicenter of the great celestial, terrestrial, geologic disaster that reshaped Tolkien's invented cosmos, and it might just be the single most formative event in the legendarium. Its importance to the myth notwithstanding, the Fall of Númenor, both as event and concept, made a surprisingly late entrance into the world it altered so drastically. In the "Myths Transformed" segment of *Morgoth's Ring* describing Tolkien's sometimes drastic revision of his mythology, Christopher Tolkien quotes a note appended by his father to the manuscripts of the *Annals of Aman*. Tolkien wrote: "This [i. e., the *Annals*] descends from the oldest forms of the mythology—when it was still intended to be no more than another primitive mythology, though more coherent and less 'savage'. It was consequently a 'Flat Earth' cosmogony (much easier to manage anyway): the Matter of Númenor had not been devised" (*MR* 370).

When was the "Matter of Númenor" devised? According to Christopher Tolkien, the original narrative of the legend of Númenor "arose in close association with *The Lost Road*" (*SD* 331), which Christopher dates to sometime around 1936. The mythology was already well along by then, but the entrance of Númenor effected some drastic modifications to Tolkien's concept. So important and so late a reconception raises what I hope are some interesting questions about the whole subject of Númenor, three of which I would like to address here. First, just how did Númenor affect the mythology? Second, what was the origin of Tolkien's interest in this particular kind of disaster? And last (and to me most important), why did Tolkien want to link such a cataclysm to a mythos already in place?

How did Númenor affect the mythology? It redirected three important elements in the legendarium, notably the cosmology that shaped it, the theology that grew out of that cosmology, and the narrative structure that supported them both. Cosmologically, the Fall of Númenor severed Valinor forever from Middle-earth and rounded Arda from a flat plane into a globe. Theologically, it was the occasion of the Fall of Men. The combination of that cosmology with that theology produced the spiritual concept of the Straight Road. On the narrative level, it also extended the history and the individual stories making up that history. According to Christopher Tolkien, the extension of the Silmarillion from the Elder Days into a Second Age of the World is a direct consequence of the entry of the concept of Númenor into the mythology. According to Tolkien himself, the existence of Númenor provided "a great function for Strider Aragorn" (*Letters* 347), linking him to the dynasties of Arnor and Gondor and giving him a kingdom to win back, thus providing the essential motive of the second plotline of *The Lord of the Rings*. Try to imagine *The Lord of The Rings* without Aragorn (not Strider—Aragorn), without the Paths of the Dead or the Dead Marshes, without Elendil, Isildur, Denethor, Boromir, or Faramir, and you will see how materially the "Matter of Númenor" contributed to the mythology.

What was the source of Tolkien's interest? There are several answers to that question, and they are not always in complete harmony with one another. Tolkien has given several versions of its genesis. According to one account, a conversation with C. S. Lewis gave him the impetus for a story about Atlantis. "When . . . Lewis and I tossed up, and he was to write on space-travel and I on time-travel, I began an abortive book of time-travel of which the end was to be the presence of my hero in the drowning of Atlantis. This was to be called *Númenor*, the Land in the West. . . . But I found my real interest was only in the upper end, the *Akallabêth* or *Atalantië* . . . so I brought all the stuff I had written on the originally unrelated legends of Númenor into relation with the main mythology" (*Letters* 347). This seems straightforward enough, but paradoxically raises the very questions it purports to answer, for despite Tolkien's reference to "originally unrelated" legends, Christopher Tolkien maintains that Númenor "was from the outset conceived in full association with 'The Silmarillion.'" "There never was a time," he maintains, "when the legends of Númenor were unrelated to the main mythology'" (*LR* 10). Yet in seeming opposition to this we have also Tolkien's statement, quoted by Christopher, that he "really wanted to make a new version of the Atlantis legend," of which only "[t]he final scene survives as *The Downfall of Númenor*" (*LR* 7).

Whatever the original impetus may have been, the commonality in all these statement is Atlantis, and it would seem obvious that Atlantis was the inspiration and the source for Númenor. Anyone who has read Tolkien's *Letters* knows of his recurrent dream of "the Great Wave, towering up, and coming in ineluctably over the trees and green fields" (*Letters* 213), and knows also that he called this his "Atlantis-haunting" (347). The source of the legend itself is Plato's *Timaeus*, where the story is told of "a great power which arrogantly advanced from its base in the Atlantic ocean to attack the cities of Europe and Asia. . . . On this island of Atlantis had arisen a powerful and remarkable dynasty of kings, who ruled the whole island, and many other islands as well, and . . . attempted to enslave. . . . all the territory" (qtd. in Settegast, App. A 279–80). The tale continues in *Critias*: "In the course of time the kings fell away from their high standards of justice and became greedy and domineering. Whereupon Zeus, wishing to chastise them, called a council of the gods and . . . there occurred violent earthquakes and floods, and in a single dreadful day and night . . . the island of Atlantis was . . . swallowed up by the sea and vanished" (qtd. in Ó Síocháin, 100–101).

It doesn't take much to see in Plato's account a clear parallel to the passage from *The Silmarillion* with which I began—an island empire, kings fallen from a high standard to greed and tyranny, attempts to dominate other lands, a council of gods, chastisement by the highest god, and the final, terrible punishment—the drowning of the land. Nevertheless, I suggest that Atlantis was *one* but not the *only* inspiration for Númenor. Plato's account is the best-known but certainly not the only legend of a drowned land with which Tolkien was acquainted. If we stop with Atlantis, we will be overlooking other available sources which will, I hope, lead to the answer to my third question— why did he attach such a cataclysm to a mythology already formed?

The Celtic legends of the British Isles, which Tolkien knew and studied, include several accounts of lands in the Western sea drowned for one reason or another in a single overwhelming cataclysm. So similar in content are these stories that scholars have attempted to correlate them and propose a theory of a great natural disaster that occurred in the distant past, the memory of which is preserved in myth and legend. The knowledge of a lost land is part of Celtic literature and history. The Welsh, the Bretons, the Irish, and the Cornish all share a parent mythology, and all have stories of sunken or engulfed lands. The Welsh *Black Book of Carmarthen* tells of the Cantref of Gwaelod, lost when the drunkard son of the king unleashed the sea to quench his thirst. Hersart de la Villemarqué's *Barsaz-Breiz*, a collection of Breton folktales, includes "Livaden Geris" (the Submersion of Ker-Ys), chronicling the drowning of that city by God in punishment for its heathen behavior. Irish legends tell of Hy-Brasil, a mysterious island that rises to the surface only once in every seven years. The lost land of Lyonesse, once a part of Cornwall, appears in the Arthurian story of Tristan, son of the king of Lyonesse and nephew of King Mark of Cornwall.

Several things are worth noting here. One is that all these stories of flood are sited on the western coast of their respective region of origin and all the drowned lands are located within a comparatively small circumference. Another is that while in all these tales the actual event is the same—the flooding of formerly inhabited land—the rationale in each case—the story behind the event—is individual and local. It would be no surprise if Tolkien saw an opportunity to add his own story to the mix. Third and most important for my argument, Tolkien had easy access to all these legends, and in some cases had the actual books in his library. I want to focus specifically on two of these accounts of lost lands, demonstrating that allusions to both, oblique or straightforward, can be found in two of Tolkien's Númenor stories. The first concerns the Cornish Lyonesse, whose presence is implied but not explicitly mentioned in *The Lost Road*. Lyonesse is equated with a region known in Cornish folklore as Lethowstow but has also been associated with the coast of Brittany. Such a cross-Channel transfer is not as unlikely as it might seem, for in the early medieval period, the Cornish and the Bretons shared a language and a culture, as well as myths and stories.

According to legend, Lyonesse filled what is now Mount's Bay and stretched west around Land's End and beyond, joining what are now the Scilly Isles to one another and to the mainland. At some indefinite time in the past, the ocean swept in, and Lyonesse has been submerged ever since. Another more fanciful legend states that following Arthur's defeat at Camlann, Mordred's forces pursued the remnants of Arthur's army to Lyonesse. The ghost of Merlin appeared and the land sank, destroying Mordred's men, but Arthur's men reached what are now the Scilly Isles. There is archeological evidence to support the event, if not the details of the story. Sunken remains of huts and walls below the high-water line suggest that some of the Scillies were joined in a single land mass as late as the early Christian era, about the time of the historical Arthur.

The second account concerns the Irish Hy-Brasil, which comes up—almost literally in fact—during the dénouement of *The Notion Club Papers*. Hy-Brasil is a little harder to pin down than Lyonesse. A legendary Atlantic island located west of Ireland, it was visible only once every seven years, and the suggestion has been made that it was an actual sunken land of which the Aran Islands in Galway Bay are the remnants. Ruairí Ó Flaithearta's seventeenth-century *A Choregraphical Description of West Connaught* told of a man named O'Ley who was kidnapped and taken to Hy-Brasil. William Butler Yeats reported in his book *The Celtic Twilight* of speaking with Irish fishermen who claimed to have sailed as far as Hy-Brasil. Under various names, Hy-Brasil is marked on medieval maps as an island to the west of Ireland.

As a fabled land reached by sailing west, Hy-Brasil clearly influenced the naming of the actual Brazil in South America, although post-Colombian maps continued to show an island of that name west of Ireland. In this context, we should not overlook a pertinent statement in Tolkien's essay "On Fairy-stories." Here he suggests that the rationalization and diminution of myth seem to have "become fashionable soon after the great voyages had begun to make the world seem too narrow to hold both men and elves; when the magic land of Hy Breasail in the West had become the mere Brazils, the land of red-dye-wood" (*MC* 111). Nor should we overlook the note Tolkien appended to that statement: "For the probability that the Irish *Hy Breasail* played a part in the naming of Brazil see Nansen, *In Northern Mists*, ii, 223–30" (*MC* 111 n2). It seems clear from this that Tolkien not only knew of Hy-Brasil but mourned its transformation from a mythic land to a merely actual one. It will not be surprising, then, if we find that he took steps in his own invented mythology to re-transform it and to widen the world so that it could again hold men and elves and magic.

Hy-Brasil seems to have been, among other things, a version of the Celtic otherworld, so often described as an island or islands somewhere in the western ocean or under the sea. One of the Irish otherworld voyage stories, *The Voyage of Bran*, recounts Bran's meeting with the sea god Manannan mac Lir, who explains that what to Bran appears to be ocean is to Manannan and his people solid land.

> Along the top of a wood
> Your coracle has sailed, over ridges,

> There is a wood of beautiful fruit
> Under the prow of your little skiff...

In the context of these legends, let us look at Tolkien's own lost land story and its position in his mythology as a whole. Although it changed over the years of its development, Tolkien's legendarium, as we know, had begun with the idea of a mythology dedicated to England, his own island nation in the western sea. And although that concept altered and its elements changed over the course of many years' writing, certain links to England remained. I believe these links are woven into the plot situations of Tolkien's two time-travel stories, *The Lost Road* and *The Notion Club Papers*, and that they intentionally connect Númenor to the lost land stories of the regions along the western coast of the British Isles.

One link is to the Cornish Lyonesse; the other, to the Irish Hy-Brasil. I cannot demonstrate a coherent scheme fulfilled in either story, first, because neither story was ever finished, and second, because Tolkien's habit of shifting among texts produced overlapping and competing versions guaranteed to frustrate scholars and make partial any conjecture of what might have been. What I can do is try to follow the link in each story to what I believe was intended to be its fictive resolution, the linking of the legendary British Isles to mythological Middle-earth through a repetition, at the "same" time and in the "same" place in each world, of the same geological disaster.

The Lost Road introduces Númenor into the mythology. This story, the time-travel result of Tolkien's agreement with C. S. Lewis, was to take Tolkien's heroes back to the drowning of Atlantis by means of successive serial identities, all with the same two names, variants on Alboin and Audoin. The opening scene is set, not by accident, in "a little house in Cornwall" overlooking the sea (*LR* 40), where Oswin Errol and his son Alboin are vacationing. The subject of drowned lands is introduced obliquely, as we are told that Oswin Errol, a historian, talks of writing a book about Cornwall. Lyonesse is never mentioned, but when Alboin, looking out over the sea one evening, sees a cloudy sunset as "the eagles of the Lords of the West coming upon Númenor" (38), we may guess that it has been implied, and that one drowned land is being identified with another. We know from subsequent chapters that Alboin has a Númenorean avatar, Herendil, and we may infer from Tolkien's notes that he intended the two identities to fuse at the time of the final cataclysm. Whether that cataclysm would have fused places as well as persons, occurring simultaneously in Cornwall/Lyonesse and in Númenor, we cannot know, for the story never got that far.

It got almost that far in Tolkien's next attempt, written some ten years later. *The Notion Club Papers* takes up the time-travel theme again, not in Cornwall this time, but in Oxford. The members of the Notion Club are interested in time- and space travel. In one conversation, they discuss the interconnection of myth and history and speculate on "the daimonic force the great myths and legends have," a force that "if suddenly detonated . . . might go off with a crash: yes: might produce a disturbance in the real primary world" (*SD* 228). One club member, Ramer, gives as an example the coming of ships "riding a storm," of men bearing "tales of catastrophe . . . the whelming of lands in some tumult of the earth" (229).

At a subsequent meeting just such a disturbance—a storm, a catastrophe, men riding a ship, the whelming of lands in tumult—erupts out of mythic Númenor into modern Oxford. A violent storm interrupts the meeting, whereupon two Notion Club members, Wilfrid Jeremy and Arry Lowdham, taking on Númenorean identities, appear to be at once in a room in Oxford and on a Númenorean ship riding out a storm at sea. They stumble out into the storm, and when they return some months later tell stories of voyages and of being shipwrecked. "We started off down in Cornwall, Land's End," says Jeremy (*SD* 266). From there they go to Wales and thence to the west coast of Ireland. "We both heard many tales," Jeremy continues, "of the huge waves . . . like phantoms, or only half real. . . . Some rolled far inland. . . . we were told of one that had rolled clean over the Aran Isles and passed up Galway Bay and so on like a cloud, drowning the land in a ghostly flood . . ." (267).

The action of *The Notion Club Papers* never progressed beyond this point. Nevertheless, it seems clear that in sending Lowdham and Jeremy on a stormy journey from Cornwall to Wales to the west of Ireland, Tolkien was intentionally incorporating locations associated with drowned lands—Cornwall at Land's End linking to Lyonesse; Wales linking to the Cantref of Gwaelod; the Aran Isles and Galway Bay linking to Hy-Brasil—in order to give his own story a kind of mythic veracity. It is a complex and complicated veracity, to be sure, and it requires a lot of inside information to appreciate. Indeed, Christopher Tolkien suggests that the conception had now become so intricate that "one need perhaps look no further for an answer to the question, why were *The Notion Club Papers* abandoned?" (*SD* 282). Certainly it is impossible to say with any surety where the story would have gone from there. But we may speculate that the investigations of Lowdham and Jeremy might, as Tolkien projected for Alboin and Audoin Errol, have spiraled back through successive identities, bringing themselves and the reader to that place in time, space, and memory where the worlds overlapped: where the submergence of

Lyonesse, the disappearance of Hy-Brasil, the destruction of Ker-Ys, and the Fall of Númenor were all embodiments of the same mythic catastrophe.

I believe that in by consciously tying Númenor to "real world" myth, by deliberately and overtly invoking the legend of Atlantis and by obliquely and covertly echoing the stories of Lyonesse, of Gwaelod, of Hy-Brasil, and of Ker-Ys, Tolkien was making a statement about myth itself. I believe he was saying that the mythic memory is always present in the human consciousness. I believe he was saying that under the right circumstances, given the right act of imagination, the daimonic force of a great myth or legend—such as that of Atlantis or Lyonesse or Hy-Brasil—might "go off with a crash," might reenact itself and produce a disturbance in the real primary world. I believe that such a disturbance was what he was working toward—probably in *The Lost Road* and almost certainly in *The Notion Club Papers*. And I believe further that had he ever finished *The Lost Road* or *The Notion Club Papers* he would have succeeded in linking the primary and secondary worlds to make it happen. He would have succeeded in introducing into the secondary world of his fiction the mythic history of the primary world in which his readers lived. If Atlantis and Lyonesse and Hy-Brasil could be identified with Númenor, then Númenor could be identified with all of them. And if that reciprocal transference were indeed to happen, then Tolkien would have accomplished the goal of all mythmakers, what in his essay "On Fairy-Stories" he called "the realisation": the making real, "independent of the conceiving mind, of imagined wonder" (*MC* 116).

Voyaging About

Tolkien and Celtic Navigatio

It will come as no secret to anyone who has read his *Letters* that J. R. R. Tolkien went out of his way on several occasions to disavow any affinity for anything Celtic (except for the Welsh language, which he loved) and, indeed, explicitly and pointedly affirmed his "distaste" (*Letters* 26). Nevertheless, there is a good deal of evidence that he made a conscious effort to link his own invented mythology to existing literary texts of Irish myth with the explicit intention of validating his myth by tying it to primary, "real-world" myth.

Both Tom Shippey in *The Road to Middle-Earth* and Norma Roche in her essay "Sailing West: Tolkien, the Saint Brendan Story, and the Idea of Paradise in the West" have examined Tolkien's use of the medieval Irish voyage tale. I would like to carry their efforts a little farther, first taking special note of Tolkien's inclusion in his unfinished time-travel story *The Notion Club Papers* of his own poetic version of the Irish *Navigatio Sancti Brendani* (unpublished at the time Roche and Shippey wrote), and second suggesting a broader influence of the voyage motif on the very earliest versions of his mythology. Making the best case for the conflict between what Tolkien said and what he did with regard to Celtic influence, we may speculate that he wanted to repair what he referred to in a 1937 letter as the madness and "fundamental unreason" of Celtic writing by restoring its sanity, by reordering the pieces of the "broken stained glass window reassembled without design" to which he likened "Celtic things" into a more coherent and reasonable mythology, remounting the stained glass, as it were, in a new window (*Letters* 26).

The irony is that Tolkien's own poem itself seemed at first to be a broken fragment of stained glass, a circumstance for which its scrambled publication history must be held responsible. The poem exists in two closely related versions: the original, called "The Voyage of St. Brendan," and a revised version, retitled "Imram." The two were published in reverse order, and only "Imram" made it into print in Tolkien's lifetime, appearing in 1955 in the 3 December issue of *Time and Tide*. In his 1977 biography of Tolkien, Humphrey Carpenter noted that "Imram" had originally been intended as a part of the then-unpublished *Notion Club Papers*, but commented that "on its own it is a little bare, a forlorn memorial to an unfinished and promising story" (Carpenter, *Tolkien* 172). For many years "Imram" was the only version known, and thus was not seen as a "version" but as a self-contained, freestanding poem. Only with the publication of *The Silmarillion* in autumn 1977 could it be related even marginally to Tolkien's major work, the Matter of Middle-earth.

Not until 1992 did the original version in its original context appear in *Sauron Defeated*, volume 9 of the History of Middle-earth, edited by Christopher Tolkien. No longer "bare" or "forlorn," far from being freestanding or allusive, the poem could now be seen as essential to the structure of *The Notion Club Papers*. Moreover, Tolkien's notes to the story suggest strongly that the general motif of the otherworld voyage was a formative element in his original mythic concept. The volume of work Tolkien put into the poem supports this hypothesis. Christopher Tolkien notes that "The Voyage of St. Brendan" was preceded by "no less than fourteen closely-written pages of initial working," and that these were followed by "four finished manuscript texts" preceding the final typescript text" (*SD* 295–96). Such painstaking labor on a subject so obviously Celtic suggests the very opposite of the "distaste" Tolkien expressed in his 1937 letter, quoted above (*Letters* 26), and argues strongly for what I have suggested was his original purpose in blending the two mythologies—to give his own myth a "real-world" foundation.

If this was the case, however, Tolkien's stained glass window fared no better than the Celtic one he disliked, for he left *The Notion Club Papers* to return to *The Lord of the Rings*, leaving St. Brendan high and dry, without a context or function, bereft of his original place in a design. We can guess that at this point, with *The Lord of the Rings* demanding his time and attention, Tolkien had abandoned, at least for the moment, the attempt to explicitly and directly link his own mythology with Irish myth, and that later on he decided to extract the poem from its original context and revise, rename, and publish it as a separate piece. In this regard, Christopher Tolkien identifies three further typescripts as "clearly" belonging to the later "Imram" version (*SD* 296). But though taken out of context, the content of the poem did not materially change, and the new title, although unfamiliar to readers unacquainted with Irish myth, tied the poem just as firmly to medieval Celtic myth as had the old.

This new title, the Irish word *immram*, translated literally as "rowing" (O hOgain 50), has the extended meaning of "sailing or voyaging about," and was glossed in Latin as *navigatio*. In medieval Celtic literature, *immram* was a term for a specific type of Irish wonder tale, the voyage to the otherworld. Together with Destructions, Cattle-raids, Wooings, Battles, Feasts, Adventures, Elopements, Slaughters, Expeditions, Invasions, and Deaths, *Immrama* (voyages), are listed by Alwyn and Brinley Rees in their book *Celtic Heritage* as part of what they call "The Storytellers Repertoire" (Rees and Rees, 208).

All *immrama* have as their subject matter fantastic accounts of voyages to the otherworld or a succession of otherworlds, places of a clearly supernatural nature usually (since these are voyages) presented as islands. The direction is explicitly westward, and the idea of the otherworld voyage, described by the Reeses as "one of the most distinctive in Celtic tradition" (Rees and Rees 314), contributed not a little to the great voyages of discovery of the fifteenth and sixteenth centuries. Among the best-known of the Irish voyage tales are the pre-Christian *immrama* of Bran mac Febhail and Maol Dúin, and the later, explicitly Christian *Navigatio Sancti Brendani*, the Voyage of St. Brendan, which is itself based on the Voyage of Maol Dúin.

Easy to identify but difficult to locate precisely, the Celtic otherworld is described by the Celtic scholar Proinsias MacCana as "a changing scene of many phases," filled with "enchanting music from bright-plumaged birds, from the swaying branches of the otherworld tree, from instruments which sound without being played" (MacCana 123–24). It is inhabited by the *Sídh*, supernatural, immortal beings that Daithi O hOgain calls "the principle otherworld race in Irish literary myth" (407). These descriptions put that world and its people very close to the realm that Tolkien called "Faërie," of which he said that it "contains many things besides elves and fays . . . it holds the seas, the sun, the moon, the sky . . . tree, bird, water and stone . . . and ourselves, mortal men, when we are enchanted" (*MC* 113). The psychological thrust of this last phrase, "when we are enchanted," is not unlike MacCana's characterization of the otherworld as "an imaginative reflex of human attitudes and aspirations" (MacCana 126), and both phrases carry the same implication: however magical the Celtic otherworld, however enchanting Tolkien's Faërie, the chief thing about both of them is that they could be and were visited by human beings, for in both cases—otherworld and Faërie—the stories about them concern humans who enter the magical realm.

I believe that as part of the creation of his mythology, Tolkien gave his Faërie world of Middle-earth its own, inner otherworld of Faërie, and that this was Valinor, known in Middle-earth as the Undying Land, also called the Land in the West, and known as the home of the immortal Elves and the godlike Valar. The Rees brothers suggest that the Celtic otherworld was connected in both pagan and Christian imagination with the land in the West and the world beyond death (324–25). While Tolkien's Valinor is not to be seen as any kind of Christian Heaven, it is certainly the home of deathless beings, and is referred to as the undying land. Moreover, its location, like that of the Celtic otherworld, is at once metaphysical and psychological. In the central conceit of Tolkien's mythology, the originally flat world was made round as the result of transgression. The consequence was that Valinor was set off from Middle-earth, to be reached only by grace after a long and arduous westward voyage, and then only by following a watery path imagined as extending straight out from the curvature of the earth and described as the Straight Road. This phrase recalls other references to the straight road in other Celtic-influenced literature. In Chrétien de Troyes's twelfth-century romance *Lancelot*, the hero is conducted into the otherworld by a maiden who guides him along a road described as "the straight way" (Trans. Cline, l. 615) and "the straight path" (l. 1507). It does not seem to be stretching things too far to suggest that Tolkien was consciously and deliberately associating all these otherworld aspects with his own Valinor.

The connections are explicit in both versions of Tolkien's poem, but only come into focus when it is read in its proper context. While he acknowledged the Irish models for Tolkien's "Imram," Shippey also found the poem to be assimilated "very closely to [Tolkien's] own fiction" through its mention of a "foundered land," a Tree, a Star, and an "old road" running to "coasts that no man knows," [*Road*, rev.ed. 326), all of which certainly sound familiar. But while he connected these elements to Tolkien's *Silmarillion*, Shippey nevertheless found "Imram" to be "an extremely private poem" (*Road*, rev.ed 326). *The Notion Club Papers*, published the same year as the second edition of *The Road to Middle-Earth*, widened our understanding by providing the previously missing evidence that Tolkien was not just assimilating St. Brendan's voyage to his own fiction but deliberately mixing the two, consciously making the poem a bridge between two mythologies. His revision and separate publication of the poem as "Imram," at a time when he must have felt that not only his time-travel story but the entire Silmarillion would never see print, enables us to see it as not just a "private poem" but a kind of wry and bitter private joke—all the meaning is there, but only Tolkien can see the connections.

It is probable that the concept of voyaging preceded the poem in Tolkien's vision, for as Norma Roche points out (18), there are hints of it in his earlier (and also unfinished) time-travel story *The Lost Road*. Tolkien's outline sketches for that story make mention of "strange tales from Ireland," of "the holy Brendan," Maelduin [sic], and "*Insula Deliciarum*" (LR 80). Nevertheless, the original position of "The Voyage of St. Brendan" in *The Notion Club Papers* is essential to an understanding not only of the poem but of the story as well. Begun as a time-travel story, *The Notion Club Papers* is very much concerned with "voyaging about" on several levels of narrative and planes of experience. Set initially in present-day Oxford, the story begins with a discussion of time travel and goes on to parallel two kinds of voyages (or three, if you count "St. Brendan"). Essential to the plot is the psychic soul journey of the story's protagonist, Arundel Lowdham, who, together with his companion, Trewyn Jeremy, travels back through history, via a series of reincarnated identities, into Tolkien's Middle-earth, and in one episode catches glimpses of a land which is clearly Tolkien's Valinor.

Just as essential to the theme are the mysterious voyages of Lowdham's father, Edwin, who sails about in his ship *The Earendel* in search of "shores a good deal further off than Sussex"—which shores, the story strongly hints, are those of Valinor, the Land in the West. Edwin Lowdham never appears in the story, but his presence broods over the later, most dramatic parts of the action. St. Brendan's voyage, then, must be seen as the key to both the others. It is the story's most explicit gesture toward the otherworld; it seems clear that Tolkien was using his "St. Brendan" poem as a kind of fingerpost to his invented world, and that he intended not just to parallel his own myth with Irish myth but also deliberately to equate his own otherworld of Valinor with the Celtic otherworld of the poem, and to use the latter to validate the former.

Strategically placed after the storm and consequent eruption of the past into the present that form the story's climax, the poem is read aloud at a meeting of the Notion Club, presented by Philip Frankley as his own composition. But it is clearly derivative, if not imitative, of the Irish *Navigatio Sancti Brendani* and just as clearly is meant to be seen as such. Among other things, the *Navigatio* describes an island with a magical tree covered with white leaves, which are revealed as birds when they take flight, leaving the branches bare. Tolkien's "Brendan" poem has an almost identical episode. The *Navigatio* suggests that the birds are fallen angels, while Tolkien's poem suggests "a third fair kindred," which can only mean his own Elves. To anyone who knows the *Navigatio*, the similarities are unmistakable, but for those of his readers who don't know it, Tolkien has taken care, in the discussion that follows the reading, to have his characters single out exactly these elements of the poem which relate his myth to that of St. Brendan.

In addition, we learn later in the story that his heroes, Lowdham and Jeremy, have traveled to Ireland in search of an explanation for the uncanny events of the night of the storm. Their report back to the Notion Club makes special mention of the fact that the storm (which we are to believe occurred simultaneously in Oxford, Ireland, and Middle-earth) sent waves inland "almost as far as Clonfert." This is more than a simple measurement of distance. Clonfert was St. Brendan's abbey, and its name, in the Irish spelling *Cluain-ferta*, is explicitly cited in the poem's opening and closing verses. Nor is this mere name-dropping. The storm that carries waves almost as far as Clonfert carries with them Tolkien's story and its part in his mythos as a whole. These narrative clues, as strategically placed as the poem itself, are persuasive evidence of Tolkien's intent to link the two mythologies.

One final clue linking the Irish voyages to Tolkien's version is the description of the transition from the "real" world to the otherworld. The very nature of phenomena can undergo mysterious alteration. In the Irish voyage of Bran, for example, Bran sails across a mysterious zone where sea and earth are one. Here he meets the sea god Manannán mac Lir, who describes the apparent paradox.

> "Speckled salmon leap from the womb
> Of the white sea, on which you look:
> They are calves, they are coloured lambs
> With friendliness, without mutual slaughter.
>
> "Along the top of a wood
> Your coracle has sailed, over ridges,
> There is a wood of beautiful fruit
> Under the prow of your little skiff."   (Rees and Rees 315)

The Voyage of Maol Dúin describes a scene not unlike the one just described to Bran by Mannanán, in which Maol Dúin floats on a thin sea like a transparent cloud and beneath it sees a fair land with a tree surrounded by cattle.

This same conflation of water and land is an essential part of the voyage to Tolkien's otherworld of Valinor, and is alluded to in the poem, where, as Shippey has pointed out, St. Brendan speaks of a place,

> "where the round world plunges steeply down,
>   but on the old road goes,
> as an unseen bridge that on arches runs
>   to coasts that no man knows" (*SD* 264).

This last phrase also clearly recalls Edwin Lowdham's voyages in search of "shores a good deal further off than Sussex." Christopher Tolkien notes that in Tolkien's sketches for the first version of *The Lost Road*, his hero, Ælfwine, "awakes on the beach of the Lonely Isle 'to find the ship being drawn by people walking in the water'" (*SD* 280), while Tolkien's own notes to *The Notion Club Papers* describe his heroes, at this point called Ælfwine and Tréowine, as seeing land below them in the water: "Tréowine sees the round world [?curve] below, and straight ahead a shining land, before the wind seizes them and drives them away. In the gathering dark . . . he sees a bright star, shining in a rent in the cloud in the West" (*SD* 278). And in a second sketch, "Tréowine sees the straight road and the world plunging down. Ælfwine's vessel seems to be taking the straight road and [he] falls in a swoon of fear and exhaustion" (*SD* 279).

These sketched-out episodes are not a perfect match with their Irish counterparts, for in the Irish voyages the real world is superimposed on the otherworld, which appears below it through the water, whereas Tolkien's voyagers see the real world below them in the water and the otherworld shining straight ahead of them, lit by a star. But it must be remembered that these are only brief jottings, ideas set down as markers for further development, and the resemblances are obvious enough to be seen as deliberate. The whole concept was left hanging, however, when Tolkien left *The Notion Club Papers* to return to *The Lord of the Rings*. Having once abandoned any idea of melding Irish myth with his own, Tolkien seems never to have taken up the concept again.

Nevertheless, the Celtic voyage tale had a perceptible influence on Tolkien's mythology, as my next and last—and also (if I can convince you) most sweeping and comprehensive examples—illustrate. These carry the concept as far back as it can go, to *The Book of Lost Tales*, Tolkien's earliest conception of his mythology, begun in 1917, way back when it might still properly be described as "a mythology for England." The conceit of that early version, and the frame for the tales contained therein, was the voyage of a mariner, Eriol, to a magical shore called in Elvish Tol Eressëa, the Lonely Isle, where he meets the Fairies and hears from them tales of the gods and the story of creation. It doesn't take much to see in Tolkien's Fairies (soon to be developed into Elves) a near-direct replication of the Irish *Sídh*, the fairy folk of the Celtic otherworld, nor to see Eriol's journey as an otherworld voyage. Neither does it take much imagination to see in the sailing career of Eärendil the Mariner, to whom there are references from the very inception of the myth, an explicit reuse of the motif. References in the story of Eärendil to "the Shadowy Seas" and especially to "the Enchanted Isles" cannot but be understood, in the light of all the foregoing information, as scarcely veiled allusions to the otherworld voyage

That these concepts went through countless adjustments and readjustments over the course of fifty years is hardly remarkable. The geography, the names, and the characters changed markedly (with the exception of Eärendil, who simply became more developed). Nevertheless, I believe it is not stretching the argument beyond the evidence to see a major element in the genesis of Tolkien's whole mythology—which was to occupy his life for fifty years, have a formative (though not always beneficial) impact on the course of modern fantasy, and feed the popular interest in medievalism—as immediately derived from and directly modeled on the medieval Irish *immram*, the voyage to the otherworld.[1]

Permissions Acknowledgments

"'There Would Always Be a Fairy-Tale': J. R. R. Tolkien and the Folklore Controversy." First published in 2003 in *Tolkien the Medievalist*, ed. Jane Chance, pp. 26–35. New York and London: Routledge.

"But What Did He Really Mean?" First published in 2014 in *Tolkien Studies* Vol. XI. © 2014 by West Virginia University Press. Reprinted with permission.

"Eucatastrophe and the Dark." First published in 2015 in *Approaches to Teaching Tolkien's* The Lord of the Rings *and Other Works*, ed. Leslie A Donovan.

"Myth, History, and Time-travel: *The Lost Road* and *The Notion Club Papers.*" First published in 2014 in *A Companion to J. R. R. Tolkien*, ed. Stuart Lee. © 2014 by John Wiley & Sons, Ltd.

"The Jewels, the Stone, the Ring, and the Making of Meaning." First published in *Tolkien in the New Century: Essays in Honor of Tom Shippey*. © 2014 Edited by John Wm. Houghton, Janet Brennan Croft, Nancy Martsch, John D. Rateliff and Robin Anne Reid by permission of McFarland & Company, Inc., Box 611, Jefferson NC 28640. www.mcfarlandpub.com.

"The Forests and the Trees: Sal and Ian in *Faërie*." First published in 2013 in *J. R. R. Tolkien: The Forest and the City*, ed. O'Briain and Hynes, Four Courts Press.

"How Trees Behave—Or Do They?" First published in 2013 in *Mythlore* Vol. 32, no. 1, Fall/Winter 2013.

"Myth and Truth in Tolkien's Legendarium." First published in Italy on the website of Associazione Italiana Studi Tolkieniani, 2012.

"Tolkien's French Connection." From *The Hobbit and Tolkien's Mythology: Essays on Revisions and Influences* © 2014. *Edited by* Bradford Lee Eden by permission of McFarland & Company, Inc., Box 611, Jefferson NC 28640. www.mcfarlandpub.com.

Notes

But What Did He Really Mean?

1. And even here his position is somewhat suspect, for his own note on this statement to Auden says, "take the Ents, for instance. I did not consciously invent them at all" (*Letters* 211).

2. The only play mentioned, and that relegated to a note, is J. M. Barrie's *Mary Rose*, a play presented not by elves to men but by men to other men, though it does deal with elven-human interaction. The note is important, however, as a clue to those "abundant records," now described as "stories telling how men and women have disappeared and spent years among the fairies, without noticing the passage of time, or appearing to grow older" (*MC* 160). Tolkien adds that "[m]any of the short folk-lore accounts of such incidents purport to be just pieces of 'evidence' about fairies, items in an agelong accumulation of 'lore' concerning them and the modes of their existence" (160). These I take to mean collections of folk and fairy lore such as *The Denham Tracts*, Thomas Keightley's *The Fairy Mythology*, John Rhys's *Celtic Folklore*, and James MacDougall and George Calder's *Folktales and Fairy Lore in Gaelic and English*.

There exist more literary, or mythic, examples as well, for instance, the Irish tale type called *echtrai* (otherworld journeys), such as that of Connla's journey to Tír na mBeo, the Land of the Living, in *Echtra Connla*. A related type is the *imramma* (voyage narratives), such as the Voyage of Bran or the Journey of Mael Diun. Tolkien was familiar with these genres; in fact, he wrote an *imram* himself, based on the *Navigatio Sancti Brendani*, included in Part Two of *The Notion Club Papers* as "The Death of St. Brendan," and there attributed to Tolkien's fictive character Frankley.

3. For more on this, see Tom Shippey's discussion of *glamour* in *The Road to Middle-earth*, 58–62.

Re-creating Reality

1. It is worth noting here that Gandalf the wizard tells Bilbo that he is looking for someone to share in an adventure (the spelling is anglicized but the medieval usage is clear), and that Bilbo reacts with predictable distaste, calling adventures "nasty, disturbing, uncomfortable things" (*H* 13), all of which is true not just in Bilbo's terms but in the medieval sense as well. It is no accident that the word *adventure* occurs twelve times in the first five pages of the book.

2. See Lewis's essay "On Stories," in *Essays Presented to Charles Williams*. "*The Hobbit* escapes the danger of degenerating into mere plot and excitement by a very curious shift of tone. As the humour and homeliness of the early chapters, the sheer 'Hobbitry', dies away we pass insensibly into the world of epic. It is as if the battle of Toad Hall had become a serious *heimsökn* and Badger had begun to talk like Njal" (Lewis, "On Stories" 104). Badger is a major character in Kenneth Grahame's *The Wind in the Willows*, a classic children's book. In genre it is a beast-fable in which animal characters—Water Rat, Mole, Badger, Toad, and Otter—typify human characteristics, but it transcends the genre by as much as *The Lord of the Rings* transcends fairy tale. Tolkien noted in his essay "On Fairy-stories" that *The Wind in the Willows* came close to qualifying as a fairy story.

3. Tolkien soon abandoned the abortive first chapter begun in response to the publisher's request for a sequel to capitalize on *The Hobbit*'s popularity, and began the story over, not for the last time. Christopher Tolkien chronicles a total of six separate attempts before Tolkien found his way to a viable beginning.

4. Tolkien's statement, in the Foreword to the second edition of *The Lord of the Rings*, that the book's composition "went on at intervals during the years 1936 to 1949" is off by one year in its starting date. *The Hobbit* was published on 21 September 1937, not 1936. According to Humphrey Carpenter, it was "a few weeks" after this publication that Tolkien and Stanley Unwin met to discuss a possible sequel (*Tolkien* 183).

5. On 19 December 1937, Tolkien wrote to Charles Furth at Allen and Unwin that he had "written the first chapter of a new story about Hobbits—'A long expected party'" (*Letters* 27). Although the first chapter subsequently underwent several revisions as Tolkien wrote his way into the darker atmosphere of *The Lord of the Rings*, it nevertheless retained, to a greater extent than the rest of the book, the more light-hearted tone of *The Hobbit*.

6. See the passage on daemons and tree-fairies in Manuscript B of "On Fairy-stories" in *Tolkien On Fairy-stories*. "For lack of a better word they may be called spirits, *daemons:* inherent powers of the created world . . . subject to Moral Law, capable of good and evil. . . . Thus a tree-fairy (or a dryad) is, or was, a minor spirit in the process of creation who aided as 'agent' in the making effective of the divine Tree-idea or some part of it, or of even of some one particular example: some tree" (*TOFS* 254–55).

7. See Verlyn Flieger, *A Question of Time: J. R. R. Tolkien's Road to* Faërie (Kent, OH: Kent State Univ. Press, 1997).

War, Death, and Fairy Stories in the Work of J. R. R. Tolkien

1. It is worth noting that in a late (1971) letter to Roger Lancelyn Green, Tolkien wrote that Frodo, like other mortals "could only dwell in *Aman* for a limited time. . . . they would eventually pass away (*die* at their own desire and of free will)" (*Letters* 411).

Words and World-making: The Particle Physics of Middle-earth

1. See Fritjof Capra's *The Tao of Physics* (Boulder, CO: Shambala Publications, 1975); and David Bohm's interview by Renée Weber, "The Enfolding-Unfolding Universe: A Conversation with David Bohm," in *The Holographic Paradigm and Other Paradoxes*, ed. Ken Wilbur (Boulder, CO: Shambala Publications, 1982), 44–104.

2. See, for example, Ernst Cassirer's *Language and Myth* (New York: Dover Books. 1953); Owen Barfield's *Poetic Diction* (Middletown, CN: Wesleyan Univ. Press, 1977) and *Saving the Appearances* (New York: Harcourt Brace Jovanovich, 1965); and Benjamin Whorf's *Language, Thought, and Reality*, ed. John B. Carroll (Cambridge, MA: M.I.T. Press, 1945).

3. For an etymological unpacking of all these names, see Christopher Gilson's etymologies in J. R. R. Tolkien's *Words, Phrases, and Passages in Various Tongues in* The Lord of the Rings, ed. Gilson, which was published as issue 17 of *Parma Eldalamberon*, a journal of the Elvish Linguistic Fellowship, a special interest group of the Mythopoeic Society.

Myth, History, and Time-travel: *The Lost Road* and *The Notion Club Papers*

1. While Atlantis is the best known, it is far from the only mythic account of the drowning of a land mass that Tolkien might have known. The country of Lyonesse, locale of some of the Arthurian Tristan material, was said to have sunk beneath the sea near what are now the Scilly Isles. The Kingdom of Ys in Brittany, ruled over by King Gradlon, was submerged under sea when the king's daughter, Dahut, stole the key to the city and gave it to the devil. A violent storm sent waves over the city, entirely submerging it. Ireland too has a tradition of a great wave, the *tonn*, that periodically sweeps over the shore and far inland. The latter portions of part 2 of *The Notion Club Papers* have club members Lowdham and Jeremy in Ireland, where they hear stories of a ghostly black wave that swept over the land on the night of the Oxford storm, reaching as far inland as Clonfert, traditional home of St. Brendan.

2. Adunaic, from all accounts the last of Tolkien's invented languages to be developed, is part of the strongly linguistic course of thought which runs through part 2 of *The Notion Club Papers* and which is almost entirely missing from *The Lost Road*. The concept of memory of unknown language is derived from Tolkien's idea of native language, by which he means language inherited through birth, as opposed to cradle tongue, by which he means language learned in infancy. In part 1 of *The Notion Club Papers*, Ramer voices this theory, explaining to the club that everyone has a native language (*SD* 201). Tolkien returned to the idea in his 1962 O'Donnell Lecture, "English and Welsh" (published in 1963), where he maintained that, "We each have a *native language*. But that is not the language that we speak, our cradle-tongue" (*A&B* 36). He went on to emphasize, in words very like Ramer's, "the difference between the first-learned language, the language of custom, and an

individual's native language, his inherent linguistic predilection" (*A&B* 36). This is the premise behind Alboin Errol's dreams of what he calls Eresseän or Elf-Latin (the few words of which quoted are Quenya and Sindarin). In similar fashion, Lowdham in *The Notion Club Papers* first dreams of individual words, and then gets fragments of a text in two languages and makes copies which he shares with the club, shouting "More than mere words. Verbs! Syntax at last!" (*SD* 246). These fragments he identifies as Avallonian (Quenya) and Adunaic, which he speculates are "passages out of some book" (*SD* 248). For further information on Adunaic, see "Lowdham's report on the Adunaic Language" in *Sauron Defeated* and Christopher's following note (*SD* 413–40).

Politically Incorrect Tolkien

1. See Scull's essay, "Open Minds, Closed Minds in *The Lord of the Rings*," and Chance's essay, "Power and Knowledge in Tolkien: The Problem of Difference in 'The Birthday Party,'" both in *Proceedings of the J. R. R. Tolkien Centenary Conference, Keble College, Oxford, 1992*, ed. Patricia Reynolds and Glen H. GoodKnight (Altadena, CA: Mythopoeic Society, 1995); and Chance's essay "Queer Hobbits: The Problem of Difference in the Shire," in *J. R. R. Tolkien's* The Lord of the Rings, ed. Harold Bloom (Philadelphia, PA: Chelsea House Publishers, 2000). Modern Critical Interpretations.

The Jewels, the Stone, the Ring, and the Making of Meaning

1. See Jonathan B. Himes, "What J. R. R. Tolkien Really Did with the Sampo," *Mythlore* 22.4 (Spring 2000): 69–85.

2. The date would place it before the 1918 appearance already discussed, except that the 1917 text exists only in an ink-over-pencil palimpsest that Christopher Tolkien places as "one of the latest elements in the composition of the *Lost Tales*" (*BLT* I 204), probably before the c. 1925 "Lay of Leithian."

3. A passage in *Unfinished Tales* alludes to Fëanor's request for a "tress" of Galadriel's silver-gilt hair, whose "gold was touched by some memory of the starlike silver of her mother," and which "the Eldar say" snared "the light of the Two Trees, Laurelin and Telperion" (*UT* 230). The passage suggests that this saying first gave Fëanor the idea of "imprisoning and blending" the two lights that "later took shape in his hands as the Silmarils" (230), a surprising complication to an already complicated concept of the connection between light and desire. Christopher Tolkien dates the passage to "certainly" after the publication of *The Road Goes Ever On* (*UT* 229).

4. For more on this interesting speculation, see "The Arkenstone as Silmaril," in *The History of* The Hobbit, part 2: *Return to Bag-End*, 603–9.

5. The ground for Bilbo's fall has been prepared by his "theft" of the Ring (at least from Gollum's point of view) and his weeks of pilfering the larder in the wood-elves' caves (for which he later apologizes to the king of wood-elves himself).

6. Wagner's "Ring of the Nibelung" is the comparison most often made, but the epitome of the search for Tolkien's possible sources is David Day's popularizing book, *Tolkien's Ring*, which ransacks literature for any and all mentions of magic rings, however near to or far from Tolkien's Ring of Power they may be.

7. There is some debate as to whether the voice that speaks out of the wheel of fire is the voice of Frodo or that of the Ring itself. I propose that at this point in Frodo's long surrender there is very little difference between the two.

The Forests and the Trees: Sal and Ian in Faërie

1. Sal and Gimli are not the only ones who ascribe conscious intent to the natural world. Jon Krakauer's account of the disastrous 1996 Everest expedition, *Into Thin Air*, tells of a climbing Sherpa who was hit by a "grapefruit sized" stone that "came whizzing down from the upper mountain" and struck him in the back of the head (250). A moment later, "a second rock came down," smashing into the same man in the same place, the back of the head. The reaction of his climbing companions was, "What's going on here? What have we done to make this mountain so angry?" (250).

2. The *-ish* suffix used here is worth examining. *The Oxford English Dictionary* defines *-ish* as, "Of or belonging to a person or thing, of the nature or character of" (def. 2), and "Of the nature of, somewhat." It also notes that in colloquial use, *-ish* added to a noun forms a nonce adjective "of a slighting or depreciatory nature" (def. 2). Merry has already commented that the forest is "frightfully tree-ish" (*TT* III, iv, 65), and we can infer that this is not a compliment but a slighting or depreciatory qualifier. Since woodlands are usually made up of trees, to describe a forest as "tree-ish" seems redundant, and as "frightfully tree-ish," even more so. The tree-ishness of Fangorn Forest is too much of a good (or, in the hobbits' view, not so good) thing. Treebeard's later addition of *-ish* to *Ent* is less pejorative, but still implies a sense of "somewhat." We might be tempted to associate Merry's usage here with Tolkien's usage of *–ish* in an early (1913) sketchbook, titled by him *The Book of Ishness*, and in the titles of two of his early pictures, "Undertenishness" and "Grownupishness." The effort in all three instances seems to have been to capture an essence or quality.

3. One is impelled to look for meaning in other such trees, both in Tolkien's mythology and in real-world mythologies. Tolkien wrote two poems about birch trees in *Songs for the Philologists*. One, "Bagme Bloma" (Flower of the Trees), praises the birch for its beauty and shows some tenuous connections to Smith's birch: "smooth, straight and white-barked, trembling she speaks a language, a bright token, a good mystery" and "the fine leaves fly free, but firm and faithful the white birch stands bare and waits" (Shippey, *Road*, rev. ed. 401). The other, "Éadig beo þu" (Good Luck to You), praises "the birch and the birch's race, the teacher, the student, and the subject" (*Road*, rev. ed. 402). Based on these lines, Tom Shippey, who reads *Smith of Wootton Major* as an allegory of Tolkien as a philologist, suggests that the birch "represents learning, severe learning, even discipline" (*Road*, rev. ed. 316).

4. These two attempts were *The Lost Road*, in 1936 or thereabouts, and *The Notion Club Papers*, in 1944–45. Christopher Tolkien has edited and published

both in his History of Middle-earth, *The Lost Road* in volume 5, *The Lost Road and Other Writings*, and *The Notion Club Papers* in volume 9, *Sauron Defeated*.

5. In this context, see Tolkien's description, in a draft of "On Fairy-stories," of the tree-fairy or dryad as "a minor spirit in the process of creation who aided as 'agent' in the making of the divine Tree-idea or some part of it, or even of some one particular example of one tree" (*TOFS* 255).

How Trees Behave—Or Do They?

1. Some etymological connections that Tolkien deleted but that nonetheless show his thoughts include "*ho, syogo; hu, khugu; = fōa*," suggesting a connection at least of sense with "√PHAW-, emit (foul breath etc.). *phawalōkō > foalóke*" (*WPP* 181). These deleted notes also cite related (or possibly related) roots/elements in the corpus:

In Tolkien's *Words, Phrases and Passages in Various Tongues in* The Lord of the Rings, published as issue 17 of *Parma Eldalamberon*, the issue's editor, Christopher Gilson, notes, "The question mark in the gloss of huorn is in the manuscript," adding, "[T]he gloss of *hō* is uncertain, and might be 'speak, show'." He continues, "Deleted: *ho, syogo; hu, khugu; = fōa*. The gloss of *hú* might be 'heart'. Cf. GL *hond >> honn* 'heart', *hû* 'dog'; Etym. KHŌ-N- 'heart (physical)', Q *hōn*, N *hûn*; *Khō-gorē*, N *Huor* 'heart-vigour; courage', KHUGAN-, Q *huan* 'hound', N *huan*; Huorns, WR 30, Galbedirs 'Talking Trees', 47, *Lamorni* >> *Ornómar*, 50, *Ornómi* 'trees with voices', 55. For orn '(tall) tree', see I 356 s.v. *mellyrn*" (*WPP* 86).

Tolkien's *Qenyaqetsa: The Qenya Phonology and Lexicon*, published as issue 12 of *Parma Eldalamberon*, discusses other roots/elements possibly related to *hu-* if having to do with voices: "HO- (OHO ?) shout, scream. *hô* an owl. *holle* a shout. *holtó-* call out. *holále* babble, chatter, conversation." "HUHU- (= *hoho*.) whoop. *hulále* = *holále*."

Etymologies (p. 365, s.v. KHUGAN-): "KHUG- bark, bay. *khugan*: Q *huan* (*húnen*) hound; N *Huan* (dog-name); Q *huo* dog; N *hû*."

Myth and Truth in Tolkien's Legendarium

1. Christopher Tolkien identifies "a small quantity of original draft material" written on "slips made from documents of the year 1955" (*MR* 304).

2. Three letters to Murray are included in the published *Letters*. The first two were written within a year of one another, the first on 2 December 1953, the second on 4 November 1954. The third, concerned almost entirely with etymology, was written on 4 May 1958. The first two letters are both in answer to Murray's questions about aspects of *The Lord of the Rings*, and both devote much time and space to a consideration of death in Tolkien's fiction.

3. This would not be the first time that Tolkien responded to inquiry from a reader by amplifying some aspect of his mythology. In a 1969 letter to Tolkien, Paul Bibire enquired "whether the River Glanduin is the same as the Swanfleet." Tolkien replied to Bibire at some length and then wrote an essay headed "Nomenclature."

The essay, titled by Christopher Tolkien "The Rivers and Beacon – hills of Gondor" and edited by Carl Hostetter, was published in *Vinyar Tengwar* 42 (July 2001): 5–31.

4. In this regard, an allusion to "P. H." in the second letter to Murray is worth noting. "As for Gandalf, surely it is not to join P. H. to voice *any* criticism" (*Letters* 201). A note identifies "P. H." as Peter Hastings. The reference seems to assume a shared opinion that "P. H." was a voice particularly critical of *The Lord of the Rings*. The letter at this point is concerned with the presentation of the return of Gandalf, which Tolkien acknowledges to be "a defect," referred to by "one other critic" (alas, unidentified) as "cheating."

Fays, Corrigans, Elves, and More: Tolkien's Dark Ladies

1. Tolkien is here slightly misquoting a line from a fifteenth-century Icelandic ballad, "Ólafur Liljurós," included in *Songs for the Philologists*. It is the story of a mortal man beguiled by an elf-maiden, who kills him when he rejects her advances. As it appears in the *Songs*, the line is "*alfamær . . . Hun var ekki Kristi kær*" ("elf-maiden . . . she was not dear to Christ") (in *SP* 5).

2. The exception to this negligence is Tom Shippey, who with characteristic thoroughness, devotes appendix B of *The Road to Middle-earth* to four "asterisk" poems from *Songs for the Philologists,* one of which is "Ides Ælfscýne."

3. Kullervo's two families, one massacred at the beginning of the story so he will be an orphan and a second still alive halfway through so he will have an unknown sister to seduce/violate (a perpetual puzzle to readers), are the result of some juggling by the story's compiler, Elias Lönnrot, who combined two separate stories but neglected to smooth out the awkward join.

4. This motif will reappear in the story of Túrin Turambar, who persistently disregards the good advice given him by well-meaning friends and even enemies.

5. I am excepting the Eldar of his Silmarillion, as they are all fays or fairies, and their interaction with humans is rare and atypical. A case might be made for Lúthien or Idril, but that would stretch the bounds of this essay.

6. Broceliande is a potent name in Celtic, and especially Arthurian, fairy lore, as the place where the mage Merlin was seduced by the fairy Nimue into giving her the secret of his magic, after which she used it to cast him into an enchanted sleep, wherein he remains to this day. Broceliande also appears prominently in Chrétien de Troyes's *Yvain* as the place where the hero pours water from a fountain onto a magic stone, unleashing a powerful storm.

7. Called the Loathly Lady, she appears in Chaucer's "Wife of Bath's Tale" and in "Sir Gawain and the Green Knight," as well as in lesser-known folktales and poems.

8. There is as well a suggestion that the fay, as a shape-changer, also appears as the white doe.

9. For an alternate reading of Tolkien's focus on the Corrigan, see Kristine Larsen's "'Alone Between the Dark and Light': 'The Lay of Aotrou and Itroun' and Lessons from the Later Legendarium."

10. See Patrick Sims-Williams's essay "Some Celtic Otherworld Terms," in *Celtic Language, Celtic Culture: A Festschrift for Eric P. Hamp,* ed. A. T. E. Matonis

and Daniel F. Melia (Van Nuys, CA: Ford and Baillie, 1990), 58–59. The "shine" etymology may connect to Tolkien's description of "Guinever": "with gleaming limbs" (*FoA* II, p. 17, l. 27).

11. For more on this, see Alyssa House-Thomas's recently completed MA thesis for Signum University, "'Fair as fay-woman and fell-minded': Tolkien's 'Guinever,'" to be published in the forthcoming anthology *The Inklings and King Arthur*, edited by Sørina Higgins.

12. Clearly derived from the *álfamær* of "Ólafur Liljurós" in my epigraph. See note 1 for this essay, above.

13. Noted in passing but omitted for reasons of space and repetition is another of Tolkien's "trapped mortal" poems from *Songs for the Philologists*, "Ofer Wídne Gársecg," where roughly the same scenario is repeated, this time with a mermaid and with comedic intent and effect.

14. See Marjorie Burns's discussion of Galadriel in her book *Perilous Realms: Celtic and Norse in Tolkien's Middle-earth* (Toronto: Univ. of Toronto Press, 2005).

15. We might note here the particular applicability of the *scyne* (bright= beautiful) element in the compound *ælfscyne* to Galadriel as Tolkien describes her, emphasizing at several points in the narrative (and in the backstory as well) the shining gold of her hair. Both Gimli in Lórien and Feänor in the Silmarillion backstory are ensnared by and desirous of strands of her hair.

Tolkien, *Kalevala*, and Middle-earth

1. In print see, for example, Jane Chance, *The Lord of the Rings: The Mythology of Power*, rev. ed. (Lexington: Univ. Press of Kentucky, 2001); Anne C. Petty, "Identifying England's Lönnrot," *Tolkien Studies* 1.1 (2004): 69–84; Matthew Bardowell, "J. R. R. Tolkien's Creative Ethic and Its Finnish Analogues," *Journal of the Fantastic in the Arts* 20.1 (Mar. 2009): 91–108; Richard West, "Setting the Rocket Off in Story," and David Elton Gay, "J. R. R. Tolkien and the *Kalevala*," both in *Tolkien and the Invention of Myth*, ed. Jane Chance (Lexington: Univ. of Kentucky Press, 2004); and David L. Dettman, "Vänämöinen in Middle-earth," in *Tolkien in the New Century*, ed. John W. Houghton et al. (Jefferson, NC: McFarland and Co., 2014). Online see the discussion in the Minas Tirith Forum, "Who or what is Tom Bombadil?" <http://www.minastirith.com/cgi-bin/ultimatebb.cgi?ubb=get_topic;f=17;t=000024;p=5>.

2. For a full discussion of this extraordinary figure, see Israel Gollancz's *Hamlet in Iceland* (London: David Nutt, 1898). With variant names Amlethus, Ambales, Amlaith, and Amlodhi, the figure was clearly well known. An early form of his name has been translated as "dullard," "simpleton," or "fool." Whatever his origin, the medieval "hero-fool" is clearly the precursor of the Renaissance prince.

3. It is worth noting that "Great Lands" (now pluralized) was a phrase added to the second manuscript of "The Cottage of Lost Play," begun by Tolkien in 1916–17. Here it means not Russia specifically but more generally "lands east of the Great Sea," by which we can suppose something not unlike continental Europe (*BLT* I 19, 21). Tolkien may have abandoned *The Story of Kullervo*, but it clearly never aban-

doned him, and its elements, especially the linguistic ones, are embedded in the later texts of the Silmarillion like fossils in rock. Many of the names in both volumes of *The Book of Lost Tales* (now recognized as precursors of Qenya, Tolkien's proto-Elvish), had their roots in *The Story of Kullervo*.

4. Only Túrin and Frodo come close, as pointed out in the next section, but both of them have friends, experience some happy moments, and enjoy some bright spots in the otherwise dark world of Middle-earth. Kullervo has no friends and only one happy moment, which rapidly turns sour; the only bright spot he encounters—the sunlight on the mountain—leads directly to his downfall.

5. See J. R. R. Tolkien, *The Story of Kullervo*, ed. Verlyn Flieger (London: HarperCollins, 2015); and Verlyn Flieger, "Tolkien, *Kalevala*, and 'The Story of Kullervo,'" in Flieger, *Green Suns and Faërie* (Kent, OH: Kent State Univ. Press, 2012).

6. For a full discussion of *Kalevala* meter, see Matti Kuusi, Keith Bosley, and Michael Branch, eds. and trans. *Finnish Folk Poetry: Epic* (Helsinki: Finnish Literature Society, 1977), 62–65.

Tolkien's French Connection

1. There is no etymological connection, but there is a clear visual and associational one.

2. The change of mode from romance to saga in the latter half of *The Hobbit* has been recognized ever since C. S. Lewis commented, in "On Stories," that "it is if Badger had begun to talk like Njal" (*EPCW* 105).

Voyaging About: Tolkien and Celtic *Navigatio*

1. I would like to point readers to Kris Swank's essay, "The Irish Otherworld Voyage of *Roverandom*," which had not been written when this paper was presented in1998 but has now been published in *Tolkien Studies* 12 (2015): 31–57.

Works Cited

Agøy, Nils Ivar. "The Fall and Man's Mortality: An Investigation of Some Theological Themes in J. R. R. Tolkien's 'Athrabeth Finrod ah Andreth.'" In *Between Faith and Fiction: Tolkien and the Powers of his World. Proceedings of the Arda Symposium at the Second Northern Tolkien Festival, Oslo, August 1997*. Ed. Nils Ivar Agøy. *Arda Special* 1 Sept. 1998. 16–27.

———. "The Christian Tolkien: A Response to Ronald Hutton." In *The Ring and the Cross: Christianity and the Writings of J. R. R. Tolkien*. Ed. Paul Kerry. Madison, NJ: Fairleigh Dickinson Univ. Press, 2011.

Amazing Stories. Ed. Hugo Gernsback. New York: Experimenter Publishing Co., 1926.

The American Heritage Dictionary of the English Language. Ed. William Morris. Boston, MA: American Heritage Publishing Co. and Houghton Mifflin, 1969.

The Awntyrs off Arthure at the Terne Wathelyn: An Edition Based on Bodleian Library MS. Douce 324. Ed. Ralph Hanna 3rd. Manchester, UK: Manchester Univ. Press, 1974.

Bardowell, Matthew. "J. R. R. Tolkien's Creative Ethic and Its Finnish Analogues." *Journal of the Fantastic in the Arts* 20.1 (Mar. 2009): 91–108.

Barfield, Owen. *Poetic Diction*. London: Faber and Gwyer, 1928.

———. *Saving the Appearances*. New York: Harcourt Brace Jovanovich, 1965.

Barzaz-Breiz: Chants Populaires de la Bretagne., Comp. Théodore Hersart de la Villemarqué. 4th ed. 2 vols. Paris: A. Franck, 1846.

Bohm, David. "The Enfolding-Unfolding Universe: A Conversation with David Bohm." In *The Holographic Paradigm and Other Paradoxes*. Ed. Ken Wilbur. Boulder: Shambala Publications, 1982. 44–104. Interview conducted by Renée Weber.

Branch, M. A. Introduction to *Kalevala*. Comp. Elias Lönnrot. Trans. W. F. Kirby. London: Athlone Press, 1985.

Bromwich, Rachel, ed. and trans. *Trioedd Ynys Prydein: The Welsh Triads*. 2nd ed. Cardiff: Univ. of Wales Press, 1978.

Burns, Marjorie. *Perilous Realms: Celtic and Norse in Tolkien's Middle-earth*. Toronto: Univ. of Toronto Press, 2005.

Campbell, Joseph. *The Hero with a Thousand Faces*. 4th ed. 1949; Novato, CA: New World Library, 2008.

Capra, Fritjof. *The Tao of Physics*. Boulder, CO: Shambala Publications, 1975.

Carpenter, Humphrey. *The Inklings*. Boston, MA: Houghton Mifflin, 1979.

———. *Tolkien: A Biography*. Boston, MA: Houghton Mifflin, 1977.

Cassirer, Ernst. *Language and Myth*. New York: Dover, 1946.
Chance, Jane. *The Lord of the Rings: The Mythology of Power*. Rev. ed. Lexington: Univ. Press of Kentucky, 2001.
———. "Power and Knowledge in Tolkien: The Problem of Difference in 'The Birthday Party.'" In *Proceedings of the J. R. R. Tolkien Centenary Conference, Keble College, Oxford, 1992*. Ed. Patricia Reynolds and Glen GoodKnight. Altadena, CA: Mythopoeic Press, 1995. 115–20.
———. "Queer Hobbits: The Problem of Difference in the Shire." In *J. R. R. Tolkien's* The Lord of the Rings. Ed. Harold Bloom. Philadelphia, PA: Chelsea House Publishers, 2000. Modern Critical Interpretations.
———, ed. *Tolkien and the Invention of Myth: A Reader*. Lexington: Univ. of Kentucky Press, 2004.
———. *Tolkien's Art: A Mythology for England*. London: Macmillan, 1979.
Charlton, Bruce. "Torturing Gollum: The Implications." Bruce Charlton's Notions (formerly Charlton's Miscellany). Weblog. 15 May 2011. Web. <http://charlton-teaching.blogspot.com/2011/05/torturing-gollum-implications.html>.
Chrétien de Troyes. *Erec and Enide*. Trans. Ruth Harwood Cline. Athens: Univ. of Georgia Press, 2000.
———. *Erec and Enide*. Trans. Dorothy Gilbert. Berkeley: Univ. of California Press, 1992.
———. *Lancelot, or the Knight of the Cart*. Trans. Ruth Harwood Cline. Athens: Univ. of Georgia Press, 1990.
———. *Yvain or The Knight with the Lion*. Trans. Ruth Harwood Cline. Athens: Univ. of Georgia Press, 1975.
Cohen, Cynthia. "The Unique Representation of Trees in *The Lord of the Rings*." *Tolkien Studies* 6.1 (2009): 91–126.
Collins, Wilkie. *The Moonstone*. New York: Heritage Press, 1959.
Comparetti, Domenico. *The Traditional Poetry of the Finns*. Trans. Isabella M. Anderton. London: Longmans, Green, and Co., 1898.
Corbet, Richard. "The Fairies Farewell, or God-a-Mercy Will." Norton Online Archive: *The Norton Anthology of English Literature* (webpage). W. W. Norton and Co. (website). <https://www.wwnorton.com/college/english/nael/noa/pdf/27636_17th_U13_Corbet-1-2.pdf>.
Curry, Patrick. *Defending Middle-Earth*. Edinburgh: Floris Books, 1997.
d'Ardenne, Simonne. "The Man and the Scholar." In *Tolkien: Scholar and Storyteller*. Ed. Mary Salu and Robert T. Farrell. Ithaca, NY: Cornell Univ. Press, 1979. 33–37.
Dasent, George Webbe, ed. and trans. *Popular Tales from the Norse*. With an Introductory Essay on the Origin and Diffusion of Popular Tales. 2nd. ed., enlarged. Edinburgh: Edmonston and Douglas, 1859. Translated from two volumes of Norwegian folk tales collected and compiled by Peter Christen Asbjørnsen and Jørgen Moe, under the title *Norske Folkeeventyr*, published in 1843 and 1844.
Day, David. *Tolkien's Ring*. New York: Barnes and Noble, 2002.
Dettman, David L. "Vänämöinen in Middle-earth." In *Tolkien in the New Century: Essays in Honor of Tom Shippey*. Ed. John W. Houghton et al. Jefferson, NC: McFarland and Co., 2014.

Dorson, Richard M. *The British Folklorists: A History.* Chicago: Univ. of Chicago Press, 1968.

———, ed. *Peasant Customs and Savage Myths*, 2 vols. Chicago: Univ. of Chicago Press, 1968.

Drout, Michael D. C. "Towards a Better Tolkien Criticism." In *Reading* The Lord of the Rings: *New Writings on Tolkien's Classic.* Ed. Robert Eaglestone. London: Continuum, 2005. 15–28.

Dunne, J. W. *An Experiment with Time.* London: Faber and Faber, 1934.

Ellis, Peter Berresford. *Celt and Saxon: The Struggle for Britain, AD 410–937.* London: Constable, 1993.

Essays Presented to Charles Williams. Oxford: Oxford University Press, 1947.

Evans-Wentz, Walter Yeeling. *The Fairy-Faith in Celtic Countries.* New York: University Books, 1966.

A Film Portrait of J. R. R. Tolkien. Narr. Judi Dench. Landseer Film and Television Productions, 1996). Film.

Finnish Folk Poetry Epic. Ed. and trans. Maatti Kuusi, Keith Bosley, and Michael Branch. Helsinki: Finnish Literature Society, 1977.

Flieger, Verlyn. *Green Suns and Faërie: Essays on Tolkien.* Kent, OH: Kent State Univ. Press, 2012.

———. *A Question of Time: J. R. R. Tolkien's Road to* Faërie. Kent, OH: Kent State Univ. Press, 1997.

———. "Whose Myth Is It?" In *Between Faith and Fiction: Tolkien and the Powers of his World. Proceedings of the Arda Symposium at the Second Northern Tolkien Festival, Oslo, August 1997.* Ed. Nils Ivar Agøy. Arda Special 1 Sept. 1998. 35–42.

———, and Carl F. Hostetter, eds. *Tolkien's Legendarium: Essays on The History of Middle-earth.* Westport, CN: Greenwood Press, 2000.

Garner, Alan. *Thursbitch.* London: Harvill Press, 2003.

Garth, John. *Tolkien and the Great War: The Threshold of Middle-earth.* New York: Houghton Mifflin, 2003.

Gay, David Elton. "J. R. R. Tolkien and the *Kalevala:* Some Thoughts on the Finnish Origins of Tom Bombadil and Treebeard." In *Tolkien and the Invention of Myth.* Ed. Jane Chance. Lexington: Univ. of Kentucky Press, 2004. 295–304.

Geoffrey of Monmouth. *History of the Kings of Britain.* Trans. Lewis Thorpe. Chatham: Folio Society, 1969.

Gollancz, Israel. *Hamlet in Iceland: Being the Icelandic Romantic Ambales Saga.* London: David Nutt, 1898.

Greer, Germaine. "The Book of the Century." *W: The Waterstone's Magazine.* Winter/Spring 1997: 2–9.

Hall, Alaric. *Elves in Anglo-Saxon England: Matters of Belief, Health, Gender and Identity.* Anglo-Saxon Studies. Woodbridge, Suffolk: Boydell and Brewer, 2007.

Hammond, Wayne, and Christina Scull. *J. R. R. Tolkien: Artist and Illustrator.* London HarperCollins, 1995.

———. *The J. R. R. Tolkien Companion and Guide.* 2 vols. London: HarperCollins, 2006.

———. *The Lord of the Rings: A Reader's Companion.* London: HarperCollins, 2005.

Helms, Randel. *Tolkien and the Silmarils.* Boston, MA: Houghton Mifflin, 1981.

Hostetter, Carl, and Arden Smith. "A Mythology for England." In *Proceedings of the J. R. R. Tolkien Centenary Conference, Keble College, Oxford, 1992*. Ed. Patricia Reynolds and Glen GoodKnight. Altadena, CA: Mythopoeic Press, 1995. 281–90.

Houghton, John W., et al. *Tolkien in the New Century: Essays in Honor of Tom Shippey*. Jefferson, NC: McFarland and Co., 2014.

"-ish." Def. 2. *The Oxford English Dictionary*. 2nd ed. 1989.

"J. R. R. Tolkien Dead at 81: Wrote 'Lord of the Rings.'" Obituary. *New York Times* 3 Sept. 1973.

Kahlas-Tarkka, Leena. "Finnish: The Land and Language of Heroes." In *A Companion to J. R. R. Tolkien*. Ed. Stuart Lee. Chichester: John Wiley and Sons, 2014.

The Kalevala. Comp. Elias Lönnrot. 1835. Länsii-Savo OY: Mikkeli, 1985.

———. Comp. Elias Lönnrot. Trans. Keith Bosley. Oxford: Oxford Univ. Press, 1989.

———. Comp. Elias Lönnrot. Trans. John Martin Crawford. 2 vols. in one. New York: John B. Alden, Publisher, 1888.

———. Comp. Elias Lönnrot. Trans. Eino Friberg. 2nd. ed. Helsinki: Otava Publishing Co., 1990.

———. Comp. Elias Lönnrot. Trans. W. F. Kirby. 2 vols. London: J. M. Dent, 1974. Everyman's Library.

———. Comp. Elias Lönnrot. Trans. Francis Magoun. Cambridge, MA: Harvard Univ. Press, 1975.

———. Comp. Elias Lönnrot. Trans. Franz Anton Schiefner. Helsingfors: Papoer, Druck Under Verlag, J. S. Franckel and Sohn, 1852.

Kane, Douglas Charles. *Arda Reconstructed: The Creation of the Published Silmarillion*. Bethlehem, PA: Lehigh Univ. Press, 2009.

Keightley, Thomas. *The Fairy Mythology*. London: George Bell and Sons, 1882.

King Arthur's Death: The Middle English Stanzaic Morte Arthur and Alliterative Morte Arthure. Ed. Larry D. Benson. Exeter, UK: Univ. of Exeter Press, 1986.

Kipling, Rudyard. *Puck of Pook's Hill*. New York: Doubleday, Page, 1906.

———. *Rewards and Fairies*. New York: Doubleday, Page, 1910.

Kirk, Robert. *The Secret Commonwealth of Elves, Fauns, and Fairies*. Stirling: Eneas MacKay, 1933.

Kocher, Paul. *Master of Middle-earth*. Boston, MA: Houghton Mifflin, 1972.

Krakauer, Jon. *Into Thin Air*. New York: Villard, 1997.

Kuusi, Matti, Keith Bosley, and Michael Branch, eds. and trans. *Finnish Folk Poetry: Epic*. Helsinki: Finnish Literature Society, 1977.

Lang, Andrew. *Custom and Myth*. London: Longmans, Green, and Co., 1893.

———. "The History of the Book and Author." In *The Secret Commonwealth of Elves, Fauns and Fairies*, by Robert Kirk. Stirling: Eneas MacKay, 1933.

Larsen, Kristine. "'Alone Between the Dark and Light': 'The Lay of Aotrou and Itroun' and Lessons from the Later Legendarium." In *Tolkien in the New Century: Essays in Honor of Tom Shippey*. Ed. John Wm. Houghton et al. Jefferson, NC: McFarland and Co., 2014.

Lee, Stuart D., ed. *A Companion to J. R. R. Tolkien*. Chichester: John Wiley and Sons, 2014.

Lewis, C. S. "On Stories." In *Essays Presented to Charles Williams*. London: Oxford Univ. Press, 1947. 90–105.

———. *Out of the Silent Planet*. New York: Macmillan, 1967.
———. *Perelandra*. New York: Macmillan, 1958.
Lindsay, David. *A Voyage to Arcturus*. London: Victor Gollancz, 1946.
Lobdell, Jared, ed. *A Tolkien Compass*. LaSalle, IL: Open Court, 1975.
The Mabinogion. Trans. Gwyn Jones and Thomas Jones. Dent: London, 1966. Everyman's Library.
MacCana, Proinsias. *Celtic Mythology*. London: Hamlyn, 1970.
MacKillop, James. *Dictionary of Celtic Mythology*. Oxford: Oxford Univ. Press, 1998.
Malory, Sir Thomas. *Works* [*Le Morte D'Arthur*]. Ed. Eugene Vinaver. London: Oxford Univ. Press, 1971.
Martsch, Nancy. "The 'Squint-eyed Southerner.'" *Beyond Bree* May 1990: 9. Newsletter of the Tolkien Special Interest Group of American Mensa. Quoted in Hammond and Scull, *Reader's Companion*, 153–54.
Matonis, A. T. E., and Daniel F. Melia, eds. *Celtic Language, Celtic Culture: A Festschrift for Eric P. Hamp*. Van Nuys, CA: Ford and Baillie, 1990.
Mendlesohn, Farah. *Rhetorics of Fantasy*. Middletown, CT: Wesleyan Univ. Press, 2008.
Muir, Edwin. "Strange Epic." Review of *The Fellowship of the Ring*, by J. R. R. Tolkien. *Observer* (London), 22 Aug. 1954: 7.
Müller, Max. *Chips from a German Workshop*. 4 vols. New York: Scribner, Armstrong and Co., 1871–76.
O hOgain, Daithi. *Myth, Legend, and Romance: An Encyclopædia of the Irish Folk Tradition*. New York: Prentice Hall Press, 1991.
Ó Síocháin, P. A. *Ireland: A Journey into Lost Time*. 3d ed. 1967; Dublin: Foilsiuchain Eireann, 1983.
Oxford English Dictionary. Ed. J. A. Simpson and E. S. C. Weiner. 2nd ed. Oxford: Oxford Univ. Press, 1989.
Pearce, Joseph. *Tolkien: Man and Myth*. London: HarperCollins, 1998.
Pentikäinen, Juha. *Kalevala Mythology*. Trans. and ed. Ritva Boom. Bloomington: Indiana Univ. Press, 1989.
Petty, Anne. "Identifying England's Lönnrot." *Tolkien Studies* 1.1 (2004): 69–84.
Plato. *Timaeus and Critias*. Trans. Desmond Lee. Rev. ed. London: Penguin Books, 1977.
Pullman, Philip. *The Amber Spyglass*. New York: Alfred A. Knopf, 2000.
———. *The Golden Compass*. New York: Alfred A. Knopf, 1995.
———. "Questions and Answers." *Philip Pullman* (website). <http://www.philip-pullman.com/qas?searchtext=&page=5>.
———. *The Subtle Knife*. New York: Alfred A. Knopf, 1997.
———. Unattributed interview. Dec. 1998. Author Interviews, Children's Books UK. ACHUKA (website). <http://www.achuka.co.uk/archive/interviews/ppint.php>.
Pwyll Pendeuic Dyuet: The First of the Four Branches of the Mabinogi,, edited from the White Book of Rhydderch, with variants from the Red Book of Hergest. Ed. R. L. Thomson. Medieval and Modern Welsh Series. Dublin: Dublin Institute for Advanced Studies, 1957.

Rateliff, John. *The History of The Hobbit*. One-vol. ed. London: HarperCollins, 2011. Contains text of original draft of J. R. R. Tolkien's *The Hobbit*.

Rees, Alwyn, and Brinley Rees. *Celtic Heritage: Ancient Tradition in Ireland and Wales*. London: Thames and Hudson, 1961.

Resnik, Henry. "An Interview with Tolkien." *Niekas* 18 (Late Spring 1967): 37–47.

Rhys, John. *Celtic Folklore: Welsh and Manx*. 2 vols. New York: Gordon Press, 1974.

Roche, Norma. "Sailing West: Tolkien, the Saint Brendan Story, and the Idea of Paradise in the West." *Mythlore* 66 (Summer 1991): 16–20.

Schakel, Peter, ed. *The Longing for a Form: Essays on the Fiction of C. S. Lewis*. Eugene, OR: Wipf and Stock, 2008.

Scull, Christina. "Open Minds, Closed Minds in *The Lord of the Rings*." In *Proceedings of the J. R. R. Tolkien Centenary Conference, Keble College, Oxford, 1992*. Ed. Patricia Reynolds and Glen GoodKnight. Altadena, CA: Mythopoeic Press, 1995. 151–57.

Settegast, Mary. *Plato Prehistorian*. Cambridge, MA: Rotenberg Press, 1987.

Shakespeare, William. *A Midsummer Night's Dream*. Ed. Harold Bloom. New York: Infobase Publishing, 2008.

Shippey, T. A. "Long Evolution: The History of Middle-earth and Its Merits." In *Arda* (1987): 18–39.

———. *The Road to Middle-earth*. Rev. ed. London: HarperCollins, 2005.

———. *The Road to Middle-earth*, 2nd ed. London: Grafton, 1992.

Sims-Williams, Patrick. "Some Celtic Otherworld Terms." In Matonis and Melia, *Celtic Language, Celtic Culture*. 57–81.

Stenström, Anders. "A Mythology? For England?" In *Proceedings of the J. R. R. Tolkien Centenary Conference, Keble College, Oxford, 1992*. Ed. Patricia Reynolds and Glen GoodKnight. Altadena, CA: Mythopoeic Press, 1995. 310–14.

Thurman, Judith. *Secrets of the Flesh: A Life of Colette*. New York: Alfred A. Knopf, 1999.

Tolkien, J. R. R. *The Adventures of Tom Bombadil*. London: George Allen and Unwin, 1962.

———. *The Annotated Hobbit*. Rev. and expanded ed. Annotated by Douglas A. Anderson. Boston, MA: Houghton Mifflin, 2002.

———. "Beowulf: The Monsters and the Critics." In *Proceedings of the British Academy* 22 (1936): 245–95.

———. "*Beowulf:* The Monsters and the Critics." In *The Monsters and the Critics and Other Essays*. Ed. Christopher Tolkien. London: George Allen and Unwin, 1983. 5–48.

———. *The Book of Lost Tales*, Part I. Ed. Christopher Tolkien. Boston, MA: Houghton Mifflin, 1984.

———. *The Book of Lost Tales*, Part II. Ed. Christopher Tolkien. Boston, MA: Houghton Mifflin, 1984.

———. "English and Welsh." In *Angles and Britons: O'Donnell Lectures*. Ed. Henry Lewis. Cardiff: Univ. of Wales Press, 1963. 1–41.

———. *The Fall of Arthur*. Ed. Christopher Tolkien. London: HarperCollins, 2013.

———. *The Fellowship of the Ring.* Vol. 1 of *The Lord of the Rings.* 2nd ed. Boston, MA: Houghton Mifflin, 1965.

———. *The Hobbit.* 2nd ed. London: George Allen and Unwin, 1951.

———. "Ides Ælfscyne." In *Songs for the Philologists,* by J. R. R. Tolkien, E. V. Gordon, and Others. London: Privately printed in the Department of English at University College, 1936. 10–11.

———. "The Lay of Aotrou and Itroun." *Welsh Review* 4.4 (Dec. 1945): 254–66.

———. *The Lay of Aotrou and Itroun.* Ed. Verlyn Flieger, with a Note on the Text by Christopher Tolkien. London: HarperCollins, 2016.

———. *The Lays of Beleriand.* The History of Middle-earth. Vol. 3. Ed. Christopher Tolkien. Boston, MA: Houghton Mifflin, 1985.

———. *The Letters of J. R. R. Tolkien.* Sel. and ed. Humphrey Carpenter, with Christopher Tolkien. Boston, MA: Houghton Mifflin, 1981.

———. "Looney." *The Oxford Magazine.* 18 Jan. 1934. 340.

———. *The Lord of the Rings.* London: HarperCollins, 1991.

———. *The Lost Road and Other Writings: Language and Legend before* The Lord of the Rings. The History of Middle-earth. Vol. 5. Ed. Christopher Tolkien. Boston, MA: Houghton Mifflin, 1987.

———. *A Middle English Vocabulary.* Oxford: Clarendon Press, 1925.

———. *The Monsters and the Critics and Other Essays.* Ed. Christopher Tolkien. London: George Allen and Unwin, 1983.

———. *Morgoth's Ring.* The History of Middle-earth. Vol. 10. Ed. Christopher Tolkien. Boston, MA: Houghton Mifflin, 1993.

———. "On Fairy-stories." In *Essays Presented to Charles Williams.* Oxford: Oxford Univ. Press, 1947. 38–89.

———. "On Fairy-stories." In *The Monsters and the Critics and Other Essays.* Ed. Christopher Tolkien. London: George Allen and Unwin, 1983. 109–61.

———. "On 'The Kalevala' or Land of Heroes." In *The Story of Kullervo.* Ed. Verlyn Flieger. London: HarperCollins, 2015.

———. *The Peoples of Middle-earth.* The History of Middle-earth. Vol. 12. Ed. Christopher Tolkien. Boston, MA: Houghton Mifflin, 1996.

———. *Qenyaqetsa: The Qenya Phonology and Lexicon.* Ed. Christopher Gilson, Carl F. Hostetter, Patrick H. Wynne, and Arden R. Smith. 1998; rev. 3rd. printing, Mountain View, CA: Parma Eldalamberon, 2011. 112 pp. Published as issue 12 of the journal *Parma Eldalamberon.*

———. *The Return of the King.* Vol. 3 of *The Lord of the Rings.* 2nd. ed. Boston, MA: Houghton Mifflin, 1965.

———. *The Return of the Shadow.* The History of Middle-earth. Vol. 6. Ed. Christopher Tolkien. Boston, MA: Houghton Mifflin, 1988.

———. "The Rivers and Beacon-hills of Gondor." *Vinyar Tengwar* 42 (July 2001): 5–31.

———. *Sauron Defeated: The End of the Third Age.* The History of Middle-earth. Vol. 9. Ed. Christopher Tolkien. London: HarperCollins, 1992.

———. *The Simarillion.* Ed. Christopher Tolkien. London: HarperCollins, 1990.

———. *Smith of Wootton Major.* Extended ed. Ed. Verlyn Flieger. London: HarperCollins, 2005.
———. *The Story of Kullervo.* Ed. Verlyn Flieger. London: HarperCollins, 2015.
———. *Tolkien On Fairy-Stories.* Expanded ed. Ed. Verlyn Flieger and Douglas A. Anderson. London: HarperCollins, 2008.
———. *The Treason of Isengard,* . The History of Middle-earth. Vol. 7. Ed. Christopher Tolkien. Boston, MA: Houghton Mifflin, 1989.
———. *Tree and Leaf, Including the Poem* "Mythopoeia." Rev. ed. London: Allen and Unwin, 1988.
———. *The Two Towers.* Vol. 2 of *The Lord of the Rings.* 2nd ed. Boston, MA: Houghton Mifflin, 1965.
———. *Unfinished Tales of Númenor and Middle-earth.* Ed. Christopher Tolkien. Boston, MA: Houghton Mifflin, 1980.
———. *The War of the Jewels.* The History of Middle-earth. Vol. 11. Ed. Christopher Tolkien. Boston, MA: Houghton Mifflin, 1994.
———. *The War of the Ring.* The History of Middle-earth. Vol. 8. Ed. Christopher Tolkien. Boston, MA: Houghton Mifflin, 1990.
———. *Words, Phrases and Passages in Various Tongues in* The Lord of the Rings. Ed. Christopher Gilson. Mountain View, CA: Parma Eldalamberon, 2007. 220 pp. Published as issue 17 of the journal *Parma Eldalamberon.*
———, E. V. Gordon, and Others. *Songs for the Philologists.* London: Privately printed in the Department of English at University College, 1936.
Twain, Mark. *The Adventures of Huckleberry Finn.* 1884. Clayton, DE: Prestwick House, 2005.
The Welsh Review 4. 4 (Dec. 1945). Ed. Gwyn Jones.
West, Richard C. "Setting the Rocket Off in Story: The Kalavala as the Germ of Tolkien's Legendarium." In *Tolkien and the Invention of Myth.* Ed. Jane Chance. Lexington: Univ. of Kentucky Press, 2004. 285–94.
Wheeler, John A. "The Universe as Home for Man." *American Scientist* 62 (Nov.–Dec. 1974): 683–91.
Whorf, Benjamin. *Language, Thought, and Reality.* Ed. John B. Carroll. Cambridge, MA: M.I.T. Press, 1945.
Wilber, Ken. *The Holographic Paradigm and Other Paradoxes.* Boulder, CO: Shambala Publications, 1982.
Wilson, Edmund. "Oo, Those Awful Orcs!" Review of *The Lord of the Rings,* by J. R. R. Tolkien. *The Nation,* 14 Apr. 1956: 312–14.
Wynne, Patrick, and Carl F. Hostetter. "Three Elvish Verse Modes." In Flieger and Hostetter, *Tolkien's Legendarium.* 113–39.

Index

ælfscyne, 165; in *Songs for the Philologists*, 166, 173, 174, 176, 237n2, 238n15
ælfshot, 165
Ælfwine: and Celtic references, 202; as Eriol-Ælfwine narrator, 158; Germanic elements and Celtic references of, 197; *The Lost Road* and *The Notion Club Papers* origin of, 76, 81; as Lowdham in *The Notion Club Papers*, 83, 85–87, 202; medieval Irish voyages compared to *The Lost Road*, 226–27
Adanel, 161–64
Adunaic language, 73, 80, 83, 84, 159, 160, 213, 233–34n2
Adventures of Tom Bombadil, The, 147–48, 245. *See also* Bombadil, Tom
"Ainulindalë": and death, 53; in "The Athrabeth," 161–64. *See also* music
Alexander, Lloyd, 46, 48
álfamær, 165, 237
Allen and Unwin, 6, 19, 196, 232
Anderson, Douglas A., and Arkenstone, 101
Andreth, 159–64
Andrew Lang Lecture, 5–7, 11–16, 145
Annals of Aman, 213–14
Annotated Hobbit, The (Anderson), 101
Aotrou, 169–72
aotrou (word), Breton meaning of, 204

Aragorn: coronation and marriage of, as happy ending, 44; death of, 54–55, 56, 58; and Galadriel, 175–76; and Gandalf in Fangorn, 31; on good and evil, 123; and second plotline of *The Lord of the Rings*, 214; and sentient landscape, 132, 137–38; as son of Arathorn, 76
Arda: and Christian belief, 161–62, 164; and Númenor myth, 157–64, 213–14
Arkenstone: as artifact, 69, 100–102, 106–8, 111–12; function in *The Hobbit*, 106–8, 111–12; as Silmaril (Rateliff), 234
"arresting strangeness": and green sun, 127; as hallmark of fantasy, 39; of Mirkwood and Smaug, 39; of Misty Mountain names, 74; in the natural world, 127
Arthur, King (English legend): *The Awnters off Arthure at the Terne Wathelyne*, 205; and Celtic references in Tolkien's works, 201; death of, 114–15; as England's mythology, 18; Grail concept in, 109–11, 211–12; and real-world accounts of lost lands, 216–17
Arwen: marriage with Aragorn, 44; and "Tale of Aragorn," 55
Aryan theory, World War II and, 7, 9–13
Asbjørnsen, Peter Christen, *Norske Folkeeventyr*, 8

Āsemo *(The Story of Kullervo)*, 186–87.
See also *Kalevala* (Lönnrot)
"Athrabeth Finrod ah Andreth," 22, 127, 159–64; theological themes in, 240
"Atlantis and Númenor," 76, 77, 86, 87, 163, 201, 213–20; as "dividing line" of myth and history, 84–85; *versus* "Eriol-Saga," 86, 87, 163; and real-world inundations, 181, 201–2, 213–20, 233n1; recurrent dream, 82, 201, 215
Aubrey, John, 8
Auden, W. H., 17, 20, 21, 24, 82, 113, 195, 231n1
Austin, Ruth, 21
Avallonian (Quenya) language, 84, 186
aventure/adventure: and Faërie, 34, 204; forest of, 34, 42, 43, 204, 207; in French romance, 207–8; in *The Hobbit*, 206–7; in Malory, 208–9; Middle English *aunter/awnter*, 205; Old Irish equivalent, 204; quest compared to, 209–12; terminology of, 204–9
Awnters off Arthure at the Terne Wathelyne, The, 205

Baggins, Bilbo: and Arkenstone, 107; as atypical hobbit, 92; compared to Launcelot, 207–12; effect of Ring on, 109; Escape, 38–40, 44; and Faërian Drama, 26–27; and fairy wife ancestor, 174; moral lapse and self-knowledge, 108, 111; and Red Book, 88, 158; and "Song of Eärendil," 101; understanding of Ring, 110
Baggins, Frodo: as atypical hobbit, 92, 93; balanced against Gollum, 98; and eucatrophe, 44–45, 61–64; in Lórien, 140–41; and moral ambiguity, 116, 118–20, 122, 123; and Old Forest as Faërian Drama, 134, 136, 148, 149; and Red Book, 88, 158; on the Straight Road, 80; as typical hobbit, 93–94; use of the Ring, 109–11
Bard the Bowman: and Arkenstone, 108; and Bilbo's armor, 206; dragon-slaying and late entry into *The Hobbit*, 40
Barfield, Owen, *Poetic Diction*, 11, 73, 233n2
Barsaz-Breiz (Villemarqué), 216
Beare, Rhona, 109

Beowulf poet, as model, 22
"*Beowulf*: The Monsters and the Critics": battle with the dark, 4; teaching *The Lord of the Rings* with, 59–65
Beren: and Silmarils, 101, 103–5; and Thingol, 96
Bilbo. *See* Baggins, Bilbo
Bingo, 147
birch tree: as dryad, 155; in *Kalevala*, 142; in *Smith of Wootton Major*, 131, 139–43, 155; in *Songs for the Philologists*, 142, 235
Black Book of Carmarthen, 216
Black Gate, 116, 121–23
Black Riders, 109, 110
Blue-robed Lady of the Forest (The Story of Kullervo), 127, 166–69, 173, 177
Bohm, David, 72, 233n1
Bombadil, Tom: compared to Väinämöinen, 190–93; effect of the Ring on, 109–10; enigmatic, 183; and Faërie concept, 60–61; and Old Forest, Willow-man, 135–37, 139, 147–48; Tolkien as, 195, 238n1; and tree-fairies, 150
"bones of the ox," 8, 12, 13, 181
Book of Lost Tales, 5; "Ainulindalë" in, 163; and Celtic references, 202, 227; Children of Ilúvatar, 197; Silmarils in, 103–4
Boromir: character of, and Ring, 102, 108, 111, 121; Galadriel, 167, 174; good and evil in, 31, 115; moral dilemma of, 69; and sentient landscape, 132
Borrow, D. N. as "linguist," pseudo editor in *The Notion Club Papers*, 84
Bounders, political incorrectness and, 92
Brandybuck, Meriadoc "Merry": as atypical hobbit, 92; and dream, 137; and Fangorn Forest, 135n2; and Harry the Gatekeeper, 94; and Huorns, 138, 139, 152–53, 154; and Lobelia, 94; and Old Forest, 42, 134, 135, 136, 148, 149–50; and Treebeard, 42, 129
Bratt, Edith, 186
Breelanders, political incorrectness and, 94
Breton folklore on Corrigans, 169
Broceliande forest, 169–72
Brooks, Terry, *Sword of Shannara*, 45
Butterbur, Barliman, 93, 94

Camden, William, 8
Campbell, Joseph, and Hero Journey, 206
Capra, Fritjof, 72, 233n1
Caradhras: as Faërian Drama, 134; names for, 74; as sentient landscape, 132–33, 136, 137, 139, 140, 149
Carpenter, Humphrey: G. B. Smith letter, 52; "Imram," 222; *Smith of Wootton Major*, 143; "The Voyage of Eärendel," Tolkien, and *Kalevala*, 14; Tolkien as "man of antitheses," xii, 30, 65; Tolkien "given my heart to be shot at," 13; Tolkien's "Gallophobia," 203, 206, 212; Tolkien's mother's conversion to Catholicism, 89; Unwin and sequel to *The Lord of the Rings*, 232n4
Cassirer, Ernst, 73, 233n2
Celtic Heritage (Rees, Rees), 223, 226
Celtic references, in Tolkien's works, 166, 172, 196–202, 204, 221–28
Cerin Amroth, 43
Chance, Jane, 90, 238n1
Charlton, Bruce, 122
Child, Francis, 8
children: and fairy stories, 7, 11, 13–14; and fantasy literature, 32–34, 38; and *The Hobbit*, 23, 38, 106, 189, 205, 210; and *The Lord of the Rings*, 33, 38, 41
"Children of Húrin," 181
Children of Ilúvatar, 197
Choregraphical Description of West Connaught, A (Ó Flaithearta), 217
Chrétien de Troyes: *Erec and Enide*, 207–9; *Lancelot*, 224; *Yvain*, 207–9
Christianity: in Arthurian world, 18, 157, 158; and Faërie, 143; intentionality in Tolkien's work, 3, 17–22, 127, 163, 164; and paganism, 171
Christmas Truce, 51–52, 57
Cirith Ungol: Frodo in, 105, 111; light in, 105; orcs of, 97, 98; Sam at, 116–18
Cohen, Cynthia, 42, 134–35, 138–39
Collins, Wilkie, *The Moonstone*, 107
Collins, William, 19
Common Speech, 43, 72, 73–75
Comparetti, Domenico, 191, 192
Cooper, Susan, 46
Corbet, Richard, 143
corrigan, defined, 166

Corrigan of Broceliande, 166, 169–72, 177; phial of, 169, 174
Cotton, Rosie, 44
Cracks of Doom, and eucastrophe, 44, 61–62, 63, 109, 111, 116
Crankshaw, Edward, comments on Silmarillion, 196
Crawford, John, *Kalevala* translation, 192
Curry, Patrick, 17–19, 29

d'Ardenne, Simonne, "The Man and the Scholar," 28–29
Dark Ladies, 127, 165–77; Blue-robed Lady of the Forest, 166–69; Corrigan of Broceliande, 166, 169–72; folklore terms for, 165–66; Galadriel, 167, 174–77; Guinever, 166, 172–73; Ides Ælfscyne (Elf-fair Lady), 167, 173–74
Dasent, George Webbe, *Popular Tales from the Norse*, 7–8, 12–13
death: of Aragorn, 55, 58; in "Athrabeth," 159, 161; in *Beowulf* essay, 4; and deathlessness, 54, 57; of Denethor, 54–55, 58; escape from, 37, 54; Gandalf on, 57; of G. B. Smith, 52–53, 54, 57; as "gift," 3, 53, 58; Hemingway on, 57; of Man of Harad, 55–57, 58; as motive for writing, 53; of Rob Gilson, 50–52, 54, 56, 57; by suicide, 117, 184, 188; of Theoden, 55, 58
Denethor: as complex character, 116, 121; as dark thread in story, 183, 188; and death, 54–55, 58; and Númenor, 214; and Ring, 102
Dolbear, Rufus, 81, 84–86
Donaldson, Stephen, 45, 48
Dorson, Richard, 6–8, 10, 11, 12, 146, 149
dragons: in fantasy, 33, 39, 40; French medieval influence of Tolkien's works, 206, 208; Müeller's theory of, 10; slaying in *The Hobbit*, 40; and *The Story of Kullervo*, 190
dream: Bilbo's dream, 39; compared to Faërian Drama, 25–28; as inherited memory, 82, 84–85, 87; of Misty Mountains, 73; as time-travel device, 77–79; waking dream, 26, 85, 115
Drout, Michael D. C., "Towards a Better Tolkien Criticism," 18

INDEX

"Drowning of Anadûne, The," 159–64
dryad, 29, 145, 146, 155, 156, 187, 232n6, 236n4
Du Maurier, George, *Peter Ibbetson*, 78
Dúnedanic mixed human-elvish mythmaking tradition, 158, 159–61
Dwarves: and Arkenstone, 106–8; and Battle of Five Armies, 40; Dwarvish (language), Sam's comment on, 73; and Faërian Drama, 26–27; grudge against Elves, 91; names for mountains, 73–75; and Thingol, 96
dyscastrophe: defined, 37; in *The Lord of the Rings*, 61–63; Tolkien's coinage, xiii, 37
Dyson, Hugo, 27, 30; Lowdham as, 81

Eärendil/Eärendel: Edwin Lowdham's ship, 225; as mariner, 5, 227–28; and Silmaril, 100, 101, 105
Elendil: ancestor of Aragorn, 76; and book, 86, 87, 88, 214; of Lowdham, 86; Númenorean counterpart of Alboin, 77, 79, 87
Elf-fair Lady (Ides Ælfscyne), 167, 173–74, 177
Elf-Latin (Eresseän), 234n2
Ellis, Peter Berresford, *Celt and Saxon*, 200–201
Elrond, 192, 209, 210
Elves: Aragorn on, 123; and Bilbo, 206, 209, 234n5; deathlessness of, 53–55, 161; dictionary definition of, 165; different categories of, 95, 146, 197; disappearance of, 143; enmity to dwarves, 91; and Faërian Drama, 133, 231; and Faërie, 223; as fairies, 86, 145, 227; magic as technology of, 47; mourned by stones, 130; mythmaking perspectives of, 157–64; and neopagans, 17; possible reality of, 17, 18, 23–25, 133, 145; Quenya language of, 73, 84, 186, 213, 234n2; and reincarnation, 22; Sindarin language of, 72–75, 153, 186, 197, 213, 234n2; Ted Sandyman skeptical of, 92; as "third kindred," 225; Three Rings, 175; Tolkien's Elves more Celtic than Germanic, 197–98, 227; as tree-people, 43, 146;
and Valinor, 223; world too narrow to hold, 217
elvish, defined, 165
Elvish drama. *See* Faërian Drama
enchantment: Faërian Drama as, 25–28, 133–34; and Faërie, 3, 7, 41, 42, 60, 198; as *fay-ery/erie*, 35, 60, 130, 205; "glamour" as, 29; and Huorns, 138; and Old Forest, 129, 134–36; and secondary world, 35, 41, 45, 46, 60; and Smith, 140; as song, 42
England, "mythology" for, 5, 14–15, 18, 87–89, 218; Arthurian world disqualified as, 18, 158; dedicated "to," 6, 181, 202, 218; and Eriol-Saga, 86; loss of, in modern life, 143–44; and loss of enchantment, 143; point of view in, 158–59; time-travel frame, 87–88; and Tolkien's personal life, 76, 77; as "true," 157
Ents: first appearance of word, 150; and Huorns, 93, 139, 152; language of, 73, 152; not consciously invented, 231n1; not trees, 42, 138, 151. *See also* Fangorn Forest
Éomer: and Galadriel, 167, 175–77; good and evil, 123
Eowyn: heroism of, 91; marriage to Faramir as happy ending, 44, 63; typical of Tolkien's women characters, 165, 177; warrior maiden and healer, 31
Eriol-Saga: and "Atlantis story," 86; and Celtic references, 202; medieval Irish voyages as otherworld voyages, 227; and mythmaking, 163. *See also* Ælfwine
Errol, Alboin/Audoin/Oswin, 77, 79, 81, 218
Eru, 161–64. *See also* Ilúvatar
escape, in fairy-stories, 15, 32–48, 61; in books inspired by Tolkien and *The Hobbit*, 45–48; from Deathlessness, 54; Great Escape, 37; and *The Hobbit*, 34–37, 39; in *The Lord of the Rings*, 38, 40–45; and "On Fairy-Stories," 33–37; overview, 32–34, 38
Essays Presented to Charles Williams, 145
eucatastrophe: and the dark, 3, 16; etymology of, 37; in *The Hobbit*, 39, 40, 61–62; in *The Lord of the Rings*, 44, 45, 59–65; as Tolkien's coinage, xiii, 15, 37, 61–62
Evans-Wentz, Walter Yeeling, 174

Faërian Drama, xvii, 18, 25–31, 130, 133; and sentient landscape, 133–36, 139, 140, 143, 144

Faërie: and *aventure*, 34, 205–12; and Celtic references, 198; death as writing inspiration for Tolkien, 49–58; enchantment as quality of, 7; etymology of, xvii, 34–35, 60, 130, 205; and folklore controversy, 5–16; *The Hobbit* as, 38, 39; and imagination, 24; in *The Lord of the Rings*, 131, 134; medieval Irish voyages compared to, 223–24; as place, xii, 17, 26, 28, 34, 41–43, 46, 47, 60–61, 90, 127; as state, 3, 34, 35; teaching "On Fairy-stories," 60–62. *See also* sub-creation

Faery, in *Smith of Wootton Major*, 143

"fairies": as Celtic, 197–98, 227; and Christianity, 143; and cold iron, 143; disappearance of, 143; as Eldar, 237; fairy-stories not about, 34; original names for Elves, 86, 145; as real, 17, 24, 29, 145; state of being, 34, 43, 205, 231n2. *See also* tree-fairy

Fall of Arthur, The, 166, 172–73, 177

Fangorn. *See* Treebeard

Fangorn Forest: as Faërie, 60, 131; "frightfully tree-ish," 235n2; Galdalf or Saruman at, 31; as sentient nature, 138. *See also* Huorns

fantasy: "arresting strangeness" of, 127; and escape, 32–36; and language, 72. *See also* sub-creation

Faramir: and Denethor, 121; on good and evil, 123; in Ithilien, 56, 109, 118, 119; marriage of, 44, 63, 101; and Númenor, 214

"Farewell Rewards and Fairies" (Corbet), 143

Farmer Cotton, 63

Farmer Maggot, 109

fate, etymological root of *fairy*, 60, 166, 205

fay, Old French *fairy*, 34; in Tolkien's fiction, 127, 165–77

Fëanor, 102–5, 108, 234n3, 238n15

Ferny, Bill, 93, 95

Finrod, 159–64

folklore controversy, 5–16; "Comparative Mythology" (Müller), 7–11; *Custom and Myth* (Lang), 10–11; Dorson on "golden century" of British folklore studies, 6–8, 10, 12; *Popular Tales from the Norse* (Dasent), 7–9, 12–13; Tolkien's Andrew Lang Lecture on, 5–7, 11–16

Forbidden Pool, Frodo and Gollum at, 118–20

Frankley, Philip: as author of Imram poem, 201, 225, 231; as C. S. Lewis, 81, 84

free will of Men, 232n1

French medieval romance, Tolkien influenced by, 34, 203–12

Frodo. *See* Baggins, Frodo

Galadhrim, 146

Galadriel: as "beautiful fay," 166, 167; compared to Virgin Mary, 20–21, 174–77; and the Corrigan, 174–76; in Lórien, 146; phial of, 105, 174; as rebel, 21; refusal of Ring, 175; Tolkien's contradictory messages about, 20–21; transformation of, 175–76; and tree-fairies, 146–47

Galahad, 212

Gamgee, Gaffer, 92, 93, 94

Gamgee, Samwise "Sam": and dwarf-language, 73; eucatastrophe, 63; and Galadriel, 167, 175–77; and Man of Harad, 54, 56–57; on Mordor orcs, 98; and Old Man Willow, 136; and political incorrectness, 91–92, 94, 98; and Ring, 111; Samwise name of, 116; Tolkien's contradictory messages about, 31

Gandalf: balanced against Saruman, 31, 98; on death, 55, 57; French medieval influence on Tolkien's works, 206, 209, 231n1; and Frodo's fate, 63; and Huorns, 154; moral dilemma of, 69, 116, 121, 122; and political incorrectness, 93; and "Quest of Erebor," 210; return of, 44, 237n4; and Ring, 109; Tolkien's contradictory messages about, 31

Gardner, John, *Grendel*, 122

Garner, Alan, *Thursbitch*, 46, 129–30

Garth, John, 203

Gawain, in Malory, 211, 212

gender, of tree-fairies, 146–47

Geoffrey of Monmouth, *The History of the Kings of Britain*, 173

Gilson, Rob, 50–54, 56–57
Gimli: Faërie as sentient landscape, 132, 137; names for the Misty Mountains, 73–75
Goldberry: and Faërie, 60; on Tom Bombadil, 190–91; as Tom's "lady," 193
"golden century" of British folklore studies, 6–8, 10, 12, 14
Gollum: and eucastrophe, 44, 61–62, 63, 210, 212; and Frodo, 93, 98, 118, 119–20; keeps promises, 120–21; mistreatment of, 122–23; as monster, 62, 63; and moral ambiguity, 116–23; and Ring, 102, 109, 111, 119; and Sam, 116–17, 118, 120, 122
"Great Wave," 82, 201, 215; in Ireland, 233n1; memory of, 83, 85, 202. *See also* "Atlantis and Númenor"
Green, Howard, discoverer and editor of *The Notion Club Papers*, 84, 86, 88
"green sun," 36, 127, 130, 131, 134; Huorns as, 139; Old Forest, Willow, Treebeard as, 135–39
Greer, Germaine, 30, 33
Grimm, Jacob and Wilhelm, 28; "The Frog-King," 8–9; "The Juniper Tree," 8–9
Grishnákh, 98
Guildford, Nicholas: and Faërian Drama, 27; and minutes, 79, 81; Tolkien as, 81, 88
Guinever/Guinevere: etymology of name, 171–72; as fay-woman, 166, 172–73, 177; and Launcelot, 207, 208, 211, 212; and Morgan le Fay, 172; Tolkien's Guinever atypical, 173

Hall, Alaric, *Elves in Anglo-Saxon England*, 165
Hammond, Wayne, 93
Harad, Man of, 54–58
Harry the gatekeeper, 94–95
Hastings, Peter, 22, 29, 162, 164, 237n4
Havard, Humphrey, as Dolbear, 81
Heisenberg's principle of indeterminacy, 71–72
Helms, Randel, 100–101
Hemingway, Ernest, 57
Henneth Annûn. *See* Forbidden Pool
Herder, Johannes Gottfried von, 8
Herendil, 77, 79, 218

Hero Path, 206–12
History of Middle-earth (ed. C. Tolkien), xiv, 6, 72, 73, 76, 144, 159, 160, 222, 236n4; *The Lost Road* and *The Notion Club Papers* in, 76; *Sauron Defeated* in, 222; on Tolkien's mythology, 159, 160
Hobbit, The: Arkenstone in, 100–102, 106–8, 111–12; as children's story, 23, 189; and Faërian Drama, 26–27; French influence on, 34, 203–12; mountain storm in, 131, 133
hobbits: and political incorrectness, 91–95. *See also* Baggins, Bilbo; Baggins, Frodo; Brandybuck, Meriadoc "Merry"; Gamgee, Samwise "Sam"; Took, Peregrin "Pippin"
Hostetter, Carl, "Three Elvish Verse Modes," 72
Huorns: as green sun, 139; as sentient landscape, 137–39; as tree-fairies, 151–55
Hy-Brasil, 217–20

Ides Ælfscyne (Elf-fair Lady), 167, 173–74, 177
Ilmarinen, *Kalevala*, 186–87
Ilmatar, *Kalevala*, 192
Ilúvatar: and Celtic references, 197; children of, 197; and death, 53, 54, 58, 161; invoked by Manwë, 213; and task of Men, 164. *See also* Eru
immrama, 181, 223, 231n
"Imram," 201, 222–28
indeterminacy, Heisenberg's principle of, 71–72
"Indo-Aryan" theory, World War II and, 7, 9–11, 12–13
Inklings, as Notion Club, 27, 81
Isengard: Battle of, 152; and death of Beechbone, 138
Itroun, 169–72

Jeremy, Wilfred: and Atlantis catastrophe, 84; Elvish Drama, 27; and Faërian Drama, 27; in Ireland, 201–2, 219; and Númenor, 84–86, 219; and reincarnation, 225; as Tréowine, 85; as Voronwë, 86. *See also* King Sheave; Tréowine
Jones, Gwyn, 198
Jones, Thomas, 198

Kahlas-Tarkka, Leena, 185
Kalevala (Lönnrot): birch in, 142; as model for Tolkien, 14, 167–69, 181, 183–95, 239n5, 239n6; and national identity, 8; and Silmarils, 103
Kalevala meter, 239n6
Kane, Douglas, *Arda Reconstructed*, 101–2, 160
Keats, John, 26
Keightley, Thomas, *The Fairy Mythology*, 8, 169, 170–71
Ker-Ys, 181, 201–2, 216, 220, 233
"King Sheave," 85, 88
Kirby, W. F., 167–68, 186, 192, 194
Kirk, Robert, *The Secret Commonwealth of Elves, Fauns and Fairies*, 169, 170–71
Kocher, Paul, *Master of Middle-earth*, 209, 210
Kuhn, Adalbert, "lightning school" theory of myth, 10
Kullervo, 184–85; comparison with Tolkien, 189; in *Kalevala*, 167, 168, 184–85; in *The Story of Kullervo*, 168–69, 183–84, 186, 188; and Túrin, 190, 191, 239n3; two families of, 237n3

Lancelot/Launcelot (King Arthur legend): in Chrétien de Troyes, 224; in *The Fall of Arthur*, 173
Lang, Andrew, 169
language: Celtic references in Tolkien's works, 197; destruction of, as bigotry, 95–96; French medieval influence in Tolkien's works, 203–12; in *The Lost Road* and *The Notion Club Papers*, 80, 84; Proto-Indo-European language theory, 141; in *The Story of Kullervo*, 185–87, 191–93; as sub-creation, 35–36. *See also* Misty Mountains; Moria
languages (invented by Tolkien): Entish, 73, 152–53; Quenya/Qenya as Proto-Eldarin, 73, 84, 186, 213, 234n2, 239n3; Sindarin, 73–74, 153, 186, 197, 213, 234n2
languages (real-world): Anglo-Saxon, 5, 60, 81, 83, 85, 87, 116, 150, 213; Breton, 166, 204; Cornish, 216; English (Common Speech), 43, 72, 73, 74, 75; Finnish, 167, 168, 185, 191–92, 194; French, 34, 35, 60, 130, 166, 204, 205, 207, 210; Greek, 12, 37, 60, 146; Icelandic, 165, 207, 237n1; Indo-European, 9, 141, 172; Irish, 172, 192, 204, 223, 226; Latin, 60, 166, 205, 210, 223; Tolkien's dislike of, 196, 203
Lay of Aotrou and Itroun, The: and Breton legend, 197, 204; Dark Lady in, 166, 169–72
"Lay of Leithian, The," 204
Legolas, and sentient landscape, 130, 137–38, 153
Leland, John, 8
Le Sieur Nan, 169
Letters of J. R. R. Tolkien, The: on Celtic references in his works, 221; contradictory messages in, 17–23; real-world accounts of lost lands, 215
Lewis, C. S.: in draft of NCP, 27; explicit Christianity in *The Lion, the Witch, and the Wardrobe*, 19; on *The Hobbit*, 39, 232n2, 239n2; as Inkling, 81; and portal-quest fantasy, 46, 48; space novels, 11, 83; Tolkien's views on works of, 19, 83; toss-up with Tolkien, 77, 214, 218
Lindsay, David, *A Voyage to Arcturus*, 26, 83
Lönnrot, Elias, 12, 14, 100, 142, 167, 181, 183–95
"Looney," 23–25, 28, 31
Lord of the Rings, The: Celtic references in, 196–202; Christianity in, 17, 18–22; citation of, xiii–xiv; contradictory messages in, 3, 17–31; critical response to, 23, 30, 33, 36, 113, 115, 124; death in, 54–58; escapism in, 38, 40–48; Faërie as sentient landscape, 140–44; French medieval influence on Tolkien's works, 209–12; inception of, 6; *The Lost Road* and *The Notion Club Papers* origin of, 76; moral ambiguity in, 113–24; mythmaking in, 160–64; political incorrectness in, 92–95; publishing of, 18, 23; real-world accounts of lost lands, 214–20; Ring of Power, 47, 100–102, 108–12; *The Story of Kullervo* characters and tragedy compared to, 188; symbolism

of light in, 105; teaching undergraduate students about, 59–65; "terrifying romance," 31; treatment of death in, 49–58; tree-fairies of, 147–55

Lórien: Celtic references, 199; and Dark Lady archetype, 175; dating of, 105; as "Dwimordene," 175, 238n; elves of, 146; escapism of, 35, 43, 47; Faërie as sentient landscape, 141; and Faërie concept, 60–61; Frodo in, 140, 141; mallorns and, 129, 130, 146; as secondary world/Faërie, 35, 43, 47, 60, 61, 98, 200; time in, 43, 199. *See also* Cerin Amroth; Galadhrim

Lost Road, The: biographical elements in, 81–83; carry-overs to *The Notion Club Papers*, 85; Celtic references in, 200; and Fall of Númenor, 160, 163–64, 214, 218, 220; importance to Tolkien's other works, 87–89; medieval Irish voyage tales compared to, 224–28; mythmaking in, 160–64; overview, 76–77; plot and characters of, 79–83; and real-world accounts of lost lands, 214–16, 218–20; as science fiction, 69, 76; "thread" concept of, 77–78; as time-travel, 77–80, 87, 181, 218; unfinished status of, 76, 85. See also *Notion Club Papers, The*

Lothlórien. *See* Lórien

Louhi, *Kalevala*, 12

Lowdham, Alwyn Arundel "Arry": as Ælfwine, 83, 85, 86, 226–27; as Dyson, 81; as Elendil, 83, 86, 87; and languages, 160; and Númenor, 84, 85, 202, 219; and reincarnation, 219, 225; and Wales, Ireland, 200, 201, 202, 225, 233n1, 234n2. *See also* Ælfwine

Lowdham, Edwin, 83, 86, 160, 225–27

Lúthien, 96, 101, 105, 177, 237n5

Lyonesse, as real-world account of lost land, 181, 201, 216–17, 218, 219–20, 233n1

MacCana, Proinsias, 198, 223

MacLean, Magnus, *Literature of the Celts*, 200

Maedhros, 102, 105

Maglor, 102, 105

Malory, Sir Thomas: *Le Morte d'Arthur*, 172–73, 207–12; "Noble Tale of Sir Launcelot Du Lake," 208; "Tale of the Sankgreal," 211

Manannán mac Lir, 217, 226

Manwë, 163, 187, 213

Martsch, Nancy, 95

Mary (Virgin), Galadriel compared to, 20–21

McKillop, James, *Dictionary of Celtic Mythology*, 166, 169, 174

Melian: and Silmarils, 102, 187; and Thingol, 95

Melko/Melkor: curse of, 190; and mythmaking, 161; and Silmarils, 104–5

Mendlesohn, Farah, *The Rhetorics of Fantasy*, 46–48

Merry. *See* Brandybuck, Meriadoc

Middle-earth: as landscape, 130; languages of, 71–75; as reflective of real world, 91. *See also individual titles of Tolkien's works*

Miöllnir, 12

Misty Mountains, names for, 73–75

Mitchison, Naomi, 115

Moe, Jørgen, *Norske Folkeeventyr*, 8

Moore, Marianne, 36

Mordred, 172–73, 216

Morgan le Fay, 172–73, 208

Morgoth: and History of the Gnomes, 49, 53, 57; and Silmarils, 102–3, 105. *See also* Melko/Melkor

Morgoth's Ring. *See* Adanel; Andreth; "Athrabeth Finrod ah Andreth"; Finrod

Moria, names for, 73–75

Muir, Edwin, 113, 115, 119

Müller, Max, 13; *Chips from a German Workshop*, 9; "Comparative Mythology," 7–11

Murray, Robert, 23, 24, 161–62, 236n2, 237n4

Murray, Sir James, 19

music, ability of Men to change, 53, 164

"Mythopoeia," 171

Naigatio Sancti Brendani, 197, 221–28

Nodens, 197

Noldor: and jewels, 104, 198; kinslaying of, 95

Notion Club Papers, The, 76–89; biographical elements in, 81–83; Celtic references in, 200; "Elvish Drama" and Faërian Drama in, 25, 27; importance to Tolkien's other works, 87–89; *The Lost Road* as precursor to, 77–78; medieval Irish voyage tales compared to, 221–28; moral ambiguity in, 113–15, 122; mythmaking in, 160–64; Númenor concept of, 76–80; overview, 76–77; plot elements and characters of, 83–88; and real-world accounts of lost lands, 217–20; unfinished status of, 76, 86, 88–89. *See also* Jeremy, Wilfred; "King Sheave"; *Lost Road, The;* Lowdham, Alwyn Arundel "Arry"; Ramer, Michael; time-travel

Númenor, 76–89; and "Atlantis complex" dream, 82, 84–87, 201–2; biographical elements of, 81–83; Dúnedanic mythmaking compared to human perspectives, 157–64; framing devices for space travel, 83–86; as missing link, 77–80; as mythology for England, 87–89; overview, 76–77; real-world accounts of lost lands, 213–20

Oakenshield, Thorin: and Arkenstone, 107, 108, 112; death of, 40, 44, 111; and Faërian Drama, 26–27; and mithril coat, 206; and stone giants, 131

Odo, 147

Ó Flaithearta, Ruairí, 217

O hOgain, Daithi, 223

Old Forest: and escapism, 41–43, 46; as secondary world/faërie, 41–42, 43, 60–61, 98, 143; as sentient landscape, 129, 131, 134–37, 139, 140, 141, 153–54; and tree-fairy, 147–50, 151

Old Man Willow: as Faërian Drama, 135–37, 139–40; and Faërie concept, 60–61; as sentient landscape, 129, 134, 140, 141; and Tom Bombadil, 19, 193

Old Noakes, 93, 94

Once and Future King, The (White), 172

"On Fairy-stories": Andrew Lang Lecture origin of, 5–7, 11–16, 145; "boiling bones" reference in, 181; contradictory messages in, 17, 23, 28; escape in, 33–37; and Faërian Drama, 133–34; Faërie and "into the Blue" *(The Hobbit)*, 207; Faërie as sentient landscape, 130–31; on French fairy tales, 203; Kirk reference in, 169; real-world accounts of lost land, 217–18, 220; on "recovery" process, 90; on sub-creation, 185; teaching *The Lord of the Rings* with, 59–65; tree-fairies of, 145–47

"On the 'Kalevala,'" 184–85

Orcs, 36, 90, 92; as goblins in *The Hobbit*, 209; of Mordor, 91, 97–98; of Moria, 97; "on both sides," 91, 92; Uruk-Hai, 91, 98, 137, 138, 155

otherworld: Celtic references and, 198–99; medieval Irish voyages compared to Tolkien's works, 221–28; real-world accounts of lost land, 217–18

Oxford English Dictionary, The, 19

Oxford Magazine, 23–25

paganism: in *Aotrou and Itroun*, 171; and Celtic otherworld, 224; and Christian blend, 19; indigenous belief in, 143; intentional in Tolkien's works, 18, 127; neo-, 17, 30; past in *Beowulf*, 22, 156

Parma Eldalamberon (journal), 153

Pearce, Joseph, 17–18, 19

pedagogical strategy, for *The Lord of the Rings*, 59–65

Pentikäinen, Juha, *Kalevala Mythology*, 192

Percy, Thomas, 8

Pippin. *See* Took, Peregrin "Pippin"

Plato: *Critias*, 215; *Timaeus*, 215

point of view and mythic tradition, 157–64

political incorrectness, 90–99; in *The Fellowship of the Ring*, 92–95; in *The Lord of the Rings*, 97–98; overview, 69, 90–92; in *The Silmarillion*, 95–97

"portal-quest" fantasy, 46–48

Proto-Indo-European language theory, 141

Pullman, Philip, *His Dark Materials* trilogy, xiii, 33, 47–48

Pwyll, Prince of Dyfed, 198–99, 200, 204

Qenyaqetsa: The Qenya phonology and Lexicon in *Parma Eldalamberon*, 12, 236n1

Qenya/Quenya, 73, 84, 186, 234n2, 239n3

Quendi, 197

Rackham, Arthur, 146, 155
Ramer, Michael, 81, 84–86, 114–15, 122; and Elvish Drama, 27–28
Rateliff, John, ed., *The History of The Hobbit*, 101, 107, 174
"Red Book of Hergest, The," 199
"Red Book of Westmarch, The," 88, 158; of Hergest, 199
Rees, Alwyn, 197, 223
Rees, Brinley, 197, 223
reincarnation: in *The Notion Club Papers*, 84, 85, 86, 201, 219; and time-travel in *The Lost Road*, 77, 79, 85, 218; Tolkien's defense of, 22
Resnick, Henry, interview with Tolkien, 21
Return of the Shadow, The, 108
Reuel: meaning of, 81; as Tolkien family name, 81
Rhys, Sir John, *Celtic Folklore*, 8, 169
Rider of Rohan, 175
Ring: and Bilbo, 234n5; compared to Arkenstone, Silmaril, 69, 102, 105, 107, 108–12; and eucatastrophe, 44, 62; and Frodo, 44, 62, 63; Galadriel, 175–76; and intrusion fantasy, 47; Tom's immunity to, 61, 109
Roche, Norma, 221, 224–25

Sackville-Baggins, Lobelia, 94
St. Andrews University, 5–7, 11–16, 145
Sam. *See* Gamgee, Samwise "Sam"
Sampo, 103, 234n1. *See also* Louhi
Sandyman, Ted, 91–93
Saruman: Faërie as sentient landscape, 137–38; Tolkien's contradictory messages about, 31
Sauron: reference to, in *Notion Club*, 84; and Ring, 102, 108–9
Sauron Defeated (History of Middle-earth; ed. C. Tolkien), 222
Schiefner, Franz Anton, 192
Scull, Christina, 90, 93, 234n1
secondary world. *See* Faërie; green sun; sub-creation
Shagrat, 97, 98
Shakespeare, William: and Birnam Wood, 139; *Hamlet*, 184; and King Lear, 197; *A Midsummer Night's Dream*, 25–26

Shelob: and escapism, 105; and moral ambiguity, 120; and symbolism of light, 105
Shippey, Tom: on birch tree, 235n3; on Elf-fair Lady, 167, 173–74, 237n2; on *glamour*, 231n3; on medieval Irish voyage tales, 221, 224, 226
Shire, political incorrectness in, 92–95. *See also* hobbits
Sídh, 223, 227
Silmarillion: Celtic references in, 196–202; publishing of, 18; real-world accounts of lost lands, 213–20; *The Story of Kullervo* compared to, 190–91; treatment of death in, 49–50, 53, 54, 57. See also *Silmarillion, The*
Silmarillion, The: Celtic references in, 197; *The Lost Road* and *The Notion Club Papers* as origin of, 80; medieval Irish voyage tales compared to, 222; mythology of, 159; political incorrectness in, 95–97; real-world accounts of lost lands, 215
Simarils, 69, 100–106, 111–12
Sindarin (Elvish) language, 72–75, 186, 197
Sir Gawain and the Green Knight, 237n7
Smith, Geoffrey, 50–54, 57
Smith of Wootton Major: birch as tree-fairy in, 155; Celtic references in, 197, 199–200; sentient landscape of, 139–44
Snaga, 97–98
solar mythology concept, 7, 9–13
"Song of Eärendil, The" (*Lord of the Rings*), 100, 101
Songs for the Philologists: "birch" poems in, 142; Ides Ælfscyne (Elf-fair Lady) as Dark Lady archetype, 167, 173–74, 177
"soup" metaphor, folklore controversies of, 8, 9, 12–13
"squint-eyed," usage of, 95
Story of Kullervo, The, 183–95; Blue-robed Lady in, 127, 166–69, 177; Kullervo and Túrin Turambar, 183, 190, 237n4, 2394; likeness to Tolkien, 188–90; overview, 181, 183–85; as sub-created secondary world, 185–87
Strider: and political incorrectness, 95; real-world accounts of lost lands, 214; and "The Tale of Tinúviel," 71. *See also* Aragorn

sub-creation, 3, 35, 69, 130; in *The Hobbit*, 131–32, 133; in *The Lord of the Rings*, 132–33, 151; in *The Story of Kullervo*, 183, 187, 188

suicide: Frodo's mission, 118; Sam Gamgee and, 116, 117, 118; in *The Story of Kullervo*, 184, 188; and Túrin, 190

"Tale of Tinúviel, The": and Silmarils, 104; and Strider, 71

Tea Club Barrows Store (TCBS), 50–52

Théoden, death of, 54–56

Thingol: political incorrectness of, 95–97; and Silmarils, 102; as Tinwelint, 104

Third Age, religious references to, 21

Thomas Covenant novels (Donaldson), 45

Thorin. *See* Oakenshield, Thorin

Thórr, nature myth of, 12

Time and Tide (magazine), 222

time-travel, Tolkien on, 11, 77–80, 201, 214–15, 218. *See also Lost Road, The; Notion Club Papers, The*

Tinwelint, Silmarils and, 104

Titmass, J. R., "historian" of *The Notion Club Papers*, 84

Tolkien, Arthur, 81

Tolkien, Christopher: on Celtic references in father's works, 200; on Cirith Ungol, 105; *The Fall of Arthur* edited and published by, 166, 172–73, 177; and father's diaries, 30; on Galadriel character, 175–76; History of Middle-earth, 76, 144, 159, 160, 222; on Huorns, 152; on Inklings, 27; on *Kalevala*, 195; on *The Lost Road* and *The Notion Club Papers*, 76, 77, 81, 84, 86–88, 226–27; military service of, 49–50; on mythmaking, 159–62; real-world accounts of lost lands and Tolkien's works, 213–15, 219–20; on Simarils, 104; on "squint-eyed" usage, 95; on "third phase" of revision, 148, 150

Tolkien, J. R.: Andrew Lang Lecture (1939), 5–7, 11–16, 145; on "arresting strangeness" of fantasy, 127; biographical information, 49–58, 81–83, 186, 189–90; Celtic references by, 196–202, 204; on Christianity in *The Lord of the Rings*, 3, 17–31; coin-toss with Lewis, 77, 214, 218; death as writing inspiration for, 49–58; diaries of, 30; on fantasy as "sub-creative art," 35; "Gallophobia" of, 203, 206; on "history," 212; and image of trees, 129, 137; influence of French medieval romance on, 34, 203–12; languages invented by, 71–75; "man of antitheses," xii, 30, 65; moral ambiguity in themes of, 113–24; mythmaking by, 127, 157–64; on Númenor concept, 214; O'Donnell lecture, 196–97; political incorrectness of, 90–99; on "primary belief," 133; on Ring, 109; science fiction genre of (see *Lost Road, The; Notion Club Papers, The*); theory and practice of fantasy by, 32–48; time-travel themes of, 11, 77–80, 201, 214–15, 218. *See also individual titles of works*

Tolkien, Michael, 82

Tolkien Reader, The, and *aventure*, 34, 204–12

Tolkien Studies (journal), 166

Took, Peregrin "Pippin": at Black Gate, 121, 188; on Denethor, 121; dream, 137; Faërie as sentient landscape, 14, 136–37; and Old Forest as Faërie, 41–42, 134–36; and Old Man Willow, 149

Treason of Isengard, The, 175–76

Treebeard: changed from giant to Ent, 150, 153, 156; Faërie as sentient nature landscape, 42, 127, 129, 137; as green sun, 139; and Huorns, 138, 139, 151, 153–54; as tree-fairy, 147, 150–51

tree-fairy, 145–56; in folklore, 146; Huorns as, 151–55; Old Man Willow as, 147–50; overview, 127, 145–47; in *Smith of Wootton Major*, 155

Tréowine, 227; Jeremy as, 64; as purgatory, 85

Triads, 172, 173

Tuatha Dé Danann, and Tolkien's Elves, 197, 200

Túrin, 96; Kullervo compared to, 183, 190, 237n4, 239n4

Two Trees, 95, 97, 104, 234n3

Tyler, Edward Burnet, *Primitive Culture*, 146

Uglúk, 97, 98
"Unique Representation of Trees in *The Lord of the Rings*, The" (Cohen), 42, 134–35
Untamo: name retained form *Kalevala*, 185; in *The Story of Kullervo*, 167–69

Väinämöinen: and birch tree, 142; and Sampo, 103; and Tom Bombadil, 183, 190–94
Valar: and Arda, 213; and brightness, 74; as gods, 19, 80, 224; as nature spirits, 187; Tolkien's contradictory messages about, 19, 21
Valinor: Elves' departure for, 143; light in, 97, 102, 106; as otherworld, 223–24, 225, 226; as purgatory, 64; and Silmarils, 104; and Straight Road, 80, 224
Villemarqué, Hersart de la, 216
Voyage of Bran, The, 217–18, 226
"Voyage of Eärendel, The," 5
"Voyage of St. Brendan, The," 181, 222–28

Waldman, Milton, 18, 19–20, 23, 102, 157, 158, 163
Walton, Evangeline, *The Mabinogion*, 45–46, 198–99, 200, 204
Webster, Deborah, Tolkien letter to, 20–21
Welsh Review, The, 166

Wheeler, John, 71–72, 74
White, T. H., 172
Whorf, Benjamin, 73, 233n2
William Collins, Sons, and Co., 18, 19
Wilson, Edmund, "Oo! Those Awful Orcs!," 23, 30, 33, 36, 113, 114, 115, 117, 118, 120, 124
Wiseman, Christopher, 50
Wood Elves, Faërian Drama and, 26–27, 146; Bilbo and, 205, 234n5
Words, Phrases and Passages in Various Tongues in *Parma Eldalamberon*, 17, 153, 233n3, 236n1
World War I: "Christmas Truce" (1914), 51–52, 57; and "golden century," 6, 7, 14; and *The Hobbit*, 40; Tolkien in, 5, 49–58, 186; and Tolkien's mythology, 5, 6
World War II: Christopher Tolkien in, 49; and "Fairy-story" lecture, 11, 15; and *The Hobbit*, 40
Wormald, W. W., "Bibliopolist" of *The Notion Club Papers*, 84
Wormtongue: on Galadriel, 175–77; and Lotho and Saruman, 188
Wynne, Patrick, "Three Elvish Verse Modes," 72

Yeats, William Butler, *The Celtic Twilight*, 217
Ys. *See* Ker-Ys